S0-AJD-158

The American Presidency

AMERICAN STUDIES INFORMATION GUIDE SERIES

Series Editor: Donald Koster, Professor of English Emeritus, Adelphi University, Garden City, New York

Also in this series:

AFRO-AMERICAN LITERATURE AND CULTURE SINCE WORLD WAR II—*Edited by Charles D. Peavy*

AMERICAN ARCHITECTURE AND ART—*Edited by David M. Sokol*

AMERICAN EDUCATION—*Edited by Richard G. Durnin*

AMERICAN LITERATURE AND LANGUAGE—*Edited by Donald N. Koster*

AMERICAN POPULAR CULTURE—*Edited by Larry N. Landrum*

AMERICAN RELIGION AND PHILOSOPHY—*Edited by Ernest R. Sandeen and Frederick Hale*

AMERICAN STUDIES—*Edited by David W. Marcell*

HISTORY OF THE UNITED STATES OF AMERICA—*Edited by Ernest Cassara*

JEWISH WRITERS OF NORTH AMERICA—*Edited by Ira Bruce Nadel*

THE RELATIONSHIP OF PAINTING AND LITERATURE—*Edited by Eugene L. Huddleston and Douglas A. Noverr*

SOCIOLOGY OF AMERICA—*Edited by Charles Mark*

TECHNOLOGY AND VALUES IN AMERICAN CIVILIZATION—*Edited by Stephen H. Cutcliffe, Judith A Mistichelli, and Christine M. Roysdon*

WOMAN IN AMERICA—*Edited by Virginia R. Terris*

The above series is part of the

GALE INFORMATION GUIDE LIBRARY

The Library consists of a number of separate series of guides covering major areas in the social sciences, humanities, and current affairs.

General Editor: Paul Wasserman, Professor and former Dean, School of Library and Information Services, University of Maryland

Managing Editor: Denise Allard Adzigian, Gale Research Company

The American Presidency

A GUIDE TO INFORMATION SOURCES

Volume 11 in the American Studies Information Guide Series

Kenneth E. Davison

Professor of History and American Studies
and
Chairperson of the American Studies Department
Heidelberg College
Tiffin, Ohio

Gale Research Company
Book Tower, Detroit, Michigan 48226

Library of Congress Cataloging in Publication Data

Davison, Kenneth E.
The American presidency.

(American studies information guide series ; v. 11)
(Gale information guide library)
Includes indexes.
1. Presidents—United States—Bibliography.
2. United States—Politics and government—Bibliography.
I. Title. II. Series.
Z1249.P7D38 1983 [E176.1] 016.973'09'92 73-17552
ISBN 0-8103-1261-1

To Virginia

Contents

Part 2. The American Presidents, 1789-1982

FOREWORD

For Americans few subjects are surrounded by as much glamour, glitter, and mystery as is the American presidency. The man in the street has been taught to believe that the most powerful individual in the world is the American president, and it is quite probable that this notion is correct. Surely, then, there is a sound basis for our ever-growing fascination with the office and the being who holds it.

When Professor Davison first mentioned to me his rapidly accumulating hoard of published materials on the subject of the presidency and the presidents, I was impressed; and when he suggested that he would be interested in organizing these materials into publishable form as a book in my series of information guides in American studies, I was delighted. I had known Ken Davison for many years when both of us served as officers of the American Studies Association, and I had come to believe that whatever he undertook to do he did well. Surely no one was better equipped than he to do the job that had to be done.

Although neither Ken nor I could quite believe that this book, which had its first stirrings in the days of Watergate, would not be completed until Ronald Reagan was well into his third year in office, I trust that he joins me in the opinion that its long period of gestation has been worth the wait and has helped to make it a much more valuable book than it could otherwise have been. I am confident that, for years to come, it will remain an incomparable resource for the study of the most fascinating of American political institutions and of the men involved with it.

Donald N. Koster
Series Editor

PREFACE

The purpose of this information guide is to assemble in a single reference volume the first comprehensive bibliography covering the American presidency and American presidents from 1787 to 1982. While much has been written about presidents and the presidency, only three guides to this growing literature have appeared since 1963. Professor Fred I. Greenstein et al. of Princeton University produced in 1977 a very useful bibliography of books, articles, and government documents pertaining to the modern presidency from the era of Franklin D. Roosevelt through the administration of Gerald R. Ford. David Heslop's critical assessment of works on the presidency, published by University Microfilms in 1969, covers only part of the subject area rather than the whole field of presidential studies. The Library of Congress selective guide to the literature on American presidents, edited by Donald H. Mugridge, was completed in 1963 just prior to the great explosion of presidential research and writing which began in the mid-sixties and continues to the present time. The Mugridge guide is notable, however, as the earliest and best attempt to survey the entire field of presidential scholarship.

This guide to the American presidency has been prepared with these earlier bibliographies in mind. It is more comprehensive in coverage and documents the quality and the wide range of presidential studies since 1945 and particularly since 1960. The table of contents has been arranged in outline form and may be used as a simplified subject index to the volume.

My bibliography did not begin with a library reference book in mind. It started as a boy's collection and continued as a professor's hobby. It took another turn when I introduced a college course on the American presidency in 1965. I needed a handy reference file to help me advise students concerning their reading and writing projects. Little did I realize how fast the field would grow in scholarly endeavor and public interest during the 1960s and 1970s.

At first I took pride in my command of the growing literature and great pleasure in acquiring <u>all</u> of the basic books on each president and any topic relating to the presidency. I even started a file cabinet to keep articles and brochures or clippings I found of interest on each president. I haunted used book stores in many American cities to make my book collection as complete as possible. Alas, I did not foresee either the great expansion in writing about presidents or the presidency, nor the gradual escalation in the cost of books. Fortunately, I began my "presidential library" soon enough that I already owned much of the basic literature before inflation became a serious factor. I suspect I now have one of the better private collections of presidential literature in the country.

I was delighted when my colleague in the American studies movement, Dr. Donald N. Koster of Adelphi University, invited me to participate in his project to edit a series of information guides designed for readers and researchers on American topics. He readily accepted my suggestion to include a volume on America's presidents and the office of president. I am grateful to him and my editors at Gale Research Company, Denise Allard Adzigian and Pamela Dear, for their patience and insistence that I complete the project. It has enabled me to organize a large number of scattered references and materials in a systematic way I would never have done otherwise. I hope those who use this guide will derive as much satisfaction as I did in putting it together.

The scope of this bibliography and study guide should be defined and explained.

1. It is selective. Generally speaking, I have cited only items published since 1945 unless an older work stands alone or is clearly superior to more recent scholarship.

2. I have concentrated on books and articles accessible in a large public or university library, plus some government documents normally available in any government depository library.

For references to books and reprints, I relied mainly upon the Library of Congress Card Distribution Service to which I subscribed between 1961 and 1981 in the subject area of presidents and the presidency. This excellent service has since given way to a new computerized data bank system.

Book reviews and advertisements I read or received in the mail were other sources of information. In some cases, as a book review editor, I got complimentary advance copies from publishers. I also examined many subject lists in BOOKS IN PRINT, CUMULATIVE BOOK INDEX, BIOGRAPHY INDEX, and similar library reference tools.

Travel and friends in the profession produced other leads. I especially wish to acknowledge assistance I have received for more than a decade from Dr. R. Gordon Hoxie, president of the Center for the Study of the Presidency in New York City. This organization and its publications have put me in touch with persons in the field of presidential studies I would not have known in any other way, including the authors of many of the works cited in this guide.

For articles about the presidency, I depended on several sources. WRITINGS ON AMERICAN HISTORY, published annually since 1902, proved invaluable. I also combed bibliography lists regularly published in AMERICA: HISTORY AND LIFE, the AMERICAN HISTORICAL REVIEW, the JOURNAL OF AMERICAN HISTORY (formerly the MISSISSIPPI VALLEY HISTORICAL REVIEW); and other professional journals in several disciplines. For more recent years, PRESIDENTIAL STUDIES QUARTERLY (1974--) and the PRESIDENCY RESEARCH GROUP NEWSLETTER (1978--) proved to be particularly good guides to periodical literature on the presidency.

In recent years the availability of data bases and information retrieval by means of computer printouts has completely transformed access to the periodical literature. I would recommend use of the Library of Congress SCORPIO system and DIALOG Information Services, Inc., 3460 Hillview Avenue, Palo Alto, Calif. 94304.

With the aid of these library tools, I gradually assembled hundreds of 4 x 6 inch cards, enough to fill a dozen or more shoebox size working files. These references were gradually reduced to about one-third of their original number. In general more articles than books were dropped from my original file. Many of the deleted articles have appeared in popular magazines or newspapers, and may be retrieved by consulting READER'S GUIDE TO PERIODICAL LITERATURE, MAGAZINE INDEX, or newspaper indexes. Other articles with primarily a local or regional focus were culled in favor of ones with a national scope.

Books intended for juvenile readers were usually passed over unless the subject matter was unusual or the work of a quality to appeal to adult readers.

I might have cited many more government documents but did not do so because the essential information from this type of material is frequently well summarized in a good secondary work. Researchers finding it necessary to go back to government documents on a particular aspect of the presidency should consult the MONTHLY CATALOG OF UNITED STATES GOVERNMENT DOCUMENTS and the CUMULATIVE INDEXES to the same.

3. This bibliography does not cover audiovisual materials. The many convenient film and record catalogs already available in libraries preempt this category.

4. Many entries are not annotated. Partly this reflects my own interests and knowledge about certain presidents or aspects of the presidency. Often the point of view or content of items cited is obvious from the title or category in which it appears. In other instances highly specialized and detailed critical bibliographies are available and I did not choose to duplicate these reference tools. Finally, considerations of space limited what I could do in a selective bibliography. I decided to include more entries rather than fewer more fully annotated citations.

5. In part 2, dealing with individual presidents and their administrations, I have followed a standard arrangement of entries. Bibliographies are listed first. This section is followed by "Source Materials." This means private or public papers of the president under review, or other contemporary records and documents relating to him or his administration. Autobiographies, diaries, memoirs, correspondence, and speeches of the president or his associates are grouped in this category. Next, I have cited biographies, occasionally separating multivolume works from one-volume treatments. The two remaining categories list important monographs and articles.

For a few recent presidents additional categories may be found. For example, books and articles on the assassination of John F. Kennedy are grouped together as are writings on Richard Nixon's Watergate scandal.

Because Ronald Reagan was still president at the time I prepared this bibliography, fewer good books and articles were in print than on other presidents. I have therefore relied upon articles appearing in the weekly NATIONAL JOURNAL to document his presidency.

No work of this kind is ever accomplished without the support of other individuals. I wish to recognize the valuable services of my student secretaries, Rebecca Baker Hill, Karen Goetz, Kim Weyand, and Carol Yarborough, who helped me greatly by typing cards and checking the accuracy of many small details encountered in a bibliographical search. The staff of Beeghly Library at Heidelberg College--Janet Strickland, director; Nancy Rubenstein, reference librarian; Rosemarie Maloney, acquisitions librarian; and Ruth Ann Weininger, senior terminal operator--helped me on more occasions than I can remember or repay, all with unremitting courtesy and professional competence.

Last, I dedicate this volume to my wife Virginia, who always believed it was something I should do and who supported my efforts at every turn.

K.E.D.
February 28, 1983

Part 1
The American Presidency, 1787-1982

Chapter 1

AIDS TO RESEARCH

A. BIBLIOGRAPHIES

Greenstein, Fred I., et al. EVOLUTION OF THE MODERN PRESIDENCY: A BIBLIOGRAPHICAL SURVEY. Washington, D.C.: American Enterprise Institute for Public Policy Research, 1977. xv, 369 p.

> A computer printout of 2,504 references for the study of the presidency from F.D. Roosevelt through Ford.

Heslop, David Alan. THE PRESIDENCY AND POLITICAL SCIENCE: A CRITIQUE OF THE WORK OF POLITICAL SCIENTISTS IN THREE AREAS OF PRESIDENTIAL POLITICS. Ann Arbor, Mich.: University Microfilms, 1969. vi, 504 p.

> A survey of major books and articles dealing with the president as chief legislator, administrative chief, and party leader.

PRESIDENTS: A CATALOG OF DOCTORAL DISSERTATIONS. Ann Arbor, Mich.: University Microfilms International, 1982. 34 p.

> Covers 915 dissertations completed between 1939 and 1982.

U.S. Library of Congress. General Reference and Bibliography Division. THE PRESIDENTS OF THE U.S., 1789-1962: A SELECTED LIST OF REFERENCES. Compiled by Donald H. Mugridge. Washington, D.C.: Government Printing Office, 1963. xviii, 159 p.

B. ENCYCLOPEDIAS AND HANDBOOKS

1. Compendiums

Barone, Michael, and Ujifusa, Grant. THE ALMANAC OF AMERICAN POLITICS, 1982. Washington, D.C.: Barone and Co., 1981. lxix, 1,258 p.

An excellent guide to the American political scene containing valuable essays on every state, their governors, senators, and representatives.

BIOGRAPHICAL DIRECTORY OF THE UNITED STATES EXECUTIVE BRANCH, 1774-1977. Edited by Robert Sobel. Westport, Conn.: Greenwood Press, 1977. x, 503 p.

Clymer, Ernest Fletcher. CABINETS OF THE PRESIDENTS AND THE SPEAKERS OF THE HOUSE OF REPRESENTATIVES, PRESIDENTIAL VOTES BY STATES, 1900-1916, SPECIAL NOTES ON THE PRESIDENTS. New York: W.E. Rudge, 1920. 38 p.

Congressional Quarterly Service. PRESIDENTIAL CANDIDATES FROM 1788 TO 1964, INCLUDING THIRD PARTIES, 1832-1964, AND POPULAR ELECTORAL VOTE: HISTORICAL REVIEW. Rev. ed. Washington, D.C.: 1964. 27 p.

______. PRESIDENTIAL ELECTIONS SINCE 1789. Washington, D.C.: Congressional Quarterly, 1975. vi, 170 p.

Cooke, Donald E. ATLAS OF THE PRESIDENTS. Rev. ed. Maplewood, N.J.: Hammond, 1977. 93 p.

Brief biographies of thirty-nine U.S. presidents. Includes a brief essay by John F. Kennedy about preparing for the presidency.

Fell, Frederick Victor. THE WIT AND WISDOM OF THE PRESIDENTS. New York: F. Fell, 1966. 206 p.

Frank, Sidney. THE PRESIDENTS: TIDBITS & TRIVIA. Maplewood, N.J.: Hammond, 1980. 160 p.

Gibson, Ronald. NAME AND SUBJECT INDEX TO THE PRESIDENTIAL CHRONOLOGY SERIES: FROM GEORGE WASHINGTON TO GERALD R. FORD. Dobbs Ferry, N.Y.: Oceana Publications, 1977. 141 p.

Harnsberger, Caroline, ed. TREASURY OF PRESIDENTIAL QUOTATIONS. Chicago: Follett Publishing Co., 1964. xix, 394 p.

Kane, Joseph Nathan. FACTS ABOUT THE PRESIDENTS: A COMPILATION OF BIOGRAPHICAL AND HISTORICAL INFORMATION. 4th ed. New York: H.W. Wilson Co., 1981. viii, 456 p.

Contains much personal and comparative data on all American presidents from George Washington to Ronald Reagan.

Lang, H. Jack, comp. LETTERS OF THE PRESIDENTS. Los Angeles: Los Angeles Times Syndicate, 1964. 39 p.

> Consists of transcriptions of letters, one apiece from Washington to Lyndon B. Johnson, each with portrait and facsimile of signature.

McKee, Thomas Hudson. THE NATIONAL CONVENTIONS AND PLATFORMS OF ALL POLITICAL PARTIES, 1789 TO 1905: CONVENTION, POPULAR, AND ELECTORAL VOTE. ALSO THE POLITICAL COMPLEXION OF BOTH HOUSES OF CONGRESS AT EACH BIENNIAL PERIOD. 6th ed., rev. and enl. Baltimore: Friedenwald Co., 1906. Reprint. New York: AMS Press, 1971. 418, 33 p. Appendix.

Miller, Carl, comp. MARCHES OF THE PRESIDENTS, 1789-1909: AUTHENTIC MARCHES AND CAMPAIGN SONGS, ARRANGED FOR PIANO. Presidential notes edited by Lee Snider. Illustrated by Rae Geswaldo. New York: Chappell, 1968. 63 p.

Morris, Richard Brandon. GREAT PRESIDENTIAL DECISIONS. Enl. ed. New York: Harper and Row, 1973. 508 p.

PRESIDENTIAL RHETORIC: 1961-1980. 2d ed. Edited by Theodore Windt. Dubuque, Iowa: Kendall, Hunt Publishing Co., 1980. xii, 283 p.

QUOTATIONS FROM OUR PRESIDENTS: BEING A COLLECTION OF QUOTATIONS FROM THE PRESIDENTS OF THE UNITED STATES OF AMERICA RELEVANT TO THEIR PERSONAL PATRIOTISM AND PHILOSOPHY OF GOVERNMENT. Mount Vernon, N.Y.: Peter Pauper Press, 1969. 62 p.

Seuling, Barbara. THE LAST COW ON THE WHITE HOUSE LAWN, AND OTHER LITTLE-KNOWN FACTS ABOUT THE PRESIDENCY. Garden City, N.Y.: Doubleday, 1978. 95 p.

> A collection of little-known facts about each of the presidents from Washington to Carter.

Smith, Don. PECULIARITIES OF THE PRESIDENTS. 4th ed. Van Wert, Ohio: Wilkinson Printing Co., 1946. 185 p.

Taylor, John M. FROM THE WHITE HOUSE INKWELL: AMERICAN PRESIDENTIAL AUTOGRAPHS. Rutland, Vt.: C.E. Tuttle Co., 1968. 147 p.

Taylor, Tim. THE BOOK OF PRESIDENTS. New York: Arno Press, 1972. viii, 703 p.

> Combines facts and figures on each president with a chronological listing of major events during each term of office.

Vexler, Robert I. THE VICE-PRESIDENTS AND CABINET MEMBERS: BIOGRAPHIES ARRANGED CHRONOLOGICALLY BY ADMINISTRATION. 2 vols. Dobbs Ferry, N.Y.: Oceana Publications, 1975.

Windt, Theodore, and Ingold, Beth, eds. ESSAYS IN PRESIDENTIAL RHETORIC. Dubuque, Iowa: Kendall, Hunt, 1983. xv, 323 p.

2. Presidential Genealogy

BURKE'S PRESIDENTIAL FAMILIES OF THE UNITED STATES OF AMERICA. Edited by Hugh Montgomery-Massingberd. London: Burke's Peerage, 1975. xix, 676 p.

Laird, Archibald. MONUMENTS MARKING THE GRAVES OF THE PRESIDENTS. North Quincy, Mass.: Christopher Publishing House, 1971. 213 p.

Perling, Joseph Jerry. PRESIDENTS' SONS: THE PRESTIGE OF NAME IN A DEMOCRACY. New York: Odyssey, 1947. Reprint. Freeport, N.Y.: Books for Libraries Press, 1971. viii, 451 p.

Tucker, Robert Whitney. THE DESCENDANTS OF THE PRESIDENTS. Charlotte, N.C.: Delmar Printing Co., 1975. vi, 222 p.

WILLS OF THE U.S. PRESIDENTS. Biographical text by Herbert R. Collins; notes on the wills by David B. Weaver. New York: Communications Channels, 1976. 287 p.

3. Presidential Statistics

Governmental Affairs Institute. Elections Research Center. AMERICA AT THE POLLS: A HANDBOOK OF AMERICAN PRESIDENTIAL ELECTION STATISTICS, 1920-1964. Compiled and edited by Richard M. Scammon. Pittsburgh: University of Pittsburgh Press, 1965. Reprint. New York: Arno Press, 1976. 521 p.

Petersen, Svend. A STATISTICAL HISTORY OF THE AMERICAN PRESIDENTIAL ELECTIONS. Introduction by Louis Filler. New York: Ungar, 1968. xxiii, 250 p.

Runyon, John H., et al., comps. SOURCE BOOK OF AMERICAN PRESIDENTIAL CAMPAIGN AND ELECTION STATISTICS, 1948-1968. Foreword by Hubert H. Humphrey. New York: F. Ungar, 1971. xiv, 380 p.

C. NEWSPAPERS

CHRISTIAN SCIENCE MONITOR. Boston: Christian Science Publishing Society, 1908-- .

Strong on international news coverage and political analysis.

NEW YORK TIMES. New York: New York Times Co., 1851-- .

Maintains a consistently high standard of independent political reporting. It normally prints complete texts of all important presidential statements.

WALL STREET JOURNAL. New York: Dow, Jones and Co., 1889-- .

The nation's best known paper for financial and business affairs.

WASHINGTON POST. Washington, D.C.: Washington Post Co., 1877-- .

Has frequently won acclaim for its investigative reporting.

D. PERIODICALS

1. Conservative Magazines

AMERICAN SPECTATOR. Bloomington, Ind.: Saturday Evening Club, 1967-- . Monthly.

A witty national journal of literary and political review.

COMMENTARY. New York: American Jewish Committee, 1945-- . Monthly.

Liberal in mid-1960s, radical in late 1960s, conservative since 1970; a journal of significant thought and opinion.

CONSERVATIVE DIGEST. Falls Church, Va.: Viguerie Communications Corp., 1975-- . Monthly.

Self-styled "magazine for the new majority."

HUMAN EVENTS. Washington, D.C.: Human Events, 1944-- . Weekly.

Consistently conservative.

NATIONAL REVIEW. New York: National Review, 1955-- . Fortnightly.

A conservative journal of fact and opinion edited by William F. Buckley.

POLICY REVIEW. Washington, D.C.: Heritage Foundation, 1977-- . Quarterly.

PUBLIC INTEREST. New York: National Affairs, 1965-- . Quarterly.

Aimed at providing solid reference materials for congressional staff members on public policy matters.

2. Liberal Magazines

ATLANTIC MONTHLY. Boston: Atlantic Monthly Co., 1857-- .

CENTER MAGAZINE. Santa Barbara, Calif.: Center for the Study of Democratic Institutions, 1968-- . Bimonthly.

HARPER'S MAGAZINE. New York: Harper's Magazine Co., 1851-- . Monthly.

NEW REPUBLIC: A JOURNAL OF POLITICS AND ARTS. Washington, D.C.: New Republic, 1914-- . Weekly.

WASHINGTON MONTHLY. Washington, D.C.: Washington Monthly, 1969-- .

3. Professional Journals

ADMINISTRATIVE SCIENCE QUARTERLY. Ithaca, N.Y.: Cornell University, 1956-- .

Academic discussion of public administration matters sponsored by Cornell Graduate School of Business and Public Administration.

AMERICAN ARCHIVIST. Chicago: Society of American Archivists, 1938-- . Quarterly.

Prints regular reports on accession of presidential papers, and occasionally has an article on the subject.

AMERICAN HERITAGE. New York: American Heritage Publishing Co., 1949-- . Bimonthly.

AMERICAN JOURNAL OF POLITICAL SCIENCE. Austin, Tex.: Midwest Political Science Association, 1957-- . Quarterly.

AMERICAN POLITICAL SCIENCE REVIEW. Washington, D.C.: American Political Science Association, 1906-- . Quarterly.

The most prestigious magazine in its field.

ANNALS OF AMERICAN ACADEMY OF POLITICAL AND SOCIAL SCIENCE. Philadelphia: American Academy of Political and Social Science, 1891-- . Bimonthly.

Normally an entire issue is devoted to a single theme.

CONGRESS & THE PRESIDENCY. Washington, D.C.: Center for Congressional and Presidential Studies, The American University, 1972-- . Semiannual.

Began as CAPITOL STUDIES until vol. 7, no. 1; then became CONGRESSIONAL STUDIES until 1982. New focus is on scholarly articles, research notes, review articles, and book reviews on the presidency, Congress, the interactions between these two institutions, and national policymaking in general.

CURRENT HISTORY. Philadelphia: Current History, 1914-- . Monthly.

A magazine of world affairs.

FOREIGN AFFAIRS. New York: Council on Foreign Relations, 1922-- . 5 times a year.

The most respected journal in its field.

JOURNAL OF AMERICAN HISTORY. Bloomington, Ind.: Organization of American Historians, 1914-- . Quarterly.

JOURNAL OF POLITICS. Gainesville, Fla.: Southern Political Science Association, 1939-- . Quarterly.

JOURNAL OF SOUTHERN HISTORY. New Orleans: Southern Historical Association, 1935-- . Quarterly.

POLITICAL SCIENCE QUARTERLY. New York: Academy of Political Science, 1886-- .

PRESIDENTIAL STUDIES QUARTERLY. New York: Center for the Study of the Presidency, 1974-- .

The leading journal in the field.

PROLOGUE. Washington, D.C.: National Archives and Records Service, 1969-- . Quarterly.

Often mentions or discusses presidential papers.

PS. Washington, D.C.: American Political Science Association, 1968-- . Quarterly.

PUBLIC ADMINISTRATION REVIEW. Washington, D.C.: American Society for Public Administration, 1940-- . Bimonthly.

Often discusses aspects of the presidency and reviews books in the field.

PUBLIC OPINION QUARTERLY. New York: American Association for Public Opinion Research, 1937-- .

Contains research articles on all phases of the subject.

WESTERN POLITICAL QUARTERLY. Salt Lake: Western Political Science Association, 1948-- .

WILSON QUARTERLY. Washington, D.C.: Woodrow Wilson International Center for Scholars, 1976-- .

Critically annotates recent periodical literature from a broad spectrum of scholarly journals.

WORLD POLITICS. Princeton: Center of International Studies, 1948-- . Quarterly.

A journal of international relations.

E. PICTURES AND PHOTOGRAPHS

THE AMERICAN HERITAGE PICTORIAL HISTORY OF THE PRESIDENTS OF THE UNITED STATES. 2 vols. By the editors of American Heritage. New York: American Heritage Publishing Co.; book trade distribution by Simon and Schuster, 1968.

Bassett, Margaret Byrd. PROFILES AND PORTRAITS OF AMERICAN PRESIDENTS. Introduction by Henry F. Graff. New York: McKay, 1976. x, 306 p.

Blaisdell, Thomas C., Jr., et al. THE AMERICAN PRESIDENCY IN POLITICAL CARTOONS, 1776-1976. Salt Lake City: Peregrine Smith, 1976. 278 p. Illus.

A museum catalog to accompany a bicentennial exhibit on American political caricature with special emphasis upon the office of the president. Very well edited.

Collins, Herbert Ridgeway. PRESIDENTS ON WHEELS. Washington, D.C.: Acropolis Books, 1971. 224 p.

A history of presidential vehicles.

CONTEST FOR POWER: THE EXCITING PICTORIAL STORY OF THE AMERICAN PRESIDENTIAL ELECTIONS, THE PERSONALITIES, THE ISSUES, THE TURNING POINTS IN U.S. POLITICAL HISTORY, FROM 1778 TO THE PRESENT. By the Editors of News Front. New York: Year, 1968. 249 p.

Durant, John, and Durant, Alice. PICTORIAL HISTORY OF AMERICAN PRESIDENTS. New York: Castle Books, 1975. 375 p.

Lorant, Stefan. THE GLORIOUS BURDEN: THE HISTORY OF THE PRESIDENCY AND PRESIDENTIAL ELECTIONS FROM GEORGE WASHINGTON TO JAMES EARL CARTER, JR. Lenox, Mass.: Authors Edition, 1976. 1,104 p.

A splendid volume of illustrations gathered from many pictorial archives. Generous commentary make this one of the finest books on the presidency.

Milhollen, Hirst Dillon, and Kaplan, Milton. PRESIDENTS ON PARADE. New York: Macmillan Co., 1948. 425 p.

Photographs to 1947, reproduced in part from material in the Library of Congress, each with a brief commentary.

Post, Robert C., ed. EVERY FOUR YEARS. Washington, D.C.: Smithsonian Exposition Books, 1980. 228 p.

An excellent volume effectively blending a text by several presidential experts with numerous illustrations from the rich collection of presidential artifacts owned by the Smithsonian.

Whitney, David C. THE GRAPHIC STORY OF THE AMERICAN PRESIDENTS. Edited by Thomas C. Jones. Chicago: J.G. Ferguson Publishing Co., 1975. xl, 543 p.

Expanded and rearranged pictorial edition of the author's THE AMERICAN PRESIDENTS (1969).

Chapter 2
THE OFFICE OF PRESIDENT

A. ORIGINS OF THE PRESIDENCY

Bowen, Catherine Drinker. MIRACLE AT PHILADELPHIA: THE STORY OF THE CONSTITUTIONAL CONVENTION. Boston: Little, Brown, 1966. xix, 346 p.

A lively account for the general reader.

Farrand, Max, ed. THE RECORDS OF THE FEDERAL CONVENTION OF 1787. 4 vols. Rev. ed. New Haven, Conn.: Yale University Press, 1966.

Madison, James. NOTES OF DEBATES IN THE FEDERAL CONVENTION OF 1787. Introduction by Adrienne Koch. Athens: Ohio University Press, 1966. xxiii, 659 p.

First published separately in 1893 under title: JOURNAL OF THE FEDERAL CONVENTION KEPT BY JAMES MADISON.

Rossiter, Clinton. 1787: THE GRAND CONVENTION. New York: Macmillan, 1966. 443 p.

Especially good on the character and lives of the men who participated in framing the Constitution.

Thach, Charles C., Jr. THE CREATION OF THE PRESIDENCY, 1775-1789: A STUDY IN CONSTITUTIONAL HISTORY. Baltimore: Johns Hopkins Press, 1922. Reprint. New York: Da Capo Press, 1969. xii, 182 p.

Wright, Benjamin Fletcher, ed. THE FEDERALIST. Cambridge, Mass.: Belknap Press of Harvard University, 1961. viii, 572 p.

The office of president is discussed in essays numbered 67 to 77.

B. INAUGURATIONS

Cable, Mary. THE AVENUE OF THE PRESIDENTS. Boston: Houghton Mifflin, 1969. xxii, 248 p.

Cathedral of St. Peter and St. Paul. Rare Book Library. Washington, D.C. PRESIDENTIAL INAUGURAL BIBLES: CATALOGUE OF AN EXHIBITION, NOVEMBER 17, 1968 THROUGH FEBRUARY 23, 1969. Washington, D.C.: 1969. 49 p.

Durbin, Louise. INAUGURAL CAVALCADE. New York: Dodd, Mead, 1971. xii, 210 p.

> Describes the inaugural ceremonies of the thirty-seven presidents from Washington to Nixon drawing on contemporary letters, diaries, newspapers, prints, and photographs.

Dusterberg, Richard B. THE OFFICIAL INAUGURAL MEDALS OF THE PRESIDENTS OF THE UNITED STATES. 2d ed. Cincinnati: Medallion Press, 1976. iv, 140 p.

Freitag, Ruth S. PRESIDENTIAL INAUGURATIONS: A SELECTED LIST OF REFERENCES. 3d ed., rev. and enl. Washington, D.C.: Government Printing Office, 1969. vii, 230 p.

> First issued in 1949 by the General Reference and Bibliography Division of the Library of Congress.

Kittler, Glenn D. HAIL TO THE CHIEF! THE INAUGURATION DAYS OF OUR PRESIDENTS. Philadelphia: Chilton Books, 1965. 242 p.

Lafontaine, Charles V. "God and Nation in Selected U.S. Presidential Inaugural Addresses, 1789-1945." Part 2. JOURNAL OF CHURCH AND STATE 18 (Autumn 1976): 503-21.

Owsley, Clifford D. INAUGURAL. New York: Olympic Press, 1964. 154 p.

> Originated as a master's thesis at the American University, Washington, D.C.

Smylie, James H. "Providence and Presidents: Types of American Piety in Presidential Inaugurals." RELIGION IN LIFE 35 (Spring 1966): 270-82.

U.S. National Archives. LIST OF MOTION PICTURES AND SOUND RECORDINGS RELATING TO PRESIDENTIAL INAUGURATIONS. Washington, D.C.: National Archives, 1960. v, 20 p.

> Special list no. 16 compiled by E. Daniel Potts.

U.S. President. INAUGURAL ADDRESSES OF THE PRESIDENTS OF THE UNITED STATES FROM GEORGE WASHINGTON, 1789, TO RICHARD MILHOUS NIXON, 1973. Washington, D.C.: Government Printing Office, 1974. vi, 283 p.

C. WHITE HOUSE

Aikman, Lonnelle. THE LIVING WHITE HOUSE. 7th ed. Washington, D.C.: White House Historical Association, 1982. 151 p.

Bryant, Traphes. DOG DAYS AT THE WHITE HOUSE: THE OUTRAGEOUS MEMOIRS OF THE PRESIDENTIAL KENNEL KEEPER. New York: Macmillan, 1975. 343 p.

Carosso, Vincent P. "Music and Musicians in the White House." NEW YORK HISTORICAL SOCIETY QUARTERLY 48 (April 1964): 101-29.

Davison, Kenneth E., comp. "White House During the Hayes Era." HAYES HISTORICAL JOURNAL 1 (Fall 1977): 263-70.

Furman, Bess. WHITE HOUSE PROFILE: A SOCIAL HISTORY OF THE WHITE HOUSE, ITS OCCUPANTS AND ITS FESTIVITIES. Indianapolis: Bobbs-Merrill Co., 1951. 368 p.

Hurd, Charles. THE WHITE HOUSE STORY. New York: Hawthorn Books, 1966. 240 p.

Jeffries, Ona Griffin. IN AND OUT OF THE WHITE HOUSE, FROM WASHINGTON TO THE EISENHOWERS: AN INTIMATE GLIMPSE INTO THE SOCIAL AND DOMESTIC ASPECTS OF THE PRESIDENTIAL LIFE. New York: W. Funk, 1960. xi, 404 p.

Jensen, Amy La Follette. THE WHITE HOUSE AND ITS THIRTY-FIVE FAMILIES. Rev. ed. New York: McGraw-Hill, 1971. 321 p.

Jones, Robert, comp. THE PRESIDENT'S OWN WHITE HOUSE COOKBOOK. Chicago: Culinary Arts Institute, 1973. 110 p.

Lawson, Don. YOUNG PEOPLE IN THE WHITE HOUSE. Rev. ed. London and New York: Abelard-Schuman, 1970. 176 p.

Leish, Kenneth W. THE WHITE HOUSE. New York: Newsweek, 1972. 170 p.

Nesbitt, Victoria Henrietta. WHITE HOUSE DIARY. Garden City, N.Y.: Doubleday and Co., 1948. 314 p.

Memoirs of FDR's housekeeper.

Parks, Lillian Rogers. IT WAS FUN WORKING AT THE WHITE HOUSE. Illustrated by Isadore Parker. New York: Fleet Press Corp., 1969. 208 p.

A maid writes of her association with White House families, from Taft through Eisenhower, in her thirty years of employment.

Reit, Seymour. GROWING UP IN THE WHITE HOUSE. New York: Crowell-Collier Press, 1968. viii, 118 p.

Ryan, William, and Guinness, Desmond. THE WHITE HOUSE: AN ARCHITECTURAL HISTORY. New York: McGraw-Hill, 1980. x, 196 p.

Sadler, Christine. CHILDREN IN THE WHITE HOUSE. New York: Putnam, 1967. 316 p.

Shaw, Maud. WHITE HOUSE NANNIE: MY YEARS WITH CAROLINE AND JOHN KENNEDY, JR. New York: New American Library, 1965. 127 p.

Singleton, Esther. THE STORY OF THE WHITE HOUSE. 2 vols. New York: McClure Co., 1907. Reprint. New York: B. Blom, 1969.

Smith, Marie D. ENTERTAINING IN THE WHITE HOUSE. Rev. and updated ed. New York: Macfadden-Bartell, 1970. 320 p.

Truman, Margaret. WHITE HOUSE PETS. New York: D. McKay, 1969. x, 174 p.

Weidenfeld, Sheila Rabb. FIRST LADY'S LADY: WITH THE FORDS AT THE WHITE HOUSE. New York: G.P. Putnam's Sons, 1979. 419 p.

West, J.B. UPSTAIRS AT THE WHITE HOUSE: MY LIFE WITH THE FIRST LADIES. New York: Coward, McCann and Geoghegan, 1973. 381 p.

Wolff, Perry. A TOUR OF THE WHITE HOUSE WITH MRS. JOHN F. KENNEDY. Garden City, N.Y.: Doubleday and Co., 1962. 255 p.

Woodall, R. "White House." HISTORY TODAY 10 (October 1960): 695-701.

Chapter 3
GENERAL WORKS ON THE PRESIDENCY

A. SURVEY TREATMENTS

1. Basic Textbooks

Binkley, Wilfred Ellsworth. THE MAN IN THE WHITE HOUSE: HIS POWERS AND DUTIES. Rev. ed. New York: Harper and Row, 1964. viii, 274 p.

The product of a lifetime of study and reflection upon the office of president. Exceptionally readable and strong in its historical approach and insights.

DiClerico, Robert E. THE AMERICAN PRESIDENT. Englewood Cliffs, N.J.: Prentice-Hall, 1979. x, 374 p.

Stresses presidential selection, power, accountability, decision making, personality, and leadership. Many examples cited from the recent past.

Egger, Rowland. THE PRESIDENT OF THE UNITED STATES. 2d ed. New York: McGraw-Hill, 1972. viii, 198 p.

Organized around the principal functions of the office.

Funderburk, Charles. PRESIDENTS AND POLITICS: THE LIMITS OF POWER. Monterey, Calif.: Brooks, Cole Publishing Co., 1982. 288 p.

Hargrove, Erwin C. THE POWER OF THE MODERN PRESIDENCY. Foreword by Harold D. Lasswell. Philadelphia: Temple University Press, 1974. xi, 353 p.

A valuable synthesis of the literature on the subject.

______. PRESIDENTIAL LEADERSHIP: PERSONALITY AND POLITICAL STYLE. New York: Macmillan, 1966. v, 153 p.

Compares six "presidents of action" (the two Roosevelts, Wilson, and to a lesser extent, Truman, Kennedy, and Johnson) with three "presidents of restraint" (Taft, Hoover, and Eisenhower) as men who have shaped the modern presidency.

Heller, Francis H. THE PRESIDENCY: A MODERN PERSPECTIVE. New York: Random House, 1960. 114 p.

A neat introduction to the field with a useful bibliographical essay on the early literature of the presidency.

Hoopes, Roy. WHAT THE PRESIDENT OF THE UNITED STATES DOES. New York: John Day Co., 1974. 128 p.

A basic introduction and handbook on the office. For the general reader.

Hughes, Arthur J. THE AMERICAN PRESIDENCY. Encino, Calif.: Benziger, 1977. ix, 318 p.

A high school textbook. Has some notable illustrations of presidents and events occurring during their administrations.

James, Dorothy Buckton. THE CONTEMPORARY PRESIDENCY. 2d ed. Indianapolis: Pegasus, 1974. xiii, 336 p.

A study of presidential power from the New Deal to Watergate.

Koenig, Louis William. THE CHIEF EXECUTIVE. 4th ed. New York: Harcourt Brace Jovanovich, 1981. viii, 472 p.

The original textbook on the subject. Notable for its organization, understanding, and literary quality.

______. OFFICIAL MAKERS OF PUBLIC POLICY: CONGRESS AND THE PRESIDENT. Glenview, Ill.: Scott, Foresman and Co., 1967. vi, 197 p.

An excellent brief study, well documented with case examples.

Lammers, William W. PRESIDENTIAL POLITICS: PATTERNS AND PROSPECTS. New York: Harper and Row, 1976. xviii, 310 p.

Deals with presidential politics since 1932. Contains good summaries of the collapse of the Nixon presidency, changing perspectives on the office, and possible reforms of the presidency as an institution.

McConnell, Grant. THE MODERN PRESIDENCY. 2d ed. New York: St. Martin's Press, 1976. vii, 133 p.

A brief introduction to the subject. See especially, chapter on the presidency as "Myth and Symbol."

Mullen, William F. PRESIDENTIAL POWER AND POLITICS. New York: St. Martin's Press, 1976. viii, 294 p.

See especially the section on "Demythologizing the Presidency," pages 251-63, and the excellent bibliography which includes seminal articles on the subject.

Murphy, John Francis. THE PINNACLE: THE CONTEMPORARY AMERICAN PRESIDENCY. Philadelphia: Lippincott, 1974. 215 p.

Contains six chapters on individual presidents and their administrations from Hoover through Nixon.

Pious, Richard M. THE AMERICAN PRESIDENCY. New York: Basic Books, 1979. xx, 491 p.

Best of the recent textbooks but not as well organized as Koenig's book (p. 18). Contains much recent information.

Polsby, Nelson W. CONGRESS AND THE PRESIDENCY. Englewood Cliffs, N.J.: Prentice-Hall, 1964. viii, 120 p.

Rossiter, Clinton. THE AMERICAN PRESIDENCY. Rev. ed. New York: Harcourt, Brace and World, 1960. 270 p.

An excellent little volume which combines both history and political science effectively. Noted for its lively and interesting style.

Shull, Steven A. PRESIDENTIAL POLICY MAKING: AN ANALYSIS. Brunswick, Ohio: King's Court Communications, 1979. xiv, 367 p.

Concentrates on the public administration and policy-making side of the presidency. Contains many excellent charts and tables. An appendix analyzes the literature and research on the presidency. Excellent bibliography.

Sickels, Robert J. THE PRESIDENCY: AN INTRODUCTION. Englewood Cliffs, N.J.: Prentice-Hall, 1980. vii, 339 p.

Examines modern presidents broadly--their selection, politics, administrative problems, domestic affairs, foreign affairs, personality, and popularity.

______. PRESIDENTIAL TRANSACTIONS. Englewood Cliffs, N.J.: Prentice-Hall, 1974. viii, 184 p.

Applies the insights of exchange theory to the study of the presidency.

Strum, Philippa. PRESIDENTIAL POWER AND AMERICAN DEMOCRACY. 2d ed. Santa Monica, Calif.: Goodyear Publishing Co., 1979. xiv, 184 p.

Discusses presidential accountability and willingness to share power with other duly constituted bodies. Examples are drawn from the Kennedy through Carter years.

Vinyard, Dale. THE PRESIDENCY. New York: Scribner's, 1971. x, 214 p.

A brief and traditional introduction to the subject.

2. Selected Readings

"The American Presidency." AMERICAN HERITAGE 15 (August 1964): entire issue.

Bach, Stanley, and Sulzner, George, comps. PERSPECTIVES ON THE PRESIDENCY. Lexington, Mass.: D.C. Heath, 1974. viii, 411 p.

A selection of seminal essays on the presidency combining description and analysis with some of the better contemporary writing and research on the subject.

Bailey, Harry A., Jr., ed. CLASSICS OF THE AMERICAN PRESIDENCY. Oak Park, Ill.: Moore Publishing Co., 1980. xi, 429 p.

A judicious sampling of some of the most basic periodical literature on the presidency and excerpts from key books on the subject.

Barber, James David, ed. CHOOSING THE PRESIDENT. Englewood Cliffs, N.J.: Prentice-Hall, 1974. vii, 208 p.

A hard, long-range look at our presidential election system by eight leading authorities on the subject. The essays were background papers for the 44th American Assembly, Arden House, New York, December 1973.

Charlesworth, James C., ed. "Meaning of the 1952 Presidential Election." ANNALS OF THE AMERICAN ACADEMY OF POLITICAL AND SOCIAL SCIENCE 283 (September 1952): 1-186.

A good preview by eighteen specialists.

Cornwell, Elmer E., ed. THE AMERICAN PRESIDENCY: VITAL CENTER. Chicago: Scott, Foresman, 1966. 166 p.

A good brief set of basic readings on the presidency. Cornwell contributes a significant concluding essay on the study of the presidency.

Cronin, Thomas E., ed. RETHINKING THE PRESIDENCY. Boston: Little, Brown, 1982. ix, 403 p.

Twenty-six essays by leading experts in the field. Very authoritative and up-to-date.

Cronin, Thomas E., and Tugwell, Rexford G., eds. THE PRESIDENCY REAPPRAISED. 2d ed. New York: Praeger, 1977. xii, 371 p.

Seventeen specialists reconsider the institutionalized presidency, the imperial presidency, and presidential government in the aftermath of Watergate. Originally issued in 1974.

Davis, Vincent, ed. THE POST-IMPERIAL PRESIDENCY. New Brunswick, N.J.: Transaction Books, 1980. xi, 190 p.

A collection of readings by well-known authorities including Aaron Wildavsky, Thomas E. Cronin, and George Reedy.

Dolce, Philip C., and Skau, George H., eds. POWER AND THE PRESIDENCY. New York: Scribner's, 1976. xii, 339 p.

An outgrowth of a CBS television series entitled "The American Presidency." Most of the contributions are by well-known scholars, journalists, and public officials who treat the historical evolution of presidential power in the United States in brief compass.

Dunn, Charles W., ed. THE FUTURE OF THE AMERICAN PRESIDENCY. Morristown, N.J.: General Learning Press, 1975. xii, 363 p.

An analysis of the presidential office since World War II by twelve authors representing academia, the U.S. Congress, and the news media. Good bibliographies after most essays and at the end of the volume.

Edwards, George C. III, and Wayne, Stephen J. STUDYING THE PRESIDENCY. Knoxville: University of Tennessee Press, 1983. 320 p.

Haight, David E., and Johnston, Larry D., eds. THE PRESIDENT: ROLES AND POWERS. Chicago: Rand McNally, 1965. x, 400 p.

Hirschfield, Robert S., ed. THE POWER OF THE PRESIDENCY: CONCEPTS AND CONTROVERSY. 2d ed. Chicago: Aldine Publishing Co., 1973. xii, 395 p.

Concentrates on the scope and limits of presidential power.

Klein, Mary, comp. THE PRESIDENCY: THE POWER AND GLORY. Minneapolis: Winston Press, 1973. x, 272 p.

A collection of essays.

Mansfield, Harvey C., Sr., ed. CONGRESS AGAINST THE PRESIDENT. New York: Academy of Political Science, 1975. vi, 200 p.

Some of the essays were given at a conference held at Columbia University on 2 June 1975.

Nikolaieff, George A., comp. THE PRESIDENT AND THE CONSTITUTION. Reference Shelf Series. New York: H.W. Wilson Co., 1974. 230 p.

Devoted to articles on executive power.

Peters, Charles, comp. INSIDE THE SYSTEM: A WASHINGTON MONTHLY READER. Introduction by Richard H. Rovere. New York: Praeger Publishers, 1970. xviii, 333 p.

The first section deals with the presidency.

Polsby, Nelson W., comp. THE MODERN PRESIDENCY. New York: Random House, 1973. xii, 236 p.

A book of readings organized by the presidents they concern from Franklin D. Roosevelt to Richard Nixon.

"The Presidency." CURRENT HISTORY 25 (September 1953): entire issue.

A special issue with eight articles by authorities on the subject.

THE PRESIDENCY IN CONTEMPORARY CONTEXT. Edited by Norman C. Thomas. New York: Dodd, Mead, 1975. viii, 348 p.

Sixteen essays on the presidency in recent years.

"The Presidency in Transition." JOURNAL OF POLITICS 11 (February 1949): 5-256.

Reedy, George, advisory ed. THE PRESIDENCY. New York: New York Times, 1975. xi, 468 p.

Saffell, David C., ed. WATERGATE: ITS EFFECTS ON THE AMERICAN POLITICAL SYSTEM. Cambridge, Mass.: Winthrop Publishers, 1974. xi, 371 p.

A well-chosen set of readings which places the Watergate affair within the context of the entire operation of American government.

Shull, Steven A., and LeLoup, Lance T. THE PRESIDENCY: STUDIES IN POLICY MAKING. Brunswick, Ohio: King's Court Communications, 1979. xii, 306 p.

A basic reader containing sixteen articles concerning approach, process, policies, and implementation and results through the Carter administration.

Thomas, Norman C., and Baade, Hans W., eds. THE INSTITUTIONALIZED PRESIDENCY. Dobbs Ferry, N.Y.: Oceana Publications, 1972. 239 p.

Originally published in LAW AND CONTEMPORARY PROBLEMS 35 (Summer 1970): 427-665. Offers an appraisal of the office of the president at the beginning of the 1970s.

Warren, Sidney. THE AMERICAN PRESIDENCY: READINGS. Englewood Cliffs, N.J.: Prentice-Hall, 1967. xii, 176 p.

Westin, Alan Furman, ed. THE ANATOMY OF A CONSTITUTIONAL LAW CASE: YOUNGSTOWN SHEET AND TUBE CO. V. SAWYER, THE STEEL SEIZURE DECISION. New York: Macmillan, 1958. viii, 183 p.

Speeches, debates, and court documents concerning the seizure of eighty-five steel companies by order of President Truman in 1952, and the decision of the Supreme Court that he lacked authority for the seizure. With comments on the "inherent powers" and emergency powers of the president, the separation of powers, and the limits of eminent domain.

Wildavsky, Aaron B., ed. PERSPECTIVES ON THE PRESIDENCY. Boston: Little, Brown, 1975. ix, 539 p.

A collection of essays on the presidency written in the early 1970s when the study of the American presidency accelerated very rapidly.

______. THE PRESIDENCY. Boston: Little, Brown, 1969. xv, 795 p.

An excellent collection of forty-eight essays gathered from a wide range of sources to document the presidency as a subject for social science analysis. The best of the anthologies published in the 1960s.

Wise, Sidney, comp. THE PRESIDENTIAL OFFICE. Edited by Sidney Wise and Richard F. Schier. New York: Crowell, 1968. vii, 248 p.

Six basic essays by Clinton Rossiter, Harold Laski, James W. Davis, James MacGregor Burns, Louis Koenig, and Neil MacNeil.

3. Symposia

Henry, L.L., ed. "The American Presidency: A Symposium." PUBLIC ADMINISTRATION REVIEW 29 (September 1969): 441-82.

Hoxie, R. Gordon, ed. THE PRESIDENCY OF THE 1970'S. Proceedings of the 1971 Montauk Symposium on the Office of the President of the United States. New York: Center for the Study of the Presidency, 1973. xv, 196 p.

Based on a symposium held at Gurney's Inn on Long Island, 29-31 October 1971, and attended by 175 leaders from business, government, and academe. Covers the period from FDR through Nixon.

______. THE WHITE HOUSE: ORGANIZATION AND OPERATIONS. Proceedings of the 1970 Montauk Symposium on the Office of the President of the United States. New York: Center for the Study of the Presidency, 1971. xxi, 218 p.

Based on a symposium held at Gurney's Inn on Long Island, 3, 4, and 5 April 1970. Speakers: senior White House staff members from every administration from the Hoover through the Nixon period.

Hoy, John C., and Bernstein, Melvin H., eds. THE EFFECTIVE PRESIDENT. Pacific Palisades, Calif.: Palisade Publishers, 1976. ix, 189 p.

Based upon a symposium held at the University of California, Irvine Campus in 1976, and attended by students and faculty from more than forty colleges and universities together with public leaders, journalists, writers, and scholars of national renown.

Livingston, William S.; Dodd, Lawrence C.; and Schott, Richard L., eds. THE PRESIDENCY AND THE CONGRESS: A SHIFTING BALANCE OF POWER? Austin, Tex.: Lyndon B. Johnson School of Public Affairs; Lyndon Baines Johnson Library, 1979. xvii, 432 p.

Papers presented at a symposium held at the University of Texas at Austin, November 1977, sponsored by the Lyndon B. Johnson Library and the Lyndon B. Johnson School of Public Affairs.

Paschal, J.F., ed. "Presidential Office: A Symposium." LAW AND CONTEMPORARY PROBLEMS 21 (Autumn 1956): 609-752.

"Presidential Power." LAW AND CONTEMPORARY PROBLEMS 40 (Spring-Summer 1976): entire issue.

Papers presented at a conference held at Duke University, 23-24 January 1976, organized by Institute of Policy Sciences and Public Affairs and Duke University School of Law.

"The Presidency." Special Issue. CURRENT HISTORY 25 (September 1953): entire issue.

Ray, Joseph M., ed. THE COATTAILLESS LANDSLIDE: EL PASO PAPERS ON THE 1972 PRESIDENTIAL CAMPAIGN. El Paso: Texas Western Press, University of Texas at El Paso, 1974. xii, 164 p.

Papers from the fourth symposium on presidential elections held at the University of Texas at El Paso on 13-14 September 1972.

______. "The President: Rex, Princeps, Imperator?" El Paso: Texas Western Press, 1969. ix, 101 p.

A study of the 1968 presidential election based upon the first three symposiums on presidential elections held at the University of Texas in El Paso.

Roberts, Charles, ed. HAS THE PRESIDENT TOO MUCH POWER? New York: Harper's Magazine Press, 1974. xii, 257 p.

The proceedings of a conference for journalists sponsored by the Washington Journalism Center, 15-18 October 1973.

B. MONOGRAPHS

Albertazzie, Ralph, and terHorst, Jerald F. THE FLYING WHITE HOUSE: THE STORY OF AIR FORCE ONE. New York: Coward, McCann and Geoghegan, 1979. 350 p.

Alley, Robert S. SO HELP ME GOD: RELIGION AND THE PRESIDENCY, WILSON TO NIXON. Richmond: John Knox Press, 1972. 160 p.

Amlund, Curtis Arthur. NEW PERSPECTIVES ON THE PRESIDENCY. New York: Philosophical Library, 1969. 113 p.

Armbruster, Maxim Ethan. THE PRESIDENTS OF THE UNITED STATES AND THEIR ADMINISTRATIONS FROM WASHINGTON TO FORD. New York: Horizon Press, 1981. 400 p.

Bailey, Thomas Andrew. PRESIDENTIAL GREATNESS: THE IMAGE AND THE MAN FROM GEORGE WASHINGTON TO THE PRESENT. New York: Appleton-Century, 1966. Reprint. New York: Irvington Publishers, 1978. xiii, 368 p.

______. PRESIDENTIAL SAINTS AND SINNERS. New York: The Free Press, 1981. viii, 304 p.

Barber, James David. THE PRESIDENTIAL CHARACTER: PREDICTING PERFORMANCE IN THE WHITE HOUSE. 2d ed. Englewood Cliffs, N.J.: Prentice-Hall, 1977. xi, 576 p.

General Works on the Presidency

Barger, Harold M. THE AMERICAN PRESIDENCY: MYTHS AND REALITIES. Written for the Robert A. Taft Institute of Government. New York: The Institute, 1979. 57 p.

Barrett, Patricia. RELIGIOUS LIBERTY AND THE AMERICAN PRESIDENCY: A STUDY IN CHURCH-STATE RELATIONS. New York: Herder and Herder, 1963. ix, 166 p.

Bell, Jack. THE PRESIDENCY: OFFICE OF POWER. Boston: Allyn and Bacon, 1967. v, 182 p.

______. THE SPLENDID MISERY: THE STORY OF THE PRESIDENCY AND POWER POLITICS AT CLOSE RANGE. Garden City, N.Y.: Doubleday, 1960. 474 p.

Bestor, Arthur E. "Thomas Jefferson and the Freedom of Books." In THREE PRESIDENTS AND THEIR BOOKS. Edited by Robert B. Downs. Urbana: University of Illinois Press, 1963. ix, 129 p.

> Part of the 1953 Windsor Lectures in Librarianship devoted to a theme that year of "Books and American Statesmanship." Originally published by the University of Illinois in 1955.

Boller, Paul F., Jr. PRESIDENTIAL ANECDOTES. New York: Oxford University Press, 1981. xvi, 410 p.

Bolles, Blair. MEN OF GOOD INTENTIONS: CRISIS OF THE AMERICAN PRESIDENCY. Garden City, N.Y.: Doubleday, 1960. x, 359 p.

Bonnell, John Sutherland. PRESIDENTIAL PROFILES: RELIGION IN THE LIFE OF AMERICAN PRESIDENTS. Philadelphia: Westminster Press, 1971. 253 p.

Brown, Ernest Francis. THE READING OF THE PRESIDENTS: AN ADDRESS DELIVERED AT A BANQUET CELEBRATING THE 25TH ANNIVERSARY OF THE TRACY W. McGREGOR LIBRARY, 1939-1964. Charlottesville: Tracy W. McGregor Library, University of Virginia, 1965. 13 p.

Brown, Stuart Gerry. THE AMERICAN PRESIDENCY: LEADERSHIP, PARTISANSHIP, AND POPULARITY. New York: Macmillan, 1966. viii, 279 p.

Brownlow, Louis. THE PRESIDENT AND THE PRESIDENCY. Chicago: University of Chicago Press, 1949. xi, 137 p.

Buchanan, Bruce. THE PRESIDENTIAL EXPERIENCE: WHAT THE OFFICE DOES TO THE MAN. Englewood Cliffs, N.J.: Prentice-Hall, 1978. ix, 198 p.

> A perceptive study which explains why the structure of the presidency promotes secrecy and deception, and how bureaucratic red tape frustrates a president's ability to work with Congress, the press, and the public to get things done. Numerous case examples are cited.

Burns, James MacGregor. PRESIDENTIAL GOVERNMENT: THE CRUCIBLE OF LEADERSHIP. New preface by the author. Boston: Houghton Mifflin, 1973. xxv, 366 p.

Originally published by Houghton Mifflin in 1966.

Califano, Joseph A. A PRESIDENTIAL NATION. New York: Norton, 1975. xii, 338 p.

Cavaioli, Frank J. WEST POINT AND THE PRESIDENCY. New York: St. John's University Press, 1962. iv, 154 p.

Collins, Herbert Ridgeway. PRESIDENTS ON WHEELS. Washington, D.C.: Acropolis Books, 1971. 224 p.

Corwin, Edward S., and Koenig, Louis W. THE PRESIDENCY TODAY. New York: New York University Press, 1956. ix, 138 p.

Cousins, Norman, ed. 'IN GOD WE TRUST': THE RELIGIOUS BELIEFS AND IDEAS OF THE AMERICAN FOUNDING FATHERS. New York: Harper, 1958. viii, 464 p.

Coyle, David Cushman. ORDEAL OF THE PRESIDENCY. Washington, D.C.: Public Affairs Press, 1960. Reprint. Westport, Conn.: Greenwood Press, 1973. v, 408 p.

Concerns personal abuse suffered by presidents.

Cronin, Thomas E. THE STATE OF THE PRESIDENCY. 2d ed. Boston: Little, Brown, 1980. vii, 417 p.

Eleven perceptive essays by a distinguished student of the presidency.

Cunliffe, Marcus. AMERICAN PRESIDENTS AND THE PRESIDENCY. 2d ed., rev. and enl. New York: McGraw-Hill, 1976. 467 p.

Published in 1968 under title: THE AMERICAN HERITAGE HISTORY OF THE PRESIDENCY.

Denton, Robert E., Jr. THE SYMBOLIC DIMENSIONS OF THE AMERICAN PRESIDENCY: DESCRIPTION AND ANALYSIS. Prospect Heights, Ill.: Waveland Press, Inc., 1982. xii, 154 p.

De Santis, Vincent P. REPUBLICANS FACE THE SOUTHERN QUESTION--THE NEW DEPARTURE YEARS, 1877-1897. Baltimore: Johns Hopkins Press, 1959. 275 p.

Dulce, Berton, and Richter, Edward J. RELIGION AND THE PRESIDENCY: A RECURRING AMERICAN PROBLEM. New York: Macmillan Co., 1962. x, 245 p.

Traces the evolution of the religious issue in American politics with particular emphasis upon John F. Kennedy's 1960 campaign for the presidency.

Durant, John, and Durant, Alice. THE PRESIDENTS OF THE UNITED STATES: A HISTORY OF THE PRESIDENTS OF THE UNITED STATES: WITH AN ENCYCLOPEDIC SUPPLEMENT ON THE OFFICE AND POWERS OF THE PRESIDENCY: CHRONOLOGIES, AND RECORDS OF PRESIDENTIAL ELECTIONS. Commemorative ed. 2 vols. Miami: A. A. Gache, 1976. 390 p.

Fincher, Ernest Barksdale. THE PRESIDENCY: AN AMERICAN INVENTION. New York: Abelard-Schuman, 1977. xi, 210 p.

Examines the office and powers of the presidency citing specific actions, decisions, and ideas of different presidents.

Flatto, Elie. THE SECOND AMERICAN REVOLUTION: DECLINE AND FALL OF THE PRESIDENCY. New York: Arica Press, 1974. xi, 93 p.

Deals with the impact of modern technology and communications media upon political institutions and the future of the American presidency.

Fuller, Edmund, and Green, David E. GOD IN THE WHITE HOUSE: THE FAITHS OF AMERICAN PRESIDENTS. New York: Crown, 1968. 246 p.

Goebel, Dorothy, and Goebel, Julius, Jr. GENERALS IN THE WHITE HOUSE. Garden City, N.Y.: Doubleday, Doran and Co., 1945. Reprint. Freeport, N.Y.: Books for Libraries Press, 1971. 276 p.

Haas, Irvin. HISTORIC HOMES OF THE AMERICAN PRESIDENTS. New York: David McKay Co., 1976. xiii, 209 p.

A traveler's guide to American presidential homes still in existence and open to the public.

Hart, James. THE AMERICAN PRESIDENCY IN ACTION, 1789: A STUDY IN CONSTITUTIONAL HISTORY. New York: Macmillan Co., 1948. xvi, 256 p.

Hecht, Marie B. BEYOND THE PRESIDENCY: THE RESIDUES OF POWER. New York: Macmillan, 1976. xvi, 348 p.

Hersey, John. ASPECTS OF THE PRESIDENCY: TRUMAN AND FORD IN OFFICE. New Haven, Conn., and New York: Ticknor and Fields, 1980. xix, 247 p.

Hughes, Emmet John. THE LIVING PRESIDENCY: THE RESOURCES AND DILEMMAS OF THE AMERICAN PRESIDENTIAL OFFICE. New York: Coward, McCann and Geoghegan, 1973. 377 p.

Hyman, Sidney. THE AMERICAN PRESIDENT. New York: Harper, 1954. Reprint. Westport, Conn.: Greenwood Press, 1974. 342 p.

_____, ed. "The Office of the American Presidency." ANNALS OF THE AMERICAN ACADEMY OF POLITICAL AND SOCIAL SCIENCE 307 (September 1956): entire issue.

An excellent special issue featuring fourteen essays by outstanding authorities on the presidency.

Isely, Bliss. THE PRESIDENTS: MEN OF FAITH. Boston: W. A. Wilde Co., 1953. 284 p.

Covers Washington through Eisenhower.

Johnson, Amandus. JOHN HANSON: FIRST PRESIDENT OF THE UNITED STATES UNDER THE ARTICLES OF CONFEDERATION. Philadelphia: Swedish Colonial Society, 1966. 24 p.

Jones, Cranston. HOMES OF THE AMERICAN PRESIDENTS. New York: McGraw-Hill Book Co., 1962. 232 p.

A pictorial survey of historic homes occupied by thirty-four American presidents from Washington through Kennedy. Richly documented by forty color plates and three hundred black and white illustrations.

Jones, Robert, comp. THE PRESIDENT'S OWN WHITE HOUSE COOKBOOK. Chicago: Culinary Arts Institute, 1973. 110 p.

Laski, Harold J. THE AMERICAN PRESIDENCY: AN INTERPRETATION. New York: Harper and Brothers, 1940. Reprint. New introduction by James MacGregor Burns. New Brunswick, N.J.: Transaction Books, 1980. ix, 278 p.

Long, John Cuthbert. THE LIBERAL PRESIDENTS: A STUDY OF THE LIBERAL TRADITION IN THE AMERICAN PRESIDENCY. New York: Thomas Y. Crowell, 1948. Reprint. Port Washington, N.Y.: Kennikat Press, 1965. 226 p.

Longaker, Richard P. THE PRESIDENCY AND INDIVIDUAL LIBERTIES. Ithaca, N.Y.: Cornell University Press, 1961. xii, 239 p.

Lurie, Leonard. PARTY POLITICS: WHY WE HAVE POOR PRESIDENTS. New York: Stein and Day, 1980. xi, 326 p.

MacNeil, Neil. THE PRESIDENT'S MEDAL, 1789-1977. New York: C.N. Potter, distributed by Crown Publishers, 1977. 160 p.

Marx, Rudolph. THE HEALTH OF THE PRESIDENTS. New York: Putnam, 1961. 376 p.

Morgan, Howard Wayne. FROM HAYES TO McKINLEY: NATIONAL PARTY POLITICS, 1877-1896. Syracuse, N.Y.: Syracuse University Press, 1969. x, 618 p.

Moses, John B., and Cross, Wilbur. PRESIDENTIAL COURAGE. New York: W.W. Norton and Co., 1980. 249 p.

Paolucci, Henry. THE SOUTH AND THE PRESIDENCY: FROM RECONSTRUCTION TO CARTER, A LONG DAY'S TASK. Whitestone, N.Y.: Published for the Bagehot Council by Griffin House Publications, 1978. 22 p.

Patterson, Caleb Perry. PRESIDENTIAL GOVERNMENT IN THE UNITED STATES. Chapel Hill: University of North Carolina Press, 1947. ix, 301 p.

Reedy, George E. THE PRESIDENCY IN FLUX. New York: Columbia University Press, 1973. vii, 133 p.

_____. THE TWILIGHT OF THE PRESIDENCY. New York: World Publishing Co., 1970. xvii, 205 p.

Reinfeld, Fred. THE BIGGEST JOB IN THE WORLD: THE AMERICAN PRESIDENCY. New York: Crowell, 1964. 229 p.

Rienow, Robert. THE LONELY QUEST: THE EVOLUTION OF PRESIDENTIAL LEADERSHIP. Chicago: Follett Publishing Co., 1966. xiv, 307 p.

Rosenman, Samuel Irving, and Rosenman, Dorothy. PRESIDENTIAL STYLE: SOME GIANTS AND A PYGMY IN THE WHITE HOUSE. Introduction by James MacGregor Burns. New York: Harper and Row, 1976. xx, 602 p.

Russell, Francis. THE PRESIDENT MAKERS: FROM MARK HANNA TO JOSEPH P. KENNEDY. Boston: Little, Brown, 1976. vi, 407 p.

A popular treatment not well founded in primary sources.

Schlesinger, Arthur Meier, Jr. THE IMPERIAL PRESIDENCY. Boston: Houghton Mifflin, 1973. x, 505 p.

Schubert, Glendon A., Jr. THE PRESIDENCY AND THE COURTS. Minneapolis: University of Minnesota Press, 1957. xi, 391 p.

Scigliano, Robert. THE SUPREME COURT AND THE PRESIDENCY. New York: Free Press, 1971. x, 233 p.

Sinkler, George. THE RACIAL ATTITUDES OF AMERICAN PRESIDENTS, FROM ABRAHAM LINCOLN TO THEODORE ROOSEVELT. Garden City, N.Y.: Doubleday, 1971. xiii, 413 p.

Small, Norman Jerome. SOME PRESIDENTIAL INTERPRETATIONS OF THE PRESIDENCY. Baltimore: Johns Hopkins Press, 1932. Reprint. New York: Da Capo Press, 1970. 208 p.

Stanwood, Edward. A HISTORY OF THE PRESIDENCY. 2 vols. Boston: Houghton Mifflin, 1928. Reprint. New ed. rev. by Charles Knowles Bolton. Clifton, N.J.: A. M. Kelley, 1975.

Steinberg, Alfred. THE FIRST TEN: THE FOUNDING PRESIDENTS AND THEIR ADMINISTRATIONS. Garden City, N.Y.: Doubleday, 1967. ix, 493 p.

Steinfield, Melvin. OUR RACIST PRESIDENTS: FROM WASHINGTON TO NIXON. San Ramon, Calif.: Consensus Publishers, 1972. 304 p.

Tourtellot, Arthur Bernon. THE PRESIDENTS ON THE PRESIDENCY. New York: Russell and Russell, 1970. xiv, 505 p.

Tugwell, Rexford Guy. OFF COURSE: FROM TRUMAN TO NIXON. New York: Praeger, 1971. ix, 326 p.

U.S. National Park Service. THE PRESIDENTS: FROM THE INAUGURATION OF JIMMY CARTER: HISTORIC PLACES COMMEMORATING THE CHIEF EXECUTIVES OF THE UNITED STATES. National Survey of Historic Sites and Buildings, vol. 20. Rev. ed. Washington, D.C.: U.S. Department of the Interior, National Park Service, U.S. Government Printing Office, 1977. x, 606 p.

Walker, Kenneth Roland. THE DAYS THE PRESIDENTS DIED. Little Rock: Arkansas Press, 1966. xi, 175 p.

Wicker, Tom. JFK AND LBJ: THE INFLUENCE OF PERSONALITY UPON POLITICS. New York: Morrow, 1968. 297 p.

Wold, Karl. MR. PRESIDENT--HOW IS YOUR HEALTH? St. Paul, Minn.: Bruce Publishing Co., 1948. x, 214 p.

C. COLLECTIVE BIOGRAPHIES ON SPECIFIC ADMINISTRATIONS

Agar, Herbert. THE PEOPLE'S CHOICE, FROM WASHINGTON TO HARDING: A STUDY IN DEMOCRACY. New York: Houghton Mifflin Co., 1933. Reprint. Dunwoody, Ga.: N. S. Berg, 1968. xxi, 337 p.

Allen, George Edward. PRESIDENTS WHO HAVE KNOWN ME. New York: Simon and Schuster, 1960. xi, 290 p.

First edition published in 1950. Includes Presidents Roosevelt, Truman, and Eisenhower, 1929-1960. A lighthearted account by a perennial court jester to the nation's chief executives.

THE AMERICAN HERITAGE BOOK OF THE PRESIDENTS AND FAMOUS AMERICANS. Created and designed by the editors of American Heritage. New York: Dell Publishing Co., 1967. 1,083 p.

Barclay, Barbara. LAMPS TO LIGHT THE WAY: OUR PRESIDENTS. Presidential Portraits by Celeste Swayne-Courtney. Glendale, Calif.: Bowmar, 1970. xi, 444 p.

Bassett, Margaret Byrd. PROFILES AND PORTRAITS OF AMERICAN PRESIDENTS AND THEIR WIVES. Introduction by Henry F. Graff. Freeport, Maine: B. Wheelwright Co., 1969. x, 449 p.

Blum, John Morton. THE PROGRESSIVE PRESIDENTS: ROOSEVELT, WILSON, ROOSEVELT, JOHNSON. New York: W.W. Norton and Co., 1980. 221 p.

A study of the strong presidency concept as practiced by four twentieth-century presidents in the progressive mold.

Booth, Edward Townsend. COUNTRY LIFE IN AMERICA AS LIVED BY TEN PRESIDENTS OF THE UNITED STATES: JOHN ADAMS, GEORGE WASHINGTON, THOMAS JEFFERSON, ANDREW JACKSON, MARTIN VAN BUREN, WILLIAM HENRY HARRISON, JAMES BUCHANAN, ABRAHAM LINCOLN, THEODORE ROOSEVELT, CALVIN COOLIDGE. New York: Knopf, 1947. Reprint. Westport, Conn.: Greenwood Press, 1973. xviii, 264 p.

Borden, Morton, ed. AMERICA'S ELEVEN GREATEST PRESIDENTS. 2d ed. Chicago: Rand McNally, 1971. xii, 295 p.

First published in 1961 under the title: AMERICA'S TEN GREATEST PRESIDENTS.

Bowers, Claude G. MAKING DEMOCRACY A REALITY: JEFFERSON, JACKSON, AND POLK. Memphis: Memphis State College Press, 1954. xi, 170 p.

The J.P. Young lectures in American history.

Bruce, David K.E. SIXTEEN AMERICAN PRESIDENTS: FROM WASHINGTON TO LINCOLN. Indianapolis: Bobbs-Merrill Co., 1962. 336 p.

A series of informal portraits by a veteran career diplomat.

Carpenter, Frank George. CARP'S WASHINGTON. Arranged and edited by Frances Carpenter. New York: McGraw-Hill, 1960. xv, 314 p.

Covers the decades after the Civil War with attention to presidential personalities and politics.

Freidel, Frank. OUR COUNTRY'S PRESIDENTS. Introduction by Jimmy Carter. Foreword by Melville Bell Grosvenor. Prepared by National Geographic Special Publications Division. 8th ed. Washington, D.C.: National Geographic Society, 1979. 278 p.

Presents brief biographies of the presidents from George Washington to Jimmy Carter.

Hess, Stephen. AMERICA'S POLITICAL DYNASTIES FROM ADAMS TO KENNEDY. Garden City, N.Y.: Doubleday, 1966. 736 p.

Hofstadter, Richard. THE AMERICAN POLITICAL TRADITION AND THE MEN WHO MADE IT. New York: Alfred A. Knopf, 1949. xi, 378 p.

A classic treatment of the American past through twelve brilliant biographical portraits, including eight presidents: Jefferson, Jackson, Lincoln, Cleveland, Theodore Roosevelt, Wilson, Hoover, and Franklin D. Roosevelt.

Krock, Arthur. MEMOIRS: SIXTY YEARS ON THE FIRING LINE. New York: Funk and Wagnalls, 1968. xii, 508 p.

Intimate recollections of twelve American presidents from Theodore Roosevelt to Richard Nixon by a famous NEW YORK TIMES observer.

Lindop, Edmund. WHITE HOUSE SPORTSMEN. Boston: Houghton Mifflin, 1964. 172 p.

McCoy, Donald R. "Trends in Viewing Herbert Hoover, Franklin D. Roosevelt, Harry S. Truman, and Dwight D. Eisenhower." MIDWEST QUARTERLY 20 (Winter 1979): 117-36.

Martin, Asa Earl. AFTER THE WHITE HOUSE. State College, Pa.: Penns Valley Publishers, 1951. 464 p.

An intimate, revealing, and human picture of what happened to twenty-four ex-presidents after their retirement from the White House. Stops with Herbert Hoover's life.

Mayo, Bernard Joseph. MYTHS AND MEN: PATRICK HENRY, GEORGE WASHINGTON, THOMAS JEFFERSON. Athens: University of Georgia Press, 1959. xii, 71 p.

Miller, Hope Ridings. SCANDALS IN THE HIGHEST OFFICE: FACTS AND FICTIONS IN THE PRIVATE LIVES OF OUR PRESIDENTS. New York: Random House, 1973. 280 p.

Morgan, James. OUR PRESIDENTS. 3d ed. New York: Macmillan, 1969. xx, 548 p.

Chapters on Kennedy and Johnson by Herbert S. Parmet.

PRESIDENTS NORTH CAROLINA GAVE THE NATION. Raleigh: Commission for a Memorial to the Three North Carolina Presidents, 1969. 61 p.

Andrew Jackson, James K. Polk, and Andrew Johnson.

Purdy, Virginia C., and Reed, Daniel J., comps. PRESIDENTIAL PORTRAITS. Edited by J. Benjamin Townsend. Washington, D.C.: Smithsonian Institution Press, 1968. 75 p.

Sievers, Harry J., ed. SIX PRESIDENTS FROM THE EMPIRE STATE. Tarrytown, N.Y.: Sleepy Hollow Restorations, 1974. x, 208 p.

Smith, A. Merriman. MERRIMAN SMITH'S BOOK OF PRESIDENTS: A WHITE HOUSE MEMOIR. Edited by Timothy G. Smith, with a foreword by Robert J. Donovan. New York: Norton, 1972. 250 p.

______. THANK YOU, MR. PRESIDENT: A WHITE HOUSE NOTEBOOK. New York: Harper, 1946. Reprint. New York: Da Capo Press, 1976. x, 304 p.

Sokolsky, Eric. OUR SEVEN GREATEST PRESIDENTS. Foreword by James A. Farley. New York: Exposition Press, 1964. 120 p.

Steinberg, Alfred. THE FIRST TEN: THE FOUNDING PRESIDENTS AND THEIR ADMINISTRATIONS. Garden City, N.Y.: Doubleday, 1967. ix, 493 p.

Stoddard, Henry Luther. AS I KNEW THEM: PRESIDENTS AND POLITICS FROM GRANT TO COOLIDGE. New York: Harper, 1927. Reprint. Port Washington, N.Y.: Kennikat Press, 1971. 571 p.

Thompson, Charles Willis. PRESIDENTS I'VE KNOWN AND TWO NEAR PRESIDENTS. Indianapolis: Bobbs-Merrill Co., 1929. Reprint. Freeport, N.Y.: Books for Libraries Press, 1970. 386 p.

Weyandt, Dorothy E. I WAS A GUIDE FOR THREE U.S. PRESIDENTS: AS TAKEN FROM THE LOG OF A FAMOUS BRULE GUIDE, STEVE WEYANDT I. Brule, Wis.: Weyandt, 1976. 298 p.

Whalen, Richard J. TAKING SIDES: A PERSONAL VIEW OF AMERICA FROM KENNEDY TO NIXON TO KENNEDY. Introduction by Robert D. Novak. Boston: Houghton Mifflin, 1974. xvi, 320 p.

Whitney, David C. THE AMERICAN PRESIDENTS. Illustrated by Richard Paul Kluga. 4th ed. Garden City, N.Y.: Doubleday, 1978. xi, 532 p.

Williams, William Appleman. SOME PRESIDENTS: WILSON TO NIXON. New York: New York Review, distributed by Vintage Books, 1972. 122 p.

World Book Encyclopedia. PRESIDENTS OF THE UNITED STATES. Illus. Chicago: Field Enterprises Educational Corp., 1973. Var. pag.

> Presidential biographies excerpted from the World Book Encyclopedia with supplemental commentaries by and about the presidents.

D. ARTICLES

Albjerg, Marguerite Hall. "Our Changing Concept of (Presidential) Leadership." CURRENT HISTORY 25 (September 1953): 157-62.

Benjamin, Mary A. "The Presidents." COLLECTOR 62 (January-April 1949): 1-4, 27-29, 49-52, 73-76.

> On the rarity and prices of autographs of presidents of the United States, 1789-1948.

_____. THE PRESIDENTS: A SURVEY OF AUTOGRAPH VALUES, 1965. New York: W.R. Benjamin, 1965. 35 p.

Binkley, Wilfred E. "The President as a National Symbol." ANNALS OF THE AMERICAN ACADEMY OF POLITICAL AND SOCIAL SCIENCE 283 (September 1952): 86-93.

_____. "The President as Chief Legislator." ANNALS OF THE AMERICAN ACADEMY OF POLITICAL AND SOCIAL SCIENCE 307 (September 1956): 92-105.

Brodie, Fawn M. "Political Hero in America: His Fate and His Future." VIRGINIA QUARTERLY REVIEW 46 (Winter 1970): 46-60.

Burns, James MacGregor. THE EMBATTLED PRESIDENCY. Urbana: University of Illinois, Department of Political Science, 1964. 14 p.

Coulter, E. Merton. "Presidential Visits to Georgia during Ante-Bellum Times." GEORGIA HISTORICAL QUARTERLY 55 (Fall 1971): 329-64.

Current, Richard N. "The Lincoln Presidents." PRESIDENTIAL STUDIES QUARTERLY 9 (Winter 1979): 25-35.

Edwards, George C., III. "The Quantitative Study of the Presidency." PRESIDENTIAL STUDIES QUARTERLY 11 (Spring 1981): 146-50.

Finch, G.A. "Need to Restrain the Treaty-Making Power of the United States within Constitutional Limits." AMERICAN JOURNAL OF INTERNATIONAL LAW 48 (January 1954): 57-82.

Freedman, Warren. "Presidential Timber: Foreign Born Children of American Parents." CORNELL LAW QUARTERLY 35 (Winter 1950): 357-66.

On eligibility for the presidency, 1787-1949.

Goldman, Eric F. "The Presidency as Moral Leadership." ANNALS OF THE AMERICAN ACADEMY OF POLITICAL AND SOCIAL SCIENCE 280 (March 1952): 37-45.

Part of a special issue on the theme "Ethical Standards in American Life."

_____. "The President, the People, and the Power to Make War." AMERICAN HERITAGE 21 (April 1970): 28-35.

Graebner, Norman A. "Political Parties and the Presidency." CURRENT HISTORY 25 (September 1953): 138-43.

Harris, Irving D. "The Psychologies of Presidents." HISTORY OF CHILDHOOD QUARTERLY 3 (Winter 1976): 337-50.

Irish, Marion D. "Organization Man in the Presidency." JOURNAL OF POLITICS 20 (May 1958): 259-77.

Jacob, C.E. "Limits of Presidential Leadership." SOUTH ATLANTIC QUARTERLY 62 (Autumn 1963): 461-73.

Koenig, Louis W. "The Presidency Today." CURRENT HISTORY 66 (June 1974): 249-53.

Kuic, V. "Theory and Practice of the American Presidency." REVIEW OF POLITICS 23 (July 1961): 307-22.

Kynerd, Tom. "An Analysis of Presidential Greatness and 'President Rating.'" SOUTHERN QUARTERLY 9 (April 1971): 309-29.

An analysis of five famous presidential evaluations (Schlesinger, 1948 and 1962; Bailey, 1966; Rossiter, 1956; and Sokolsky, 1964).

Landis, B.Y. "American Presidency: An Ethical Evaluation." RELIGION IN LIFE 18, no. 4 (1949): 533-41.

Long, Norton E. "Party Government and the United States." JOURNAL OF POLITICS 13 (May 1951): 208-14.

Discusses how urban masses have become the constituency of the presidency.

McMurray, H.J. "President: Leader or Institution?" WESTERN POLITICAL QUARTERLY 14 (September 1961): 47-48.

An abstract.

Maranell, Gary M. "The Evaluation of Presidents: An Extension of the Schlesinger Polls." JOURNAL OF AMERICAN HISTORY 57 (June 1970): 104-13.

Maranell, Gary M., and Dodder, Richard A. "Political Orientation and the Evaluation of Presidential Prestige: A Study of American Historians." SOCIAL SCIENCE QUARTERLY 51 (September 1970): 415-21.

Mowry, George E. "The Uses of History by Recent Presidents." JOURNAL OF AMERICAN HISTORY 53 (June 1966): 5-18.

Neustadt, Richard E. "Presidency and Legislation: Planning the President's Program." AMERICAN POLITICAL SCIENCE REVIEW 49 (December 1955): 980-1021.

______. "Presidency and Legislation: The Growth of Central Clearance." AMERICAN POLITICAL SCIENCE REVIEW 48 (September 1954): 641-71.

Peabody, Robert L.; Ornstein, Norman J.; and Rohde, David W. "The United States Senate as a Presidential Incubator: Many Are Called but Few Are Chosen." POLITICAL SCIENCE QUARTERLY 91 (Summer 1976): 237-58.

Pious, Richard M. "The Evolution of the Presidency: 1798-1932." CURRENT HISTORY 66 (June 1974): 242-45, 271-72.

Plischke, E. "The President's Right to Go Abroad." ORBIS 15 (Fall 1971): 755-83.

Analyzes the constitutional questions involved.

Prothro, James Warren. "Verbal Shifts in the American Presidency: A Content Analysis." AMERICAN POLITICAL SCIENCE REVIEW 50 (September 1956): 726-50.

Reedy, George E. "The Presidency in 1976: Focal Point of Political Unity?" JOURNAL OF POLITICS 38 (August 1976): 228-38.

Rossiter, Clinton L. "Constitutional Dictatorship in the Atomic Age." REVIEW OF POLITICS 11 (October 1949): 395-418.

_____. "War, Depression, and the Presidency, 1933-1950." SOCIAL RESEARCH 17 (December 1950): 417-40.

Russ, William A., Jr. "Who Was the First Woman to Run for President?" SUSQUEHANNA UNIVERSITY STUDIES 9 (June 1971): 41 ff.

Victoria Woodhull versus Belva Lockwood.

Sayre, Wallace S. "Studies of the Chief Executive." PUBLIC ADMINISTRATION REVIEW 16 (Fall 1956): 307-12.

A review article.

Schlesinger, Arthur M. "Historians Rate United States Presidents." LIFE, 1 November 1948, pp. 65 ff.

_____. "Our Presidents: A Rating by Seventy-Five Historians." NEW YORK TIMES MAGAZINE, 29 July 1962, pp. 12 ff.

Schubert, Glendon A., Jr. "Judicial Review of the Subdelegation of Presidential Power." JOURNAL OF POLITICS 12 (November 1950): 668-93.

_____. "Presidential Subdelegation Act of 1950." JOURNAL OF POLITICS 13 (November 1951): 647-74.

Seligman, L.G. "Developments in the Presidency and the Conception of Political Leadership." AMERICAN SOCIOLOGICAL REVIEW 20 (December 1955): 706-12.

Shull, Steven A., and LeLoup, Lance T. "Reassessing the Reassessment: Comment on Sigelman's Note on the 'Two Presidencies' Thesis." JOURNAL OF POLITICS 43 (May 1981): 563-64.

Spracher, William C. "Some Reflections on Improving the Study of the Presidency." PRESIDENTIAL STUDIES QUARTERLY 9 (Winter 1979): 71-80.

Stamps, N.L. "American Presidential System." POLITICAL QUARTERLY 25 (April 1954): 155-65.

Thomas, Norman C. "Studying the Presidency: Where and How Do We Go from Here?" PRESIDENTIAL STUDIES QUARTERLY 7 (Fall 1977): 169-75.

Truman, David B. "The Presidency and Congressional Leadership: Some Notes on Our Changing Constitution." PROCEEDINGS OF THE AMERICAN PHILOSOPHICAL SOCIETY 103 (October 1959): 687-92.

Covers the years 1900-1957.

Tugwell, Rexford Guy. "The Historians and the Presidency: An Essay Review." POLITICAL SCIENCE QUARTERLY 86 (June 1971): 183-204.

Discusses three books on the Lyndon Johnson period: Eric Goldman's TRAGEDY OF LYNDON JOHNSON (1969), Lady Bird Johnson's WHITE HOUSE DIARY (1970), and George Reedy's TWILIGHT OF THE PRESIDENCY (1970).

"Two Presidents and a Haberdasher, 1948." AMERICAN JEWISH ARCHIVES 20 (April 1968): 3-15.

Concerns the long and warm friendship between President Truman and his army and business associate, Eddie Jacobson, and their mutual regard for Dr. Chaim Weizman, the first president of Israel.

Warren, Sidney. "The President in the Constitution." CURRENT HISTORY 25 (September 1953): 133-37.

Wells, Ronald A. "American Presidents as Political and Moral Leaders: A Report on Four Surveys." FIDES ET HISTORIA 11 (Fall 1978): 39-53.

Chapter 4
FIRST LADIES

A. COLLECTIVE BIOGRAPHIES

Barzman, Sol. THE FIRST LADIES. New York: Cowles Book Co., 1970. xiii, 370 p.

> Profiles of thirty-seven first ladies from Martha Washington to Patricia Nixon.

Faber, Doris. THE PRESIDENTS' MOTHERS. New York: St. Martin's Press, 1978. xv, 316 p.

> Thirty-eight profiles of the women whose sons reached America's highest office.

Gerlinger, Irene. MISTRESSES OF THE WHITE HOUSE: NARRATOR'S TALE OF A PAGEANT OF FIRST LADIES. New York: French, 1950. Reprint. Freeport, N.Y.: Books for Libraries Press, 1970. xx, 125 p.

Gordon, Lydia L. FROM FIRST LADY WASHINGTON TO MRS. CLEVELAND. Boston: Lee and Shepard, 1889. Reprint. Freeport, N.Y.: Books for Libraries Press, 1972. 448 p.

James, Edward T.; James, Janet Wilson; and Boyer, Paul S., eds. NOTABLE AMERICAN WOMEN, 1607-1950: A BIOGRAPHICAL DICTIONARY. 3 vols. Cambridge, Mass.: Belknap Press of Harvard University, 1971.

> Excellent biographical sketches of thirty first ladies from Martha Washington through Lou Henry Hoover.

Klapthor, Margaret Brown. THE FIRST LADIES. Washington, D.C.: White House Historical Association, 1975. 84 p. Illus.

> Published with the cooperation of the National Geographic Society.

Langford, Laura Carter Holloway. THE LADIES OF THE WHITE HOUSE. Philadelphia: A. Gorton, 1882. Reprint. New York: AMS Press, 1976. 736 p.

Loots, Barbara Kunz. FASCINATING FIRST LADIES: MEMORABLE MOMENTS IN THE LIVES OF FIFTEEN PRESIDENTS' WIVES. Kansas City, Mo.: Hallmark Cards, 1977. 61 p.

McConnell, Jane, and McConnell, Burt. OUR FIRST LADIES: FROM MARTHA WASHINGTON TO PAT RYAN NIXON. Portraits by Isabel Dawson. Rev. ed. New York: Crowell, 1969. 379 p.

Prindeville, Kathleen. FIRST LADIES. Rev. ed. New York: Macmillan, 1954. 309 p.

Intended for younger readers.

Sicherman, Barbara, and Green, Carl Hurd, eds. NOTABLE AMERICAN WOMEN: THE MODERN PERIOD. Cambridge, Mass.: Belknap Press of Harvard University Press, 1980. xxii, 773 p.

Contains sketches of Edith Bolling Galt Wilson, Grace Coolidge, and Eleanor Roosevelt.

Whitton, Mary Ormsbee. FIRST FIRST LADIES, 1789-1865: A STUDY OF THE WIVES OF THE EARLY PRESIDENTS. New York: Hastings House, 1948. Reprint. Freeport, N.Y.: Books for Libraries Press, 1969. x, 341 p.

B. INDIVIDUAL BIOGRAPHIES

Arranged chronologically by presidential administrations.

Martha Washington

Fields, Joseph Edward. "The Correspondence of the First First Lady." MANUSCRIPTS 8 (Fall 1956): 287-90.

Lewis, Robert. "A Journey from Fredricksburg, Virginia, to New York." Edited by Richard Walsh. MARYLAND HISTORICAL MAGAZINE 52 (June 1957): 180-85.

A nephew of George Washington escorts Martha Washington.

Thane, Elswyth. WASHINGTON'S LADY. New York: Dodd, Mead, 1960. Reprint. Mettituck, N.Y.: Aeonian Press, 1977. 306 p.

Abigail Adams

Adams, Abigail. NEW LETTERS OF ABIGAIL ADAMS, 1788-1801. Edited, with an introduction by Stewart Mitchell. Boston: Houghton Mifflin Co., 1947. 281 p.

Akers, Charles W. ABIGAIL ADAMS, AN AMERICAN WOMAN. Library of American Biography Series. Boston: Little, Brown, 1980. x, 207 p.

Butler, Lorine Letcher. "Abigail Adams--Correspondent of History." D.A.R. MAGAZINE 90 (July 1956): 623-27.

On the marriage and correspondence of Abigail Smith and John Adams, 1764-1801.

Coit, Margaret L. "Dearest Friends: With Excerpts from Letters during Courtship and Marriage." AMERICAN HERITAGE 19 (October 1968): 9-13.

Pulley, Judith. "The Bittersweet Friendship of Thomas Jefferson and Abigail Adams." ESSEX INSTITUTE HISTORICAL COLLECTIONS 108 (July 1972): 193-216.

Randolph, Sarah N. THE DOMESTIC LIFE OF THOMAS JEFFERSON. New York: Harper, 1871. Reprint. New York: Frederick Ungar, 1958. 432 p.

Compiled from family letters and reminiscences by Jefferson's great-granddaughter.

Whitney, Janet Payne. ABIGAIL ADAMS. Boston: Little, Brown, 1947. Reprint. Westport, Conn.: Greenwood Press, 1970. xii, 357 p.

Dolley Madison

Madison, Dolley. MEMOIRS AND LETTERS OF DOLLEY MADISON, WIFE OF JAMES MADISON, PRESIDENT OF THE UNITED STATES. Edited by Lucia Cutts. Boston: Houghton Mifflin, 1886. Reprint. Port Washington, N.Y.: Kennikat Press, 1971. 210 p.

Cutts is a grand-niece of Dolly Madison.

Anthony, Katherine. DOLLEY MADISON: HER LIFE AND TIMES. New York: Doubleday and Co., 1949. x, 426 p.

Arnett, Ethel Stephens. MRS. JAMES MADISON: THE INCOMPARABLE DOLLEY. Greensboro, N.C.: Piedmont Press, 1972. xiii, 520 p.

Klapthor, Margaret Brown. "Benjamin Latrobe and Dolley Madison Decorate the White House, 1809-1811." UNITED STATES NATIONAL MUSEUM BULLETIN 241 (1965): 153-64.

Moore, Virginia. THE MADISONS: A BIOGRAPHY. New York: McGraw-Hill, 1979. xvii, 568 p.

Sifton, Paul G. "'What a Dread Prospect. . .': Dolley Madison's Plague Year (1793-1795)." PENNSYLVANIA MAGAZINE OF HISTORY AND BIOGRAPHY 87 (April 1963): 182-88.

Thane, Elswyth. DOLLEY MADISON, HER LIFE AND TIMES. New York: Crowell-Collier Press, 1970. viii, 184 p.

Whitridge, A. "Dolley Madison." HISTORY TODAY 8 (January 1958): 3-9.

Louisa Adams

Kerr, Laura. LOUISA: THE LIFE OF MRS. JOHN QUINCY ADAMS. New York: Wilfred Funk, 1964. 186 p.

Anna Symmes Harrison

Symmes, John Cleves. THE INTIMATE LETTERS OF JOHN CLEVES SYMMES AND HIS FAMILY, INCLUDING THOSE OF HIS DAUGHTER, MRS. WILLIAM HENRY HARRISON, WIFE OF THE NINTH PRESIDENT OF THE UNITED STATES. Edited by Beverley W. Bond, Jr. Cincinnati: Historical and Philosophical Society of Ohio, 1956. xxxiii, 174 p.

Wood, Clarence A. "Riverhead Boasts First Lady, Too." LONG ISLAND FORUM 13 (August 1950): 149-51.

> On Anna Symmes (1775-1864), wife of President William Henry Harrison, and the Symmes and Cleves families on Long Island, 1637 ff.

Priscilla Tyler

Coleman, Elizabeth Tyler. PRISCILLA COOPER TYLER AND THE AMERICAN SCENE, 1816-1889. University: University of Alabama Press, 1955. xiii, 203 p.

> Priscilla Tyler, daughter-in-law of the president, served as First Lady from 1841 to 1844 in place of Tyler's invalid first wife, Letitia Christian Tyler.

Julia Gardiner Tyler

Bradshaw, Herbert Clarence. "A President's Bride at 'Sherwood Forest.'" VIRGINIA CAVALCADE 7 (Spring 1958): 30-39.

On the estate in Charles City County purchased by John Tyler in 1842 and occupied by him and his second wife, Julia Gardiner Tyler, and their seven children from 1845 until his death in 1862.

Seager, Robert II. AND TYLER TOO: A BIOGRAPHY OF JOHN AND JULIA TYLER. New York: McGraw-Hill, 1963. xvii, 681 p.

The fullest biographical account based upon all known manuscript letters.

Sarah Childress Polk

Polk, Sarah Childress. "Letters of Mrs. James K. Polk to Her Husband, 1839-1843." TENNESSEE HISTORICAL QUARTERLY 11 (June-September 1952): 180-91; 282-88.

Dated at Columbia and Nashville, 1839-43.

Nelson, Anson, and Nelson, Fanny. MEMORIALS OF SARAH CHILDRESS POLK: WIFE OF THE ELEVENTH PRESIDENT OF THE UNITED STATES. 1892. Reprint. Spartanburg, S.C.: Reprint Co., 1974. xiv, 284 p.

Contains the fullest account of Sarah Polk.

Jane Appleton Pierce

Nichols, Roy Franklin. FRANKLIN PIERCE: YOUNG HICKORY OF THE GRANITE HILLS. 2d ed., completely rev. Philadelphia: University of Pennsylvania Press, 1958. xvii, 625 p.

Contains the fullest account of Mrs. Pierce's married life.

Taylor, Lloyd C., Jr. "A Wife for Mr. Pierce." NEW ENGLAND QUARTERLY 28 (September 1955): 339-48.

Harriet Lane

Hostetter, Ida L.K. "Harriet Lane." LANCASTER COUNTY HISTORICAL SOCIETY JOURNAL 33 (1929): 97-112.

Harriet Lane, the president's niece, served as First Lady in the Buchanan administration.

Taylor, Lloyd C. "Harriet Lane--Mirror of an Age." PENNSYLVANIA HISTORY 30 (April 1963): 213-25.

Mary Todd Lincoln

Lincoln, Mary Todd. "Mary Lincoln Writes to Noah Brooks." Edited by Francis Whiting Hatch. JOURNAL OF THE ILLINOIS STATE HISTORICAL SOCIETY 48 (Spring 1955): 45-51.

> Two letters, Chicago, 16 December 1875 and 11 May 1866, on the writer's money troubles and her wish to sell three shares of mining stock.

______. "The Mary Lincoln Letters to Mrs. Felician Slataper (1868-74)." Edited by Justin G. Turner. JOURNAL OF THE ILLINOIS STATE HISTORICAL SOCIETY 49 (Spring 1956): 7-33.

______. MARY TODD LINCOLN: HER LIFE AND LETTERS. Edited by Justin G. Turner and Linda Lovitt Turner. Introduction by Fawn M. Brodie. New York: Knopf, 1972. xxv, 750 p.

Hackensmith, C.W. "Family Background and Education of Mary Todd." REGISTER OF THE KENTUCKY HISTORICAL SOCIETY 69 (July 1971): 187-96.

Helm, Katherine. THE TRUE STORY OF MARY, WIFE OF LINCOLN. New York: Harper, 1928. 309 p.

> The recollections of Mary Lincoln's sister Emilie (Mrs. Ben Hardin Helm), extracts from Emilie's war-time diary, numerous letters, and other documents as published by Katherine Helm, niece of Mary Lincoln.

James, Jeannie H., and Temple, Wayne C. "Mrs. Lincoln's Clothing." LINCOLN HERALD 62 (Summer 1960): 54-65.

Keckley, Elizabeth Hobbs. BEHIND THE SCENES: THIRTY YEARS A SLAVE AND FOUR YEARS IN THE WHITE HOUSE. New York: Arno Press, 1968. xvi, 371 p.

> Contains intimate recollections of Mrs. Lincoln, by her seamstress.

Ostendorf, Lloyd. "The Photographs of Mary Todd Lincoln." JOURNAL OF THE ILLINOIS STATE HISTORICAL SOCIETY 61 (Autumn 1968): 269-332.

Randall, Ruth Painter. MARY LINCOLN: BIOGRAPHY OF A MARRIAGE. Boston: Little, Brown, 1953. xiv, 555 p.

> The most comprehensive biography. Includes a detailed bibliography.

______. "Mary Lincoln: Judgment Appealed." ABRAHAM LINCOLN QUARTERLY 5 (September 1949): 379-404.

Data warranting reconsideration of previous views of Mrs. Lincoln's character, 1840-66.

Rhodes, James A. THE TRIAL OF MARY TODD LINCOLN. Indianapolis: Bobbs-Merrill, 1959. 200 p.

Ross, Ishbel. THE PRESIDENT'S WIFE: MARY TODD LINCOLN, A BIOGRAPHY. New York: Putnam, 1973. 378 p.

Ross, Rodney A. "Mary Todd Lincoln, Patient as Bellevue Place, Batavia." JOURNAL OF THE ILLINOIS STATE HISTORICAL SOCIETY 63 (Spring 1970): 5-34.

Day-by-day physician's records of Mrs. Lincoln's behavior during her stay in the sanitarium.

Squires, James Duane. "Mrs. Abraham Lincoln's Visit to Mount Washington in 1863." APPALACHIA 33 (15 December 1961): 452-57.

Temple, Wayne C. "Mary Todd Lincoln as a Sailor." LINCOLN HERALD 61 (Fall 1959): 101-10.

______. "Mary Todd Lincoln's Travels." JOURNAL OF THE ILLINOIS STATE HISTORICAL SOCIETY 52 (Spring 1959): 180-94.

On her interest in boats and water travel and her penchant for keeping the newspaper reporters guessing about her plans.

Julia Grant

Ross, Ishbel. THE GENERAL'S WIFE: THE LIFE OF MRS. ULYSSES S. GRANT. New York: Dodd, Mead, 1959. xii, 372 p.

Contains a full bibliography.

Lucy Webb Hayes

Geer, Emily Apt. "Lucy Webb Hayes: An Unexceptionable Woman." Ph.D. dissertation, Western Reserve University, 1962.

______. "Lucy Webb Hayes and Her Family." OHIO HISTORY 77 (Winter-Spring-Summer 1968): 33-57.

Marchman, Watt Pearson. "Autographs--A Testimonial to a First Lady." AUTOGRAPH COLLECTORS JOURNAL 4 (Winter 1952): 20-21.

______, ed. "Lucy Webb (Hayes) in Cincinnati: The First Five Years, 1848-1852." BULLETIN OF THE HISTORICAL AND PHILOSOPHICAL SOCIETY OF OHIO 13 (January 1955): 38-60.

Letters from and to her during the period of her attendance at the Wesleyan Female College of Cincinnati, Ohio, February 1848 to May 1850.

Scott, George Tressler. ILLINOIS' TESTIMONIAL TO MRS. RUTHERFORD B. HAYES (1880-81). Springfield: Illinois State Historical Society, 1953. 21 p.

Describes six volumes of autograph messages to Lucy Hayes, 1881, commending the courage she displayed in the administration of the hospitalities of the executive mansion by not serving alcoholic beverages.

Lucretia Garfield

Comer, Lucretia Garfield. "My Grandmother Garfield's Balldress." D.A.R. MAGAZINE 92 (November 1958): 881-84.

On the social activities of the Garfield family during the week of the inauguration of James Garfield, March 1881, and the rich lavender satin dress trimmed with point lace worn at the inaugural ball by Lucretia Garfield.

______. STRANDS FROM THE WEAVING. New York: Vantage Press, 1959. 73 p.

A valuable source by Mrs. Garfield's grand-daughter.

Garfield, James A. THE DIARY OF JAMES A. GARFIELD. Edited by Harry J. Brown and Frederick D. Williams. 4 vols. East Lansing: Michigan State University Press, 1967-81.

Quite full on Mrs. Garfield and family life.

Ellen Arthur (died before her husband's term)

Reeves, Thomas C. "The Diaries of Malvina (Mrs. Chester Alvin) Arthur: Windows into the Past of Our 21st President." VERMONT HISTORY 38 (Summer 1970): 177-88.

Caroline Scott Harrison

Smith, Ophia. "Caroline Scott Harrison: A Daughter of Old Oxford." NATIONAL HISTORICAL MAGAZINE 75 (April 1941).

On first wife of Benjamin Harrison.

Ida McKinley

Leech, Margaret. IN THE DAYS OF McKINLEY. New York: Harper and Brothers, 1959. viii, 686 p.

Provides the best discussion of Mrs. McKinley's personality and health problems.

Edith Roosevelt

Churchill, Allen. THE ROOSEVELTS: AMERICAN ARISTOCRATS. New York: Harper and Row, 1965. 341 p.

Hagedorn, Hermann. THE ROOSEVELT FAMILY OF SAGAMORE HILL. New York: Macmillan Co., 1954. 435 p.

Helen Taft

Taft, Helen Herron. RECOLLECTIONS OF FULL YEARS. New York: Dodd, Mead and Co., 1914. x, 395 p.

Ellen Axson Wilson

Wilson, Woodrow. THE PRICELESS GIFT: THE LOVE LETTERS OF WOODROW WILSON AND ELLEN AXSON WILSON. Edited by Eleanor Wilson McAdoo. New York: McGraw-Hill, 1962. 324 p.

A selection of letters between Woodrow Wilson and his first wife, edited by their daughter.

Bicknell, Mrs. Ernest P. "The Home-Maker of the White House." SURVEY 33 (3 October 1914): 19-22.

On Ellen Wilson, the first wife of Woodrow Wilson.

McAdoo, Eleanor Wilson. THE WOODROW WILSONS. New York: Macmillan Co., 1937. x, 301 p.

A family memoir.

McKelway, A.J. "The Social Activities of the White House." HARPER'S WEEKLY 58 (25 April 1914): 26-27.

Concerns Ellen Wilson and the first Wilson administration.

Edith Galt Wilson

Wilson, Edith Bolling. MY MEMOIR. Indianapolis: Bobbs-Merrill Co., 1939. 386 p.

Anecdotal and often unreliable.

Ross, Ishbel. POWER WITH GRACE: THE LIFE STORY OF MRS. WOODROW WILSON. New York: Putnam, 1975. 374 p.

Smith, Gene. WHEN THE CHEERING STOPPED: THE LAST YEARS OF WOODROW WILSON. New York: William Morrow, 1964. xi, 307 p.

Florence Harding

Adams, Samuel Hopkins. INCREDIBLE ERA: THE LIFE AND TIMES OF WARREN GAMALIEL HARDING. Boston: Houghton Mifflin, 1939. ix, 457 p.

Grace Coolidge

Ross, Ishbel. GRACE COOLIDGE AND HER ERA: THE STORY OF A PRESIDENT'S WIFE. New York: Dodd, Mead and Co., 1962. ix, 370 p.

The best biography. Based on family letters and reminiscences and recollections of Mrs. Coolidge's intimate friends.

Lou Henry Hoover

Pryor, Helen B. LOU HENRY HOOVER: GALLANT FIRST LADY. New York: Dodd, Mead and Co., 1969. 271 p.

Eleanor Roosevelt

Roosevelt, Eleanor. THE AUTOBIOGRAPHY OF ELEANOR ROOSEVELT. New York: Harper and Row, 1961. xix, 454 p.

An abbreviated composite of Eleanor Roosevelt's three earlier volumes: THIS IS MY STORY (1937), THIS I REMEMBER (1949), and ON MY OWN (1958), plus a final section on her later life and activities.

Roosevelt, Elliott. AN UNTOLD STORY: THE ROOSEVELTS OF HYDE PARK. New York: G.P. Putnam's Sons, 1973. 318 p.

A son's account of his parents.

Roosevelt, James. MY PARENTS: A DIFFERING VIEW. Chicago: Playboy Press, 1976. xi, 369 p.

Davis, Kenneth S. "Miss Eleanor Roosevelt." AMERICAN HERITAGE 22 (October 1971): 48-59.

Hareven, Tamara K. ELEANOR ROOSEVELT: AN AMERICAN CONSCIENCE. Chicago: Quadrangle Books, 1968. xx, 326 p.

Harrity, Richard, and Martin, Ralph G. ELEANOR ROOSEVELT: HER LIFE IN PICTURES. New York: Duell, Sloan, and Pearce, 1958. 212 p.

Kearney, James R. ANNA ELEANOR ROOSEVELT: THE EVOLUTION OF A REFORMER. Boston: Houghton Mifflin Co., 1968. xvi, 332 p.

Lash, Joseph P. ELEANOR: THE YEARS ALONE. New York: W.W. Norton, 1972. 368 p.

______. ELEANOR AND FRANKLIN: THE STORY OF THEIR RELATIONSHIP. New York: W.W. Norton, 1971. 765 p.

Steinberg, Alfred. MRS. R: THE LIFE OF ELEANOR ROOSEVELT. New York: Putnam, 1958. 384 p.

Whiteman, M.M. "Mrs. Franklin D. Roosevelt and the Human Rights Commission." AMERICAN JOURNAL OF INTERNATIONAL LAW 62 (October 1968): 918-21.

Bess Truman

Truman, Margaret. SOUVENIR: MARGARET TRUMAN'S OWN STORY. New York: McGraw-Hill Book Co., 1956. 365 p.

Mamie Doud Eisenhower

Brandon, Dorothy Barrett. MAMIE DOUD EISENHOWER: A PORTRAIT OF A FIRST LADY. New York: Charles Scribner's Sons, 1954. 307 p.

Jacqueline Kennedy

Gallagher, Mary Barelli. MY LIFE WITH JACQUELINE KENNEDY. Edited by Frances Spatz Leighton. New York: David McKay, 1969. x, 396 p.

Kelley, Kitty. JACKIE OH! Secaucus, N.J.: Lyle Stuart, 1978. 352 p.

Thayer, Mary Van Rensselaer. JACQUELINE KENNEDY, THE WHITE HOUSE YEARS. Boston: Little, Brown, 1971. xx, 362 p.

Claudia Alta Taylor Johnson

Johnson, Claudia Alta Taylor. A WHITE HOUSE DIARY. New York: Holt, Rinehart and Winston, 1970. ix, 806 p.

Carpenter, Liz. RUFFLES AND FLOURISHES: THE WARM AND TENDER STORY OF A SIMPLE GIRL WHO FOUND ADVENTURE IN THE WHITE HOUSE. New York: Doubleday, 1970. 341 p.

Montgomery, Ruth. MRS. L.B.J.: AN INTIMATE PORTRAIT OF THE FIRST LADY. New York: Holt, Rinehart and Winston, 1964. 212 p.

Patricia Nixon

David, Lester. THE LONELY LADY OF SAN CLEMENTE: THE STORY OF PAT NIXON. New York: Thomas Y. Crowell, 1978. 235 p.

Betty Ford

Feinman, Jeffrey. BETTY FORD. New York: Universal-Award House, Inc., 1976. 171 p.

Ford, Betty, and Chase, Chris. THE TIMES OF MY LIFE. New York: Harper and Row, 1978. xi, 305 p.

Cassiday, Bruce Bingham. BETTY FORD: WOMAN OF COURAGE. Waterbury, Conn.: Dale Books, 1978. 162 p.

Rosalynn Carter

Langford, Edna, and Maddox, Linda. ROSALYNN: FRIEND AND FIRST LADY. Old Tappan, N.J.: Fleming H. Revell Co., 1980. 180 p.

Norton, Howard. ROSALYNN. Plainfield, N.J.: Logos, 1977. x, 220 p.

Nancy Reagan

Elwood, Roger. NANCY REAGAN: A SPECIAL KIND OF LOVE. New York: Pocket Books, 1976. 159 p.

Reagan, Nancy. NANCY. New York: Berkley Books, 1981. 234 p.

C. SPECIAL TOPICS

Brown, Margaret W. THE DRESSES OF THE FIRST LADIES OF THE WHITE HOUSE. Washington, D.C.: Smithsonian Institution, 1952. ix, 149 p.

Klapthor, Margaret Brown. THE FIRST LADIES COOK BOOK: FAVORITE RECIPES OF ALL THE PRESIDENTS OF THE UNITED STATES. New York: Parents' Magazine Press, 1975. 228 p.

National Museum of History and Technology. THE FIRST LADIES HALL. Washington, D.C.: Smithsonian Institution Press, 1973. 24 p.

Smith, Marie, and Durbin, Louise. WHITE HOUSE BRIDES. Washington, D.C.: Acropolis Books, 1966. 208 p.

Truett, Randle Bond. FIRST LADIES IN FASHION. New York: Hastings House, 1965. 84 p.

Chapter 5
PRESIDENTIAL ELECTIONS

A. OVERVIEWS

Abels, Jules. THE DEGENERATION OF OUR PRESIDENTIAL ELECTION: A HISTORY AND ANALYSIS OF AN INSTITUTION IN TROUBLE. New York: Macmillan, 1968. 306 p.

American Political Parties Project. PRESIDENTIAL NOMINATING PROCEDURES: A COMPENDIUM OF ELECTION PRACTICES IN 1972. 2 vols. American Political Parties Project, William J. Crotty, project director. New York: National Municipal League, 1974.

Barber, James David. THE PULSE OF POLITICS: ELECTING PRESIDENTS IN THE MEDIA AGE. New York: Norton and Co., 1980. 342 p.

> A study of the cycles of twentieth-century politics. Barber identifies three steps in twelve-year patterns: the politics of conflict; the politics of conscience; and the politics of conciliation.

Bean, Louis Hyman. HOW AMERICA VOTES IN PRESIDENTIAL ELECTIONS. Metuchen, N.J.: Scarecrow Press, 1968. v, 152 p.

Boyd, Richard W. "Presidential Elections: An Explanation of Voting Defection." AMERICAN POLITICAL SCIENCE REVIEW 63 (June 1969): 498-514.

Brams, Steven J. THE PRESIDENTIAL ELECTION GAME. New Haven, Conn.: Yale University Press, 1978. xix, 242 p.

Broder, David S. THE PARTY'S OVER. New York: Harper and Row, 1972. xxv, 280 p.

Brown, W. Burlie. "The Cincinnatus Image in Presidential Politics." AGRICULTURAL HISTORY 31 (January 1957): 23-29.

> On the honorific effects of a farm boyhood.

Burnham, W. Dean. PRESIDENTIAL BALLOTS, 1836-1892. Baltimore: Johns Hopkins Press, 1955. xix, 956 p.

Byrne, Gary C., and Marx, Paul. THE GREAT AMERICAN CONVENTION: A POLITICAL HISTORY OF PRESIDENTIAL ELECTIONS. Palo Alto, Calif.: Pacific Books, 1976. 168 p.

Cantor, Robert D. VOTING BEHAVIOR AND PRESIDENTIAL ELECTIONS. Itasca, Ill.: F.E. Peacock Publishers, 1975. 139 p.

Carleton, William G. "Six Year Term for the President?" SOUTH ATLANTIC QUARTERLY 71 (Spring 1972): 165-76.

Congressional Quarterly Service. HISTORICAL REVIEW OF PRESIDENTIAL CANDIDATES FROM 1788 TO 1968; INCLUDING THIRD PARTIES, 1832 TO 1968, WITH POPULAR AND ELECTORAL VOTE. 5th ed. Washington, D.C.: 1969. 26 p.

CRUCIAL AMERICAN ELECTIONS; SYMPOSIUM PRESENTED AT THE AUTUMN GENERAL MEETING OF THE AMERICAN PHILOSOPHICAL SOCIETY, NOVEMBER 10, 1972. Memoirs of the American Philosophical Society, vol. 99. Philadelphia: American Philosophical Society, 1973. vii, 77 p.

De Santis, Vincent P. "Catholicism and Presidential Elections, 1865-1900." MID-AMERICA 42 (April 1960): 67-79.

Divine, Robert A. FOREIGN POLICY AND U.S. PRESIDENTIAL ELECTIONS, 1940-1948. New York: New Viewpoints, 1974. xii, 353 p.

_____. FOREIGN POLICY AND U.S. PRESIDENTIAL ELECTIONS, 1952-1960. New York: New Viewpoints, 1974. x, 359 p.

Everett, R.O., ed. "Electoral Process." LAW AND CONTEMPORARY PROBLEMS 27 (Spring-Summer 1962): 157-536.

Ewing, Cortez Arthur Milton. PRESIDENTIAL ELECTIONS FROM ABRAHAM LINCOLN TO FRANKLIN D. ROOSEVELT. Norman: University of Oklahoma Press, 1940. Reprint. Westport, Conn.: Greenwood Press, 1972. xiii, 226 p.

Garrison, Lloyd W., comp. AMERICAN POLITICS AND ELECTIONS: SELECTED ABSTRACTS OF PERIODICAL LITERATURE, 1964-1968. Edited by Lloyd W. Garrison and Kathleen M. Curran. Santa Barbara, Calif.: ABC-Clio, 1968. iii, 45 p.

> Extracted from volumes 1 through 4 of AMERICA, HISTORY AND LIFE (1964-67).

Ghnebom, George. "Election to the Presidency (1789-1933)." SOCIAL STUDIES 39 (November 1948): 291-302.

Goldman, Eric F. "Just Plain Folks." AMERICAN HERITAGE 23 (June 1972): 4-8, 90-91.

Concerns populism in presidential elections.

Gray, Lee Learner. HOW WE CHOOSE A PRESIDENT: THE ELECTION YEAR. Illustrated by Stanley Stamaty. 2d rev. ed. New York: St. Martin's Press, 1972. 175 p.

Keech, William R., and Matthews, Donald R. THE PARTY'S CHOICE. Studies in Presidential Selection Series. Washington, D.C.: Brookings Institution, 1976. xii, 258 p.

Key, Vladimir Orlando, Jr., with the assistance of Milton C. Cummings, Jr. THE RESPONSIBLE ELECTORATE: RATIONALITY IN PRESIDENTIAL VOTING, 1936-1960. Foreword by Arthur Maass. Cambridge: Belknap Press of Harvard University Press, 1966. xxi, 158 p.

King, James D. "Comparing Local and Presidential Elections." AMERICAN POLITICS QUARTERLY 9 (July 1981): 277-90.

Lavender, David. "How to Make it to the White House without Really Trying." AMERICAN HERITAGE 18 (June 1967): 26-27, 80-86.

League of Women Voters of the United States. Education Fund. CHOOSING THE PRESIDENT. Nashville: Published for the League of Women Voters Education Fund by T. Nelson, 1980. 106 p.

Lichtman, Allan J. "Critical Election Theory and the Reality of American Presidential Politics, 1916-1940." AMERICAN HISTORICAL REVIEW 81 (April 1976): 317-51.

Marcus, Robert D. "Presidential Elections in the American Political System." REVIEW OF POLITICS 33 (January 1971): 3-23.

Matthews, Donald R., ed. PERSPECTIVES ON PRESIDENTIAL SELECTION. Washington, D.C.: Brookings Institution, 1973. xii, 246 p.

Mazmanian, Daniel A. THIRD PARTIES IN PRESIDENTIAL ELECTIONS. Washington, D.C.: Brookings Institution, 1974. viii, 163 p.

Menendez, Albert J. RELIGION AT THE POLLS. Philadelphia: Westminster Press, 1977. 248 p.

Moos, Malcolm. POLITICS, PRESIDENTS, AND COATTAILS. Baltimore: Johns Hopkins Press, 1952. Reprint. Westport, Conn.: Greenwood Press, 1969. xxi, 237 p.

National Portrait Gallery. Historian's Office. Washington, D.C. "IF ELECTED": UNSUCCESSFUL CANDIDATES FOR THE PRESIDENCY, 1796-1968. By Lillian B. Miller et al. Washington, D.C.: Published for the National Portrait Gallery, Smithsonian Institution, by the Smithsonian Institution Press; for sale by the Superintendent of Documents, Government Printing Office, 1972. 512 p.

Ogden, Daniel M. ELECTING THE PRESIDENT. Rev. ed. San Francisco: Chandler Publishing Co., 1968. ix, 335 p.

100 YEARS OF PRESIDENTIAL ELECTIONS, 1864-1964 COVERED IN THE EVENING AND SUNDAY STAR. Washington, D.C.: Evening Star Newspaper Co., 1968. Unpaged.

Pedersen, Johannes T. "Political Involvement and Partisan Change in Presidential Elections." AMERICAN JOURNAL OF POLITICAL SCIENCE 22 (February 1978): 18-30.

Petersen, William J. "Cartoons in Presidential Elections." PALIMPSEST 49 (November 1968): 449-544.

Polsby, Nelson W., and Wildavsky, Aaron. PRESIDENTIAL ELECTIONS: STRATEGIES OF AMERICAN ELECTORAL POLITICS. 5th ed. New York: Scribner, 1980. xviii, 300 p.

Pomper, Gerald M. ELECTIONS IN AMERICA: CONTROL AND INFLUENCE IN DEMOCRATIC POLITICS. New York: Dodd, Mead and Co., 1968. 485 p.

Press, Charles. "Voting Statistics and Presidential Coattails." AMERICAN POLITICAL SCIENCE REVIEW 52 (December 1958): 1041-50.

Ra, Jong Oh. LABOR AT THE POLLS: UNION VOTING IN PRESIDENTIAL ELECTIONS, 1952-1976. Amherst: University of Massachusetts Press, 1978. x, 182 p.

RACE FOR THE PRESIDENCY: THE MEDIA AND THE NOMINATING PROCESS. Englewood Cliffs, N.J.: Prentice-Hall, 1978. viii, 205 p.

> Essays prepared for an American Assembly on Presidential Nominations and the Media held at Seven Springs Center, Mt. Kisco, New York, May 1978.

Ranney, Austin, ed. THE PAST AND FUTURE OF PRESIDENTIAL DEBATES. Washington, D.C.: American Enterprise Institute for Public Policy Research, 1979. 226 p.

Discusses the arguments for and against mandatory nationally televised debates for major party candidates.

Rayback, Joseph G. "Presidential Nominations Made in Pennsylvania." COMMONWEALTH 2 (31 June 1948): 609.

Roseboom, Eugene H., and Eckes, Alfred E., Jr. A HISTORY OF PRESIDENTIAL ELECTIONS FROM GEORGE WASHINGTON TO JIMMY CARTER. 4th ed. New York: Macmillan, 1979. vii, 355 p.

Schlesinger, Arthur Meier, Jr., ed. THE COMING TO POWER: CRITICAL PRESIDENTIAL ELECTIONS IN AMERICAN HISTORY. New York: Chelsea House Publishers, 1972. xxi, 550 p.

Schlesinger, Arthur Meier, Jr., and Israel, Fred L., eds. HISTORY OF AMERICAN PRESIDENTIAL ELECTIONS, 1789-1968. 4 vols. New York: Chelsea House, 1971.

Seitz, Don Carlos. THE "ALSO RANS": GREAT MEN WHO MISSED MAKING THE PRESIDENTIAL GOAL. New York: Thomas Y. Crowell Co., 1928. Reprint. Freeport, N.Y.: Books for Libraries Press, 1968. xxiv, 356 p.

Shade, William L. SOCIAL CHANGE AND THE ELECTORAL PROCESS. University of Florida monographs, social sciences, no. 49. Gainesville: University of Florida Press, 1973. vii, 73 p.

Shogan, Robert. NONE OF THE ABOVE: WHY PRESIDENTS FAIL--AND WHAT CAN BE DONE ABOUT IT. New York: New American Library, 1982. viii, 312 p.

Skau, George H. "A Critical Analysis of the Presidential Election System." PRESIDENTIAL STUDIES QUARTERLY 6 (Fall 1976): 42-48.

Smith, Bryant. "Third Term and the Dead Hand." SOUTHWESTERN SOCIAL SCIENCE QUARTERLY 29 (March 1949): 273-79.

Stein, Charles W. THE THIRD-TERM TRADITION: ITS RISE AND COLLAPSE IN AMERICAN POLITICS. New York: Columbia University Press, 1943. Reprint. Westport, Conn.: Greenwood Press, 1972. xvi, 382 p.

Stoddard, Henry Luther. PRESIDENTIAL SWEEPSTAKES: THE STORY OF POLITICAL CONVENTIONS AND CAMPAIGNS (1840-1944). Edited by Francis W. Leary. New York: G.P. Putnam's Sons, 1948. 224 p.

Includes the author's personal reminiscences as a campaign reporter, 1884-1948.

Stone, Irving. THEY ALSO RAN: THE STORY OF THE MEN WHO WERE DEFEATED FOR THE PRESIDENCY. Garden City, N.Y.: Doubleday, 1966. xi, 434 p.

Trent, Judith S. "Presidential Surfacing: The Ritualistic and Crucial First Act." SPEECH MONOGRAPHS 45 (November 1978): 281-92.

Tugwell, Rexford Guy. HOW THEY BECAME PRESIDENT: THIRTY-FIVE WAYS TO THE WHITE HOUSE. New York: Simon and Schuster, 1965. 587 p.

Weaver, David H.; Graber, Doris A.; McCombs, Maxwell E.; and Eyal, Chaim H. MEDIA AGENDA-SETTING IN A PRESIDENTIAL ELECTION. New York: Praeger, 1981. 227 p.

Zikmund, Joseph. "Suburban Voting in Presidential Elections, 1948-1964." MIDWEST JOURNAL OF POLITICAL SCIENCE 12 (May 1968): 239-58.

B. MONOGRAPHS AND ARTICLES

1. Party Caucuses

Carleton, William G. "The Collapse of the Caucus." CURRENT HISTORY 25 (September 1953): 144-50.

THE CAUCUS SYSTEM IN AMERICAN POLITICS. New York: Arno Press, 1974. 27, 107, 46 p.

> Reprint of CAUCUS SYSTEM, by Frederick W. Whitridge, first published 1883 by the Society for Political Education, New York; of THE AMERICAN CAUCUS SYSTEM, by George W. Lawton, first published 1885 by Putnam, New York; and of AN ESSAY ON THE RISE AND FALL OF THE CONGRESSIONAL CAUCUS AS A MACHINE FOR NOMINATING CANDIDATES FOR THE PRESIDENCY, by Charles S. Thompson, first issued in 1902.

2. Nominating Conventions

a. GENERAL STUDIES

Angle, Paul M. "Conventions and Candidates." CHICAGO HISTORY 8 (Summer 1968): 225-48.

> Lists nominating conventions held in Chicago by major political parties since 1860.

Bain, Richard C., and Parris, Judith H. CONVENTION DECISIONS AND VOTING RECORDS. 2d ed. Washington, D.C.: Brookings Institution, 1973. x, 350 p.

Chase, James Staton. EMERGENCE OF THE PRESIDENTIAL NOMINATING CONVENTION, 1789-1832. Urbana: University of Illinois Press, 1973. xvii, 332 p.

______. "Jacksonian Democracy and the Rise of the Nominating Convention." MID-AMERICA 45 (October 1963): 229-49.

Collat, Donald C.; Kelley, Stanley, Jr.; and Rogowski, Ronald. "The End Game in Presidential Nominations." AMERICAN POLITICAL SCIENCE REVIEW 75 (June 1981): 426-35.

Congressional Quarterly. NATIONAL PARTY CONVENTIONS, 1831-1972. Washington, D.C.: 1976. 216 p.

A compendium including state delegation voting, disputes over platforms and procedures, profiles of political parties, a listing of nominees, and brief biographies of candidates.

David, Paul T. "Role of Governors at the National Party Conventions." STATE GOVERNMENT 33 (Spring 1960): 103-10.

David, Paul T., and Goldman, Ralph M. "Presidential Nominating Patterns." WESTERN POLITICAL QUARTERLY 8 (September 1955): 465-80.

Covers national party conventions, 1832-1952.

David, Paul T.; Goldman, Ralph M.; Bain, Richard C. THE POLITICS OF NATIONAL PARTY CONVENTIONS. Washington, D.C.: Brookings Institution, 1960. xv, 592 p.

Eaton, Herbert. PRESIDENTIAL TIMBER: A HISTORY OF NOMINATING CONVENTIONS, 1868-1960. New York: Free Press of Glencoe, 1964. 528 p.

Epstein, Leon D. "Political Science and Presidential Nominations." POLITICAL SCIENCE QUARTERLY 93 (Summer 1978): 177-95.

Hammond, Mary K. "The National Convention." CURRENT HISTORY 25 (September 1953): 151-56.

Lucy, W.H. "Polls, Primaries, and Presidential Nominations." JOURNAL OF POLITICS 35 (November 1973): 830-48.

McGregor, E.G., Jr. "Rationality and Uncertainty at National Nominating Conventions." JOURNAL OF POLITICS 35 (May 1973): 459-78.

McKeough, Kevin L., and Bibby, John F. THE COSTS OF POLITICAL PARTICIPATION: A STUDY OF NATIONAL CONVENTION DELEGATES. Princeton, N.J.: Citizen's Research Foundation, 1968. 100 p.

Marshall, Thomas R. PRESIDENTIAL NOMINATIONS IN A REFORM AGE. New York: Praeger, 1981. 240 p.

Menez, J.F. "Case for the National Nomination Convention." SOUTH ATLANTIC QUARTERLY 70 (Autumn 1971): 546-59.

Miles, Edwin A. "The Keynote Speech at National Nominating Conventions." QUARTERLY JOURNAL OF SPEECH 46 (February 1960): 26-31.

Covers period 1896-1956.

Niemi, Richard G., and Jennings, M. Kent. "Intraparty Communications and the Selection of Delegates to a National Convention." WESTERN POLITICAL QUARTERLY 22 (March 1969): 29-46.

O'Lessker, Karl. THE NATIONAL NOMINATING CONVENTIONS. Practical Politics Pamphlet, no. 2. Written for the Robert A. Taft Institute of Government. New York: Robert A. Taft Institute of Government, 1968. 56 p.

Paletz, David L., and Elson, Martha. "Television Coverage of Presidential Conventions: Now You See It, Now You Don't." POLITICAL SCIENCE QUARTERLY 91 (Spring 1976): 109-31.

Parris, Judith H. THE CONVENTION PROBLEM: ISSUES IN REFORM OF PRESIDENTIAL NOMINATING PROCEDURES. Studies in Presidential Selection. Washington, D.C.: Brookings Institution, 1972. xi, 194 p.

Pomper, Gerald. NOMINATING THE PRESIDENT: THE POLITICS OF CONVENTION CHOICE, WITH A NEW POSTSCRIPT ON 1964. New York: W.W. Norton, 1966. xii, 304 p.

Ranney, Austin. PARTICIPATION IN AMERICAN PRESIDENTIAL NOMINATIONS, 1976. AEI Studies, no. 149. Washington, D.C.: American Enterprise Institute for Public Policy Research, 1977. 37 p.

Ritter, Kurt W. "American Political Rhetoric and the Jeremiad Tradition: Presidential Nomination Acceptance Addresses, 1960-1976." CENTRAL STATES SPEECH JOURNAL 31 (Fall 1980): 153-71.

Sullivan, Denis G., et al. EXPLORATIONS IN CONVENTION DECISION MAKING: THE DEMOCRATIC PARTY IN THE 1970S. San Francisco: W.H. Freeman and Co., 1976. xi, 147 p.

Wildavsky, Aaron. "On the Superiority of National Conventions." REVIEW OF POLITICS 24 (July 1962): 307-19.

b. SPECIFIC CONVENTIONS

1840

Wright, Martha R. "The Log Cabin Convention of 1840 Sixty Years Later: Vermonters Correct the Record." VERMONT HISTORY 40 (Autumn 1972): 237-45.

1844

Lambert, Robert S. "The Democratic National Convention of 1844." TENNESSEE HISTORICAL QUARTERLY 14 (March 1955): 3-23.

1848

McMillan, M.C., ed. "Joseph Glover Baldwin Reports on the Whig National Convention of 1848." JOURNAL OF SOUTHERN HISTORY 25 (August 1959): 366-82.

1860

Greeman, Betty Dix. "The Democratic Convention of 1860: Prelude to Secession." MARYLAND HISTORICAL MAGAZINE 67 (Fall 1972): 225-53.

Lorenz, Alfred L., Jr. "Lincoln, (Joseph) Medill and the Republican Nomination of 1860." LINCOLN HERALD 68 (Winter 1966): 199-204.

"The Republican Convention of 1860." CHICAGO HISTORY 5 (Spring 1965): 321-40.

1872

Downey, Matthew T. "Horace Greeley and the Politicians: The Liberal Republican Convention of 1872." JOURNAL OF AMERICAN HISTORY 53 (March 1967): 727-50.

1876

Cochran, William C. "'Dear Mother: . . .' An Eyewitness Report on the Republican National Convention of 1876." Edited by Kenneth E. Davison. HAYES HISTORICAL JOURNAL 1 (Fall 1976): 88-97.

Davison, Kenneth E. "The Nomination of Rutherford Hayes for the Presidency." OHIO HISTORY 77 (Winter, Spring, Summer 1968): 95-110.

Webb, Ross A. "The Bristow Presidential Boom of 1876." HAYES HISTORICAL JOURNAL 1 (Fall 1976): 78-87.

1880

Evans, Frank B. "Wharton Barker and the Republican National Convention of 1880." PENNSYLVANIA HISTORY 27 (January 1960): 28-43.

1908

"Denver's Democratic Invasion." COLORADO MAGAZINE 41 (Summer 1964): 185-97.

1912

Dick, Charles W.F. "Organizing a National Convention: A Lesson from Senator Dick." Edited by Thomas E. Felt. OHIO HISTORICAL QUARTERLY 67 (January 1958): 50-62.

1920

Bagby, Wesley Marvin, Jr. "William Gibbs McAdoo and the 1920 Presidential Nomination." EAST TENNESSEE HISTORICAL SOCIETY PUBLICATIONS 31 (1959): 43-58.

Wadsworth, James W. "The Smoke-Filled Room." AMERICAN HERITAGE 23 (June 1972): 109-10.

> Senator Wadsworth of New York was the sole survivor of the original smoke-filled room. His story of what happened was recorded shortly before his death in 1952 for the Oral History Research Office of Columbia University. He claims no decision was made in the room.

1924

Prude, James C. "Notes and Documents: William Gibbs McAdoo and the National Democratic Convention of 1924." JOURNAL OF SOUTHERN HISTORY 38 (November 1972): 621-28.

Stratton, David H. "Splattered with Oil: William G. McAdoo and the 1924 Democratic Presidential Nomination." SOUTHWESTERN SOCIAL SCIENCE QUARTERLY 44 (June 1963): 62-76.

1968

Walker, Daniel. RIGHTS IN CONFLICT: CONVENTION WEEK IN CHICAGO, AUGUST 25-29, 1968: A REPORT. New York: E.P. Dutton, 1968. xx, 362 p.

1976

"Exploring the 1976 Republican Convention: Five Perspectives." POLITICAL SCIENCE QUARTERLY 92 (Winter 1977-78): 633-82.

3. Presidential Primaries

Beniger, James R. "Winning the Presidential Nomination: National Polls and State Primary Elections, 1936-1972." PUBLIC OPINION QUARTERLY 40 (Spring 1976): 22-38.

Davis, James W. PRESIDENTIAL PRIMARIES: ROAD TO THE WHITE HOUSE. Westport, Conn.: Greenwood Press, 1980. xv, 395 p.

A new edition of the most comprehensive book on the subject. In the interim since 1967, the number of state primaries has increased from fifteen to thirty-five. Almost 75 percent of all convention delegates are now chosen in the primary states.

Felson, Marcus, and Sudman, Seymour. "The Accuracy of Presidential Primary Polls." PUBLIC OPINION QUARTERLY 39 (Summer 1975): 232-36.

Hadley, Arthur Twining. THE INVISIBLE PRIMARY. Englewood Cliffs, N.J.: Prentice-Hall, 1976. xv, 317 p.

Lucy, William H. "Polls, Primaries, and Presidential Nominations." JOURNAL OF POLITICS 35 (November 1973): 830-48.

Overacker, Louise. THE PRESIDENTIAL PRIMARY. New York: Macmillan, 1926. Reprint. New York: Arno Press, 1974. ix, 308 p.

Ranney, Austin. THE FEDERALIZATION OF PRESIDENTIAL PRIMARIES. Studies in Political and Social Processes. Washington, D.C.: American Enterprise Institute for Public Policy Research, 1978. 40 p.

4. Campaigns

a. GENERAL STUDIES

Agranoff, Robert, comp. THE NEW STYLE IN ELECTION CAMPAIGNS. Boston: Holbrook Press, 1972. vii, 392 p.

Albert, Lillian Smith, and Adams, Jane F. "Buttons and Politics." ANTIQUES 58 (November 1950): 390-91.

Mainly confined to decorations found in New England, New York, and Ohio.

Alexander, Herbert E. FINANCING POLITICS: MONEY, ELECTIONS AND POLITICAL REFORM. Washington, D.C.: Congressional Quarterly Press, 1976. 299 p.

A study of the financing of electoral politics with emphasis upon the 1970s, including abuses and the successes and failures of reform legislation and the Federal Election Commission.

Bloom, Melvyn H. PUBLIC RELATIONS AND PRESIDENTIAL CAMPAIGNS: A CRISIS IN DEMOCRACY. New York: Crowell, 1973. viii, 349 p.

Burnham, Walter Dean. PRESIDENTIAL BALLOTS, 1836-1892. Baltimore: Johns Hopkins Press, 1955. Reprint. New York: Arno Press, 1976. xix, 956 p.

Congressional Quarterly Service. PRESIDENTIAL CANDIDATES FROM 1788 TO 1964, INCLUDING THIRD PARTIES, 1832-1964, AND POPULAR ELECTORAL VOTE: HISTORICAL REVIEW. Rev. ed. Washington, D.C.: 1964. 27 p.

Declerq, Eugene R.; Hurley, Thomas L.; and Luttbeg, Norman R. "Presidential Voting Change in the South: 1956-1972." JOURNAL OF POLITICS 39 (May 1977): 480-92.

Dunn, Delmer D. FINANCING PRESIDENTIAL CAMPAIGNS. Washington, D.C.: Brookings Institution, 1972. xiii, 168 p.

______. "Paying for Politics; Highlights of Financing Presidential Campaigns." Washington, D.C.: Brookings Institution, 1972. 9 p.

Hess, Stephen. THE PRESIDENTIAL CAMPAIGN: AN ESSAY. Rev. ed. Washington, D.C.: Brookings Institution, 1978. 123 p.

Jensen, Richard. "Armies, Admen, and Crusaders: Types of Presidential Election Campaigns." HISTORY TEACHER 2 (January 1969): 33-50.

Kelley, S., Jr. "Campaign Debates: Some Facts and Issues." PUBLIC OPINION QUARTERLY 26 (Fall 1962): 351-66.

Lazarsfeld, Paul F., et al. THE PEOPLE'S CHOICE: HOW THE VOTER MAKES UP HIS MIND IN A PRESIDENTIAL CAMPAIGN. 3d ed. New York: Columbia University Press, 1968. xlv, 178 p.

Mayo, Bernard. "The Presidential Candidate: Apotheosis of American Ideals." VIRGINIA QUARTERLY REVIEW 36 (Autumn 1960): 629-35.

Review of William Burlie Brown, THE PEOPLE'S CHOICE--THE PRESIDENTIAL IMAGE IN THE CAMPAIGN BIOGRAPHY (1960).

Miles, William. THE IMAGE MAKERS: A BIBLIOGRAPHY OF AMERICAN PRESIDENTIAL CAMPAIGN BIOGRAPHIES. Metuchen, N.J.: Scarecrow Press, 1979. xvii, 254 p.

Page, Benjamin I. CHOICES AND ECHOES IN PRESIDENTIAL ELECTIONS. Chicago: University of Chicago Press, 1978. xvi, 336 p.

An analysis of presidential campaigns from Franklin Roosevelt to Carter; examines the relations between voters and their political environment.

Papale, Henry, comp. BANNERS, BUTTONS AND SONGS: A PICTORIAL REVIEW AND CAPSULE ALMANAC OF AMERICA'S PRESIDENTIAL CAMPAIGNS. Cincinnati: World Library Publications, 1968. 92 p.

Robinson, Lloyd. THE HOPEFULS: TEN PRESIDENTIAL CAMPAIGNS. Garden City, N.Y.: Doubleday, 1966. 192 p.

Salant, R.S. "Television Debates: A Revolution that Deserves a Future." PUBLIC OPINION QUARTERLY 26 (Fall 1962): 335-50.

Weisbord, Marvin Ross. CAMPAIGNING FOR PRESIDENT: A NEW LOOK AT THE ROAD TO THE WHITE HOUSE. Rev. and exp. ed. New York: Washington Square Press, 1966. xv, 447 p.

White, Theodore H. AMERICA IN SEARCH OF ITSELF: THE MAKING OF THE PRESIDENT 1956-1980. New York: Harper and Row, 1982. viii, 465 p.

b. SELECTED CONTESTS

1824

Hay, Robert P. "The Presidential Question: Letters to Southern Editors, 1823-24." TENNESSEE HISTORICAL QUARTERLY 31 (Summer 1972): 170-86.

Tankard, James W., Jr. "Public Opinion Polling by Newspapers in the Presidential Election Campaign of 1824." JOURNALISM QUARTERLY 49 (Summer 1972): 361-65.

1832

Gammon, Samuel Rhea. THE PRESIDENTIAL CAMPAIGN OF 1832. Baltimore: Johns Hopkins Press, 1922. Reprint. St. Clair Shores, Mich.: Scholarly Press, 1972. 180 p.

1840

Gunderson, Robert Gray. THE LOG-CABIN CAMPAIGN. Lexington: University of Kentucky Press, 1957. viii, 292 p.

1844

Miles, E.A. "Fifty-four Forty or Fight--An American Political Legend." MISSISSIPPI VALLEY HISTORICAL REVIEW 44 (September 1957): 291-309.

Sperber, H. "Fifty-four Forty or Fight: Facts and Fictions." AMERICAN SPEECH 32 (February 1957): 5-11.

1860

Fite, Emerson David. THE PRESIDENTIAL CAMPAIGN OF 1860. Port Washington, N.Y.: Kennikat Press, 1967. xiii, 356 p.

1876

Baetzhold, Howard G. "Mark Twain Stumps for Hayes." HAYES HISTORICAL JOURNAL 1 (Fall 1976): 111-14.

1896

Fite, Gilbert. "Republican Strategy and the Farm Vote in the Presidential Campaign of 1896." AMERICAN HISTORICAL REVIEW 65 (July 1960): 787-806.

1920

Bagby, Wesley M. THE ROAD TO NORMALCY: THE PRESIDENTIAL CAMPAIGN AND ELECTION OF 1920. Johns Hopkins University Studies in Historical and Political Science, series 80. Baltimore: Johns Hopkins Press, 1962. 206 p.

Downes, Randolph C. "Negro Rights and White Backlash in the Campaign of 1920." OHIO HISTORY 75 (Spring-Summer 1966): 85-107.

1924

Allen, Lee N. "The McAdoo Campaign for the Presidential Nomination in 1924." JOURNAL OF SOUTHERN HISTORY 29 (May 1963): 211-28.

1928

Moore, Edmund Arthur. A CATHOLIC RUNS FOR PRESIDENT: THE CAMPAIGN OF 1928. New York: Ronald Press, 1956. Reprint. Gloucester, Mass.: P. Smith 1968. xv, 220 p.

Peel, Roy Victor, and Donnelly, Thomas. THE 1928 CAMPAIGN: AN ANALYSIS. New York: R.R. Smith, 1931. Reprint. Westport, Conn.: Greenwood Press, 1975. xii, 183 p.

1948

Ross, Irwin. THE LONELIEST CAMPAIGN: THE TRUMAN VICTORY OF 1948. New York: New American Library, 1968. 304 p.

1952

Campbell, Angus, et al. THE VOTER DECIDES. Evanston, Ill.: Row, Peterson, 1954. Reprint. Westport, Conn.: Greenwood Press, 1971. xiii, 242 p.

Based upon a survey of the 1952 election conducted by the Survey Research Center at the University of Michigan.

1956

Thomson, Charles A.H., and Shattuck, Frances M. THE 1956 PRESIDENTIAL CAMPAIGN. Washington, D.C.: Brookings Institution, 1960. xv, 592 p.

1960

Ellsworth, J.W. "Rationality and Campaigning: A Content Analysis of the 1960 Presidential Campaign Debates." WESTERN POLITICAL QUARTERLY 18 (December 1965): 794-802.

1960, 1964

Pool, Ithiel de Sola. CANDIDATES, ISSUES AND STRATEGIES: A COMPUTER SIMULATION OF THE 1960 AND 1964 PRESIDENTIAL ELECTIONS. Rev. ed. Cambridge: MIT Press, 1965. xi, 193 p.

1968

Chester, Lewis, et al. AN AMERICAN MELODRAMA: THE PRESIDENTIAL CAMPAIGN OF 1968. New York: Viking Press, 1969. xv, 814 p.

Grabner, Doris. "Press as Opinion Resource during the 1968 Presidential Campaign." PUBLIC OPINION QUARTERLY 35 (Summer 1971): 168-82.

McGinniss, Joe. THE SELLING OF THE PRESIDENT 1968. New York: Trident Press, 1969. 253 p.

1972

Fraser, Janet, and May, Ernest R., eds. CAMPAIGN '72; THE MANAGERS SPEAK. Cambridge, Mass.: Harvard University Press, 1973. ix, 318 p.

Harvard Conference on Campaign Decision-Making, Cambridge, Massachusetts, 1973.

1976

Becker, Samuel L. "The Study of Campaign '76: An Overview." SPEECH MONOGRAPHS 45 (November 1978): 265-67.

Bermann, Ernest G.; Koester, Jolene; and Bennett, Janet. "Political Cartoons and Salient Rhetorical Fantasies: An Empirical Analysis of the '76 Presidential Campaign." SPEECH MONOGRAPHS 45 (November 1978): 51-63.

Cross, Mercer, ed. CANDIDATES '76: TIMELY REPORTS TO KEEP JOURNALISTS, SCHOLARS, AND THE PUBLIC ABREAST OF DEVELOPING ISSUES, EVENTS, AND TRENDS. Washington, D.C.: Congressional Quarterly, 1976. vi, 110 p.

Freshley, Dwight L. "Manipulating Public Expectations: Pre- and Postprimary Statements in the '76 Campaign." SOUTHERN SPEECH COMMUNICATION JOURNAL 45 (Spring 1980): 223-39.

Maloney, Gary D., and Buss, Terry F. "Information, Interest, and Attitude Change: Carter and the 1976 Post-Convention Campaign." CENTRAL STATES SPEECH JOURNAL 31 (Spring 1980): 63-73.

Moore, Jonathan, and Fraser, Janet, eds. CAMPAIGN FOR PRESIDENT: THE MANAGERS LOOK AT '76. Cambridge, Mass.: Ballinger Publishing Co., 1977. viii, 194 p.

Proceedings of a conference held in Cambridge, Massachusetts, 3-5 December 1976.

Schram, Martin. RUNNING FOR PRESIDENT, 1976: THE CARTER CAMPAIGN. New York: Stein and Day, 1977. 406 p.

Swanson, David L. "And That's the Way It Was? Television Covers the 1976 Presidential Campaign." QUARTERLY JOURNAL OF SPEECH 63 (October 1977): 239-48.

1976

Tiemens, Robert K. "Television's Portrayal of the 1976 Presidential Debates: An Analysis of Visual Content." SPEECH MONOGRAPHS 45 (November 1978): 362-70.

1980

Berquist, Goodwin F., and Golden, James L. "Media Rhetoric, Criticism, and the Public Perception of the 1980 Presidential Debates." QUARTERLY JOURNAL OF SPEECH 67 (May 1981): 125-37.

Ferguson, Thomas, and Rogers, Joel, eds. THE HIDDEN ELECTION: POLITICS AND ECONOMICS IN THE 1980 PRESIDENTIAL CAMPAIGN. New York: Pantheon, 1981. x, 342 p.

Moore, Jonathan, ed. THE CAMPAIGN FOR PRESIDENT: 1980 IN RETROSPECT. Cambridge, Mass.: Ballinger Publishing Co., 1981. xxiii, 304 p.

Stacks, John F. WATERSHED: THE CAMPAIGN FOR THE PRESIDENCY, 1980. New York: Times Books, 1981. 267 p.

Watson, Richard Abernathy. THE PRESIDENTIAL CONTEST: WITH A GUIDE TO THE 1980 RACE. New York: Wiley, 1980. xii, 159 p.

5. Specific Elections

1800

Borden, Morton. "The Election of 1800: Charge and Counter-Charge." DELAWARE HISTORY 5 (March 1952): 42-62.

Deals particularly with activities of James A. Bayard of Delaware.

Lerche, Charles O., Jr. "Jefferson and the Election of 1800: A Case Study in the Political Smear." WILLIAM AND MARY QUARTERLY 5 (October 1948): 467-91.

1820

Turner, Lynn W. "The Electoral Vote against Monroe in 1820--An American Legend." MISSISSIPPI VALLEY HISTORICAL REVIEW 42 (September 1955): 250-73.

1824

Ames, William E., and Olson, S. Dean. "Washington's Political Press and the Election of 1824." JOURNALISM QUARTERLY 40 (Summer 1963): 343-50.

Nagel, Paul C. "The Election of 1824: A Reconsideration Based on Newspaper Opinion." JOURNAL OF SOUTHERN HISTORY 26 (August 1960): 315-29.

1828

Weston, Florence. THE PRESIDENTIAL ELECTION OF 1828. Washington, D.C.: Ruddick Press, 1938. Reprint. Philadelphia: Porcupine Press, 1974. 217 p.

1840

Gilbert, Abby L. "Of Banks and Politics: The Bank and the Election of 1840." WEST VIRGINIA HISTORY 34 (October 1972): 18-45.

1848

Serio, Anne Marie. POLITICAL CARTOONS IN THE 1848 ELECTION CAMPAIGN. Smithsonian Studies in History and Technology, no. 14. Washington, D.C.: Smithsonian Institution Press, 1972. 21 p.

1860

Crenshaw, Ollinger. THE SLAVE STATES IN THE PRESIDENTIAL ELECTION OF 1860. Johns Hopkins University, Studies in Historical and Political Science, series 63, no. 3. Gloucester, Mass.: P. Smith, 1969. 332 p.

Cross, Jasper W. "The Forty-Eighters and the Election of 1860." HISTORICAL BULLETIN 27 (May 1949): 79-80, 87-89.

On the belief that the Republican victory of 1860 resulted from votes by the foreign-born.

Knoles, George Harmon, ed. THE CRISIS OF THE UNION, 1860-1861. Baton Rouge: Louisiana State University Press, 1965. vi, 115 p.

Papers of a conference sponsored by the Institute of American History and held at Stanford University 1-2 March 1963.

Porter, David. "The Southern Press and the Presidential Election of 1860." WEST VIRGINIA HISTORY 33 (October 1971): 1-13.

Potterf, Rex M. PRESIDENTIAL ELECTION OF 1860. Prepared by the staff of the Public Library of Fort Wayne and Allen County. Fort Wayne: The Library, 1960. 31 p.

1864

Julian, Paul H. "William Lloyd Garrison and the Election of 1864." HISTORICAL JOURNAL OF WESTERN MASSACHUSETTS 1 (Spring 1972): 19-27.

Owsley, Harriet Chappell. "Peace and the Presidential Election of 1864." TENNESSEE HISTORICAL QUARTERLY 18 (March 1959): 3-19.

Zornow, William. "Lincoln's Influence in the Election of 1864." LINCOLN HERALD 51 (June 1949): 22-32.

1868

Coleman, Charles Hubert. THE ELECTION OF 1868: THE DEMOCRATIC EFFORT TO REGAIN CONTROL. Studies in History, Economics, and Public Law, no. 392. New York: Octagon Books, 1971. 407 p.

Perzel, Edward S. "Alexander Long, Salmon P. Chase, and the Election of 1868." CINCINNATI HISTORICAL SOCIETY BULLETIN 23 (January 1965): 3-18.

1872

Lunde, Erik S. "The Ambiguity of the National Idea: The Presidential Campaign of 1872." CANADIAN REVIEW OF STUDIES IN NATIONALISM 5 (Spring 1978): 1-23.

Papy, Mariano D. "Horace Greeley, Presidential Candidate: A Floridian's View." Edited by Willard E. Wight. FLORIDA HISTORICAL QUARTERLY 35 (January 1957): 271-75.

Riddleberger, P.W. "Bread in the Radical Ranks: Liberals vs. Stalwarts in the Election of 1872." JOURNAL OF NEGRO HISTORY 44 (April 1959): 136-57.

1876

Bishop, Robert L., and Friedman, Stephen. "Campaign Coverage--1876 Style by the CHICAGO TRIBUNE." JOURNALISM QUARTERLY 45 (Autumn 1968): 481-86, 495.

Davison, Kenneth E. "The Presidential Election of 1876." HAYES HISTORICAL JOURNAL 1 (Fall 1976): 115-22.

Kleber, L.C. "Presidential Election of 1876." HISTORY TODAY 20 (November 1970): 806-13.

Lucey, William L. "'Our Beloved Country is in Danger': Some Comments on the 1876 Election." RECORDS OF THE AMERICAN CATHOLIC HISTORICAL SOCIETY OF PHILADELPHIA 89 (June 1968).

Payne, Alma J. "The ASHTABULA SENTINEL and the Election of 1876." HAYES HISTORICAL JOURNAL 1 (Fall 1976): 98-110.

Polakoff, Keith Ian. THE POLITICS OF INERTIA: THE ELECTION OF 1876 AND THE END OF RECONSTRUCTION. Baton Rouge: Louisiana State University Press, 1973. xiv, 343 p.

Robinson, Lloyd. THE STOLEN ELECTION: HAYES VERSUS TILDEN, 1876. Garden City, N.Y.: Doubleday, 1968. 240 p.

Theisen, Lee Scott. "A 'Fair Count' in Florida: General Lew Wallace and the Contested Presidential Election of 1876." HAYES HISTORICAL JOURNAL 2 (Spring 1978): 20-32.

Vaughan, Harold Cecil. THE HAYES-TILDEN ELECTION OF 1876: A DISPUTED PRESIDENTIAL ELECTION IN THE GILDED AGE. New York: Franklin Watts, 1972. 89 p.

Woodward, C. Vann. REUNION AND REACTION: THE COMPROMISE OF 1877 AND THE END OF RECONSTRUCTION. Boston: Little, Brown, 1951. xii, 263 p.

1880

Clancy, Herbert J. THE PRESIDENTIAL ELECTION OF 1880. Chicago: Loyola University Press, 1958. ix, p. 294.

1892

Knoles, George Harmon. THE PRESIDENTIAL CAMPAIGN AND ELECTION OF 1892. New York: AMS Press, 1971. 268 p.

1896

Hollingsworth, J. Rogers. "The Historian, Presidential Elections, and 1896." MID-AMERICA 45 (July 1963): 185-92.

1900

Tweton, D. Jerome. "Imperialism versus Prosperity in the Election of 1900." NORTH DAKOTA QUARTERLY 30 (Spring 1962): 50-55.

1904

Snyder, J. Richard. "The Election of 1904: An Attempt at Reform." COLORADO MAGAZINE 45 (Winter 1968): 16-26.

1908

Hornig, Edgar A. "Campaign Issues in the Presidential Election of 1908." INDIANA MAGAZINE OF HISTORY 54 (September 1958): 237-64.

Morgan, H. Wayne. "Red Special: Eugene V. Debs and the Campaign of 1908." INDIANA MAGAZINE OF HISTORY 54 (September 1958): 211-36.

On Debs's activities as the Socialist candidate for president.

1912

Parker, James R. "Beveridge and the Election of 1912: Progressive Idealist or Political Realist." INDIANA MAGAZINE OF HISTORY 63 (June 1967): 103-14.

Pitkin, William A. "Issues in the Roosevelt-Taft Contest of 1912." MID-AMERICA 34 (October 1952): 219-32.

1916

Cuddy, Edward. "Irish-Americans and the 1916 Election: An Episode in Immigrant Adjustment." AMERICAN QUARTERLY 21 (Summer 1969): 228-43.

Huston, James A. "The Election of 1916." CURRENT HISTORY 47 (October 1964): 205-9, 242.

Leary, William M., Jr. "Woodrow Wilson, Irish Americans, and the Election of 1916." JOURNAL OF AMERICAN HISTORY 54 (June 1967): 57-72.

1920

Murray, Lawrence L. "General John J. Pershing's Bid for the Presidency in 1920." NEBRASKA HISTORY 53 (Summer 1972): 217-52.

1924

Murray, Robert K. THE 103RD BALLOT: DEMOCRATS AND THE DISASTER IN MADISON SQUARE GARDEN. New York: Harper and Row, 1976. 336 p.

> A study of the struggle between Alfred E. Smith and William Gibbs McAdoo for the democratic presidential nomination. A traditional but very solid book.

1928

Blair, John L. "'I Do Not Choose to Run in Nineteen Twenty Eight.'" VERMONT HISTORY 30 (July 1962): 177-94.

Carlson, Earland I. "Franklin D. Roosevelt's Postmortem of the 1928 Election." AMERICAN JOURNAL OF POLITICAL SCIENCE 8 (August 1964): 298-308.

Carter, Paul A. "The Other Catholic Candidate: The 1928 Presidential Bid of Thomas J. Walsh." PACIFIC NORTHWEST QUARTERLY 55 (January 1964): 1-7.

Clubb, Jerome M., and Allen, Howard W. "The Cities and the Election of 1928: Partisan Realignment?" AMERICAN HISTORICAL REVIEW 74 (April 1969): 1205-20.

Lichtman, Allan J. PREJUDICE AND THE OLD POLITICS: THE PRESIDENTIAL ELECTION OF 1928. Chapel Hill: University of North Carolina Press, 1979. xiii, 366 p.

Moore, Edmund A. A CATHOLIC RUNS FOR PRESIDENT: THE CAMPAIGN OF 1928. New York: Ronald Press Co., 1956. xv, 220 p.

Watson, R.L. "Some Recent Interpretations of the Election of 1928." HIGH SCHOOL JOURNAL 50 (May 1967): 428-48.

1932

Blair, John L. "The (Edward) T. Clark-Coolidge Correspondence and the Election of 1932." VERMONT HISTORY 34 (April 1966): 83-114.

Feinman, Ronald L. "The Progressive Republican Senate Bloc and the Presidential Election of 1932." MID-AMERICA 59 (April-July 1977): 73-91.

1936

Powell, David O. "The Union Party of 1936: Campaign Tactics and Issues." MID-AMERICA 46 (April 1964): 126-41.

1944

Melosi, Martin V. "Political Tremors from a Military Disaster: 'Pearl Harbor' and the Election of 1944." DIPLOMATIC HISTORY 1 (Winter 1977): 79-95.

1948

Bogardus, E.S. "Public Opinion and the Presidential Election of 1948." SOCIAL FORCES 28 (October 1949): 79-83.

Divine, R.A. "Cold War and the Election of 1948." JOURNAL OF AMERICAN HISTORY 59 (June 1972): 90-110.

Huston, James A. "The Election of 1948 in the Light of History." SOCIAL STUDIES 40 (October 1949): 245-50.

Shogan, Robert. "1948 Election." AMERICAN HERITAGE 19 (June 1968): 22-31, 104-11.

Williams, Oliver P. "The Commodity Credit Corporation and the 1948 Presidential Election." MIDWEST JOURNAL OF POLITICAL SCIENCE 1 (August 1957): 111-24.

Yarnell, Allen. DEMOCRATS AND PROGRESSIVES: THE 1948 PRESIDENTIAL ELECTION AS A TEST OF POSTWAR LIBERALISM. Berkeley and Los Angeles: University of California Press, 1974. xii, 155 p.

1952

Collier, Everett. "Rayburn for President: A Footnote to the 1952 Election." TEXAS QUARTERLY 9 (Winter 1966): 102-6.

De Santis, Vincent P. "The Presidential Election of 1952." REVIEW OF POLITICS 15 (April 1953): 131-50.

Includes analogies to earlier elections, 1828-1948.

Hacker, L.M. "Presidency and the Election." ACADEMY OF POLITICAL SCIENCE PROCEEDINGS 25 (May 1952): 78-87.

Janowitz, Morris, and Marvick, Dwaine. COMPETITIVE PRESSURE AND DEMOCRATIC CONSENT: AN INTERPRETATION OF THE 1952 PRESIDENTIAL ELECTION. Ann Arbor: Bureau of Government Institute of Public Administration, University of Michigan, 1956. Reprint. Westport, Conn.: Greenwood Press, 1975. viii, 122 p.

1956

Thomson, Charles Alexander Holmes, and Shattuck, Frances M. THE 1956 PRESIDENTIAL CAMPAIGN. Washington, D.C.: Brookings Institution, 1960. Reprint. Westport, Conn.: Greenwood Press, 1974. xv, 382 p.

1960

Alexander, Herbert E. FINANCING THE 1960 ELECTION. Study no. 5. Princeton, N.J.: Citizen's Research Foundation, 1962. 108 p.

Dawidowicz, Lucy S., and Goldstein, Leon J. POLITICS IN A PLURALIST DEMOCRACY; STUDIES OF VOTING IN THE 1960 ELECTION. New York: Institute of Human Relations Press, 1963. Reprint. With a foreword by Richard M. Scammon. Westport, Conn.: Greenwood Press, 1974. xii, 100 p.

Hattery, John W. "The Presidential Election Campaigns of 1928 and 1960: A Comparison of the CHRISTIAN CENTURY and AMERICA." JOURNAL OF CHURCH AND STATE 9 (Winter 1967): 36-50.

Kehl, James A. "The Presidential Sweepstakes in Review: Seen from the 1960 Starting-Gate." PENNSYLVANIA HISTORY 31 (April 1964): 216-28.

Kraus, Sidney, ed. THE GREAT DEBATES: BACKGROUND, PERSPECTIVE, EFFECTS. Gloucester, Mass.: P. Smith, 1968. 439 p.

Includes the text of the four televised debates between John F. Kennedy and Richard M. Nixon, in the 1960 presidential campaign.

Pool, Ithiel de Sola, et al. CANDIDATES, ISSUES, AND STRATEGIES: A COMPUTER SIMULATION OF THE 1960 PRESIDENTIAL ELECTION. Cambridge: MIT Press, 1964. xii, 167 p.

Watson, Richard A. "Religion and Politics in Mid-America: Presidential Voting in 1928 and 1960." MIDCONTINENT AMERICAN STUDIES JOURNAL 5 (Spring 1964): 33-55.

White, Theodore H. THE MAKING OF THE PRESIDENT 1960. New York: Atheneum Publishers, 1961. 400 p.

1960, 1964

Ogden, Daniel M., Jr., and Peterson, Arthur L. ELECTING THE PRESIDENT. Rev. ed. San Francisco: Chandler Publishing Co., 1968. ix, 335 p.

Pool, Ithiel de Sola, et al. CANDIDATES, ISSUES AND STRATEGIES: A COMPUTER SIMULATION OF THE 1960 AND 1964 PRESIDENTIAL ELECTIONS. MIT Paperback Series, no. 33. Rev. ed. Cambridge: MIT, 1965. xi, 193 p.

1964

Alexander, Herbert E. FINANCING THE 1964 ELECTION. Citizens' Research Foundation, study no. 9. Princeton, N.J.: Citizens Research Foundation, 1966. 137 p.

Cummings, Milton C., Jr., ed. THE NATIONAL ELECTION OF 1964. By Paul Tillett et al. Washington, D.C.: Brookings Institution, 1966. xi, 295 p.

Faber, Harold, ed. THE ROAD TO THE WHITE HOUSE: THE STORY OF THE 1964 ELECTION. New York: McGraw-Hill, 1965. xvi, 305 p.

Lamb, Karl A., and Smith, Paul A. CAMPAIGN DECISION-MAKING: THE PRESIDENTIAL ELECTION OF 1964. Belmont, Calif.: Wadsworth Publishing Co., 1968. xii, 238 p.

Myers, David Samuel. FOREIGN AFFAIRS AND THE 1964 PRESIDENTIAL ELECTION IN THE UNITED STATES. International Humanistic Studies and Social Sciences Monograph Series. Meerut, India: Sadhana Prakashan, 1972. viii, 107 p.

National Broadcasting Company. NBC News. SOMEHOW IT WORKS: A CANDID PORTRAIT OF THE 1964 PRESIDENTIAL ELECTION. Edited by Gene Shalit and Lawrence K. Grossman. Photographs by David Hollander and Paul Seligman. Designed by John Graham. Garden City, N.Y.: Doubleday, 1965. 223 p.

New York Times. THE ROAD TO THE WHITE HOUSE: THE STORY OF THE 1964 ELECTION. Edited by Harold Faber. New York: McGraw-Hill, 1965. xvi, 305 p.

U.S. Information Agency. AMERICAN ELECTIONS, 1964: PRIMARIES, CONVENTIONS, CAMPAIGN, VOTING. Washington, D.C.: 1964. 50 p.

White, Theodore Harold. THE MAKING OF THE PRESIDENT, 1964. New York: Atheneum Publishers, 1965. xi, 431 p.

1968

Baker, Russell. OUR NEXT PRESIDENT: THE INCREDIBLE STORY OF WHAT HAPPENED IN THE 1968 ELECTIONS. New York: Atheneum, 1968. 108 p.

Driscoll, James G. ELECTIONS 1968. Silver Spring, Md.: National Observer, 1968. 156 p.

English, David, with the staff of London Daily Express. DIVIDED THEY STAND. Englewood Cliffs, N.J.: Prentice-Hall, 1969. x, 428 p.

Frost, David. THE PRESIDENTIAL DEBATE, 1968: DAVID FROST TALKS WITH VICE-PRESIDENT HUBERT H. HUMPHREY AND OTHERS. New York: Stein and Day, 1968. 126 p.

Nicholas, H.G. "The 1968 Presidential Elections." JOURNAL OF AMERICAN STUDIES 3 (July 1969): 1-15.

THE PRESIDENT: REX, PRINCEPS, IMPERATOR? Edited by Joseph M. Ray. El Paso: Texas Western Press, 1969. ix, 101 p.

White, Theodore Harold. THE MAKING OF THE PRESIDENT, 1968. New York: Atheneum Publishers, 1969. xii, 459 p.

1972

Alexander, Herbert E. FINANCING THE 1972 ELECTION. Lexington, Mass.: Lexington Books, 1976. xxiii, 771 p.

THE COATTAILLESS LANDSLIDE: EL PASO PAPERS ON THE 1972 PRESIDENTIAL CAMPAIGN. Edited by Joseph M. Ray. Symposium on Presidential Elections, 4th, University of Texas at El Paso, 1972. El Paso: Texas Western Press, 1974. xii, 164 p.

Congressional Quarterly. CANDIDATES '72. Edited by Mercer Cross. Washington, D.C.: 1971. 92 p.

Congressional Quarterly. CONGRESSIONAL QUARTERLY GUIDE TO THE 1972 ELECTIONS. Edited by Mercer Cross. Washington, D.C.: 1972. 64 p.

Crouse, Timothy. THE BOYS ON THE BUS. New York: Random House, 1973. 383 p.

Ladd, Everett Carll, Jr., and Lipset, Seymour M. ACADEMICS, POLITICS, AND THE 1972 ELECTION. Domestic Affairs Study, no. 15. Washington, D.C.: American Enterprise Institute for Public Policy Research, 1973. 99 p.

Lubell, Samuel. THE FUTURE WHILE IT HAPPENED. New York: Norton, 1973. 162 p.

Mendelsohn, Harold A., and O'Keefe, Garrett J. THE PEOPLE CHOOSE A PRESIDENT: INFLUENCES ON VOTER DECISION MAKING. New York: Praeger, 1976. xvii, 251 p.

Miller, Arthur H., and Miller, Warren E. "Issues, Candidates and Partisan Divisions in the 1972 American Presidential Election." BRITISH JOURNAL OF POLITICAL SCIENCE 5 (October 1975): 393-434.

Nicholas, H.G. "The 1972 Elections." JOURNAL OF AMERICAN STUDIES 7 (April 1973): 1-15.

Novak, Michael. CHOOSING OUR KING: POWERFUL SYMBOLS IN PRESIDENTIAL POLITICS. New York: Macmillan, 1974. xviii, 324 p.

Paysinger, Mildred A., comp. YOU MAY QUOTE ME--THE POLITICIANS: AN ANALYTICAL ANTHOLOGY OF THE PRESIDENTIAL CAMPAIGN. Hicksville, N.Y.: Exposition Press, 1974. xii, 372 p.

Pearl, Arthur. LANDSLIDE: THE HOW & WHY OF NIXON'S VICTORY. Secaucus, N.J.: Citadel Press, 1973. 240 p.

Perry, James Morehead. US AND THEM: HOW THE PRESS COVERED THE 1972 ELECTION. New York: C.N. Potter; distributed by Crown Publishers, 1973. xiii, 279 p.

Sobel, Lester A., comp. MONEY AND POLITICS: CONTRIBUTIONS, CAMPAIGN ABUSES AND THE LAW. New York: Facts on File, 1974. 204 p.

Thompson, Hunter S. FEAR AND LOATHING: ON THE CAMPAIGN TRAIL '72. San Francisco: Straight Arrow Books, 1973. 506 p.

White, Theodore Harold. THE MAKING OF THE PRESIDENT, 1972. New York: Atheneum Publishers, 1973. xix, 391 p.

1972, 1976

Miller, Arthur H. "Partisan Reinstated? A Comparison of the 1972 and 1976 U.S. Presidential Elections." BRITISH JOURNAL OF POLITICAL SCIENCE 8 (April 1978): 129-52.

1976

Jennings, Genelle. INTO THE JAWS OF POLITICS: THE CHARGE OF THE PEANUT BRIGADE. Huntsville, Ala.: Strode Publishers, 1979. 215 p.

Myers, David S. "Editorials and Foreign Affairs in the 1976 Presidential Campaign." JOURNALISM QUARTERLY 55 (Spring 1978): 92-99.

Pomper, Marlene M., ed. THE ELECTION OF 1976: REPORTS AND INTERPRETATIONS. New York: David McKay Co., 1977. viii, 184 p.

> An early evaluation of the results and the meaning of the 1976 election by five political scientists from the faculty of Rutgers University.

Roberts, Churchill L. "From Primary to the Presidency: A Panel Study of Images and Issues in the 1976 Election." WESTERN JOURNAL OF SPEECH COMMUNICATION 45 (Winter 1981): 60-70.

Shaw, Malcolm. "Reinstatement: The American Presidential Election of 1976." PARLIAMENTARY AFFAIRS 30 (Summer 1977): 241-57.

Smith, Raymond G. "The Carter-Ford Debates: Some Perceptions from Academe." CENTRAL STATES SPEECH JOURNAL 28 (Winter 1977): 250-57.

1980

Drew, Elizabeth. PORTRAIT OF AN ELECTION: THE 1980 PRESIDENTIAL CAMPAIGN. New York: Simon and Schuster, 1981. 356 p.

Germond, Jack W., and Witcover, Jules. BLUE SMOKE AND MIRRORS: HOW REAGAN WON AND WHY CARTER LOST THE ELECTION OF 1980. New York: Viking, 1981. xviii, 337 p.

Ladd, Everett Carll. "The Brittle Mandate: Electoral Dealignment and the 1980 Presidential Election." POLITICAL SCIENCE QUARTERLY 96 (Spring 1981): 1-26.

Pomper, Gerald, et al. THE ELECTION OF 1980: REPORTS AND INTERPRETATIONS. Edited by Marlene Pomper. Chatham, N.J.: Chatham House Publishers, 1981. viii, 199 p.

Ranney, Austin, ed. THE AMERICAN ELECTION OF 1980. Washington, D.C.: American Enterprise Institute, 1981. xiii, 391 p.

Sandoz, Ellis, and Crabb, Cecil V., Jr., eds. A TIDE OF DISCONTENT: THE 1980 ELECTIONS AND THEIR MEANING. Washington, D.C.: Congressional Quarterly Press, 1981. 254 p.

6. Electoral College

Abbasi, Ali Jaffar. THE POLITICAL PANACEA: A CRITICAL EXAMINATION OF THE AMERICAN ELECTORAL COLLEGE. Qausain, Lahore: Abbasi, 1975. viii, 42 p.

Barta, Marc, and Edwards, George. AN AMERICAN GAMBLE: THE POLITICS OF ELECTORAL REFORM. Dallas: Edwards, Barta and Rowe, 1974. 198 p.

Best, Judith. THE CASE AGAINST DIRECT ELECTION OF THE PRESIDENT: A DEFENSE OF THE ELECTORAL COLLEGE. Ithaca, N.Y.: Cornell University Press, 1975. 235 p.

Bickel, Alexander M. REFORM AND CONTINUITY: THE ELECTORAL COLLEGE, THE CONVENTION, AND THE PARTY SYSTEM. New York: Harper and Row, 1971. 122 p.

> A revised and expanded edition of THE NEW AGE OF POLITICAL REFORM (1968).

Diamond, Martin. THE ELECTORAL COLLEGE AND THE AMERICAN IDEA OF DEMOCRACY. Studies in Political and Social Processes. Washington, D.C.: American Enterprise Institute for Public Policy Research, 1977. 22 p.

Joyner, C., and Pedderson, Ronald. "Electoral College Revisited." SOUTH-WESTERN SOCIAL SCIENCE QUARTERLY 45 (June 1964): 26-36.

Michener, James Albert. PRESIDENTIAL LOTTERY: THE RECKLESS GAMBLE IN OUR ELECTORAL SYSTEM. New York: Random House, 1969. viii, 240 p.

Mullen, James Morfit. "The Electoral College and Presidential Vacancies (1787-1947)." MARYLAND LAW REVIEW 9 (Winter 1948): 28-54.

Peirce, Neal R. THE PEOPLE'S PRESIDENT: THE ELECTORAL COLLEGE IN AMERICAN HISTORY AND THE DIRECT-VOTE ALTERNATIVE. Foreword by Tom Wicker. New York: Simon and Schuster, 1968. 400 p.

Sayre, Wallace Stanley, and Parris, Judith H. VOTING FOR PRESIDENT: THE ELECTORAL COLLEGE AND THE AMERICAN POLITICAL SYSTEM. Studies in Presidential Selection. Washington, D.C.: Brookings Institution, 1970. 169 p.

Sterling, Carleton W. "The Electoral College Biases Revealed: The Conventional Wisdom and Game Theory Models Notwithstanding." WESTERN POLITICAL QUARTERLY 31 (June 1978): 159-77.

Szekely, Kalman S. ELECTORAL COLLEGE: A SELECTIVE ANNOTATED BIBLIOGRAPHY. Littleton, Colo.: Libraries Unlimited, 1970. 125 p.

U.S. Electoral Commission, 1877. PROCEEDINGS OF THE ELECTORAL COMMISSION AND OF THE TWO HOUSES OF CONGRESS IN JOINT MEETING RELATIVE TO THE COUNT OF ELECTORAL VOTES CAST DECEMBER 6, 1876 FOR THE PRESIDENTIAL TERM COMMENCING MARCH 4, 1877. New York: Da Capo Press, 1970. 1,087 p.

Wilmerding, Lucius, Jr. THE ELECTORAL COLLEGE. New Brunswick, N.J.: Rutgers University Press, 1958. xiii, 224 p.

7. Recommended Reforms

American Bar Association. Special Committee on Election Reform. ELECTING THE PRESIDENT. 1967. Rev. ed. Chicago: American Bar Association, 1977. xi, 64 p.

American Enterprise Institute for Public Policy Research. DIRECT ELECTION OF THE PRESIDENT. Washington, D.C.: 1977. 28 p.

Chamber of Commerce of the United States of America. Public Affairs Department. SHOULD THE PRESENT SYSTEM OF ELECTING THE PRESIDENT AND VICE PRESIDENT OF THE UNITED STATES BE CHANGED THROUGH ELECTORAL COLLEGE REFORM? Washington, D.C.: 1963. 24 p.

Cronin, Thomas E. "The Direct Vote and the Electoral College: The Case for Meshing Things Up!" PRESIDENTIAL STUDIES QUARTERLY 9 (Spring 1979): 144-63.

HOW CAN PRESIDENTIAL NOMINATING CONVENTIONS BE IMPROVED? HIGHLIGHTS OF THE CONVENTION PROBLEM, ISSUES IN REFORM OF PRESIDENTIAL NOMINATING PROCEDURES. By Judith H. Parris. Washington, D.C.: Brookings Institution, 1972. 9 p.

Jenkins, William S., Jr. "Shall the People Elect the President?" SOUTH ATLANTIC QUARTERLY 47 (July 1948): 331-41.

Proposed limitation to two terms.

Longley, Lawrence D., and Braun, Alan G. THE POLITICS OF ELECTORAL COLLEGE REFORM. Foreword by Birch Bayh. New Haven, Conn.: Yale University Press, 1972. xii, 222 p.

Silva, Ruth C. "Reform of the Electoral System." REVIEW OF POLITICS 14 (July 1952): 394-407.

U.S. Congress. House. Committee on the Judiciary. ELECTORAL COLLEGE REFORM. HEARINGS ON H.J. RES. 179, H.J. RES. 181, AND SIMILAR PROPOSALS. 91st Cong., 1st sess. Washington, D.C.: Government Printing Office, 1969. vii, 1,009 p.

U.S. Congress. Senate. Committee on the Judiciary. THE ELECTORAL COLLEGE AND DIRECT ELECTION: HEARINGS BEFORE THE COMMITTEE ON THE JUDICIARY, UNITED STATES SENATE, NINETY-FIFTH CONGRESS, FIRST SESSION ON S.J. RES. 1, 8, AND 18. Washington, D.C.: Government Printing Office, 1977. vi, 608 p.

Hearings held January 27-February 10, 1977.

_____. ELECTORAL COLLEGE REFORM. HEARINGS, APRIL 15, 16, AND 17, 1970. 91st Cong., 2d sess. Washington, D.C.: Government Printing Office, 1970. iii, 371 p.

U.S. Congress. Senate. Committee on the Judiciary. Subcommittee on Constitutional Amendments. ELECTORAL REFORM. HEARING ON S.J. RES. 1. 93d Cong., 1st sess. Washington, D.C.: Government Printing Office, 1973. iii, 227 p.

Ward, Jean M., and Hunt, Steve B., eds. DEMOCRATIC ALTERNATIVES: A CRITICAL ANALYSIS OF POLITICAL REFORM. Skokie, Ill.: National Textbook Co., 1974. 305 p.

Contains essays by public figures and academic specialists.

Zeidenstein, Harvey G. DIRECT ELECTION OF THE PRESIDENT. Lexington, Mass.: Lexington Books, 1973. xi, 118 p.

Chapter 6

FUNCTIONS AND POWERS OF THE PRESIDENT

A. GENERAL WORKS

"American Political Institutions after Watergate--A Discussion." POLITICAL SCIENCE QUARTERLY 89 (Winter 1974-75): 713-49.

Bessette, Joseph M., and Tulis, Jeffrey, eds. THE PRESIDENCY IN THE CONSTITUTIONAL ORDER. Baton Rouge: Louisiana State University Press, 1981. xii, 349 p.

Boyett, Gene W. "Developing the Concept of the Republican Presidency, 1787-1788." PRESIDENTIAL STUDIES QUARTERLY 7 (Fall 1977): 199-208.

Buchanan, Bruce. "The Senior Executive Service: How We Can Tell If It Works." PUBLIC ADMINISTRATION REVIEW 41 (May-June 1981): 349-58.

Califano, Joseph A., Jr. GOVERNING AMERICA: AN INSIDER'S REPORT FROM THE WHITE HOUSE AND THE CABINET. New York: Simon and Schuster, 1981. 474 p.

Corwin, Edward S. THE PRESIDENT, OFFICE AND POWERS, 1787-1957: HISTORY AND ANALYSIS OF PRACTICE AND OPINION. New York: New York University Press, 1957. xiii, 519 p.

A classic study.

Cotter, Cornelius P., and Smith, John Malcolm. POWERS OF THE PRESIDENT DURING NATIONAL CRISES. Washington, D.C.: Public Affairs Press, 1961. viii, 184 p.

Davis, James W., Jr. THE NATIONAL EXECUTIVE BRANCH. New York: Free Press, 1970. x, 228 p.

Donovan, John C. THE POLICY-MAKERS. Indianapolis: Pegasus, 1970. 255 p.

Eagleton, Thomas F. WAR AND PRESIDENTIAL POWER: A CHRONICLE OF CONGRESSIONAL SURRENDER. New York: Liveright, 1974. xiv, 240 p.

Earle, Chester B.; Earle, Valerie A.; and Lynch, John A. THE PRESIDENT'S POWERS: SHOULD THE POWER OF THE PRESIDENCY BE SIGNIFICANTLY CURTAILED? Washington, D.C.: American Enterprise Institute for Public Policy Research, 1974. iii, 92 p.

Franck, Thomas M., ed. THE TETHERED PRESIDENCY. New York: Columbia University Press, 1981. xiii, 299 p.

Genovese, Michael A. "The Supreme Court as a Check on Presidential Power." PRESIDENTIAL STUDIES QUARTERLY 6 (Winter-Spring 1976): 40-44.

Goldsmith, William M. THE GROWTH OF PRESIDENTIAL POWER: A DOCUMENTED HISTORY. 3 vols. Introductory essay by Arthur M. Schlesinger, Jr. New York: Chelsea House Publishers, 1974.

Hardin, Charles M. PRESIDENTIAL POWER AND ACCOUNTABILITY: TOWARD A NEW CONSTITUTION. Chicago: University of Chicago Press, 1974. 257 p.

Havard, William C. "The Presidency: the Office, the Man, and the Constituencies." VIRGINIA QUARTERLY REVIEW 50 (Autumn 1974): 497-514.

Heclo, Hugh, and Salamon, Lester. THE ILLUSION OF PRESIDENTIAL GOVERNMENT. Boulder, Colo.: Westview, 1981. xiv, 359 p.

Heineman, Ben W., Jr., and Hessler, Curtis A. MEMORANDUM FOR THE PRESIDENT: A STRATEGIC APPROACH TO DOMESTIC AFFAIRS IN THE 1980'S. New York: Random House, 1980. xxv, 404 p.

Herring, Edward Pendleton. PRESIDENTIAL LEADERSHIP: THE POLITICAL RELATIONS OF CONGRESS AND THE CHIEF EXECUTIVE. New York: Farrar and Rinehart, 1940. xiv, 173 p.

Hoy, John C., and Bernstein, Melvin H. THE EFFECTIVE PRESIDENT. Pacific Palisades, Calif.: Palisades Publishers, 1976. ix, 189 p.

Johnson, Walter. THE AMERICAN PRESIDENT AND THE ART OF COMMUNICATION: AN INAUGURAL LECTURE DELIVERED BEFORE THE UNIVERSITY OF OXFORD ON MAY 13, 1958. Oxford, Engl.: Clarendon Press, 1958. 21 p.

Kallenbach, Joseph Ernest. THE AMERICAN CHIEF EXECUTIVE: THE PRESIDENCY AND THE GOVERNORSHIP. New York: Harper and Row, 1966. xii, 622 p.

Kessler, Frank. THE DILEMMAS OF PRESIDENTIAL LEADERSHIP: OF CARETAKERS AND KINGS. Englewood Cliffs, N.J.: Prentice-Hall, 1982. xii, 404 p.

Keyser, Carl A. SPARE NONE: THE FEDERAL OCTOPUS: HOW IT GREW AND OTHER TALES. Amherst, Mass.: Amherst Press, 1972. 410 p.

Kurland, Gerald. THE GROWTH OF PRESIDENTIAL POWER. Topics of Our Times, no. 12. Charlottesville, N.Y.: SamHar Press, 1973. 32 p.

Lea, James F. "The Presidency: Auxiliary and Primary Limits." SOUTHERN QUARTERLY 14 (January 1976): 133-49.

Loss, Richard. "Dissolving Concepts of the Presidency." PRESIDENTIAL STUDIES QUARTERLY 6 (Winter-Spring 1976): 64-84.

Manley, John F. "Presidential Power and White House Lobbying." POLITICAL SCIENCE QUARTERLY 93 (Summer 1978): 255-75.

Masters, Nicholas Arthur, and Baluss, Mary E. THE GROWING POWERS OF THE PRESIDENCY. With documents and commentaries by Bradford Chambers. New York: Parents' Magazine Press, 1968. 256 p.

Meltsner, Arnold J., ed. POLITICS AND THE OVAL OFFICE. New Brunswick, N.J.: Transaction Books, 1981. 332 p.

Miller, Arthur Selwyn. PRESIDENTIAL POWER IN A NUTSHELL. St. Paul, Minn.: West Publishing Co., 1977. xix, 328 p.

Milton, George Fort. THE USE OF PRESIDENTIAL POWER, 1789-1943. Boston: Little, Brown, 1944. Reprint. New York: Octagon Book, 1965. xiii, 349 p.

Mondale, Walter F. THE ACCOUNTABILITY OF POWER: TOWARD A RESPONSIBLE PRESIDENCY. New York: D. McKay Co., 1975. xix, 284 p.

"National Emergencies and the President's Inherent Powers (1890-1949)." STANFORD LAW REVIEW 2 (February 1950): 303-20.

Neustadt, Richard E. PRESIDENTIAL POWER: THE POLITICS OF LEADERSHIP FROM FDR TO CARTER. New York: John Wiley and Sons, 1980. xv, 286 p.

A classic study by a former Truman and Kennedy aide. Originally published in 1960, this edition offers three new chapters covering the five recent American presidents.

Orman, John M. PRESIDENTIAL SECRECY AND DECEPTION: BEYOND THE POWER TO PERSUADE. Westport, Conn.: Greenwood Press, 1980. 256 p.

A study of secret presidential actions from Kennedy to Ford with case studies of Kennedy's involvement in plots to eliminate Castro, Johnson's secret ground and air war in Laos, Nixon's program to depose Allende in Chile, and Ford's involvement in Angola.

Pious, Richard M. "Is Presidential Power 'Poison'?" POLITICAL SCIENCE QUARTERLY 89 (Fall 1974): 627-43.

"Presidential Powers and Duties." PUBLIC ADMINISTRATION REVIEW 16 (Winter 1956): 65.

Rienow, Robert. THE LONELY QUEST: THE EVOLUTION OF PRESIDENTIAL LEADERSHIP. Chicago: Follett Publishing Co., 1966. xiv, 307 p.

Rose, Richard. "The President: A Chief but Not an Executive." PRESIDENTIAL STUDIES QUARTERLY 7 (Winter 1977): 5-20.

Seligman, L.G. "Presidential Leadership: The Inner Circle and Institutionalization." JOURNAL OF POLITICS 18 (August 1956): 410-26.

______. "President is Many Men." ANTIOCH REVIEW 16 (Fall 1956): 305-18.

Smith, John Malcolm, and Cotter, Cornelius P. POWERS OF THE PRESIDENT DURING CRISES. Washington, D.C.: Public Affairs Press, 1960. Reprint. New York: Da Capo Press, 1972. viii, 184 p.

Sorensen, Theodore C. WATCHMAN IN THE NIGHT: PRESIDENTIAL ACCOUNTABILITY AND WATERGATE. Cambridge: MIT Press, 1975. xviii, 178 p.

Stokes, William S. "Whig Conceptions of Executive Power." PRESIDENTIAL STUDIES QUARTERLY 6 (Winter-Spring 1976): 16-35.

Sundquist, James L. POLITICS AND POLICY: THE EISENHOWER, KENNEDY AND JOHNSON YEARS. Washington, D.C.: Brookings Institution, 1968. viii, 560 p.

Thompson, Kenneth W. THE PRESIDENT AND THE PUBLIC PHILOSOPHY. Baton Rouge: Louisiana State University Press, 1981. 219 p.

Weiss, Stuart L. "American Foreign Policy and Presidential Power: the Neutrality Act of 1935." JOURNAL OF POLITICS 30 (August 1968): 672-95.

Wildavsky, Aaron. "The Past and Future Presidency." PUBLIC INTEREST 41 (Fall 1975): 56-76.

B. SPECIFIC FUNCTIONS

1. Chief Administrator

Arnold, Peri E. "The First Hoover Commission and the Managerial Presidency." JOURNAL OF POLITICS 38 (February 1976): 46-70.

Blackman, John L., Jr. PRESIDENTIAL SEIZURE IN LABOR DISPUTES. Cambridge, Mass.: Harvard University Press, 1967. xvi, 351 p.

Clark, Keith C., and Legere, Laurence J., eds. THE PRESIDENT AND THE MANAGEMENT OF NATIONAL SECURITY: A REPORT BY THE INSTITUTE FOR DEFENSE ANALYSES. New York: Frederick A. Praeger, 1969. ix, 274 p.

Grundstein, Nathan D. "Presidential Power, Administration, and Administrative Law." GEORGE WASHINGTON LAW REVIEW 18 (April 1950): 285-326.

> On changing relations between public administration and executive power, 1894-1950.

Haider, Donald. "Management and the Presidency: From Preparation to Performance." PRESIDENTIAL STUDIES QUARTERLY 6 (Winter-Spring 1976): 4-15.

Hart, James. THE ORDINANCE MAKING POWERS OF THE PRESIDENT OF THE UNITED STATES. Studies in Historical and Political Science, Series 43, no. 3. Baltimore: Johns Hopkins University Press, 1925. Reprint. New York: Da Capo Press, 1970. 339 p.

Jackson, Carlton. PRESIDENTIAL VETOES, 1792-1945. Athens: University of Georgia Press, 1967. x, 254 p.

Kaufman, Lois, and Wolf, John B. "An Inspection System to Monitor White House Subordinates Compliance with Presidential Directives." PRESIDENTIAL STUDIES QUARTERLY 11 (Winter 1981): 92-98.

Kleiler, F.M. "Presidential Seizures in Labor Disputes." INDUSTRIAL AND LABOR RELATIONS REVIEW 6 (July 1953): 547-56.

_____. "White House Intervention in Labor Disputes." POLITICAL SCIENCE QUARTERLY 68 (June 1953): 227-40.

Kurland, Philip B. WATERGATE AND THE CONSTITUTION. Chicago: University of Chicago Press, 1978. x, 261 p.

Lee, Jong R. "Presidential Vetoes from Washington to Nixon." JOURNAL OF POLITICS 37 (May 1975): 522-46.

Light, Paul C. "The President's Agenda: Notes on the Timing of Domestic Choice." PRESIDENTIAL STUDIES QUARTERLY 11 (Winter 1981): 67-82.

Long, N.E. "Power and Administration." PUBLIC ADMINISTRATION REVIEW 9, no. 4 (1949): 257-64.

McConnell, Grant. STEEL AND THE PRESIDENCY. New York: Norton, 1963. 119 p.

Martin, C.E. "Executive Determination of Legal Questions; with Discussion." AMERICAN SOCIETY OF INTERNATIONAL LAW PROCEEDINGS 42 (1948): 53-83.

Morgan, Ruth P. THE PRESIDENT AND CIVIL RIGHTS: POLICY-MAKING BY EXECUTIVE ORDER. New York: St. Martin's Press, 1970. ix, 107 p.

Nathan, Richard P. THE ADMINISTRATIVE PRESIDENCY. New York: John Wiley and Sons, 1983. xi, 180 p.

Oh, John C.H. "The Presidency and Public Welfare Policy." PRESIDENTIAL STUDIES QUARTERLY 8 (Fall 1978): 377-90.

Pederson, William D. "Amnesty and Presidential Behavior: A 'Barberian' Test." PRESIDENTIAL STUDIES QUARTERLY 7 (Fall 1977): 175-83.

Relyea, Harold C. "Declaring and Terminating a State of National Emergency." PRESIDENTIAL STUDIES QUARTERLY 6 (Fall 1976): 36-42.

Rose, Richard. MANAGING PRESIDENTIAL OBJECTIVES. New York: Free Press, 1976. x, 180 p.

Rowen, Hobart. THE FREE ENTERPRISERS: KENNEDY, JOHNSON, AND THE BUSINESS ESTABLISHMENT. New York: Putnam, 1964. 319 p.

Sorensen, Theodore C. DECISION-MAKING IN THE WHITE HOUSE: THE OLIVE BRANCH OR THE ARROWS. New York: Columbia University Press, 1963. xvi, 94 p.

SUMMARY OF EXECUTIVE ORDERS IN TIME OF WAR AND NATIONAL EMERGENCY: A WORKING PAPER. Prepared by the Staff of the Special Committee on National Emergencies and Delegated Emergency Powers, U.S. Senate, August 1974. 93d Cong., 2d sess. Washington, D.C.: Government Printing Office, 1974. vi, 69 p.

Thomas, Norman C. "The Presidency and Policy Studies." POLICY STUDIES JOURNAL 9 (Summer 1981): 1072-82.

Tugwell, Rexford G. THE ENLARGEMENT OF THE PRESIDENCY. Garden City: Doubleday, 1960. 508 p.

U.S. National Archives. PAPERS OF THE UNITED STATES SENATE RELATING TO PRESIDENTIAL NOMINATIONS, 1789-1901. Record group, 46. Washington, D.C.: 1964. xiii, 111 p.

Waldo, Clifford D., and Pincus, W. "Statutory Obligations of the President: Executive Necessity and Administrative Burden." PUBLIC ADMINISTRATION REVIEW 6, no. 4 (1946): 339-47.

Wann, A.J. THE PRESIDENT AS CHIEF ADMINISTRATOR. Washington, D.C.: Public Affairs Press, 1968. v, 219 p.

A study of Franklin D. Roosevelt.

White, Leonard D. THE FEDERALISTS: A STUDY IN ADMINISTRATIVE HISTORY. New York: Macmillan Co., 1956. xii, 538 p.

______. THE JACKSONIANS: A STUDY IN ADMINISTRATIVE HISTORY, 1829-1861. New York: Macmillan, 1954. xii, 593 p.

______. THE JEFFERSONIANS: A STUDY IN ADMINISTRATIVE HISTORY, 1801-1829. New York: Macmillan, 1951. xiv, 572 p.

______. THE REPUBLICAN ERA: 1869-1901, A STUDY IN ADMINISTRATIVE HISTORY. New York: Macmillan Co., 1958. 406 p.

Wormuth, Francis Dunham. THE VIETNAM WAR: THE PRESIDENT VERSUS THE CONSTITUTION. Center occasional paper, vol. 1, no. 3. Santa Barbara, Calif.: Center for the Study of Democratic Institutions, 1968. 63 p.

2. Commander-in-Chief

Bulmer, Charles, and Carmichael, John L. "The War Powers Resolution: A Limitation on Presidential Power?" GEORGIA POLITICAL SCIENCE ASSOCIATION JOURNAL 3 (Fall 1975): 53-68.

Hassler, Warren W., Jr. THE PRESIDENT AS COMMANDER IN CHIEF. Menlo Park, Calif.: Addison-Wesley, 1971. 168 p.

Hoxie, R. Gordon. COMMAND DECISION AND THE PRESIDENCY: A STUDY OF NATIONAL SECURITY POLICY AND ORGANIZATION. New York: Reader's Digest Press, 1977. xix, 505 p.

Basic work on the subject.

Mueller, John E. WAR, PRESIDENTS, AND PUBLIC OPINION. New York: Wiley, 1973. xxiv, 300 p.

Potter, P.B. "Power of the President of the United States to Utilize Its Armed Forces Abroad." AMERICAN JOURNAL OF INTERNATIONAL LAW 48 (July 1954): 458-59.

U.S. Congress. Senate. Committee on Government Operations. THE NATIONAL SECURITY COUNCIL. 89th Cong., 1st sess. Edited by Henry M. Jackson. New York: Praeger, 1965. xvi, 311 p.

Westwood, Howard C. "The Joint Committee on the Conduct of the War--A Look at the Record." LINCOLN HERALD 80 (Spring 1978): 3-15.

3. Chief Diplomat

Destler, I.M. PRESIDENTS, BUREAUCRATS, AND FOREIGN POLICY: THE POLITICS OF ORGANIZATIONAL REFORM. Princeton, N.J.: Princeton University Press, 1972. xii, 329 p.

Driggs, D.W. "President as Chief Educator on Foreign Affairs." WESTERN POLITICAL QUARTERLY 11 (December 1958): 813-19.

George, Alexander L. PRESIDENTIAL DECISIONMAKING IN FOREIGN POLICY: THE EFFECTIVE USE OF INFORMATION AND ADVICE. Boulder, Colo.: Westview Press, 1980. xviii, 267 p.

Gilbert, Amy M. EXECUTIVE AGREEMENTS AND TREATIES, 1946-1973: FRAMEWORK OF THE FOREIGN POLICY OF THE PERIOD. Endicott, N.Y.: Thomal-Newell, 1973. x, 213 p.

Graber, Doris Appel. PUBLIC OPINION, THE PRESIDENT, AND FOREIGN POLICY: FOUR CASE STUDIES FROM THE FORMATIVE YEARS. New York: Holt, Rinehart and Winston, 1968. viii, 374 p.

Halperin, Morton H. BUREAUCRATIC POLITICS AND FOREIGN POLICY. Washington, D.C.: Brookings Institution, 1974. xvii, 340 p.

Halperin, Morton H., and Hoffman, Daniel N. TOP SECRET: NATIONAL SECURITY AND THE RIGHT TO KNOW. Washington, D.C.: New Republic Books, 1977. vi, 168 p.

A critique of abuses in the intelligence field. Argues against executive secrecy and for greater protection of First Amendment values.

Hoxie, R. Gordon. "Presidential Leadership and American Foreign Policy: Some Reflections on the Taiwan Issue, with Particular Considerations on Alexander Hamilton, Dwight Eisenhower, and Jimmy Carter." PRESIDENTIAL STUDIES QUARTERLY 9 (Spring 1979): 131-43.

Levitt, Albert. THE PRESIDENT AND THE INTERNATIONAL AFFAIRS OF THE UNITED STATES. Introduction by Roscoe Pound. Los Angeles: Parker, 1954. xi, 87 p.

Nuechterlein, Donald E. NATIONAL INTERESTS AND PRESIDENTIAL LEADERSHIP: THE SETTING OF PRIORITIES. Boulder, Colo.: Westview Press, 1978. xvi, 246 p.

A study of U.S. involvement in foreign wars from Wilson to Nixon. Examines presidential decisions and identifies sixteen cost and risk and value factors vital to the national interest.

Paolucci, Henry. WAR, PEACE, AND THE PRESIDENCY. New York: McGraw-Hill, 1968. x, 241 p.

Plischke, E. "Summit Diplomacy: Its Uses and Limitations." VIRGINIA QUARTERLY REVIEW 48 (Summer 1972): 321-44.

Pressman, Jeffrey, and Wildavsky, Aaron. IMPLEMENTATION. Berkeley and Los Angeles: University of California Press, 1973. xviii, 182 p.

An examination of the economic development administration.

Raphalides, Samuel J. "The President's Use of Troops in Civil Disorder." PRESIDENTIAL STUDIES QUARTERLY 8 (Spring 1978): 180-87.

Stuart, G.H. "President's Role in Foreign Policy." INSTITUTE OF WORLD AFFAIRS PROCEEDINGS 23 (1946): 57-60.

Warren, Sidney. THE PRESIDENT AS WORLD LEADER. Philadelphia: Lippincott, 1964. xii, 480 p.

4. Chief Legislator

Edwards, George C., III. PRESIDENTIAL INFLUENCE IN CONGRESS. San Francisco: W.H. Freeman and Co., 1980. x, 216 p.

Holtzman, Abraham. LEGISLATIVE LIAISON: EXECUTIVE LEADERSHIP IN CONGRESS. Chicago: Rand McNally, 1970. xi, 308 p.

Wayne, Stephen J. THE LEGISLATIVE PRESIDENCY. New York: Harper and Row, 1978. xiv, 240 p.

An excellent study of legislative policymaking by the executive branch from Franklin D. Roosevelt to Carter.

Chapter 7
THE INSTITUTIONALIZED PRESIDENCY

A. GENERAL STUDIES

Burger, Edward J., Jr. SCIENCE AT THE WHITE HOUSE: A POLITICAL LIABILITY. Baltimore: Johns Hopkins University Press, 1981. xx, 180 p.

U.S. Congress. House. Committee on Government Operations. PRESIDENTIAL RECORDS ACT OF 1978. Hearings. 95th Cong., 2d sess. Feb. 23-Mar. 7, 1978. Washington, D.C.: Government Printing Office, 1978.

______. PRESIDENTIAL RECORDS ACT OF 1978. 95th Cong., 2d sess., 1978. House Report no. 95-1487, part 1. Washington, D.C.: Government Printing Office, 1978. 24 p.

U.S. Executive Office of the President. Office of Science and Technology Policy. INFORMATION SYSTEMS NEEDS IN THE EXECUTIVE OFFICE OF THE PRESIDENT: FINAL REPORT OF THE ADVISORY GROUP ON WHITE HOUSE INFORMATION SYSTEMS. Washington, D.C.: 1977. 22 p.

Vose, Clement E. "Nixon's Archival Legacy." PS 10 (Fall 1977): 432-38.

______. "Presidential Papers as a Political Science Concern." PS 8 (Winter 1975): 8-18.

B. CABINET

Best, James J. "Presidential Cabinet Appointments: 1953-76." PRESIDENTIAL STUDIES QUARTERLY 11 (Winter 1981): 62-66.

Donald, David, ed. INSIDE LINCOLN'S CABINET: THE CIVIL WAR DIARIES OF SALMON P. CHASE. New York: Longmans, Green, 1954. ix, 342 p.

Fenno, Richard F., Jr. "President-Cabinet Relations: A Pattern and a Case Study." AMERICAN POLITICAL SCIENCE REVIEW 52 (June 1958): 388-405.

______. THE PRESIDENT'S CABINET: AN ANALYSIS IN THE PERIOD FROM WILSON TO EISENHOWER. Harvard Political Studies. Cambridge, Mass.: Harvard University Press, 1959. xii, 327 p.

Heller, Deane, and Heller, David. THE KENNEDY CABINET: AMERICA'S MEN OF DESTINY. Foreword by A.S. Mike Monroney. Derby, Conn.: Monarch Books, 1961. Reprint. Freeport, N.Y.: Books for Libraries Press, 1969. 159 p.

Hendrick, Burton J. LINCOLN'S WAR CABINET. Boston: Little, Brown and Co., 1946. 559 p.

An excellent study of one of the strongest and most able cabinets in American history.

Longaker, Richard P. "Was Jackson's Kitchen Cabinet a Cabinet (1829-36)?" MISSISSIPPI VALLEY HISTORICAL REVIEW 44 (June 1957): 94-108.

Nicolay, Helen. "Lincoln's Cabinet." ABRAHAM LINCOLN QUARTERLY 5 (March 1949): 255-92.

Pratt, Fletcher. STANTON: LINCOLN'S SECRETARY OF WAR. Westport, Conn.: Greenwood Press, 1970. xiii, 520 p.

Richardson, Elmo R., and Farley, Alan W. JOHN PALMER USHER: LINCOLN'S SECRETARY OF THE INTERIOR. Lawrence: University of Kansas Press, 1960. 152 p.

Thomas, Benjamin P., and Hyman, Harold M. STANTON: THE LIFE AND TIMES OF LINCOLN'S SECRETARY OF WAR. New York: Alfred A. Knopf, 1962. xvii, 642 p.

Wilson, William Lyne. THE CABINET DIARY OF WILLIAM L. WILSON, 1896-1897. Chapel Hill: University of North Carolina Press, 1957. vii, 276 p.

C. WHITE HOUSE STAFF AND ADVISERS

Anderson, Patrick. THE PRESIDENTS' MEN: WHITE HOUSE ASSISTANTS OF FRANKLIN D. ROOSEVELT, HARRY S. TRUMAN, DWIGHT D. EISENHOWER, JOHN F. KENNEDY, AND LYNDON B. JOHNSON. Garden City, N.Y.: Doubleday, 1968. viii, 420 p.

Beale, Howard K., ed. DIARY OF GIDEON WELLES, SECRETARY OF THE NAVY UNDER LINCOLN AND JOHNSON. New York: W.W. Norton and Co., 1960. xvi, 653 p.

Blegen, Theodore C., ed. "Lincoln's Secretary Goes West: Two Reports by John G. Nicolay on Frontier Indian Troubles, 1862." La Crosse, Wis.: Sumac Press, 1965. 69 p.

Bonafede, Dom. THE PRESIDENCY: THE CARTER WHITE HOUSE AND POST-WATERGATE PRESIDENCY. Washington, D.C.: Government Research Corporation, 1977. 44 p.

Key articles reprinted from the NATIONAL JOURNAL as selected and introduced by Thomas E. Cronin.

Brown, Wilson. "Aide for Four Presidents." AMERICAN HERITAGE 6 (February 1955): 66-96.

Excerpts from Admiral Brown's manuscript, "Four Presidents as I Saw Them" (Coolidge, Hoover, FDR, and Truman).

Carey, W.D. "Presidential Staffing in the Sixties and Seventies." PUBLIC ADMINISTRATION REVIEW 29 (September 1969): 450-58.

This was a special issue on "The American Presidency."

Casserly, John J. THE FORD WHITE HOUSE: THE DIARY OF A SPEECHWRITER. Boulder: Colorado Associated University Press, 1977. xi, 374 p.

Cronin, Thomas E., and Greenberg, Sanford D., eds. THE PRESIDENTIAL ADVISORY SYSTEM. New York: Harper and Row, 1969. xx, 375 p.

Ecroyd, Donald H. "Recording the President." QUARTERLY JOURNAL OF SPEECH 48 (1962): 336-40.

Discusses the career of Jack Romagna of the White House staff who served as shorthand reporter for Presidents Roosevelt, Truman, Eisenhower, and Kennedy.

Eisenhower, Milton Stover. THE PRESIDENT IS CALLING. Garden City, N.Y.: Doubleday, 1974. xxiii, 598 p.

Hess, Stephen. ORGANIZING THE PRESIDENCY. Washington, D.C.: Brookings Institution, 1976. ix, 228 p.

Johnson, Haynes Bonner. THE WORKING WHITE HOUSE. New York: Praeger, 1975. 185 p.

Kessel, John Howard. THE DOMESTIC PRESIDENCY: DECISION-MAKING IN THE WHITE HOUSE. North Scituate, Mass.: Duxbury Press, 1975. ix, 149 p.

Koenig, Louis W. THE INVISIBLE PRESIDENCY. New York: Rinehart and Co., 1960. viii, 438 p.

McPherson, Harry C. A POLITICAL EDUCATION. Boston: Atlantic-Little, Brown, 1972. 467 p.

Memoir of a Lyndon Johnson aide, 1963-67.

Magruder, Jeb Stewart. AN AMERICAN LIFE: ONE MAN'S ROAD TO WATERGATE. New York: Atheneum, 1974. 405 p.

Medved, Michael. THE SHADOW PRESIDENTS: THE SECRET HISTORY OF THE CHIEF EXECUTIVES AND THEIR TOP AIDES. New York: Times Books, 1979. xi, 401 p.

Mondale, W.F. "Social Advisers, Social Accounting, and the Presidency." LAW AND CONTEMPORARY PROBLEMS 35 (Summer 1970): 496-504.

Nash, Bradley D.; Eisenhower, Milton S.; Hoxie, R. Gordon; and Spragens, William C. ORGANIZING AND STAFFING THE PRESIDENCY. New York: Center for the Study of the Presidency, 1980. xvii, 196 p.

Argues for less staff and more effective use of the cabinet. Nash proposes upgrading the director of the Office of Management and Budget to a supra-cabinet post and absorbing within it the position of cabinet secretary created under President Eisenhower.

O'Brien, Lawrence. NO FINAL VICTORIES: FROM JOHN F. KENNEDY TO WATERGATE. Garden City, N.Y.: Doubleday, 1974. 394 p.

Tugwell, Rexford G. "President and His Helpers: A Review Article." POLITICAL SCIENCE QUARTERLY 82 (June 1967): 253-67.

D. EXECUTIVE OFFICE OF THE PRESIDENT

Falk, Stanley. "The National Security Council under Truman, Eisenhower, and Kennedy." POLITICAL SCIENCE QUARTERLY 79 (September 1964): 403-34.

Federal Executive Institute. THE CHALLENGES OF LEADERSHIP FOR AMERICAN FEDERAL EXECUTIVES: FOUR LECTURES. Spring Conference of Executives, Charlottesville, Va., 1970. Edited by Donald E. Nuechterlein. Charlottesville: 1970. ii, 49 p.

Golden, William T., ed. SCIENCE ADVICE TO THE PRESIDENT. Elmsford, N.Y.: Pergamon Press, 1980. ix, 256 p.

Published as volume 2, nos. 1 and 2 of TECHNOLOGY IN SOCIETY.

Graham, G.A. "Presidency and the Executive Office of the President." JOURNAL OF POLITICS 12 (November 1950): 599-621.

Henley, Wallace. THE WHITE HOUSE MYSTIQUE. Old Tappan, N.J.: Fleming H. Revell Co., 1976. 126 p.

Hobbs, Edward. BEHIND THE PRESIDENT: A STUDY OF EXECUTIVE OFFICE AGENCIES. Washington, D.C.: Public Affairs Press, 1954. vi, 248 p.

Keyserling, Leon H. "The Council of Economic Advisers since 1946: Its Contributions and Failures." ATLANTIC ECONOMIC JOURNAL 6 (March 1978): 17-35.

Murphy, Thomas P.; Nuechterlein, Donald E.; and Stupak, Ronald J., eds. THE PRESIDENT'S PROGRAM DIRECTORS, THE ASSISTANT SECRETARIES: A SYMPOSIUM. Charlottesville, Va.: Federal Executive Institute, 1977. iii, 112 p.

National Academy of Public Administration. A PRESIDENCY FOR THE 1980S: A REPORT ON PRESIDENTIAL MANAGEMENT BY A PANEL OF THE NATIONAL ACADEMY OF PUBLIC ADMINISTRATION. Washington, D.C.: The Academy, 1980. 11, 49 pp.

Porter, Roger B. PRESIDENTIAL DECISION MAKING: THE ECONOMIC POLICY BOARD. Cambridge, Engl.: Cambridge University Press, 1980. xii, 265 p.

Redford, Emmette S., and Blissett, Marlan. ORGANIZING THE EXECUTIVE BRANCH: THE JOHNSON PRESIDENCY. Chicago: University of Chicago Press, 1981. 272 p.

Relyea, Harold C. "Development and Organization of White House Conferences." PRESIDENTIAL STUDIES QUARTERLY 6 (Winter-Spring 1976): 36-39.

Sparks, Will. WHO TALKED TO THE PRESIDENT LAST? New York: W.W. Norton, 1971. 127 p.

Thomas, Norman C., and Baade, Hans W., eds. THE INSTITUTIONALIZED PRESIDENCY. Dobbs Ferry, N.Y.: Oceana Publications, 1972. 239 p.

Originally published as the Summer 1970 issue of LAW AND CONTEMPORARY PROBLEMS, Duke University School of Law.

Udall, Morris K. A REPORT ON THE GROWTH OF THE EXECUTIVE OFFICE OF THE PRESIDENT, 1955-1973. Washington, D.C.: Government Printing Office, 1972. iii, 39 p.

Walton, Richard J. CONGRESS AND AMERICAN FOREIGN POLICY: A BACKGROUND BOOK ON THE PRESIDENTIAL-CONGRESSIONAL STRUGGLE. New York: Parents' Magazine Press, 1972. 234 p.

Wayne, Stephen J.; Cole, Richard L.; and Hyde, James F.C., Jr. "Advising the President on Enrolled Legislation: Patterns of Executive Influence." POLITICAL SCIENCE QUARTERLY 95 (Summer 1979): 303-18.

Wildavsky, Aaron. THE POLITICS OF THE BUDGETARY PROCESS. Boston: Little, Brown, 1964. xi, 216 p.

Zeidenstein, Harvey G. "The Reassertion of Congressional Power: New Curbs on the President." POLITICAL SCIENCE QUARTERLY 93 (Fall 1978): 393-409.

Zurcher, Arnold J. "The Presidency, Congress, and Separation of Powers (1817-1949): A Reappraisal." WESTERN POLITICAL QUARTERLY 3 (March 1950): 75-97.

E. VICE PRESIDENCY

Barzman, Sol. MADMEN AND GENIUSES: THE VICE-PRESIDENTS OF THE UNITED STATES. Chicago: Follett, 1974. xi, 335 p.

Bolt, Robert. "Vice President Richard M. Johnson of Kentucky: Hero of the Thames--Or the Great Amalgamator?" REGISTER OF THE KENTUCKY HISTORICAL SOCIETY 75 (July 1977): 191-203.

Curtis, Richard, and Wells, Maggie. NOT EXACTLY A CRIME: OUR VICE PRESIDENTS FROM ADAMS TO AGNEW. New York: Dial Press, 1972. xii, 202 p.

DiSalle, Michael V. SECOND CHOICE. New York: Hawthorn Books, 1966. 253 p.

Dorman, Michael. THE SECOND MAN: THE CHANGING ROLE OF THE VICE PRESIDENCY. New York: Delacorte Press, 1970. 305 p.

Durham, G. Homer. "The Vice-Presidency (1787-1948)." WESTERN POLITICAL QUARTERLY 1 (September 1948): 311-15.

Eastburn, Walter N. "Vice-Presidents of the United States." MANUSCRIPTS 8 (Fall 1956): 295-99.

Harwood, Michael. IN THE SHADOW OF PRESIDENTS: THE AMERICAN VICE-PRESIDENCY AND SUCCESSION SYSTEM. Philadelphia: Lippincott, 1966. x, 239 p.

Hatch, Louis Clinton. A HISTORY OF THE VICE-PRESIDENCY OF THE UNITED STATES. Rev. and edited by Earl L. Shoup. New York: American Historical Society, 1934. Reprint. Westport, Conn.: Greenwood Press, 1970. viii, 437 p.

Lincoln, A. "Theodore Roosevelt, Hiram Johnson, and the Vice-Presidential Nomination of 1912." PACIFIC HISTORICAL REVIEW 28 (August 1959): 267-83.

Sindler, Allan P. UNCHOSEN PRESIDENTS: THE VICE PRESIDENT AND OTHER FRUSTRATIONS OF PRESIDENTIAL SUCCESSION. Berkeley and Los Angeles: University of California Press, 1976. x, 118 p.

An informed discussion of presidential succession and the special problems of vice presidents.

Vexler, Robert I., ed. THE VICE-PRESIDENTS AND CABINET MEMBERS: BIOGRAPHIES ARRANGED CHRONOLOGICALLY BY ADMINISTRATION. 2 vols. Dobbs Ferry, N.Y.: Oceana Publications, 1975.

Waugh, Edgar Wiggins. SECOND CONSUL, THE VICE PRESIDENCY: OUR GREATEST POLITICAL PROBLEM. Indianapolis: Bobbs-Merrill, 1956. 244 p.

Williams, Irving G. THE RISE OF THE VICE PRESIDENCY. Washington, D.C.: Public Affairs, 1956. viii, 266 p.

Wilmerding, Lucius, Jr. "Vice Presidency." POLITICAL SCIENCE QUARTERLY 68 (March 1953): 17-41.

Young, Donald. AMERICAN ROULETTE, THE HISTORY AND DILEMMA OF THE VICE PRESIDENCY. Rev. and updated. New York: Holt, Rinehart and Winston, 1972. xiv, 433 p.

Young, Klyde H., and Middleton, Lamar. HEIRS APPARENT: THE VICE PRESIDENTS OF THE UNITED STATES. New York: Prentice-Hall, 1948. Reprint. Freeport, N.Y.: Books for Libraries Press, 1969. vi, 314 p.

F. PRESIDENTIAL COMMISSIONS

"Presidential Advisory Commissions." PUBLIC ADMINISTRATION REVIEW 13, no. 1 (1953): 65.

Wolanin, Thomas R. PRESIDENTIAL ADVISORY COMMISSIONS: TRUMAN TO NIXON. Madison: University of Wisconsin Press, 1975. xii, 298 p.

Chapter 8
PROBLEMS OF THE PRESIDENCY

A. CONGRESSIONAL RELATIONS

Amlund, C.A. "Executive-Legislative Imbalance: Truman to Kennedy?" WESTERN POLITICAL QUARTERLY 18 (September 1965): 640-45.

Binkley, Wilfred E. PRESIDENT AND CONGRESS. 3d rev. ed. New York: Random House, 1967. x, 403 p.

Chamberlain, Lawrence H. THE PRESIDENT, CONGRESS AND LEGISLATION. New York: Columbia University Press, 1946. 478 p.

Cronin, Thomas E. "A Resurgent Congress and the Imperial Presidency." POLITICAL SCIENCE QUARTERLY 95 (Summer 1980): 209-37.

Davis, James W., and Ringquist, Delbert. THE PRESIDENT AND CONGRESS: TOWARD A NEW POWER BALANCE. Woodbury, N.Y.: Barron's Educational Series, 1975. xvi, 206 p.

A survey of the executive-legislative relationship from early congressional supremacy to the "imperial presidency."

De Grazia, Alfred. REPUBLIC IN CRISIS: CONGRESS AGAINST THE EXECUTIVE FORCE. New York: Federal Legal Publications, 1965. 303 p.

Edwards, George C., III. "The President and Congress: The Inevitability of Conflict." PRESIDENTIAL STUDIES QUARTERLY 8 (Summer 1978): 245-57.

______. "Presidential Influence in the House: Presidential Prestige as a Source of Presidential Power." AMERICAN POLITICAL SCIENCE REVIEW 70 (March 1976): 101-13.

Fainsod, Merle. "Presidency and Congress." PUBLIC ADMINISTRATION REVIEW 11, no. 2 (1951): 119-24.

A review article.

Fisher, Louis. THE CONSTITUTION BETWEEN FRIENDS: CONGRESS, THE PRESIDENT, AND THE LAW. New York: St. Martin's Press, 1978. xii, 274 p.

_____. THE POLITICS OF SHARED POWER: CONGRESS AND THE EXECUTIVE. Washington, D.C.: Congressional Quarterly Press, 1981. 217 p.

_____. PRESIDENT AND CONGRESS: POWER AND POLICY. New York: Free Press, 1971. xvi, 347 p.

_____. "Presidential Spending Discretion and Congressional Controls." LAW AND CONTEMPORARY PROBLEMS 37 (Winter 1972): 135-72.

Griffith, Ernest S. THE AMERICAN PRESIDENCY: THE DILEMMAS OF SHARED POWER AND DIVIDED GOVERNMENT. New York: New York University Press, 1976. viii, 241 p.

An excellent study of the institutional presidency from FDR to Ford.

Grundstein, Nathan D. "Presidential Subdelegation of Administrative Authority in Wartime." GEORGE WASHINGTON LAW REVIEW 16 (April-June 1948): 301-41, 478-507.

Heaphy, Maura E. "Executive Legislative Liaison." PRESIDENTIAL STUDIES QUARTERLY 5 (Fall 1975): 42-46.

Hilsman, Roger. "Congressional Executive Relations and the Foreign Policy Consensus." AMERICAN POLITICAL SCIENCE REVIEW 52 (September 1958): 725-44.

Javits, Jacob. WHO MAKES WAR: THE PRESIDENT VERSUS CONGRESS. New York: Morrow, 1973. xx, 300 p.

Johannes, John R. "Where Does the Buck Stop? Congress, President, and the Responsibility for Legislative Initiation." WESTERN POLITICAL QUARTERLY 25 (September 1972): 396-415.

Kessler, Frank. "Presidential-Congressional Battles: Toward a Truce on the Foreign Policy Front." PRESIDENTIAL STUDIES QUARTERLY 8 (Spring 1978): 115-27.

Kraines, Oscar. "The President versus Congress: The Keep Commission, 1905-1909, First Comprehensive Presidential Inquiry into Administration." WESTERN POLITICAL QUARTERLY 23 (March 1970): 5-54.

Lane, Gary. THE PRESIDENT VERSUS THE CONGRESS: FREEDOM OF INFORMATION. Jamaica, N.Y.: Lanco Press, 1971. iv, 86 p.

Printed by permission of the National Law Center of the George Washington University.

Lawton, Frederick J. "Legislative-Executive Relationships in Budgeting as Viewed by the Executive." PUBLIC ADMINISTRATION REVIEW 13, no. 3 (1953): 169-76.

"Legislative-Executive Relationships." PUBLIC ADMINISTRATION REVIEW 14, no. 3 (1954): 219.

Lepawsky, Albert, ed. THE PROSPECT FOR PRESIDENTIAL-CONGRESSIONAL GOVERNMENT. Berkeley: Institute of Governmental Studies, University of California, 1977. xiii, 110 p.

Moe, Ronald C., ed. CONGRESS AND THE PRESIDENT: ALLIES AND ADVERSARIES. Pacific Palisades, Calif.: Goodyear Publishing Co., 1971. ix, 324 p.

A collection of twenty-one provocative essays on the relationship between Congress and the president.

Parker, Glenn R. POLITICAL BELIEFS ABOUT THE STRUCTURE OF GOVERNMENT: CONGRESS AND THE PRESIDENCY. Beverly Hills, Calif.: Sage Publications, 1974. 42 p.

Revised version of a paper presented at the 1973 annual meeting of the American Political Science Association.

Schick, Allen. "The Battle of the Budget." PROCEEDINGS OF THE ACADEMY OF POLITICAL SCIENCE 32, no. 1 (1975): 51-70.

Congress versus the president.

Spanier, John, and Mogee, Joseph L., eds. CONGRESS, THE PRESIDENCY, AND AMERICAN FOREIGN POLICY. Elmsford, N.Y.: Pergamon Press, 1981. xxxii, 211 p.

Sundquist, James. "Four More Years: Is Deadlock the Only Prospect?" PUBLIC ADMINISTRATION REVIEW 33 (May 1973): 279-84.

Tidmarch, Charles, and Sabatt, Charles M. "Presidential Leadership Change and Foreign Policy Roll-Call Voting in the United States Senate." WESTERN POLITICAL QUARTERLY 25 (December 1972): 613-25.

B. MEDIA AND PUBLIC RELATIONS

Balutis, Alan P. "Congress, the President and the Press (1958-74)." JOURNALISM QUARTERLY 53 (Autumn 1976): 509-15.

Becker, Samuel L. "Presidential Power: The Influence of Broadcasting." QUARTERLY JOURNAL OF SPEECH 47 (February 1961): 10-18.

Blair, John L. "Coolidge the Image-Maker: The President and the Press, 1923-1929." NEW ENGLAND QUARTERLY 46 (December 1973): 499-522.

Burkholder, Donald R. "The Caretakers of the Presidential Image." PRESIDENTIAL STUDIES QUARTERLY 4 (Summer and Fall 1974): 35-43.

Cater, Douglas. "The President and the Press." ANNALS OF THE AMERICAN ACADEMY OF POLITICAL AND SOCIAL SCIENCE 307 (September 1956): 55-65.

Ceaser, James W.; Thurow, Glen E.; Tulis, Jeffrey; and Bessette, Joseph M. "The Rise of the Rhetorical Presidency." PRESIDENTIAL STUDIES QUARTERLY 11 (Spring 1981): 158-71.

Chaffee, Stephen H. "Presidential Debates--Are They Helpful to Voters? COMMUNICATIONS MONOGRAPHS 45 (November 1978): 330-46.

Cornwell, Elmer E., Jr. "The President and the Press: Phases in the Relationship." ANNALS OF THE AMERICAN ACADEMY OF POLITICAL AND SOCIAL SCIENCE 427 (September 1976): 53-64.

_____. PRESIDENTIAL LEADERSHIP OF PUBLIC OPINION. Bloomington: Indiana University Press, 1965. Reprint. Westport, Conn.: Greenwood Press, 1979. x, 370 p.

Edwards, George C. III. THE PUBLIC PRESIDENCY: THE PURSUIT OF POPULAR SUPPORT. New York: St. Martin's Press, 1983. x, 276 p.

Felson, Marcus, and Sudman, Seymour. "The Accuracy of Presidential Primary Polls." PUBLIC OPINION QUARTERLY 39 (Summer 1975): 232-36.

Grossman, Michael Baruch, and Kumar, Martha Joynt. PORTRAYING THE PRESIDENT: THE WHITE HOUSE AND THE NEWS MEDIA. Baltimore: Johns Hopkins Press, 1981. x, 358 p.

______. "The White House and the News Media: The Phases of Their Relationship." POLITICAL SCIENCE QUARTERLY 94 (Spring 1979): 37-54.

Grossman, Michael Baruch, and Rourke, Francis E. "The Media and the Presidency: An Exchange Analysis." POLITICAL SCIENCE QUARTERLY 91 (Fall 1976): 455-70.

Johnson, Miles Beardsley. THE GOVERNMENT SECRECY CONTROVERSY, A DISPUTE INVOLVING THE GOVERNMENT AND THE PRESS IN THE EISENHOWER, KENNEDY, AND JOHNSON ADMINISTRATIONS. New York: Vantage Press, 1967. 136 p.

Johnson, Walter. "The American President and the Art of Communication: An Inaugural Lecture Delivered before the University of Oxford on 13 May 1958." Oxford, Engl.: Clarendon Press, 1958. 21 p.

On the performances of Truman, Roosevelt, and Eisenhower.

Juergens, George. NEWS FROM THE WHITE HOUSE: THE PRESIDENTIAL PRESS RELATIONSHIP IN THE PROGRESSIVE ERA. Chicago: University of Chicago Press, 1981. 344 p.

Kampelman, Max M. "Congress, the Media, and the President." PROCEEDINGS OF THE ACADEMY OF POLITICAL SCIENCE 32, no. 1 (1975): 85-97.

Kelley, Stanley, Jr. PRESIDENTIAL PUBLIC RELATIONS AND POLITICAL POWER. Baltimore: Johns Hopkins University Press, 1956. 247 p.

Keogh, James. PRESIDENT NIXON AND THE PRESS. New York: Funk and Wagnalls, 1972. 212 p.

Lammers, William W. "Presidential Press Conference Schedules: Who Hides, and When?" POLITICAL SCIENCE QUARTERLY 96 (Summer 1981): 301-18.

Landecker, Manfred. THE PRESIDENT AND PUBLIC OPINION: LEADERSHIP IN FOREIGN AFFAIRS. Washington, D.C.: Public Affairs Press, 1968. v, 133 p.

Lawrence, Bill. SIX PRESIDENTS, TOO MANY WARS. New York: Saturday Review Press, 1972. 307 p.

Locander, Robert. "The Adversary Relationship: A New Look at an Old Idea." PRESIDENTIAL STUDIES QUARTERLY 9 (Summer 1979): 266-74.

______. "Carter and the Press: The First Two Years." PRESIDENTIAL STUDIES QUARTERLY 10 (Winter 1980): 106-20.

_____. "The President, the Press, and the Public: Friends and Enemies of Democracy." PRESIDENTIAL STUDIES QUARTERLY 8 (Spring 1978): 140-50.

Manheim, Jarol B. "The News Conference and Presidential Leadership of Public Opinion: Does the Tail Wag the Dog?" PRESIDENTIAL STUDIES QUARTERLY 11 (Spring 1981): 177-88.

Minow, Newton N. PRESIDENTIAL TELEVISION. New York: Basic Books, 1973. xv, 232 p.

Montgomery, Ruth. HAIL TO THE CHIEFS: MY LIFE AND TIMES WITH SIX PRESIDENTS. New York: Coward-McCann, 1970. 320 p.

Anecdotes and personalities from the Franklin Roosevelt era through the Nixon years.

Morgan, Edward P., et al. THE PRESIDENCY AND THE PRESS CONFERENCE. Washington, D.C.: American Enterprise Institute for Public Policy Research, 1971. 56 p.

Mueller, John E. "Presidential Popularity from Truman to Johnson." AMERICAN POLITICAL SCIENCE REVIEW 64 (March 1970): 18-34.

_____. WAR, PRESIDENTS AND PUBLIC OPINION. New York: Wiley, 1973. xxiv, 300 p.

Nevins, Allan. AMERICAN PRESS OPINION: WASHINGTON TO COOLIDGE: A DOCUMENTARY RECORD OF EDITORIAL LEADERSHIP AND CRITICISM, 1785-1927. 2 vols. Port Washington, N.Y.: Kennikat Press, 1969.

Orr, C. Jack. "Reporters Confront the President: Sustaining a Counterpoised Situation." QUARTERLY JOURNAL OF SPEECH 66 (February 1980): 17-32.

Pierson, James E. "Presidential Popularity and Midterm Voting at Different Electoral Levels." AMERICAN JOURNAL OF POLITICAL SCIENCE 19 (November 1979): 683-94.

Pollard, James Edward. THE PRESIDENTS AND THE PRESS. New York: Macmillan, 1947. Reprint. New York: Octagon Books, 1973. xiii, 866 p.

_____. THE PRESIDENTS AND THE PRESS, TRUMAN TO JOHNSON. Washington, D.C.: Public Affairs Press, 1964. 125 p.

Purvis, Hoyt, ed. THE PRESIDENCY AND THE PRESS. Austin: Lyndon B. Johnson School of Public Affairs, University of Texas, 1976. iii, 113 p.

Includes the remarks of participants in two panel discussions during a symposium sponsored by the Lyndon Baines Johnson Library and the Lyndon B. Johnson School of Public Affairs, Austin, 23 April 1976.

Reedy, George E. "The President and the Press: Struggle for Dominance." ANNALS OF THE AMERICAN ACADEMY FOR POLITICAL AND SOCIAL SCIENCE 427 (September 1976): 65-72.

Relyea, Harold C., et al. THE PRESIDENCY AND INFORMATION POLICY. Foreword by R. Gordon Hoxie. Proceedings Series, vol. 4, no. 1. New York: Center for the Study of the Presidency, 1981. xxv, 216 p.

Smith, Howard E. NEWSMAKERS: THE PRESS AND THE PRESIDENTS. Reading, Mass.: Addison-Wesley, 1974. 124 p.

Spragens, William C. FROM SPOKESMAN TO PRESS SECRETARY: WHITE HOUSE MEDIA OPERATIONS. Lanham, Md.: University Press of America, 1980. xiii, 243 p.

Analyzes White House press secretaries and their role from James C. Hagerty to Jody Powell (1953-80). Comments from press secretaries and Washington correspondents as well as staff colleagues are included. Also valuable for pictures of each press secretary from George Akerson to Powell.

_____. THE PRESIDENCY AND THE MASS MEDIA IN THE AGE OF TELEVISION. Washington, D.C.: University Press of America, 1978. vi, 425 p.

Stein, Meyer L. WHEN PRESIDENTS MEET THE PRESS. New York: Messner, 1969. 109 p.

Discusses the relationship between the presidency and the American press, describing in detail the influence of some recent president-press secretary teams on the success or failure of the administration.

Strout, Richard L. TRB: VIEWS AND PERSPECTIVES ON THE PRESIDENCY. New York: Macmillan, 1979. xiv, 526 p.

A collection of columns from the NEW REPUBLIC written by a long-time Washington correspondent for the CHRISTIAN SCIENCE MONITOR.

Thomas, Helen. DATELINE: WHITE HOUSE. New York: Macmillan, 1975. xviii, 298 p.

A White House correspondent's memoir of the Kennedy to Ford period.

Wicker, Tom. JFK AND LBJ: THE INFLUENCE OF PERSONALITY UPON POLITICS. New York: Morrow, 1968. 297 p.

Woodruff, Judy. "THIS IS JUDY WOODRUFF AT THE WHITE HOUSE." Reading, Mass.: Addison-Wesley Publishing Co., 1982. xv, 229 p.

C. PROTECTION OF THE PRESIDENT

Blum, Herman. "The Mystery of the Dying President's Attendants." LINCOLN HERALD 69 (Spring 1967): 22-25.

Brooks, Stewart M. OUR MURDERED PRESIDENTS: THE MEDICAL STORY. New York: F. Fell, 1966. 234 p.

Committee to Investigate Assassinations. AMERICAN POLITICAL ASSASSINATIONS: A BIBLIOGRAPHY OF WORKS PUBLISHED, 1963-1970, RELATED TO THE ASSASSINATION OF JOHN F. KENNEDY, MARTIN LUTHER KING, ROBERT F. KENNEDY. Washington, D.C.: Georgetown University Library, 1973. 28 p.

Dietze, Gottfried. "Will the Presidency Incite Assassination?" ETHICS 76 (October 1965): 14-32.

Donovan, Robert J. THE ASSASSINS. New York: Popular Library, 1964. 254 p.

Edelman, Murray, and Simon, Rita James. "Presidential Assassinations: Their Meaning and Impact on American Society." ETHICS 79 (April 1969): 199-221.

Kieser, Paul W. OUR MARTYRED PRESIDENTS. Franklin, N.H.: Hillside Press, 1965. Unpaged.

Potter, John Mason. PLOTS AGAINST PRESIDENTS. New York: Astor-Honor, 1968. 310 p.

Roos, Charles A. "Physicians to the Presidents and Their Patients." MEDICAL LIBRARY ASSOCIATION BULLETIN 49 (July 1961): 302-3.

Starling, Edmund William, as told to Thomas Sugrue. STARLING OF THE WHITE HOUSE. New York: Simon and Schuster, 1946. xvi, 334 p.

> The story of the man whose secret service detail guarded five presidents from Woodrow Wilson to F.D. Roosevelt.

U.S. Congress. Senate. Committee on the Judiciary. PROTECTION OF THE PRESIDENT; REPORT TOGETHER WITH INDIVIDUAL VIEWS, TO ACCOMPANY S. 2896. 91st Cong., 2d sess. Washington, D.C.: Government Printing Office, 1970. 20 p.

Wilson, Frank John, and Day, Beth. SPECIAL AGENT: TWENTY-FIVE YEARS WITH THE U.S. TREASURY DEPARTMENT AND SECRET SERVICE. London: Muller, 1966. 258 p.

Youngblood, Rufus W. 20 YEARS IN THE SECRET SERVICE: MY LIFE WITH FIVE PRESIDENTS. New York: Simon and Schuster, 1973. 256 p.

> A lively behind-the-scenes look at the secret service by the man who protected Vice President Lyndon B. Johnson in the immediate aftermath of the shooting of President John F. Kennedy.

D. TENURE

Association of the Bar of the City of New York. Committee on Federal Legislation. THE LAW OF PRESIDENTIAL IMPEACHMENT. New York: Harper and Row, 1974. 57 p.

Berger, Raoul. EXECUTIVE PRIVILEGE: A CONSTITUTIONAL MYTH. Cambridge, Mass.: Harvard University Press, 1974. xvi, 430 p.

______. IMPEACHMENT: THE CONSTITUTIONAL PROBLEMS. Cambridge, Mass.: Harvard University Press, 1973. xii, 345 p.

Brant, Irving. IMPEACHMENT: TRIALS AND ERRORS. New York: Knopf, 1972. vii, 202 p.

Ehrlich, Walter. PRESIDENTIAL IMPEACHMENT: AN AMERICAN DILEMMA. St. Charles, Mo.: Forum Press, 1974. xxxvi, 136 p.

Schnapper, Morris Bartel. PRESIDENTIAL IMPEACHMENT: A DOCUMENTARY OVERVIEW. Washington, D.C.: Public Affairs Press, 1974. v, 144 p.

U.S. Congress. House. Committee on the Judiciary. CONSTITUTIONAL GROUNDS FOR PRESIDENTIAL IMPEACHMENT: REPORT. Washington, D.C.: Government Printing Office, 1974. v, 60 p.

E. TRANSITIONS AND SUCCESSION

Bayh, Birch Evans. ONE HEARTBEAT AWAY: PRESIDENTIAL DISABILITY AND SUCCESSION. Indianapolis: Bobbs-Merrill, 1968. ix, 372 p.

Blackman, Paul H. "Presidential Disability and the Bayh Amendment." WESTERN POLITICAL QUARTERLY 20 (June 1967): 440-55.

Brown, Everett S., and Silva, Ruth C. "Presidential Succession and Inability." JOURNAL OF POLITICS 11 (February 1949): 236-56.

Christian, George. THE PRESIDENT STEPS DOWN: A PERSONAL MEMOIR OF THE TRANSFER OF POWER. New York: Macmillan, 1970. 282 p.

Christian was press secretary to Lyndon B. Johnson.

Committee for Economic Development. Research and Policy Committee. PRESIDENTIAL SUCCESSION AND INABILITY: A STATEMENT ON NATIONAL POLICY. New York: 1965. 41 p.

Feerick, John D. FROM FAILING HANDS: THE STORY OF PRESIDENTIAL SUCCESSION. Foreword by Paul A. Freund. New York: Fordham University Press, 1965. xiv, 368 p.

______. THE TWENTY-FIFTH AMENDMENT, ITS COMPLETE HISTORY AND EARLIEST APPLICATIONS. Foreword by Birch Bayh. New York: Fordham University Press, 1976. xii, 270 p.

Continues the author's FROM FAILING HANDS (see previous entry).

Haider, Donald H. "Presidential Transitions: Critical If Not Decisive." PUBLIC ADMINISTRATION REVIEW 41 (March-April 1981): 207-11.

Henry, Laurin L. PRESIDENTIAL TRANSITIONS. Washington, D.C.: Brookings Institution, 1960. viii, 755 p.

______. "Presidential Transitions: The 1968-69 Experience in Perspective." PUBLIC ADMINISTRATION REVIEW 29 (September 1969): 471-82.

Rankin, Robert S. "Presidential Succession in the United States." JOURNAL OF POLITICS 8 (February 1946): 44-56.

Riccards, Michael P. "The Presidency in Sickness and in Health." PRESIDENTIAL STUDIES QUARTERLY 7 (Fall 1977): 215-31.

Schlesinger, Arthur M., Jr. "On the Presidential Succession." POLITICAL SCIENCE QUARTERLY 89 (Fall 1974): 475-505.

Silva, Ruth Garidad. PRESIDENTIAL SUCCESSION. Ann Arbor: University of Michigan Press, 1951. Reprint. New York: Greenwood Press, 1968. viii, 213 p.

______. "Presidential Succession and Disability." LAW & CONTEMPORARY PROBLEMS 21 (Fall 1956): 646-62.

Sobel, Lester A., ed. PRESIDENTIAL SUCCESSION: FORD, ROCKEFELLER, & THE 25TH AMENDMENT. New York: Facts on File, 1975. 225 p.

Tomkins, Dorothy Louise Culver, comp. PRESIDENTIAL SUCCESSION: A BIBLIOGRAPHY. Rev. ed. Berkeley: Institute of Government Studies, University of California, 1965. vii, 29 p.

U.S. Congress. House. Committee on Government Operations. PRESIDENTIAL TRANSITION ACT OF 1962. 87th Cong., 2d sess., 1962. Washington, D.C.: Government Printing Office, 1962. iii, 19 p.

_____. PRESIDENTIAL TRANSITION ACT OF 1963. 88th Cong., 1st sess., 1963. Washington, D.C.: Government Printing Office, 1963. iii, 32 p.

U.S. Congress. House. Committee on the Judiciary. IMPEACHMENT INQUIRY: HEARINGS BEFORE THE COMMITTEE ON THE JUDICIARY, HOUSE OF REPRESENTATIVES, NINETY-THIRD CONGRESS, SECOND SESSION, PURSUANT TO H. RES. 803. Washington, D.C.: Government Printing Office, 1975. iii, 2,258 p.

_____. PRESIDENTIAL INABILITY. Hearings. 89th Cong., 1st sess., 1965. Washington, D.C.: Government Printing Office, 1965. iv, 292 p.

_____. PROCEDURES FOR HANDLING IMPEACHMENT INQUIRY MATERIAL. NINETY-THIRD CONGRESS, SECOND SESSION. FEBRUARY, 1974. Washington, D.C.: Government Printing Office, 1974. iii, 2 p.

_____. STATEMENT OF INFORMATION: HEARINGS BEFORE THE COMMITTEE ON THE JUDICIARY, HOUSE OF REPRESENTATIVES, NINETY-THIRD CONGRESS, SECOND SESSION, PURSUANT TO H. RES. 803, A RESOLUTION AUTHORIZING AND DIRECTING THE COMMITTEE ON THE JUDICIARY TO INVESTIGATE WHETHER SUFFICIENT GROUNDS EXIST FOR THE HOUSE OF REPRESENTATIVES TO EXERCISE ITS CONSTITUTIONAL POWER TO IMPEACH RICHARD M. NIXON, PRESIDENT OF THE UNITED STATES OF AMERICA. MAY-JUNE 1974. 12 vols. in 21. Washington, D.C.: Government Printing Office, 1974.

U.S. Congress. House. Committee on the Judiciary. Subcommittee on Crime. ONE SIX-YEAR PRESIDENTIAL TERM: HEARING BEFORE THE SUBCOMMITTEE ON CRIME OF THE COMMITTEE ON THE JUDICIARY, HOUSE OF REPRESENTATIVES, NINETY-THIRD CONGRESS, FIRST SESSION, ON ONE SIX-YEAR PRESIDENTIAL TERM, SEPTEMBER 26, 1973. Washington, D.C.: Government Printing Office, 1974. iii, 66 p.

U.S. Congress. Senate. Committee on the Judiciary. PRESIDENTIAL INABILITY AND VACANCIES IN THE OFFICE OF THE VICE PRESIDENT: REPORT, TO-

GETHER WITH INDIVIDUAL VIEWS TO ACCOMPANY S.J. RES. 139. 88th Cong., 2d sess., 1964. Washington, D.C.: Government Printing Office, 1964. 21 p.

_____. PRESIDENTIAL INABILITY AND VACANCIES IN THE OFFICE OF THE VICE PRESIDENT: REPORT, TOGETHER WITH INDIVIDUAL VIEWS, TO ACCOMPANY S.J. RES. 1. 89th Cong., 1st sess., 1965. Washington, D.C.: Government Printing Office, 1965. 24 p.

U.S. Congress. Senate. Committee on the Judiciary. Subcommittee on Constitutional Amendments. SINGLE SIX-YEAR TERM FOR PRESIDENT. HEARING, NINETY-SECOND CONGRESS, FIRST SESSION, ON S.J. RES. 77, OCTOBER 28 AND 29, 1971. Washington, D.C.: Government Printing Office, 1972. v, 247 p.

U.S. General Accounting Office. FEDERAL ASSISTANCE FOR PRESIDENTIAL TRANSITIONS: RECOMMENDATIONS FOR CHANGES IN LEGISLATION. Report to Congress. Washington, D.C.: 1975. ii, 38 p.

Virginia. Commission of Constitutional Government. A COUNTRY WITHOUT A MAN. Richmond: 1965. 15 p.

Wilmerding, Lucius, Jr. "Presidential Inability." POLITICAL SCIENCE QUARTERLY 72 (June 1957): 616-81.

Zentner, Joseph L. "Presidential Transitions and the Perpetuation of Programs: The Johnson-Nixon Experience." WESTERN POLITICAL QUARTERLY 25 (March 1972): 5-15.

F. REORGANIZATION

Arnold, Peri E. "Executive Reorganization and the Origins of the Managerial Presidency." POLITY 13 (Summer 1981): 568-99.

Aspen Systems Corp. THE POWERS AND RESPONSIBILITIES OF THE UNITED STATES. Pittsburgh: 1970. 297 p.

Prepared for the President's Advisory Council on Executive Reorganization.

Fisher, Louis, and Moe, Ronald C. "Presidential Reorganization Authority: Is It Worth the Cost?" POLITICAL SCIENCE QUARTERLY 96 (Summer 1981): 301-18.

Polenberg, Richard. "Roosevelt, Carter, and Executive Reorganization: Lessons of the 1930s." PRESIDENTIAL STUDIES QUARTERLY 9 (Winter 1979): 35-46.

Tugwell, Rexford Guy. THE ENLARGEMENT OF THE PRESIDENCY. Garden City, N.Y.: Doubleday, 1960. Reprint. New York: Octagon Books, 1977. 508 p.

Chapter 9

PRESIDENTIAL DOCUMENTS

A. GUIDES

MONTHLY CATALOG OF U.S. GOVERNMENT PUBLICATIONS. Washington, D.C.: Government Printing Office, 1895-- .

> The basic index to the thousands of pamphlets, books, and periodicals published by the Government Printing Office, for many years the major paperback publisher in the United States.

Schmeckebier, Laurence F., and Eastin, Ray B. GOVERNMENT PUBLICATIONS AND THEIR USE. 2d rev. ed. Washington, D.C.: Brookings Institution, 1969. viii, 502 p.

> The best guide to government publications. Especially helpful in explaining the rapid changes and growth in the number of such publications in recent years; also calls attention to many special series.

UNITED STATES GOVERNMENT ORGANIZATION MANUAL. Washington, D.C.: Government Printing Office, 1935-- . Annual.

> A publication which describes the current organization and functions of each of the departments and agencies in the executive branch, as well as the legislative and judicial branches. It also is helpful in understanding the transfer of responsibilities from discontinued or reorganized government agencies.

B. PUBLIC PAPERS

FEDERAL REGISTER. Washington, D.C.: Government Printing Office, 1936-- . Daily, Mon.-Fri.

> Includes presidential executive orders, proclamations, reorganization plans, and rules and regulations issued by executive departments and agencies.

PUBLIC PAPERS OF THE PRESIDENTS OF THE UNITED STATES. Washington, D.C.: Government Printing Office, 1958-- .

A series inaugurated by publication of the 1957 Eisenhower volume. Now complete for Hoover (1929-33); Truman (1945-53); Eisenhower (1953-61); Kennedy (1961-63); Johnson (1963-69); Nixon (1969-74); Ford (1974-77); and Carter (1977-81). (F.D. Roosevelt's PUBLIC PAPERS AND ADDRESSES were published commercially between 1938 and 1950.) Volume 1 of Reagan (1981--) is out.

WEEKLY COMPILATION OF PRESIDENTIAL DOCUMENTS. Washington, D.C.: Government Printing Office, 1965-- .

Published every Monday by the Office of the Federal Register. Contains presidents' addresses, remarks, announcements, appointments and nominations, executive orders, memoranda, meetings with foreign leaders, and proclamations, as well as reports to the president, released by the White House up to 5:00 P.M. the preceding Friday.

C. EDITED COLLECTIONS

Brayman, Harold. THE PRESIDENT SPEAKS OFF-THE-RECORD. Princeton, N.J.: Dow Jones Books, 1976. xviii, 870 p.

From Grover Cleveland to Gerald Ford. Historic evenings with America's leaders, the press, and other men of power at Washington's exclusive Gridiron Club.

Cook, J. Frank. "Private Papers of Public Officials." AMERICAN ARCHIVIST 38 (July 1975): 299-324.

Filler, Louis. THE PRESIDENT SPEAKS: FROM WILLIAM McKINLEY TO LYNDON B. JOHNSON. New York: Putnam, 1964. 416 p.

Fridley, Russell. "Should Public Papers Be Private Property?" MINNESOTA HISTORY 44 (Spring 1974): 37-39.

Graebner, Norman A. THE RECORDS OF PUBLIC OFFICIALS. New York: American Assembly, Columbia University, 1975. 40 p.

Holmes, Oliver W. "'Public Records'--Who Knows What They Are?" AMERICAN ARCHIVIST 14 (January 1960): 3-26.

Horn, David. "Who Owns Our History?" LIBRARY JOURNAL 100 (1 April 1975): 635-39.

Lewis, Anthony. "Who Really Owns the Papers of Departing Federal Officials?" THE NEW YORK TIMES 6 February 1977, Sec. IV, p. 3, col. 1.

Rhoads, James B. "Who Should Own the Documents of Public Officials?" PROLOGUE 7 (Spring 1975): 32-35.

U.S. National Study Commission on Records and Documents of Federal Officials. FINAL REPORT. Washington, D.C.: Government Printing Office, 1977. 137 p.

U.S. President. THE STATE OF THE UNION MESSAGES OF THE PRESIDENTS, 1790-1966. 3 vols. Introduction by Arthur M. Schlesinger. Edited by Fred L. Israel. New York: Chelsea House, 1966. xli, 3,264 p.

Weisberger, Bernard A. "The Paper Trust." AMERICAN HERITAGE 22 (April 1971): 38-41, 104-7.

D. ARTICLES AND REPORTS

Album, Michael T. "Government Control of Richard Nixon's Presidential Material." YALE LAW JOURNAL 87 (July 1978): 1601-35.

Bullock, Helen D. "The Robert Todd Lincoln Collection of the Papers of Abraham Lincoln." LIBRARY OF CONGRESS QUARTERLY JOURNAL 5 (November 1947): 3-9.

Duckett, Kenneth, and Russell, Francis. "The Harding Papers: How Some Were Burned . . . and Some Were Saved." AMERICAN HERITAGE 16 (February 1965): 24-31.

Flato, Linda. "Automation at the White House." DATAMATION 24 (January 1978): 190-93.

Heclo, Hugh. STUDYING THE PRESIDENCY: A REPORT TO THE FORD FOUNDATION. New York: Ford Foundation, 1979. 54 p.

McDonough, John; Hoxie, R. Gordon; and Jacobs, Richard. "Who Owns Presidential Papers?" MANUSCRIPTS 27 (Winter 1975): 2-11.

"The Presidency in the Information Age: New Directions." BULLETIN OF THE AMERICAN SOCIETY FOR INFORMATION SCIENCE 5 (December 1978): 13-27.

Reid, Warren R. "Public Papers of the Presidents." AMERICAN ARCHIVIST 25 (October 1962): 435-39.

Rowland, Buford. "The Papers of the Presidents." AMERICAN ARCHIVIST 13 (July 1950): 195-211.

On the locations of the papers of the individual presidents, 1879-1950.

Schlesinger, Arthur M., Jr. "Who Owns a President's Papers?" MANUSCRIPTS 27 (Summer 1975): 178-82.

Shelley, Fred. "The Presidential Papers Program of the Library of Congress." AMERICAN ARCHIVIST 25 (October 1962): 429-33.

Spencer, Patricia L. "Separation of Powers--Bills of Attainder--Presidential Papers--Chief Executive's Right to Privacy." AKRON LAW REVIEW 11 (Fall 1977): 373-86.

Chapter 10
PRESIDENTIAL LIBRARIES AND MUSEUMS

A. GENERAL REFERENCES

Aeschbacher, W.D. "Presidential Libraries: New Dimension in Research Facilities." MIDWEST QUARTERLY 6 (January 1965): 205-14.

Cappon, Lester J. "Why Presidential Libraries?" YALE REVIEW 68 (October 1978): 11-34.

Drewry, Elizabeth B. "The Role of Presidential Libraries." MIDWEST QUARTERLY 7 (October 1965): 53-65.

Grover, Wayne C. "Presidential Libraries: A New Feature of the Archival System of the United States." INDIAN ARCHIVES 1 (January-December 1957).

Hardesty, Robert L. "The President's Papers." THE NEW YORK TIMES 29 April 1979, Sec. IV, p. 19, col. 1.

Hirshon, Arnold. "The Scope, Accessibility and History of Presidential Papers." GOVERNMENT PUBLICATIONS REVIEW 1 (Fall 1974): 363-90.

Jones, H.G. "Presidential Libraries: Is There a Case for a National Presidential Library?" AMERICAN ARCHIVIST 38 (July 1975): 325-28.

Kahn, Herman. "The Presidential Library." SPECIAL LIBRARIES 50 (March 1959): 106-13.

Illustrations from the Franklin D. Roosevelt Library.

Kirkendall, Richard S. "Presidential Libraries--One Researcher's Point of View." AMERICAN ARCHIVIST 25 (October 1962): 441-48.

An overview by a scholar who worked in the Roosevelt Library.

______. "A Second Look at Presidential Libraries." AMERICAN ARCHIVIST 29 (July 1966): 371-86.

Lewis, Finlay. "Presidential Papers: An Attempt to Own History." NATION 219 (19 October 1974): 366-69.

Lloyd, David Demerest. "Presidential Papers and Presidential Libraries." MANUSCRIPTS 8 (Fall 1955): 4-9.

Lovely, Sister Louise. "The Evolution of Presidential Libraries." GOVERNMENT PUBLICATIONS REVIEW 6, no. 1 (1979): 27-35.

O'Neill, James E. "Will Success Spoil the Presidential Libraries?" AMERICAN ARCHIVIST 36 (July 1973): 339-51.

U.S. Congress. House. Committee on Government Operations. PRESIDENTIAL LIBRARIES. 84th Cong., 1st sess., 1955. Washington, D.C.: Government Printing Office, 1955. 11 p.

______. TO PROVIDE FOR THE ACCEPTANCE AND MAINTENANCE OF PRESIDENTIAL LIBRARIES AND OTHER PURPOSES. Hearings. 84th Cong., 1st sess., 1955. Washington, D.C.: Government Printing Office, 1955. 64 p.

B. SPECIFIC PRESIDENTS

1. Rutherford B. Hayes

HAYES PRESIDENTIAL CENTER, 1337 Hayes Avenue, Fremont, OH 43420. Founded: 1911.

> Prototype of the first presidential library and museum. Founded by Webb C. Hayes in honor of his parents, Rutherford and Lucy Hayes. Operated by the State of Ohio and the Hayes Foundation rather than by the federal government. Library has 100,000 volumes plus manuscripts on the career of Hayes.

2. Herbert Hoover

HERBERT HOOVER PRESIDENTIAL LIBRARY MUSEUM, 234 South Downey, West Branch, IA 52358. Founded: 1962.

> Located on site of Hoover's 1871 birthplace. Library has 25,000 books and 6 million manuscripts covering the span of Hoover's life.

3. Franklin D. Roosevelt

FRANKLIN D. ROOSEVELT LIBRARY AND MUSEUM, Albany Post Road, Hyde Park, NY 12538. Founded: 1939.

Library has 38,000 books and 16 million pages of manuscripts devoted to Franklin and Eleanor Roosevelt.

Connor, Robert D.W. "The FDR Library." AMERICAN ARCHIVIST 3 (April 1940): 83-92.

Kahn, Herman. "The Long-Range Implications for Historians and Archivists of the Charges against the Franklin D. Roosevelt Library." AMERICAN ARCHIVIST 34 (July 1971): 265-75.

Leland, Waldo. "The Creation of the Franklin D. Roosevelt Library: A Personal Narrative." AMERICAN ARCHIVIST 18 (January 1955): 11-29.

McCoy, Donald R. "The Beginnings of the Franklin D. Roosevelt Library." PROLOGUE 7 (Fall 1975): 137-50.

Stewart, William J. "Opening Closed Material in the Roosevelt Library." PROLOGUE 7 (Winter 1975): 239-41.

4. Harry S. Truman

HARRY S. TRUMAN LIBRARY AND MUSEUM, U.S. 24 and Delaware Streets, Independence, MO 64050. Founded: 1957.

Library has 46,000 books and over 13 million manuscripts relating to Harry S. Truman and his presidency.

Brooks, Philip C. "The Harry S. Truman Library--Plans and Reality." AMERICAN ARCHIVIST 25 (January 1962): 25-37.

______. "Understanding the Presidency: The Harry S. Truman Library." PROLOGUE 1 (Winter 1969): 3-12.

Larson, Cedric Eugene Arthur. "The Museum of the Presidency at the Harry S. Truman Library, Independence, Missouri." ANTIQUES JOURNAL 14 (July 1959): 10-12.

Lloyd, David D. "The Harry S. Truman Library." AMERICAN ARCHIVIST 18 (April 1955): 99-110.

5. Dwight D. Eisenhower

DWIGHT D. EISENHOWER LIBRARY, Abilene, KS 67410. Founded: 1946.

Library has 21,000 books and 19 million manuscripts relating to the career of Eisenhower.

6. John F. Kennedy

JOHN F. KENNEDY LIBRARY, Morrissey Boulevard, Boston, MA 02125. Founded: 1969.

Library has 50,000 books and 35 million manuscripts concerning Kennedy.

7. Lyndon Baines Johnson

LYNDON BAINES JOHNSON LIBRARY AND MUSEUM, 2313 Red River Street, Austin, TX. 78705. Founded: 1971.

Library has over 34 million manuscripts and audiovisual collection pertaining to Johnson.

Frantz, Joe B. "The Lyndon Baines Johnson Library." STIRPES: TEXAS STATE GENEALOGICAL SOCIETY QUARTERLY 10 (March-June 1970): 3-6, 45-46.

8. Gerald R. Ford

GERALD R. FORD LIBRARY, 1000 Beal Avenue, Ann Arbor, MI 48109. Founded: 1976.

Library has books and 15 million manuscripts pertaining to the political career of Ford as a congressman, vice president, and president.

GERALD R. FORD MUSEUM, 303 Pearl Street, N.W., Grand Rapids, MI 49504. Founded: 1976.

The Ford Library in Ann Arbor and the Ford Museum in Grand Rapids are under the same administration. The purpose in having two separate buildings is to divide scholars more interested in research from tourist visitors more interested in museum exhibits.

Chapter 11

PRIVATE ORGANIZATIONS AND PUBLISHERS

A. CONTEMPORARY AFFAIRS AND THE PRESIDENCY

One private organization, one professional association, and two well-known Washington, D.C., publishers conduct extensive research and analysis of the contemporary presidency.

CENTER FOR THE STUDY OF THE PRESIDENCY, 208 East Seventy-fifth Street, New York, NY 10021. Founded: 1969.

> Formerly the Library of Presidential Papers, the center conducts several outstanding lectures and symposia each year, featuring distinguished political scientists and historians, and leaders of government, business, and the media. It issues PRESIDENTIAL STUDIES QUARTERLY, excellent annotated bibliographies on the presidency, and occasional books including conference proceedings. Recent publications include ORGANIZING AND STAFFING THE PRESIDENCY (1980) and THE PRESIDENCY AND INFORMATION POLICY (1981).

CONGRESSIONAL QUARTERLY, 1414 Twenty-second Street, NW, Washington, D.C. 20037. Founded: 1945.

> Publisher of CONGRESSIONAL QUARTERLY WEEKLY REPORT (Washington, D.C.: Congressional Quarterly, 1945-- .). Provides an easy to use and authoritative source of information on Congress. The president's position on all major legislation and roll-call votes is given, plus his messages to Congress, press conferences and vetoes. An annual digest is published under the title CONGRESSIONAL QUARTERLY ALMANAC. Other special publications include: CONGRESS AND THE NATION, a resume of congressional and presidential actions from 1945 to 1980; the semi-annual CONGRESSIONAL QUARTERLY GUIDE TO CURRENT AMERICAN GOVERNMENT; and the weekly EDITORIAL RESEARCH REPORTS on current controversial issues.

GOVERNMENT RESEARCH CORPORATION, 1730 M Street, NW, Washington, D.C. 20036. Founded: 1969.

Publisher of the NATIONAL JOURNAL, THE WEEKLY ON POLITICS AND GOVERNMENT. Widely read by government bureaucrats and media people.

PRESIDENCY RESEARCH GROUP, c/o Department of Political Science, Towson State University, Towson, MD 21204. Founded: 1978.

A professional organization open to persons who write and teach about the presidency. It issues a newsletter several times a year and arranges panels at the American Political Science Association annual meeting that treat presidency research, the teaching of the presidency, and common methodological problems in studying the presidency.

B. THINK TANKS AND THE PRESIDENCY

Of the many research organizations in the United States, a few have special significance for the presidency and public policymaking. They may be divided into conservative and liberal groups.

1. Conservative Research Organizations

AMERICAN ENTERPRISE INSTITUTE FOR PUBLIC POLICY RESEARCH, 1150 Seventeenth Street, NW, Washington, D.C. 20036. Founded: 1943.

A staff of 135 publishes books and monographs and produces television programs. Former President Ford is a board member of AEI.

HERITAGE FOUNDATION, 513 C Street, NE, Washington, D.C. 20002. Founded: 1974.

Concentrates on public policy research dedicated to the principles of free competitive enterprise, limited government, individual liberty, and a strong national defense.

HOOVER INSTITUTION ON WAR, REVOLUTION AND PEACE, Stanford University, Stanford, CA 94305. Founded: 1919.

Established by Herbert Hoover. At first it was concerned only with international affairs but domestic studies began in the 1960s. Among its publications is THE UNITED STATES IN THE 1980S (1980). Hoover Institution staff people have served under President Reagan in California government and in his administration in Washington.

INSTITUTE FOR CONTEMPORARY STUDIES, 260 California Street, Suite 811, San Francisco, CA 94111. Founded: 1972.

Established by a group close to President Reagan including Edwin Meese. Publishes about five studies per year including a 1981 study on POLITICS AND THE OVAL OFFICE.

2. Liberal Research Organizations

BROOKINGS INSTITUTION, 1775 Massachusetts Avenue, NW, Washington, D.C. 20036. Founded: 1927.

A staff of 220 is devoted to research, education, and publication in the areas of economic, governmental, and foreign policy. Emphasis in recent years has tended to be more conservative.

HUDSON INSTITUTE, Quaker Ridge Road, Croton-on-Hudson, NY 10520. Founded: 1961.

Established by Herman Kahn. Especially interested in future studies.

ROBERT MAYNARD HUTCHINS CENTER FOR THE STUDY OF DEMOCRATIC INSTITUTIONS, Box 4068, Santa Barbara, CA 93103. Founded: 1959.

Conducts dialogues, conferences, and convocations. Among its publications is CENTER MAGAZINE, a bimonthly.

ROOSEVELT CENTER FOR AMERICAN POLICY STUDIES, 316 Pennsylvania Ave., Suite 500, Washington, D.C. 20003. Founded: 1982.

C. UNIVERSITY CENTERS

CENTER FOR CONGRESSIONAL AND PRESIDENTIAL STUDIES, College of Public and International Affairs, American University, Washington, D.C. 20016. Founded: 1979.

Initiated in response to a need for an integrated teaching, research and study program in Washington, D.C. Focuses on Congress, the presidency, and their interaction. Conducts colloquiums and seminars. Publishes CONGRESS & THE PRESIDENCY.

CENTER FOR STRATEGIC AND INTERNATIONAL STUDIES, Georgetown University, 1800 K Street, NW, Washington, D.C. 20006. Founded: 1962.

Has fifty full-time professionals weighted more toward government than academe. Henry Kissinger has served on the staff. Research results in books, monographs, and special reports. The center holds frequent professional conferences and seminars. Influential in the Reagan administration.

WHITE BURKETT MILLER CENTER FOR PUBLIC AFFAIRS, University of Virginia, Charlottesville, Virginia 22904. Founded: 1973.

Established to contribute to the deeper understanding of public issues and to the solution of major national problems. Special emphasis upon the role of the presidency in the American political system. Sponsors conferences, seminars, and workshops. Publishes proceedings in Miller Center Series on the American Presidency.

Part 2
The American Presidents, 1789-1982

Chapter 12

GEORGE WASHINGTON, 1789-97

BIBLIOGRAPHIES

Baker, William Spohn. BIBLIOTHECA WASHINGTONIA: A DESCRIPTIVE LIST OF THE BIOGRAPHIES AND BIOGRAPHICAL SKETCHES OF GEORGE WASHINGTON. 1889. Reprint. Detroit: Gale Research Co., 1967. xv, 179 p.

Bremer, Howard F., ed. GEORGE WASHINGTON, 1732-1799: CHRONOLOGY-DOCUMENTS-BIBLIOGRAPHICAL AIDS. Presidential Chronologies Series. Dobbs Ferry, N.Y.: Oceana Publications, 1967. 90 p.

SOURCE MATERIALS

Washington, George. THE DIARIES OF GEORGE WASHINGTON. 6 vols. Edited by Donald Jackson. Charlottesville: University Press of Virginia, 1976-80.

______. THE GEORGE WASHINGTON PAPERS. Selected, edited, and interpreted by Frank Donovan. New York: Dodd, Mead, 1964. vii, 310 p.

______. THE LETTERS OF GEORGE WASHINGTON IN THE ROBERT HUDSON TANNAHILL RESEARCH LIBRARY. Edited by Jerome Irving Smith. Dearborn, Mich.: Greenfield Village and Henry Ford Museum, 1976. 29 p.

______. THE WASHINGTON PAPERS: BASIC SELECTIONS FROM THE PUBLIC AND PRIVATE WRITINGS OF GEORGE WASHINGTON. Edited and arranged with an introduction by Saul K. Padover. New York: Harper, 1955. 430 p.

> Includes all of his annual messages to Congress and his last will and testament.

______. THE WRITINGS OF GEORGE WASHINGTON FROM THE ORIGINAL MANUSCRIPT SOURCES, 1745-1799. Prepared under the direction of the United States George Washington Bicentennial Commission and published by authority of Congress. Edited by John C. Fitzpatrick. 39 vols. Washington, D.C.: Government Printing Office, 1931-44. Reprint. Westport, Conn.: Greenwood Press, 1970.

BIOGRAPHIES

Multivolume

Flexner, James Thomas. GEORGE WASHINGTON: THE FORGE OF EXPERIENCE, 1732-1775. Boston: Little, Brown, 1965. x, 390 p.

_____. GEORGE WASHINGTON IN THE AMERICAN REVOLUTION, 1775-1783. Boston: Little, Brown, 1968. xvii, 599 p.

_____. GEORGE WASHINGTON AND THE NEW NATION, 1783-1793. Boston: Little, Brown, 1970. xi, 466 p.

_____. GEORGE WASHINGTON: ANGUISH AND FAREWELL, 1793-1799. Boston: Little, Brown, 1972. xii, 554 p.

Comprehensive treatment with both praise and blame.

Freeman, Douglas Southall. GEORGE WASHINGTON: A BIOGRAPHY. 6 vols. New York: Scribner's Sons, 1948-51.

Classic study emphasizing Washington's human qualities. Bibliographical notes excellent. A one-volume abridgement, WASHINGTON, edited by Richard Harwell, was issued by Scribner's in 1968.

Stephenson, Nathaniel Wright, and Dunn, Waldo Hilary. GEORGE WASHINGTON. 2 vols. New York: Oxford University Press, 1940.

Detailed treatment except for the presidential period.

Single-Volume

Bellamy, Francis Rufus. THE PRIVATE LIFE OF GEORGE WASHINGTON. New York: Thomas Y. Crowell, 1951. v, 409 p.

Borden, Morton, comp. GEORGE WASHINGTON. Great Lives Observed Series. Englewood, N.J.: Prentice-Hall, 1969. vi, 154 p.

Callahan, North. GEORGE WASHINGTON, SOLDIER AND MAN. New York: Morrow, 1972. xiii, 296 p.

Washington the military leader.

Carroll, John Alexander, and Ashworth, Mary Wells. GEORGE WASHINGTON: FIRST IN PEACE, 1793-1799. New York: Charles Scribner's Sons, 1957. xxiv, 729 p.

Completes the Douglas Southall Freeman Washington biography (see p. 134).

Cunliffe, Marcus. GEORGE WASHINGTON, MAN AND MONUMENT. Boston: Little, Brown, 1958. xiv, 234 p.

A brief interpretive biography by a noted British historian.

Decatur, Stephen. PRIVATE AFFAIRS OF GEORGE WASHINGTON. Boston: Houghton Mifflin, 1933. Reprint. New York: DaCapo Press, 1969. xv, 356 p.

Based upon the records and accounts of Tobias Lear, Esquire, Washington's secretary.

Emery, Noemi. WASHINGTON: A BIOGRAPHY. New York: Putnam, 1976. 432 p.

Fitzpatrick, John Clement. GEORGE WASHINGTON HIMSELF: A COMMON-SENSE BIOGRAPHY WRITTEN FROM HIS MANUSCRIPTS. Indianapolis: Bobbs-Merrill, 1933. Reprint. Westport, Conn.: Greenwood Press, 1975. xiii, 544 p.

Flexner, James Thomas. WASHINGTON: THE INDISPENSABLE MAN. Boston: Little, Brown, 1974. xvii, 423 p.

Jones, Robert Francis. GEORGE WASHINGTON. Boston: Twayne Publishers, 1979. 178 p.

Ketchum, Richard M. THE WORLD OF GEORGE WASHINGTON. New York: American Heritage Publishing Co., 1974. 275 p.

Kinnaird, Clark. GEORGE WASHINGTON: THE PICTORIAL BIOGRAPHY. New York: Hastings House, 1967. vi, 265 p.

Knollenberg, Bernhard. GEORGE WASHINGTON: THE VIRGINIA PERIOD, 1732-1775. Durham, N.C.: Duke University Press, 1964. x, 238 p.

Smith, James Morton, ed. GEORGE WASHINGTON: A PROFILE. New York: Hill and Wang, 1969. xxx, 289 p.

Washington, George. GEORGE WASHINGTON: A BIOGRAPHY IN HIS OWN WORDS. Edited by Ralph K. Andrist with an introduction by Donald Jackson. New York: Newsweek, 1972. 416 p.

Weems, Mason Locke. A HISTORY OF THE LIFE AND DEATH, VIRTUES AND EXPLOITS OF GENERAL GEORGE WASHINGTON. Cleveland: World Publishing Co., 1965. 374 p.

_____. THE LIFE OF WASHINGTON THE GREAT. New York: Garland Publishing, 1977. 174 p.

Wilson, Woodrow. GEORGE WASHINGTON. New York: Harper and Brothers, 1896. Reprint. Introduction by Marcus Cunliffe. New York: Schocken Books, 1969. xviii, 333 p.

MONOGRAPHS

Ambler, Charles Henry. GEORGE WASHINGTON AND THE WEST. Chapel Hill: University of North Carolina Press, 1936. Reprint. New York: Russell and Russell, 1971. 270 p.

Bryan, William Alfred. GEORGE WASHINGTON IN AMERICAN LITERATURE, 1775-1865. New York: Columbia University Press, 1952. xii, 280 p.

Camp, Norma Cournow. GEORGE WASHINGTON: MAN OF COURAGE AND PRAYER. Milford, Mich.: Mott Media, 1977. 169 p.

Examines George Washington's religious beliefs and attitude toward God as reflected in his diaries and letters.

Christensen, Lois E. WASHINGTON'S EXPERIENCE AND THE CREATION OF THE PRESIDENCY. Ann Arbor, Mich.: University Microfilms, 1957. 425 l.

DeConde, Alexander. ENTANGLING ALLIANCE: POLITICS AND DIPLOMACY UNDER GEORGE WASHINGTON. Durham, N.C.: Duke University Press, 1958. xiv, 536 p.

Hart, James. THE AMERICAN PRESIDENCY IN ACTION, 1789: A STUDY IN CONSTITUTIONAL HISTORY. New York: Macmillan, 1948. xv, 256 p.

Kaufman, Burton Ira, comp. WASHINGTON'S FAREWELL ADDRESS: THE VIEW FROM THE 20TH CENTURY. Chicago: Quadrangle Books, 1969. 192 p.

McDonald, Forrest. THE PRESIDENCY OF GEORGE WASHINGTON. American Presidency Series. Lawrence: University Press of Kansas, 1974. xi, 210 p.

Nettels, Curtis P. GEORGE WASHINGTON AND AMERICAN INDEPENDENCE. Boston: Little, Brown, 1951. 338 p.

Wilson, Hazel. THE YEARS BETWEEN: WASHINGTON AT HOME AT MOUNT VERNON, 1783-1789. New York: Knopf, 1969. 148 p.

An account of Washington's life at Mount Vernon, based largely on his own diaries and letters, from the end of the Revolution in 1783 to his election as first president of the United States in 1789.

Wright, Esmond. WASHINGTON AND THE AMERICAN REVOLUTION. New York: Macmillan, 1957. 192 p.

ARTICLES

Campbell, Janet. "The First Americans' Tribute to the First President." CHRONICLES OF OKLAHOMA 57 (Summer 1979): 190-95.

Clarfield, Gerard. "Protecting the Frontiers: Defense Policy and the Tariff Question in the First Washington Administration." WILLIAM AND MARY QUARTERLY 32 (July 1975): 443-64.

Cullen, Joseph P. "Washington at Mount Vernon." AMERICAN HISTORY ILLUSTRATED 9 (May 1974): 4-11, 45-48.

Eaton, Dorothy S. "George Washington Papers." QUARTERLY JOURNAL OF THE LIBRARY OF CONGRESS 22 (January 1965): 3-28.

Jones, Robert F. "George Washington and the Politics of the Presidency." PRESIDENTIAL STUDIES QUARTERLY 10 (Winter 1980): 28-34.

Marx, Rudolph. "A Medical Profile of George Washington." AMERICAN HERITAGE 6 (August 1955): 43-57, 106-7.

Indicates that Washington would not have passed a present-day army physical examination because of his health history.

Partin, Robert. "The Changing Images of George Washington from Weems to Freeman." SOCIAL STUDIES 56 (February 1965): 52-59.

Smith, Merritt Row. "George Washington and the Establishment of the Harper's Ferry Armory." VIRGINIA MAGAZINE OF HISTORY AND BIOGRAPHY 81 (October 1973): 415-36.

George Washington

Smylie, James H. "The President as Republican Prophet and King: Clerical Reflections on the Death of Washington." JOURNAL OF CHURCH AND STATE 18 (Spring 1976): 233-52.

Chapter 13

JOHN ADAMS, 1797-1801

BIBLIOGRAPHY

Bremer, Howard F., ed. JOHN ADAMS, 1735-1826: CHRONOLOGY DOCUMENTS-BIBLIOGRAPHICAL AIDS. Presidential Chronologies Series. Dobbs Ferry, N.Y.: Oceana Publications, 1967. 88 p.

SOURCE MATERIALS

Adams, Abigail Smith. THE BOOK OF ABIGAIL AND JOHN: SELECTED LETTERS OF THE ADAMS FAMILY, 1762-1784. Edited and with an introduction by L.H. Butterfield, Marc Friedlaender, and Mary-Jo Kline. Cambridge, Mass.: Harvard University Press, 1975. ix, 411 p.

Adams, John. THE ADAMS-JEFFERSON LETTERS: THE COMPLETE CORRESPONDENCE BETWEEN THOMAS JEFFERSON AND ABIGAIL AND JOHN ADAMS. 2 vols. Edited by Lester J. Cappon. Chapel Hill: University of North Carolina Press, 1959. li, 638 p.

______. DIARY AND AUTOBIOGRAPHY. 4 vols. Edited by Lyman H. Butterfield. Cambridge: Harvard University Press, 1961.

> The first major publication after the opening of the Adams Family Papers in 1952. See volume 1 for the story of the Adams Papers as told by Lyman H. Butterfield.

______. THE JOHN ADAMS PAPERS. Selected, edited, and interpreted by Frank Donovan. New York: Dodd, Mead, 1965. 335 p.

______. THE POLITICAL WRITINGS OF JOHN ADAMS: REPRESENTATIVE SELECTIONS. Edited with an introduction by George A. Peek, Jr. New York: Liberal Arts Press, 1954. 223 p.

_____. THE WORKS OF JOHN ADAMS, SECOND PRESIDENT OF THE UNITED STATES. 10 vols. Edited by Charles Francis Adams. Boston: Little, Brown, 1856. Reprint. New York: AMS Press, 1971.

Incomplete and selective by modern standards.

BIOGRAPHIES

Adams, John. JOHN ADAMS: A BIOGRAPHY IN HIS OWN WORDS. Edited by James Bishop Peabody with an introduction by L.H. Butterfield. New York: Newsweek, 1973. 416 p.

Burleigh, Anne Husted. JOHN ADAMS. New Rochelle, N.Y.: Arlington House, 1969. vii, 437 p.

A good overview of Adams's personal and political life.

Chinard, Gilbert. HONEST JOHN ADAMS. Boston: Little, Brown, 1933. xii, 359 p.

Good for Adams's political philosophy.

East, Robert Abraham. JOHN ADAMS. Boston: Twayne Publishers, 1979. 126 p.

Smith, Page. JOHN ADAMS. 2 vols. Garden City, N.Y.: Doubleday, 1962. xx, 1,170 p.

Authoritative, but hard reading. First comprehensive biography based upon the Adams Family Papers which were opened in 1952.

MONOGRAPHS

Allison, John Murray. ADAMS AND JEFFERSON: THE STORY OF A FRIENDSHIP. Norman: University of Oklahoma Press, 1966. xiii, 349 p.

Bowen, Catherine Drinker. JOHN ADAMS AND THE AMERICAN REVOLUTION. Boston: Little, Brown, 1950. xvii, 699 p.

A "fictionalized" biography which ends in 1776.

Brown, Ralph A. THE PRESIDENCY OF JOHN ADAMS. American Presidency Series. Lawrence: University Press of Kansas, 1975. x, 248 p.

Written for the general reader and based upon secondary rather than primary materials.

Charles, Joseph. THE ORIGINS OF THE AMERICAN PARTY SYSTEM, 1789-1801. Williamsburg: Institute of Early American History and Culture, 1956. 147 p.

Dauer, Manning Julian. THE ADAMS FEDERALISTS. Baltimore: Johns Hopkins Press, 1968. xxix, 292 p.

An excellent analysis for the contrasts between the Adams and the Hamilton political philosophy.

Howe, John R. THE CHANGING POLITICAL THOUGHT OF JOHN ADAMS. Princeton, N.J.: Princeton University Press, 1966. xv, 259 p.

Shows how Adams adapted his thinking to specific events during his long public career.

Iacuzzi, Alfred. JOHN ADAMS, SCHOLAR. New York: S.F. Vanni, 1952. xiv, 306 p.

Kurtz, Stephen G. THE PRESIDENCY OF JOHN ADAMS: THE COLLAPSE OF FEDERALISM, 1795-1800. Philadelphia: University of Pennsylvania Press, 1957. 448 p.

Nagel, Paul C. DESCENT FROM GLORY: FOUR GENERATIONS OF THE JOHN ADAMS FAMILY. New York: Oxford University Press, 1983. xiv, 400 p.

Oliver, Andrew. PORTRAITS OF JOHN AND ABIGAIL ADAMS. Cambridge, Mass.: Belknap Press of Harvard University Press, 1967. xxxvi, 284 p.

Peterson, Merrill D. ADAMS AND JEFFERSON: A REVOLUTIONARY DIALOGUE. Athens: University of Georgia Press, 1976. xiv, 146 p.

Shaw, Peter. THE CHARACTER OF JOHN ADAMS. Chapel Hill: University of North Carolina Press, 1976. ix, 324 p.

Shepherd, Jack. THE ADAMS CHRONICLES: FOUR GENERATIONS OF GREATNESS. Introduction by Daniel Boorstin. Boston: Little, Brown, 1975. xxxi, 448 p.

Prepared in conjunction with the production of a television series of the same name.

Vaughan, Harold Cecil. THE XYZ AFFAIR, 1797-98: THE DIPLOMACY OF THE ADAMS ADMINISTRATION AND AN UNDECLARED WAR WITH FRANCE. New York: Franklin Watts, 1972. 90 p.

John Adams

ARTICLES

Anderson, William G. "John Adams, the Navy, and the Quasi-War with France." AMERICAN NEPTUNE 30 (April 1970): 117-32.

Appleby, Joyce. "The New Republican Synthesis and the Changing Political Ideas of John Adams." AMERICAN QUARTERLY 25 (December 1973): 578-95.

Carr, James A. "John Adams and the Barbary Problem: the Myth and the Record." AMERICAN NEPTUNE 26 (October 1966): 231-57.

Charles, Joseph. "Adams and Jefferson: The Origins of the American Party System." WILLIAM AND MARY QUARTERLY 12 (July 1955): 410-46.

Clarfield, Gerard. "John Adams: The Marketplace and American Foreign Policy." NEW ENGLAND QUARTERLY 52 (September 1979): 345-57.

Hayes, Frederic H. "John Adams and American Sea Power." AMERICAN NEPTUNE 25 (January 1965): 35-45.

Kramer, Eugene F. "John Adams, Elbridge Gerry, and the Origins of the XYZ Affair." ESSEX INSTITUTE HISTORICAL COLLECTIONS 94 (January 1958): 57-68.

Murphy, William J., Jr. "John Adams: The Politics of the Additional Army." NEW ENGLAND QUARTERLY 52 (June 1979): 234-49.

Peterson, Merrill D. "Adams and Jefferson: A Revolutionary Dialogue." WILSON QUARTERLY 1 (Autumn 1976): 108-25.

Rossiter, Clinton. "The Legacy of John Adams." YALE REVIEW 46 (Summer 1957): 528-50.

Deals with the political theory of Adams.

Stewart, Donald H., and Clark, George P. "Misanthrope or Humanitarian? John Adams in Retirement." NEW ENGLAND QUARTERLY 28 (June 1955): 216-36.

Chapter 14

THOMAS JEFFERSON, 1801-09

BIBLIOGRAPHY

Bishop, Arthur, ed. THOMAS JEFFERSON, 1743-1826: CHRONOLOGY-DOCUMENTS-BIBLIOGRAPHICAL AIDS. Presidential Chronologies Series. Dobbs Ferry, N.Y.: Oceana Publications, 1971. 122 p.

SOURCE MATERIALS

Adams, John, and Jefferson, Thomas. THE ADAMS-JEFFERSON LETTERS: THE COMPLETE CORRESPONDENCE BETWEEN THOMAS JEFFERSON AND ABIGAIL AND JOHN ADAMS. 2 vols. Edited by Lester J. Cappon. Chapel Hill: University of North Carolina Press, 1959. li, 638 p.

Jefferson, Thomas. AUTOBIOGRAPHY. Introduction by Dumas Malone. New York: Capricorn Books, 1959. 119 p.

______. BASIC WRITINGS (1760-1826) OF THOMAS JEFFERSON. Edited by Philip S. Foner. Garden City, N.Y.: Halcyon House, 1950. xviii, 816 p.

______. THE COMPLETE JEFFERSON: CONTAINING HIS MAJOR WRITINGS, PUBLISHED AND UNPUBLISHED, EXCEPT HIS LETTERS. Assembled and arranged by Saul K. Padover. Freeport, N.Y.: Books for Libraries Press, 1969. xxix, 1,322 p.

______. THE FAMILY LETTERS OF THOMAS JEFFERSON. Edited by Edwin Morris Betts and James Adam Bear, Jr. Columbia: University of Missouri Press, 1966. 506 p.

> Nearly six hundred letters between Jefferson and his family written from 1783 to 1826.

_____. THE PAPERS OF THOMAS JEFFERSON. 20 vols. Edited by Julian P. Boyd. Princeton, N.J.: Princeton University Press, 1950-74.

The definitive edition bringing together all known writings of Jefferson to August 1791.

_____. THE POLITICAL WRITINGS OF THOMAS JEFFERSON: REPRESENTATIVE SELECTIONS. Edited with an introduction by Edward Dumbauld. Indianapolis: Bobbs-Merrill, 1955. xii, 204 p.

_____. THE PORTABLE THOMAS JEFFERSON. Edited and with an introduction by Merrill D. Peterson. New York: Viking Press, 1975. xlv, 589 p.

_____. THOMAS JEFFERSON PAPERS. Washington, D.C.: Library of Congress, 1974. 65 reels.

_____. THE WRITINGS. Selected and edited by Saul K. Padover. Luneburg, Vt.: Printed for the members of the Limited Editions Club at the Stinehour Press, 1967. x, 362 p.

U.S. Declaration of Independence. THE JEFFERSON DRAFTS OF THE DECLARATION OF INDEPENDENCE. Compilation and design by Gerald Force. Washington, D.C.: Colortone Press, 1963. 8 p.

Virginia. University of. THE JEFFERSON PAPERS OF THE UNIVERSITY OF VIRGINIA. Charlottesville: University Press of Virginia, 1973. xvi, 495 p.

Includes manuscripts acquired through 1970.

Virginia. University of. Library. GUIDE TO THE MICROFILM EDITION OF THE JEFFERSON PAPERS OF THE UNIVERSITY OF VIRGINIA, 1732-1828. Edited by Douglas W. Tanner, Elizabeth C. Fake, Laura M. Brubaker, and Robin Wagner. Charlottesville: 1977. 96 p.

BIOGRAPHIES

Multivolume

Bowers, Claude G. JEFFERSON AND HAMILTON: THE STRUGGLE FOR DEMOCRACY IN AMERICA. Boston: Houghton Mifflin, 1925. xvii, 531 p.

_____. JEFFERSON IN POWER: THE DEATH STRUGGLE OF THE FEDERALISTS. Boston: Houghton Mifflin, 1936. xix, 538 p.

_____. THE YOUNG JEFFERSON. Boston: Houghton Mifflin, 1945. xxx, 544 p.

Jefferson, Thomas. THOMAS JEFFERSON: A BIOGRAPHY IN HIS OWN WORDS. 2 vols. New York: Newsweek; distributed by Harper and Row, 1974. 416 p.

Kimball, Marie. JEFFERSON: THE ROAD TO GLORY, 1743 TO 1776. New York: Coward-McCann, 1943. Reprint. Westport, Conn.: Greenwood Press, 1977. ix, 358 p.

_____. JEFFERSON, WAR AND PEACE, 1776-1784. New York: Coward-McCann, 1947. ix, 398 p.

_____. JEFFERSON: THE SCENE OF EUROPE, 1784-1789. New York: Coward-McCann, 1950. ix, 357 p.

Malone, Dumas. JEFFERSON AND HIS TIME. 6 vols. Boston: Little, Brown, 1948-81.

> Definitive treatment by a master historian. Volumes 4 and 5 cover the presidential years. Extensive bibliographies in each volume.

Randall, Henry S. THE LIFE OF THOMAS JEFFERSON. 3 vols. New York: Derby and Jackson, 1858.

> Best of the early biographies. The author interviewed some of Jefferson's grandchildren and used some letters and papers no longer in existence.

Schachner, Nathan. THOMAS JEFFERSON: A BIOGRAPHY. 2d ed. 2 vols. New York: Thomas Yoseloff, 1957. xiv, 1,070 p.

> Deals with Jefferson's many activities in law, government, diplomacy, art, literature, science and invention, and education.

Single-Volume

Chinard, Gilbert. THOMAS JEFFERSON: THE APOSTLE OF AMERICANISM. Rev. ed. Ann Arbor: University of Michigan Press, 1957. 548 p.

Fleming, Thomas J. THE MAN FROM MONTICELLO: AN INTIMATE LIFE OF THOMAS JEFFERSON. New York: Morrow, 1969. 409 p.

> A well-written and well-researched volume.

Jefferson, Thomas. JEFFERSON HIMSELF; THE PERSONAL NARRATIVE OF A MANY-SIDED AMERICAN. Edited by Bernard Mayo. Charlottesville: University Press of Virginia, 1970. xv, 384 p.

Koch, Adrienne, comp. JEFFERSON. Great Lives Observed Series. Englewood Cliffs, N.J.: Prentice-Hall, 1971. viii, 180 p.

Nock, Albert Jay. JEFFERSON. Introduction by Merrill D. Peterson. New York: Hill and Wang, 1960. ix, 210 p.

Padover, Saul K. JEFFERSON. New York: Harcourt, Brace, 1942. 459 p.

______, ed. A JEFFERSON PROFILE AS REVEALED IN HIS LETTERS. New York: J. Day Co., 1956. xxiv, 359 p.

Pancake, John S. THOMAS JEFFERSON AND ALEXANDER HAMILTON. Woodbury, N.J.: Barron's Educational Series, 1974. viii, 521 p.

Peterson, Merrill D. THOMAS JEFFERSON AND THE NEW NATION. New York: Oxford University Press, 1970. ix, 1,072 p.

Stresses the many contributions of Jefferson to the nation.

______, comp. THOMAS JEFFERSON: A PROFILE. New York: Hill and Wang, 1967. xx, 262 p.

Rosenberger, Francis Coleman, ed. JEFFERSON READER; A TREASURY OF WRITING ABOUT THOMAS JEFFERSON. New York: E.P. Dutton, 1953. 349 p.

Smith, Page. JEFFERSON: A REVEALING BIOGRAPHY. New York: American Heritage Publishing Co.; distribution by McGraw-Hill, 1976. 310 p.

Wibberly, Leonard Patrick O'Connor. MAN OF LIBERTY: A LIFE OF THOMAS JEFFERSON. New York: Farrar, Straus and Giroux, 1968. vii, 404 p.

A revised edition in one volume of Wibberly's original four-volume biography of Jefferson (1963-66), also published by Farrar.

MONOGRAPHS

Adams, Henry. HISTORY OF THE UNITED STATES OF AMERICA DURING THE ADMINISTRATIONS OF JEFFERSON AND MADISON. Abridged and edited by Ernest Samuels. Chicago: University of Chicago Press, 1967. xx, 425 p.

Allison, John Murray. ADAMS AND JEFFERSON: THE STORY OF A FRIENDSHIP. Norman: University of Oklahoma Press, 1966. xiii, 349 p.

Banning, Lance. THE JEFFERSONIAN PERSUASION: EVOLUTION OF A PARTY IDEOLOGY. Ithaca, N.Y.: Cornell University Press, 1978. 307 p.

Bear, James Adam, comp. JEFFERSON AT MONTICELLO. Edited with an introduction by James A. Bear, Jr. Charlottesville: University Press of Virginia, 1967. xiv, 144 p.

Boorstin, Daniel J. THE LOST WORLD OF THOMAS JEFFERSON. New York: Henry Holt and Co., 1948. xii, 306 p.

Brodie, Fawn M. THOMAS JEFFERSON, AN INTIMATE HISTORY. New York: Norton, 1974. 591 p.

Probes the inner feelings and psychology of Jefferson.

Brown, Stuart Gerry. THOMAS JEFFERSON. Great American Thinkers Series. New York: Washington Square Press, 1966. viii, 247 p.

Cohen, I. Bernard, ed. THOMAS JEFFERSON AND THE SCIENCES. New York: Arno Press, 1980. 450 p.

Cunningham, Noble E. THE JEFFERSONIAN REPUBLICANS: THE FORMATION OF PARTY ORGANIZATION, 1789-1801. Chapel Hill: University of North Carolina Press, 1957. x, 279 p.

______. THE JEFFERSONIAN REPUBLICANS IN POWER: PARTY OPERATIONS, 1801-1809. Chapel Hill: University of North Carolina Press, 1963. ix, 318 p.

Daniels, Jonathan. ORDEAL OF AMBITION: JEFFERSON, HAMILTON, BURR. Garden City, N.Y.: Doubleday, 1970. x, 446 p.

Douty, Esther. MR. JEFFERSON'S WASHINGTON. Champaign, Ill.: Garrard Publishing Co., 1970. 96 p.

Traces the history of Washington, D.C., until 1809, with emphasis on the people, schools, amusements, food, and way of life during the administration of Thomas Jefferson.

Ellis, Richard E. THE JEFFERSONIAN CRISIS: COURTS AND POLITICS IN THE YOUNG REPUBLIC. New York: Oxford University Press, 1971. xii, 377 p.

Johnstone, Robert M. JEFFERSON AND THE PRESIDENCY: LEADERSHIP IN THE YOUNG REPUBLIC. Ithaca, N.Y.: Cornell University Press, 1978. 332 p.

Kaplan, Lawrence S. JEFFERSON AND FRANCE: AN ESSAY ON POLITICS AND ON POLITICAL IDEAS. New Haven, Conn.: Yale University Press, 1967. x, 175 p.

Koch, Adrienne. JEFFERSON AND MADISON: THE GREAT COLLABORATION. New York: Knopf, 1950. xv, 294 p.

McDonald, Forrest. THE PRESIDENCY OF THOMAS JEFFERSON. American Presidency Series. Lawrence: University Press of Kansas, 1976. xi, 201 p.

Malone, Dumas. THOMAS JEFFERSON AS POLITICAL LEADER. Berkeley and Los Angeles: University of California Press, 1963. viii, 75 p.

A series of three lectures by the great Jefferson scholar.

Norton, Paul F. LATROBE, JEFFERSON, AND THE NATIONAL CAPITOL. New York: Garland Publishing, 1977. 362 p. Appendix.

Peterson, Merrill D. THE JEFFERSONIAN IMAGE IN THE AMERICAN MIND. New York: Oxford University Press, 1960. x, 548 p.

Randolph, Sarah Nicholas. THE DOMESTIC LIFE OF THOMAS JEFFERSON. Introduction by Dumas Malone. New York: Ungar, 1958. 432 p.

Compiled from family letters and reminiscences by his great-grand daughter.

Sanford, Charles B. THOMAS JEFFERSON AND HIS LIBRARY: A STUDY OF HIS LITERARY INTERESTS AND OF THE RELIGIOUS TITLES IN HIS LIBRARY. Hamden, Conn.: Archon Books, 1977. 211 p.

Sears, Louis Martin. JEFFERSON AND THE EMBARGO. New York: Octagon Books, 1966. ix, 340 p.

Stuart, Reginald C. THE HALF-WAY PACIFIST: THOMAS JEFFERSON'S VIEW OF WAR. Toronto and Buffalo: University of Toronto Press, 1978. x, 93 p.

THOMAS JEFFERSON AND THE WORLD OF BOOKS: A SYMPOSIUM HELD AT THE LIBRARY OF CONGRESS, SEPTEMBER 21, 1976. Washington, D.C.: Library of Congress, 1977. 37 p.

Van der Linden, Frank. THE TURNING POINT: JEFFERSON'S BATTLE FOR THE PRESIDENCY. Washington, D.C.: Robert B. Luce, 1962. x, 371 p.

White, Leonard D. THE JEFFERSONIANS: A STUDY IN ADMINISTRATIVE HISTORY, 1801-1829. New York: Macmillan, 1951. xi, 572 p.

Wiltse, Charles Maurice. THE JEFFERSONIAN TRADITION IN AMERICAN DEMOCRACY. New York: Hill and Wang, 1960. xii, 273 p.

Woolery, William Kirk. THE RELATION OF THOMAS JEFFERSON TO AMERICAN FOREIGN POLICY, 1783-1793. Baltimore: Johns Hopkins Press, 1927. ix, 128 p.

ARTICLES

Banning, Lance. "Jeffersonian Ideology and the French Revolution; A Question of Liberticide at Home." STUDIES IN BURKE AND HIS TIMES 17 (Winter 1976): 5-26.

Bellot, H. Hale. "Thomas Jefferson in American Historiography." TRANSACTIONS OF THE ROYAL HISTORICAL SOCIETY, 5th series, 4 (1954): 135-55.

> Deals "not with the progress of Jeffersonian studies, but the light which is thrown upon historians who have dealt with him, by their treatment of him."

Bowman, Albert H. "Jefferson, Hamilton and American Foreign Policy." POLITICAL SCIENCE QUARTERLY 71 (March 1956): 18-41.

> On "the question of realism versus idealism," 1790-95, indicating that "Hamilton's concept of the national interest . . . was grossly in error."

Boyd, Julian P. "The Relevance of Thomas Jefferson for the Twentieth Century." AMERICAN SCHOLAR 22 (Winter 1953): 61-76.

______. "Thomas Jefferson Survives." AMERICAN SCHOLAR 20 (Spring 1951): 163-73.

Brodie, Fawn M. "Jefferson Biographers and the Psychology of Canonization." JOURNAL OF INTERDISCIPLINARY HISTORY 2 (Summer 1971): 155-72.

Butterfield, Lyman H. "The Jefferson-Adams Correspondence in the Adams Manuscript Trust [1777-1826]." LIBRARY OF CONGRESS QUARTERLY JOURNAL 5 (February 1948): 3-6.

______. "The Papers of Thomas Jefferson: Progress and Procedures in the Enterprise at Princeton." AMERICAN ARCHIVIST 12 (April 1949): 131-45.

Chiang, C.Y. Jesse. "Understanding Thomas Jefferson." INTERNATIONAL REVIEW OF HISTORY AND POLITICAL SCIENCE 14 (August 1977): 51-61.

Chuinard, E.G. "Thomas Jefferson and the Corps of Discovery: Creating the Lewis and Clark Expedition." AMERICAN WEST 12 (November 1975): 4-13.

Colbourn, H. Trevor. "Thomas Jefferson's Use of the Past." WILLIAM AND MARY QUARTERLY 15 (January 1958): 56-70.

D'Elia, Donald J. "Jefferson, Rush, and the Limits of Philosophical Friendship." PROCEEDINGS OF THE AMERICAN PHILOSOPHICAL SOCIETY 117 (October 1973): 333-43.

Garrett, Wendell D. "The Monumental Friendship of Jefferson and Adams." HISTORIC PRESERVATION 28 (April-June 1976): 28-35.

Graham, Pearl M. "Thomas Jefferson and Sally Hemings." JOURNAL OF NEGRO HISTORY 46 (April 1961): 89-103.

Jahoda, Gloria. "John Beckley: Jefferson's Campaign Manager." BULLETIN OF THE NEW YORK PUBLIC LIBRARY 64 (May 1960): 247-60.

Kaplan, Lawrence S. "Consensus of 1789: Jefferson and Hamilton on American Foreign Policy." SOUTH ATLANTIC QUARTERLY 71 (Winter 1972): 91-105.

______. "Jefferson, the Napoleonic Wars, and the Balance of Power." WILLIAM AND MARY QUARTERLY, 3d series, 14 (April 1957): 196-217.

______. "Jefferson's Foreign Policy and Napoleon's Ideologues." WILLIAM AND MARY QUARTERLY 19 (July 1962): 344-59.

Lerche, Charles O., Jr. "Jefferson and the Election of 1800: A Case Study in the Political Smear." WILLIAM AND MARY QUARTERLY 5 (October 1948): 467-91.

McColley, Robert. "Jefferson's Rivals: The Shifting Character of the Federalists." MIDCONTINENT AMERICAN STUDIES JOURNAL 9 (Spring 1968): 23-33.

McLoughlin, William G. "Thomas Jefferson and the Beginning of Cherokee Nationalism, 1806 to 1809." WILLIAM AND MARY QUARTERLY 32 (October 1975): 547-80.

Malone, Dumas. "Mr. Jefferson and the Traditions of Virginia." VIRGINIA MAGAZINE OF HISTORY AND BIOGRAPHY 75 (April 1967): 131-42.

_____. "Mr. Jefferson's Private Life." PROCEEDINGS OF THE AMERICAN ANTIQUARIAN SOCIETY 84 (April 1974): 65-72.

_____. "Presidential Leadership and National Unity: The Jeffersonian Example." JOURNAL OF SOUTHERN HISTORY 35 (February 1969): 3-17.

_____. "The Relevance of Mr. Jefferson." VIRGINIA QUARTERLY REVIEW 37 (Summer 1961): 334-49.

Midgley, Louis. "The Brodie Connection: Thomas Jefferson and Joseph Smith." BRIGHAM YOUNG UNIVERSITY STUDIES 19 (Fall 1979): 59-67.

Parks, Edd Winfield. "Jefferson's Attitude toward History." GEORGIA HISTORICAL QUARTERLY 36 (December 1952): 336-41.

Peterson, Merrill D. "Henry Adams on Jefferson the President." VIRGINIA QUARTERLY REVIEW 39 (Spring 1963): 187-201.

_____. "Thomas Jefferson and the National Purpose." PROCEEDINGS OF THE AMERICAN PHILOSOPHICAL SOCIETY 105 (15 December 1961): 517-20.

Pulley, Judith. "The Bittersweet Friendship of Thomas Jefferson and Abigail Adams." ESSEX INSTITUTE HISTORICAL COLLECTIONS 108 (July 1972): 193-216.

Shimakawa, Masashi. "Thomas Jefferson and the Indian Problem." AMERICAN REVIEW 12 (1978): 214-15.

Shurr, Georgia Hooks. "Thomas Jefferson and the French Revolution." AMERICAN SOCIETY LEGION OF HONOR MAGAZINE 50 (Winter 1979-80): 161-82.

Stuart, Reginald C. "Thomas Jefferson and the Origins of War." PEACE AND CHANGE 4 (Spring 1977): 22-27.

Tauber, Gisela. "Reconstruction in Psychoanalytic Biography: Understanding Thomas Jefferson." JOURNAL OF PSYCHOHISTORY 7 (Fall 1979): 189-207.

Thomas Jefferson

Chapter 15

JAMES MADISON, 1809-17

BIBLIOGRAPHY

Elliot, Ian, ed. JAMES MADISON, 1751-1836: CHRONOLOGY-DOCUMENTS-BIBLIOGRAPHICAL AIDS. Presidential Chronologies Series. Dobbs Ferry, N.Y.: Oceana Publications, 1969. 115 p.

SOURCE MATERIALS

Madison, James. CALENDAR OF THE CORRESPONDENCE OF JAMES MADISON. New York: B. Franklin, 1970. vii, 739 p.

______. THE COMPLETE MADISON: HIS BASIC WRITINGS. Edited by Saul K. Padover. New York: Harper and Brothers, 1953. ix, 361 p.

______. DRAFTING THE FEDERAL CONSTITUTION; A REARRANGEMENT OF MADISON'S NOTES GIVING CONSECUTIVE DEVELOPMENTS OF PROVISIONS IN THE CONSTITUTION OF THE UNITED STATES, SUPPLEMENTED BY DOCUMENTS PERTAINING TO THE PHILADELPHIA CONVENTION AND TO RATIFICATION PROCESSES, AND INCLUDING INSERTIONS BY THE COMPILER. Compiled by Arthur Prescott. New York: Greenwood Press, 1968. xix, 838 p.

______. THE FEDERALIST PAPERS BY JAMES MADISON, ALEXANDER HAMILTON, AND JOHN JAY. Introduction by Willmoore Kendall and George W. Carey. New Rochelle, N.Y.: Arlington House, 1966. 527 p.

______. JOURNAL OF THE FEDERAL CONVENTION, KEPT BY JAMES MADISON. Edited by E.H. Scott. Freeport, N.Y.: Books for Libraries Press, 1970. 805 p.

______. LETTERS AND OTHER WRITINGS OF JAMES MADISON. 4 vols. New York: R. Worthington, 1884.

______. NOTES OF DEBATES IN THE FEDERAL CONVENTION OF 1787, REPORTED BY JAMES MADISON. With an introduction by Adrienne Koch. Athens: Ohio University Press, 1966. xxiii, 659 p.

______. THE PAPERS OF JAMES MADISON. Edited by William T. Hutchinson et al. 13 vols. Chicago: University of Chicago Press, 1962-81.

> Cover the years from 1751 to 1791. The definitive edition of Madison's papers.

BIOGRAPHIES

Brant, Irving. THE FOURTH PRESIDENT: A LIFE OF JAMES MADISON. Indianapolis: Bobbs-Merrill, 1970. 681 p.

> Abridgment of the author's earlier (1941-61) six-volume life of Madison. Definitive and sympathetic.

______. JAMES MADISON. 6 vols. Indianapolis: Bobbs-Merrill, 1941-61.

> The most basic and thorough study of Madison's public and private life.

Ketcham, Ralph. JAMES MADISON: A BIOGRAPHY. New York: Macmillan, 1971. xiv, 753 p.

> Massive detail and thorough acquaintance with source materials.

Madison, James. JAMES MADISON, A BIOGRAPHY IN HiS OWN WORDS. Edited by Merrill D. Peterson, with an introduction by Robert A. Rutland. New York: Newsweek; distributed by Harper and Row, 1974. 416 p.

Moore, Virginia. THE MADISONS: A BIOGRAPHY. New York: McGraw-Hill, 1979. xviii, 568 p.

Schultz, Harold Seessel. JAMES MADISON. New York: Twayne Publishers, 1970. 241 p.

MONOGRAPHS

Adams, Henry. HISTORY OF THE UNITED STATES OF AMERICA DURING THE ADMINISTRATIONS OF JEFFERSON AND MADISON. Abridged and edited by Ernest Samuels. Chicago: University of Chicago Press, 1967. xx, 425 p.

> Part 2 deals with Madison's years in office, with major stress upon the war of 1812.

Brant, Irving. THE BOOKS OF JAMES MADISON, WITH SOME COMMENTS ON THE READING OF FDR AND JFK; AN ADDRESS DELIVERED DURING THE CELEBRATION OF THE 25TH ANNIVERSARY OF THE TRACY W. McGREGOR LIBRARY, 1929-1964. Charlottesville: University of Virginia, 1965. 19 p.

Burns, Edward McNall. JAMES MADISON: PHILOSOPHER OF THE CONSTITUTION. New York: Octagon Books, 1968. x, 240 p.

Fredman, Lionel E. JAMES MADISON, AMERICAN PRESIDENT AND CONSTITUTIONAL AUTHOR. Outstanding Personalities Series, no. 78. Edited by Gerald Kurland and D. Steve Rahmas. Compiled with the assistance of the research staff of SamHar Press. Charlotteville, N.Y.: SamHar Press, 1974. 32 p.

Hunt-Jones, Conover. DOLLEY AND THE "GREAT LITTLE MADISON." Washington, D.C.: American Institute of Architects Foundation, 1977. xvii, 148 p.

Ketcham, Ralph Louis. THE MIND OF JAMES MADISON. Ann Arbor, Mich.: University Microfilms, 1956. xiv, 216 l.

D.S.S. thesis, Syracuse University.

Koch, Adrienne. JEFFERSON AND MADISON: THE GREAT COLLABORATION. New York: Knopf, 1950. xv, 294 p.

Riemer, Neal. JAMES MADISON. Great American Thinkers Series. New York: Washington Square Press, 1968. 238 p.

ARTICLES

Bell, Rudolph M. "Mr. Madison's War and Long-Term Congressional Voting Behavior." WILLIAM AND MARY QUARTERLY 36 (July 1979): 373-95.

Branson, Roy. "James Madison and the Scottish Enlightenment." JOURNAL OF THE HISTORY OF IDEAS 40 (April-June 1979): 235-50.

Brant, Irving. "James Madison and His Times." AMERICAN HISTORICAL REVIEW 57 (July 1952): 853-70.

______. "Madison and the War of 1812." VIRGINIA MAGAZINE OF HISTORY AND BIOGRAPHY 74 (January 1966): 51-67.

______. "Timid President? Futile War?" AMERICAN HERITAGE 10, no. 6 (October 1959): 46-47, 85-89.

Dangerfield, George Bubb. "If Only Mr. Madison Had Waited." AMERICAN HERITAGE 7, no. 3 (April 1956): 8-10, 92-94.

> Gambling on a diplomatic coup with a wily Napoleon, Madison maneuvered America into the needless war of 1812.

Ketcham, Ralph Louis, ed. "An Unpublished Sketch of James Madison by James K. Paulding." VIRGINIA MAGAZINE OF HISTORY AND BIOGRAPHY 67 (October 1959): 432-37.

_____. "James Madison and Judicial Review: 1787-1834." SYRACUSE LAW REVIEW 8 (Spring 1956): 158-65.

_____. "James Madison and Religion: A New Hypothesis." JOURNAL OF PRESBYTERIAN HISTORICAL SOCIETY 38 (June 1960): 65-90.

_____. "The Madison Family Papers: Case Study in a Search for Historical Manuscripts." MANUSCRIPTS 11 (Summer 1959): 49-55.

Young, John Wesley. "Madison's Answer to Machiavelli: Concerning the Legal Relation of Organized Religion to Government in a Republic." FREEMAN 27 (July 1977): 421-31.

Chapter 16
JAMES MONROE, 1817-25

BIBLIOGRAPHY

Elliot, Ian, ed. JAMES MONROE, 1758-1831: CHRONOLOGY-DOCUMENTS-BIBLIOGRAPHIC AIDS. Presidential Chronologies Series. Dobbs Ferry, N.Y.: Oceana Publications, 1969. 86 p.

SOURCE MATERIALS

Monroe, James. THE AUTOBIOGRAPHY OF JAMES MONROE. Edited by Stuart Gerry Brown. Syracuse: Syracuse University Press, 1959. xi, 236 p.

Ends in 1807 before his presidency.

______. THE WRITINGS OF JAMES MONROE, INCLUDING A COLLECTION OF HIS PUBLIC AND PRIVATE PAPERS AND CORRESPONDENCE, NOW FOR THE FIRST TIME PRINTED. 7 vols. New York: G.P. Putnam's Sons, 1898-1903. Reprint. New York: AMS Press, 1969.

BIOGRAPHIES

Ammon, Harry. JAMES MONROE: THE QUEST FOR NATIONAL IDENTITY. New York: McGraw-Hill, 1971. xi, 706 p.

Especially good on Monroe's relationship with Jefferson and Madison.

Cresson, William P. JAMES MONROE. Chapel Hill: University of North Carolina, 1946. xiv, 577 p.

Strong on foreign affairs.

Hoyt, Edwin Palmer. JAMES MONROE. Chicago: Reilly and Lee Co., 1968. 127 p.

Intended for younger readers.

Morgan, George. THE LIFE OF JAMES MONROE. Boston: Small, Maynard and Co., 1921. Reprint. New York: AMS Press, 1969. xvi, 484 p.

Good for the early life of Monroe.

Styron, Arthur. THE LAST OF THE COCKED HATS: JAMES MONROE AND THE VIRGINIA DYNASTY. Norman: University of Oklahoma Press, 1945. xiii, 480 p.

A solid biography, good on the background of Monroe's period.

MONOGRAPHS

Dangerfield, George. THE AWAKENING OF AMERICAN NATIONALISM: 1815-1818. New American Nation Series. New York: Harper and Row, 1965. xiii, 331 p.

Deals with many of the events in the Monroe administration.

_____. THE ERA OF GOOD FEELINGS. New York: Harcourt, Brace, 1952. xiv, 525 p.

Excellent personal and political history covering the years 1814 to 1829.

Wilmerding, Lucius. JAMES MONROE, PUBLIC CLAIMANT. New Brunswick, N.J.: Rutgers University Press, 1960. viii, 144 p.

On Monroe's character for integrity in the management of public money, the claims presented by him in 1825 against the United States for alleged uncompensated services since 1794, and the reluctance of Congress to recognize the full validity of the claims.

ARTICLES

Ammon, Harry. "James Monroe and the Era of Good Feelings." VIRGINIA MAGAZINE OF HISTORY AND BIOGRAPHY 66 (October 1958): 387-98.

Moore, Glover. "Monroe's Re-Election in 1820." MISSISSIPPI QUARTERLY 11 (Summer 1958): 131-40.

Sydnor, Charles S. "The One-Party Period in American History." AMERICAN HISTORICAL REVIEW 51 (April 1946): 439-51.

Turner, L.W. "The Electoral Vote Against Monroe in 1820-- American Legend." MISSISSIPPI VALLEY HISTORICAL REVIEW 42 (September 1955): 250-73.

Wilmerding, Lucius, Jr. "James Monroe and the Furniture Fund." NEW YORK HISTORICAL SOCIETY QUARTERLY 44 (April 1960): 132-49.

On "an appropriation of $20,000 made by Congress for the purpose of furnishing the President's House, the unorthodox loans from the Fund made by Monroe to himself, the unwise conduct of his agent in intermingling personal financial transactions with those of the White House and Treasury, the agent's death and investigations by Congress, Monroe's refusal to submit detailed information to Congress about his use of the Fund, his presentation of claims against the Government in 1825, and the failure of Congress to accept Monroe's invitation to make a further study of this ancient scandal."

Chapter 17

JOHN QUINCY ADAMS, 1825-29

BIBLIOGRAPHY

Jones, Kenneth V., ed. JOHN QUINCY ADAMS, 1767-1848: CHRONOLOGY-DOCUMENTS-BIBLIOGRAPHICAL AIDS. Presidential Chronologies Series. Dobbs Ferry, N.Y.: Oceana Publications, 1970. 82 p.

SOURCE MATERIALS

Adams, John Quincy. THE DIARY OF JOHN QUINCY ADAMS, 1794-1845: AMERICAN DIPLOMACY, AND POLITICAL, SOCIAL, AND INTELLECTUAL LIFE, FROM WASHINGTON TO POLK. Edited by Allan Nevins. New York: Longmans, Green, 1951. Reprint. New York: F. Ungar Publishing Co., 1969. xxxv, 586 p.

A selection from his memoirs, (see below).

_____. MEMOIRS OF JOHN QUINCY ADAMS, COMPRISING PORTIONS OF HIS DIARY FROM 1795 TO 1848. 12 vols. Philadelphia: J.B. Lippincott and Co., 1874-77. Reprint. Freeport, N.Y.: Books for Libraries Press, 1969.

Accurate for dates and events, but not complete as the editor left out considerable material.

_____. JOHN QUINCY ADAMS AND AMERICAN CONTINENTAL EMPIRE: LETTERS, PAPERS AND SPEECHES. Edited by Walter LaFeber. Chicago: Quadrangle Books, 1965. 157 p.

_____. THE SELECTED WRITINGS OF JOHN AND JOHN QUINCY ADAMS. Edited and with an introduction by Adrienne Koch and William Peden. New York: A.A. Knopf, 1946. xxxix, 413 p.

See introduction and pages 225-413, for material on John Quincy Adams.

_____. WRITINGS OF JOHN QUINCY ADAMS. 7 vols. Edited by Worthington Chauncey Ford. New York: Macmillan, 1913-17. Reprint. New York: Greenwood Press, 1968.

Covers only the years 1779-1823.

BIOGRAPHIES

Adams, James Truslow. THE ADAMS FAMILY. Boston: Little, Brown, 1930. 364 p.

Bemis, Samuel Flagg. JOHN QUINCY ADAMS AND THE FOUNDATIONS OF AMERICAN FOREIGN POLICY. New York: Knopf, 1949-56. xix, 588 p.

_____. JOHN QUINCY ADAMS AND THE UNION. New York: Knopf, 1949-56. xv, 546 p.

Pulitzer Prize winner. One of President Kennedy's favorite biographies. Bemis had access to the Adams papers. First volume covers boyhood and diplomatic career; second volume deals with presidency and career in the House of Representatives.

Clark, Bennett Champ. JOHN QUINCY ADAMS, "OLD MAN ELOQUENT." Boston: Little, Brown, 1932. 437 p.

Concentrates on Adams's congressional years.

Falkner, Leonard. THE PRESIDENT WHO WOULDN'T RETIRE. New York: Coward-McCann, 1967. 319 p.

Another book dealing with Adams in the House of Representatives.

Oliver, Andrew. PORTRAITS OF JOHN QUINCY ADAMS AND HIS WIFE. Cambridge, Mass.: Belknap Press of Harvard University Press, 1970. xli, 335 p.

MONOGRAPHS

Lipsky, George A. JOHN QUINCY ADAMS: HIS THEORY AND IDEAS. New York: Thomas Y. Crowell, 1950. xii, 347 p.

Sprague, Waldo Chamberlain. THE PRESIDENT JOHN ADAMS AND PRESIDENT JOHN QUINCY ADAMS BIRTHPLACES, QUINCY, MASS.: THEIR ORIGIN, EARLY HISTORY, AND CHANGES DOWN TO THE PRESENT TIME. Quincy, Mass.: Quincy Historical Society, 1959. 54 p.

ARTICLES

Bergquist, Harold E., Jr. "John Quincy Adams and the Promulgation of the Monroe Doctrine, October-December 1823." ESSEX INSTITUTE HISTORICAL COLLECTIONS 111 (January 1975): 37-52.

Crapol, Edward P. "John Quincy Adams and the Monroe Doctrine: Some New Evidence." PACIFIC HISTORICAL REVIEW 48 (August 1979): 413-19.

Glick, Wendall. "The Best Possible World of John Quincy Adams." NEW ENGLAND QUARTERLY 37 (March 1964): 3-17.

Goodfellow, Donald M. "First Boylston Professor of Rhetoric and Oratory." NEW ENGLAND QUARTERLY 19 (September 1946): 372-89.

Miles, E.A. "President Adams' Billiard Table." NEW ENGLAND QUARTERLY 45 (March 1972): 31-42.

Morgan, H. Wayne. "John Quincy Adams as Minister to Russia, 1809-1814." WESTERN HUMANITIES REVIEW 10 (Autumn 1956): 375-82.

Morgan, William G. "The 'Corrupt Bargain' Charge against Clay and Adams: An Historiographical Analysis." FILSON CLUB HISTORICAL QUARTERLY 42 (April 1968): 132-49.

_____. "John Quincy Adams versus Andrew Jackson: Their Biographers and the 'Corrupt Bargain' Charge." TENNESSEE HISTORICAL QUARTERLY 26 (Spring 1967): 43-58.

Parsons, Lynn Hudson. "A Perpetual Harrow upon My Feeling: John Quincy Adams and the American Indian." NEW ENGLAND QUARTERLY 46 (September 1973): 339-79.

Smoot, Joseph G. "A Presbyterian Minister Calls on President John Quincy Adams." NEW ENGLAND QUARTERLY 34 (September 1961): 379-82.

Chapter 18

ANDREW JACKSON, 1829-37

BIBLIOGRAPHIES

Cave, Alfred A. JACKSONIAN DEMOCRACY AND THE HISTORIANS. Gainesville: University of Florida Press, 1964. 86 p.

Surveys the literature during three eras: the nineteenth century; 1900-1945; and 1945-62.

Sellers, Charles Grier, Jr. JACKSONIAN DEMOCRACY. Washington, D.C.: American Historical Association, 1958. 18 p.

A bibliographical essay issued by the American Historical Association's Service Center for Teachers of History.

Shaw, Ronald E., ed. ANDREW JACKSON, 1767-1845; CHRONOLOGY-DOCUMENTS-BIBLIOGRAPHICAL AIDS. Presidential Chronologies Series. Dobbs Ferry, N.Y.: Oceana Publications, 1969. 123 p.

SOURCE MATERIALS

Jackson, Andrew. CORRESPONDENCE OF ANDREW JACKSON. 7 vols. Edited by John Spencer Bassett. Washington, D.C.: Carnegie Institute of Washington, 1926-35. Reprint. New York: Kraus Reprint Co., 1969.

The basic printed source since Jackson's papers were not kept intact after his lifetime.

______. MESSAGES TO THE UNITED STATES CONGRESS: WITH A BIOGRAPHICAL SKETCH OF HIS LIFE. Cincinnati: Day, 1837. 428 p.

BIOGRAPHIES

Bassett, John Spencer. THE LIFE OF ANDREW JACKSON. New York: Macmillan, 1928. Reprint. Hamden, Conn.: Archon Books, 1967. xix, 766 p.

The first biography to make extensive use of Jackson's papers and those of his associates.

Coit, Margaret L. ANDREW JACKSON. Boston: Houghton Mifflin, 1965. 154 p.

A brief survey.

Curtis, James C. ANDREW JACKSON AND THE SEARCH FOR VINDICATION. The Library of American Biography. Boston: Little, Brown, 1976. xi, 194 p.

Davis, Burke. OLD HICKORY: A LIFE OF ANDREW JACKSON. New York: Dial Press, 1977. 386 p.

Popular treatment for the general audience. About half of the volume is devoted to the presidential years.

James, Marquis. ANDREW JACKSON: PORTRAIT OF A PRESIDENT. Indianapolis: Bobbs-Merrill, 1937. 627 p.

Well-written biography by a journalist. Stresses Jackson's personal and family life in the White House years.

_____. ANDREW JACKSON, THE BORDER CAPTAIN. New York: Grosset and Dunlap, 1933. 461 p.

Covers Jackson's life and career as a frontier army officer before the presidency.

Johnson, Gerald W. ANDREW JACKSON: AN EPIC IN HOMESPUN. New York: Minton, Balch and Co., 1927. viii, 303 p.

Lindsey, David. ANDREW JACKSON AND JOHN C. CALHOUN. Woodbury, N.Y.: Barron's Educational Series, 1973. x, 438 p.

Bibliography, pages 420-23.

Myers, Elisabeth P. ANDREW JACKSON. Chicago: Reilly and Lee Books, 1970. 179 p.

A biography for young people.

Remini, Robert Vincent. ANDREW JACKSON. New York: Harper and Row, 1969. 212 p.

A very good brief biography.

_____. ANDREW JACKSON AND THE COURSE OF AMERICAN EMPIRE, 1767-1821. New York: Harper and Row, 1977. xxii, 502 p.

_____. ANDREW JACKSON AND THE COURSE OF AMERICAN FREEDOM, 1822-1832. New York: Harper and Row, 1981. xvi, 469 p.

The first two volumes of a new biography by the scholar called the "foremost Jacksonian scholar of our time." Brings together the best of recent scholarship by Remini and others.

Sellers, Charles Grier, comp. ANDREW JACKSON, A PROFILE. New York: Hill and Wang, 1971. xxi, 231 p.

A collection of essays by eleven authorities on the career of Jackson.

MONOGRAPHS

Benson, Lee. THE CONCEPT OF JACKSONIAN DEMOCRACY: NEW YORK AS A TEST CASE. Princeton, N.J.: Princeton University Press, 1961. xi, 351 p.

Suggests an egalitarian interpretation.

Herd, Elmer Don, Jr. ANDREW JACKSON, SOUTH CAROLINIAN: A STUDY OF THE ENIGMA OF HIS BIRTH. Lancaster, S.C.: Lancaster County Historical Commission, 1963. viii, 64 p.

Hugins, Walter Edward. JACKSONIAN DEMOCRACY AND THE WORKING CLASS: A STUDY OF THE NEW YORK WORKINGMEN'S MOVEMENT, 1829-1937. Stanford, Calif.: Stanford University Press, 1960. vi, 286 p.

Illustrates the sympathy of New York workingmen with the American capitalistic system and the desire to rise within it.

Meyers, Marvin. THE JACKSONIAN PERSUASION: POLITICS AND BELIEF. Stanford, Calif.: Stanford University Press, 1957. vi, 231 p.

Parton, James. THE PRESIDENCY OF ANDREW JACKSON. Edited with an introduction and notes by Robert V. Remini. New York: Harper and Row, 1967. xxxvii, 468 p.

Abridged from Parton's LIFE OF ANDREW JACKSON published originally in 1859-60. Hostile.

Pessen, Edward. JACKSONIAN AMERICA: SOCIETY, PERSONALITY, AND POLITICS. Homewood, Ill.: Dorsey Press, 1969. xi, 408 p.

A very good overview of the period by one of the leading authorities.

_____. NEW PERSPECTIVES ON JACKSONIAN PARTIES AND POLITICS. Boston: Allyn and Bacon, 1969. viii, 291 p.

______, ed. THE MANY-FACETED JACKSONIAN ERA: NEW INTERPRETATIONS. Westport, Conn.: Greenwood Press, 1977. 331 p.

A collection of readings offering a more than political account of the period. Sixteen essays deal with society, the economy, and reform, in addition to political trends.

Remini, Robert Vincent. ANDREW JACKSON AND THE BANK WAR: A STUDY IN THE GROWTH OF PRESIDENTIAL POWER. New York: Norton, 1967. 192 p.

The struggle between Nicholas Biddle and Andrew Jackson.

______. THE ELECTION OF ANDREW JACKSON. Philadelphia: J.B. Lippincott, 1963. Reprint. Westport, Conn.: Greenwood Press, 1980. 232 p.

Points up the influence of party organization in Jackson's victory over Adams.

______. THE REVOLUTIONARY AGE OF ANDREW JACKSON. New York: Harper and Row, 1976. x, 205 p.

A very lively recreation of the issues and personalities prominent in the age of Jackson.

Rogin, Michael Paul. FATHERS AND CHILDREN: ANDREW JACKSON AND THE SUBJUGATION OF THE AMERICAN INDIANS. New York: Knopf, 1975. xii, 373 p.

Satz, Ronald N. AMERICAN INDIAN POLICY IN THE JACKSONIAN ERA. Lincoln: University of Nebraska Press, 1974. xii, 343 p.

Schlesinger, Arthur M., Jr. THE AGE OF JACKSON. Boston: Little, Brown, 1945. xiv, 577 p.

Pulitzer Prize winner. Pictures Jackson as an intelligent as well as courageous champion of the laborer and the farmer against speculative capital and entrenched privilege.

Syrett, Harold Coffin. ANDREW JACKSON: HIS CONTRIBUTION TO THE AMERICAN TRADITION. Westport, Conn.: Greenwood Press, 1971. 298 p.

Includes letters, presidential messages, and addresses of Jackson.

Van Deusen, Glyndon B. THE JACKSONIAN ERA, 1828-1848. New York: Harper and Brothers, 1959. xvi, 291 p.

Standard political history of the Jacksonian-Whig rivalry.

Ward, John William. ANDREW JACKSON: SYMBOL FOR AN AGE. New York: Oxford University Press, 1955. xii, 274 p.

A good introductory treatment which utilizes social science insights into the nature of Jacksonian democracy.

White, Leonard D. THE JACKSONIANS: A STUDY IN ADMINISTRATIVE HISTORY, 1829-1861. New York: Macmillan, 1954. xii, 593 p.

A very basic work on the presidency, the cabinet, Congress and the courts during the Jacksonian period.

ARTICLES

Barbee, David Rankin. "Andrew Jackson and Peggy O'Neale from 1823 to 1837." TENNESSEE HISTORICAL QUARTERLY 15 (March 1956): 37-52.

Belohlavek, John M. "Andrew Jackson and the Malaysian Pirates: A Question of Diplomacy and Politics." TENNESSEE HISTORICAL QUARTERLY 36 (Spring 1977):, 19-29.

______. "'Let the Eagle Soar!': Democratic Constraints on the Foreign Policy of Andrew Jackson." PRESIDENTIAL STUDIES QUARTERLY 10 (Winter 1980): 36-50.

Brasington, George Figures. "Jackson, Calhoun, and State Rights." EMORY UNIVERSITY QUARTERLY 15 (October 1959): 168-75.

Brent, Robert A. "The Triumph of Jacksonian Democracy in the United States." SOUTHERN QUARTERLY 7 (October 1968): 43-57.

Burke, John Emmett. "Andrew Jackson as Seen by Foreigners." TENNESSEE HISTORICAL QUARTERLY 10 (March 1951): 25-45.

Cain, Marvin R. "William Wirt against Andrew Jackson: Reflections on an Era." MID-AMERICA 47 (April 1965): 113-38.

Chase, James Staton. "Jacksonian Democracy and the Rise of the Nominating Convention." MID-AMERICA 45 (October 1963): 229-49.

Chroust, Anton-Hermann. "Did President Jackson Actually Threaten the Supreme Court of the United States with the Nonenforcement of Its Injunction against the State of Georgia?" AMERICAN JOURNAL OF LEGAL HISTORY 4 (January 1960): 76-78.

Evidence, 1831, interpreted by the author as supporting an affirmative answer.

Curtis, James C. "Andrew Jackson and His Cabinet: Some New Evidence." TENNESSEE HISTORICAL QUARTERLY 27 (Summer 1968): 157-64.

DeRosier, Arthur H., Jr. "Andrew Jackson and Negotiations for the Removal of the Choctaw Indians." HISTORIAN 29 (May 1967): 342-62.

Dorfman, Joseph. "The Jackson Wage-Earner Thesis." AMERICAN HISTORICAL REVIEW 54 (January 1949): 296-306.

Argues that the "workingmen's movement" of the Jackson era did not represent urban labor at all. Instead of labor reform, they actually favored better business conditions.

Downes, Randoph Chandler, ed. "How Andrew Jackson Settled the Ohio-Michigan Boundary Dispute of 1835." NORTHWESTERN OHIO QUARTERLY 23 (Autumn 1951): 186-90.

Farrell, Brian. "Bellona and the General: Andrew Jackson and the Affair of Mrs. Eaton." HISTORY TODAY 8 (July 1958): 474-84.

Goff, Reda C. "A Physical Profile of Andrew Jackson." TENNESSEE HISTORICAL QUARTERLY 28 (Fall 1969): 297-309.

Green, F.M. "On Tour with President Andrew Jackson." NEW ENGLAND QUARTERLY 36 (June 1963): 209-28.

Hammond, Bray. "Jackson, Biddle, and the Bank of the United States." JOURNAL OF ECONOMIC HISTORY 7 (May 1947): 1-23.

_____. "Jackson's Fight with the 'Money Power': Old Hickory's Attack on Biddle's Bank Had Some Unexpected Consequences." AMERICAN HERITAGE 7 (June 1956): 8-11, 100-103.

Hoffman, William S. "Andrew Jackson, State Rightist: The Case of the Georgia Indians." TENNESSEE HISTORICAL QUARTERLY 11 (December 1952): 329-45.

On litigation involving Georgia and the Supreme Court.

Hoogenboom, Ari, and Ershkowitz, Herbert. "Levi Woodbury's 'Intimate Memoranda' of the Jackson Administration." PENNSYLVANIA MAGAZINE OF HISTORY AND BIOGRAPHY 92 (October 1968): 507-15.

Horn, Stanley F. "The Hermitage: Home of Andrew Jackson." TENNESSEE HISTORICAL QUARTERLY 20 (March 1961): 3-19.

Jackson, Carlton. "Another Time, Another Place: The Attempted Assassination of Andrew Jackson." TENNESSEE HISTORICAL QUARTERLY 26 (Summer 1967): 184-90.

_____. "The Internal Improvement Vetoes of Andrew Jackson." TENNESSEE HISTORICAL QUARTERLY 25 (Fall 1966): 261-80.

Kupfer, Barbara Stern. "A Presidential Patron of the Sport of Kings: Andrew Jackson." TENNESSEE HISTORICAL QUARTERLY 29 (Fall 1970): 243-55.

Ladies' Hermitage Association. "The Historic Hermitage Properties." Hermitage, Tenn.: 1972. 54 p.

A handbook.

Longaker, Richard P. "Andrew Jackson and the Judiciary." POLITICAL SCIENCE QUARTERLY 71 (September 1956): 341-64.

_____. "Was Jackson's Kitchen Cabinet a Cabinet?" MISSISSIPPI VALLEY HISTORICAL REVIEW 44 (June 1957): 94-108.

McBride, Robert M. "Andrew Jackson and the Bank of the United States: A Footnote." TENNESSEE HISTORICAL QUARTERLY 21 (December 1962): 377-78.

McCormick, Richard Patrick. "New Perspectives on Jacksonian Politics." AMERICAN HISTORICAL REVIEW 65 (January 1960): 288-301.

Evidence that none of the Jackson elections (1824-36) involved a mighty democratic uprising.

Marshall, Lynn L. "The Authorship of Jackson's Bank Veto Message." MISSISSIPPI VALLEY HISTORICAL REVIEW 50 (December 1963): 466-77.

Meyers, Marvin. "The Jacksonian Persuasion." AMERICAN QUARTERLY 5 (Spring 1953): 3-15.

On the political doctrines of Andrew Jackson, 1828-37.

Morris, Richard B. "Andrew Jackson, Strikebreaker." AMERICAN HISTORICAL REVIEW 55 (October 1949): 54-68.

Intervention of the federal government in a labor dispute near Williamsport, Maryland, 1834.

Owsley, Harriet Chappell. "Discoveries Made in Editing the Papers of Andrew Jackson." MANUSCRIPTS 27 (Fall 1975): 275-79.

"The Papers of Andrew Jackson." GEORGIA HISTORICAL QUARTERLY 56 (Winter 1972): 587-88.

Pessen, Edward. "Did Labor Support Jackson? The Boston Story." POLITICAL SCIENCE QUARTERLY 64 (June 1949): 262-74.

_____. "Should Labor Have Supported Jackson? Or Questions the Quantitative Studies Do Not Answer." LABOR HISTORY 13 (Summer 1972): 427-37.

Plous, Harold J. "Jackson, the Bank War, and Liberalism." SOUTHWESTERN SOCIAL SCIENCE QUARTERLY 38 (September 1957): 99-110.

Evidence against Jackson as a liberal in the economic sense (1817-36).

Prucha, Francis P. "Andrew Jackson's Indian Policy: A Reassessment." JOURNAL OF AMERICAN HISTORY 56 (December 1969): 527-39.

Robbins, Peggy. "Andrew and Rachel Jackson." AMERICAN HISTORY ILLUSTRATED 12 (August 1977): 22-28.

Satz, Ronald N. "Remini's Andrew Jackson (1767-1821): Jackson and the Indians." TENNESSEE HISTORICAL QUARTERLY (Summer 1979): 158-66.

Sellers, Charles Grier, Jr. "Andrew Jackson Versus the Historians." MISSISSIPPI VALLEY HISTORICAL REVIEW 44 (March 1958): 615-34.

_____. "Jackson Men with Feet of Clay." AMERICAN HISTORICAL REVIEW 62 (April 1957): 537-51.

On the motives of four Tennessee leaders in promoting the prospective candidacy of Andrew Jackson for president.

Sharp, James Roger. "Andrew Jackson and the Limits of Presidential Power." CONGRESSIONAL STUDIES 7 (Winter 1980): 63-80.

Smith, Elbert B. "Francis P. Blair and the GLOBE: Nerve Center of the Jacksonian Democracy." REGISTER OF THE KENTUCKY HISTORICAL SOCIETY 57 (October 1957): 340-53.

_____. "'Now Defend Yourself, You Damned Rascal.'" AMERICAN HERITAGE 9 (February 1958): 44-47, 106.

Somit, Albert. "Andrew Jackson: Legend and Reality." TENNESSEE HISTORICAL QUARTERLY 22 (December 1948): 291-313.

_____. "Andrew Jackson as Administrator." PUBLIC ADMINISTRATION REVIEW 8 (Summer 1948): 188-96.

_____. "Andrew Jackson as an Administrative Reformer." TENNESSEE HISTORICAL QUARTERLY 13 (September 1954): 204-23.

_____. "Andrew Jackson as Political Theorist." TENNESSEE HISTORICAL QUARTERLY 8 (June 1949): 99-120.

_____. "New Papers: Some Sidelights upon Jacksonian Administration." MISSISSIPPI VALLEY HISTORICAL REVIEW 35 (June 1948): 91-98.

Stickley, J.W. "Catholic Ceremonies in the White House, 1832-1833: Andrew Jackson's Forgotten Ward, Mary Lewis." CATHOLIC HISTORICAL REVIEW 51 (July 1965): 192-98.

Thomas, Robert Charles. "Andrew Jackson versus France: American Policy toward France, 1834-36." TENNESSEE HISTORICAL QUARTERLY 35 (Spring 1976): 51-64.

Tucker, Edward L., ed. "The Attempted Assassination of President Jackson: A Letter by Richard Henry Wilde." GEORGIA HISTORICAL QUARTERLY 58 (suppl. 1974): 193-99.

Wallace, Sarah Agnes, ed. "Opening Days of Jackson's Presidency as Seen in Private Letters." TENNESSEE HISTORICAL QUARTERLY 9 (December 1950): 367-71.

Two letters by Alfred Mordecai dated Washington, D.C., 11 February and 5 March 1829.

Wilson, Major L. "Andrew Jackson: The Great Compromiser." TENNESSEE HISTORICAL QUARTERLY 26 (Spring 1967): 64-78.

Wyllie, J.C. "Footnote for an Andrew Jackson Bibliography." PAPERS OF THE BIBLIOGRAPHICAL SOCIETY OF AMERICA 59 (October 1965): 437.

Young, Mary Elizabeth. "Indian Removal and Land Allotment: The Civilized Tribes and Jacksonian Justice." AMERICAN HISTORICAL REVIEW 64 (October 1958): 31-45.

Chapter 19

MARTIN VAN BUREN, 1837-41

BIBLIOGRAPHY

Sloan, Irving J., ed. MARTIN VAN BUREN, 1782-1862: CHRONOLOGY-DOCUMENTS-BIBLIOGRAPHICAL AIDS. Presidential Chronologies Series. Dobbs Ferry, N.Y.: Oceana Publications, 1969. 116 p.

SOURCE MATERIAL

Van Buren, Martin. THE AUTOBIOGRAPHY OF MARTIN VAN BUREN. Vol. 2, Annual Report of the American Historical Association for the Year 1918. Edited by John C. Fitzpatrick. Washington, D.C.: Government Printing Office, 1920. Reprint. New York: A.M. Kelley, 1969. 808 p.

BIOGRAPHIES

Alexander, Holmes Moss. THE AMERICAN TALLEYRAND: THE CAREER AND CONTEMPORARIES OF MARTIN VAN BUREN, EIGHTH PRESIDENT. New York: Russell and Russell, 1968. 430 p.

Critical of Van Buren.

Lynch, Denis Tilden. AN EPOCH AND A MAN: MARTIN VAN BUREN AND HIS TIMES. New York: H. Liveright, 1929. Reprint. Port Washington, N.Y.: Kennikat Press, 1971. 566 p.

Shepard, Edward Morse. MARTIN VAN BUREN. Boston: Houghton Mifflin, 1899. Reprint. New York: AMS Press, 1972. vii, 499 p.

Sympathetic and still useful.

MONOGRAPHS

Curtis, James C. THE FOX AT BAY: MARTIN VAN BUREN AND THE PRESIDENCY, 1837-1841. Lexington: University Press of Kentucky, 1970. xi, 233 p.

The first detailed examination of the Van Buren presidency.

Gunderson, Robert Gray. THE LOG-CABIN CAMPAIGN. Lexington: University of Kentucky Press, 1957. viii, 292 p.

Remini, Robert Vincent. MARTIN VAN BUREN AND THE MAKING OF THE DEMOCRATIC PARTY. New York: Columbia University Press, 1959. viii, 271 p.

Smith, Richard Williams. THE CAREER OF MARTIN VAN BUREN IN CONNECTION WITH THE SLAVERY CONTROVERSY FROM 1814 THROUGH THE ELECTION OF 1840. Ann Arbor, Mich.: University Microfilms, 1959. iii, 379 p.

Van Deusen, Glyndon G. THE JACKSONIAN ERA, 1828-1848. New York: Harper, 1959. xvi, 291 p.

Good synthesis of many monographs on the period.

ARTICLES

Carleton, William G. "Political Aspects of the Van Buren Era." SOUTH ATLANTIC QUARTERLY 1 (April 1951): 167-85.

Carson, Gerald. "The Speech That Toppled a President." AMERICAN HERITAGE 15 (August 1964): 108-11.

Gatell, Frank Otto. "Sober Second Thoughts on Van Buren, the Albany Regency, and the Wall Street Conspiracy." JOURNAL OF AMERICAN HISTORY 53 (June 1966): 19-40.

Harrison, Joseph Hobson, Jr. "Martin Van Buren and His Southern Supporters." JOURNAL OF SOUTHERN HISTORY 22 (November 1956): 438-58.

Koenig, Louis W. "Rise of the Little Magician." AMERICAN HERITAGE 13 (June 1962): 29-31.

McCracken, George Englert. "The Ancestry of President Martin Van Buren." AMERICAN GENEALOGIST 35 (April 1956): 73-75.

Mintz, Max M. "The Political Ideas of Martin Van Buren." NEW YORK HISTORY 30 (October 1949): 422-48.

Murray, Anne Wood. "Van Buren versus Harrison: The Campaign of 1840." AMERICAN COLLECTOR 17 (October 1948): 24-25.

On souvenirs of the election in stoneware, glass, cloth, and other materials.

Nigro, Felix A. "The Van Buren Confirmation before the Senate." WESTERN POLITICAL QUARTERLY 14 (March 1961): 148-59.

Rayback, Joseph G. "Martin Van Buren's Break with James K. Polk: the Record." NEW YORK HISTORY 34 (January 1955): 51-62.

_____. "Martin Van Buren's Desire for Revenge in the Campaign of 1848." MISSISSIPPI VALLEY HISTORICAL REVIEW 40 (March 1954): 707-16.

Remini, Robert Vincent. "The Albany Regency." NEW YORK HISTORY 39 (October 1958): 341-55.

_____. "Martin Van Buren and the Tariff of Abominations." AMERICAN HISTORICAL REVIEW 63 (July 1958): 903-17.

Van Buren, Martin. "A Father's Advice on How to Become President." Edited by Nathaniel E. Stein. MANUSCRIPTS 9 (Fall 1957): 261-64.

Van Buren to his son John.

Chapter 20

WILLIAM HENRY HARRISON, 1841

BIBLIOGRAPHY

Durfee, David A. WILLIAM HENRY HARRISON, 1773-1841; John Tyler 1790-1862: CHRONOLOGY-DOCUMENTS-BIBLIOGRAPHICAL AIDS. Presidential Chronologies Series. Dobbs Ferry, N.Y.: Oceana Publications, 1970. 144 p.

BIOGRAPHIES

Cleaves, Freeman. OLD TIPPECANOE: WILLIAM HENRY HARRISON AND HIS TIME. New York: Scribner, 1939. xiv, 422 p.

Standard treatment. Well-researched. Good on both the military and political activities of Harrison.

Goebel, Dorothy Burne. WILLIAM HENRY HARRISON: A POLITICAL BIOGRAPHY. Indianapolis: Historical Bureau of the Indiana Library and Historical Department, 1926. Reprint. Philadelphia: Porcupine Press, 1974. xi, 456 p.

MONOGRAPH

Gunderson, Robert Gray. THE LOG-CABIN CAMPAIGN. Lexington: University of Kentucky Press, 1957. Reprint. Westport, Conn.: Greenwood Press, 1977. viii, 292 p.

Colorful account of the famous Whig triumph in which they outwitted the Democrats (1840).

ARTICLES

Bond, Beverly, Jr. "William Henry Harrison and the Old Northwest." BULLETIN OF THE HISTORICAL AND PHILOSOPHICAL SOCIETY OF OHIO 7 (January 1949): 10-17.

Dowdey, Clifford. "The Harrisons of Berkeley Hundred." AMERICAN HERITAGE 8 (April 1957): 58-70.

Fabian, Monroe H. "A Portrait of William Henry Harrison." PROLOGUE 1 (Winter 1969): 29-32.

Gunderson, Robert Gray. "Webster in Linsey-Woolsey." QUARTERLY JOURNAL OF SPEECH 27 (February 1951): 23-30.

On Daniel Webster's speeches in support of William Henry Harrison, 1840.

Marshall, Lynn L. "The Strange Stillbirth of the Whig Party." AMERICAN HISTORICAL REVIEW 72 (January 1967): 445-68.

Miles, Edwin A. "The Whig Party and the Menace of Caesar." TENNESSEE HISTORICAL QUARTERLY 27 (Winter 1968): 361-79.

The conflict within the Whig party, which feared militarism, when Harrison emerged as their candidate.

Peckham, Howard Henry. "Tears for Old Tippecanoe: Religious Interpretations of President Harrison's Death." PROCEEDINGS OF THE AMERICAN ANTIQUARIAN SOCIETY 69 (15 April 1959): 17-36.

Reaction to the death of Harrison, the first president to die in office.

Volwiler, Albert Tangeman. "The Early Empire Days of the United States." WEST VIRGINIA HISTORY 18 (January 1957): 116-27.

Walker, Kenneth R. "The Death of a President." NORTHWEST OHIO QUARTERLY 28 (Summer 1956): 157-62.

Chapter 21

JOHN TYLER, 1841-45

BIBLIOGRAPHY

Durfee, David A., ed. WILLIAM HENRY HARRISON, 1773-1841; JOHN TYLER, 1790-1862: CHRONOLOGY-DOCUMENTS-BIBLIOGRAPHICAL AIDS. Presidential Chronologies Series. Dobbs Ferry, N.Y.: Oceana Publications, 1970. 144 p.

SOURCE MATERIAL

Tyler, Lyon Gardiner. THE LETTERS AND TIMES OF THE TYLERS. 3 vols. 1884-86. Reprint. New York: DaCapo Press, 1970.

The most valuable published source of material on John Tyler.

BIOGRAPHIES

Chitwood, Oliver Perry. JOHN TYLER, CHAMPION OF THE OLD SOUTH. New York: Appleton-Century, 1939. xv, 496 p.

Very favorable interpretation based on family papers.

Hoyt, Edwin Palmer. JOHN TYLER. London: Abelard-Schuman, 1969. 159 p.

Biography for young readers.

Seager, Robert. AND TYLER TOO. New York: McGraw-Hill, 1963. xvii, 681 p.

Excellent social history of President Tyler, his wife Julia Gardiner, and their large family. Based largely upon the Gardiner Papers held at Yale University.

John Tyler

MONOGRAPHS

Fraser, Hugh Russell. DEMOCRACY IN THE MAKING: THE JACKSON-TYLER ERA. Indianapolis: Bobbs-Merrill, 1938. 334 p.

Lambert, Oscar Doane. PRESIDENTIAL POLITICS IN THE UNITED STATES, 1841-1844. Durham, N.C.: Duke University Press, 1936. ix, 220 p.

Political history from the election of W.H. Harrison to the campaign of 1844 and Tyler's difficulties as the first vice president to become president on the death of his running mate.

Merk, Frederick, with the collaboration of Lois Bannister Merk. FRUITS OF PROPAGANDA IN THE TYLER ADMINISTRATION. Cambridge, Mass.: Harvard University Press, 1971. x, 259 p.

Morgan, Robert J. A WHIG EMBATTLED: THE PRESIDENCY UNDER JOHN TYLER. Lincoln: University of Nebraska Press, 1954. Reprint. Hamden, Conn.: Archon Books, 1974. xxi, 199 p.

Perling, J.J. A PRESIDENT TAKES A WIFE. Middleburg, Va.: Denlinger's, 1959. 369 p.

Fiction, but worth reading for period and personalities.

Poage, George Rawlings. HENRY CLAY AND THE WHIG PARTY. Chapel Hill: University of North Carolina Press, 1936. 295 p.

The Tyler administration as viewed by the Whigs.

ARTICLES

Barbee, David Rankin, ed. "Tyler's Intentions Become Achievements." TYLER'S QUARTERLY OF HISTORY AND GENEALOGICAL MAGAZINE 31 (April 1950): 219-21.

Bradshaw, Herbert Clarence. "A President's Bride at 'Sherwood Forest.'" VIRGINIA CAVALCADE 7 (Spring 1958): 30-39.

Discusses the estate in Virginia bought by Tyler in 1842, where he lived with his second wife, Julia Gardiner, and their seven children from 1845 to his death in 1862.

Dinnerstein, Leonard. "The Accession of John Tyler to the Presidency." VIRGINIA MAGAZINE OF HISTORY AND BIOGRAPHY 70 (October 1962): 447-58.

Gotleib, Howard Bernard, and Grimes, Gail. "President Tyler and the Gardiners: A New Portrait." YALE UNIVERSITY LIBRARY GAZETTE 34 (July 1959): 2-12.

> Information from the Gardiner family papers about John Tyler and Julia Gardiner, his second wife, from 1844 to 1862.

Hampton, Vernon B. "Intimate Associations of John Tyler and Julia Gardiner Tyler with Staten Island." STATEN ISLAND HISTORIAN, July-September 1959.

Kleber, Louis C. "John Tyler." HISTORY TODAY 25 (October 1975): 697-703.

Krueger, David W. "The Clay-Tyler Feud, 1841-1842." FILSON CLUB HISTORICAL QUARTERLY 42 (April 1968): 162-77.

Maness, Lonnie E., and Chesteen, Richard D. "The First Attempt at Presidential Impeachment: Partisan Politics and Intra-Party Conflict at Loose [1843]." PRESIDENTIAL STUDIES QUARTERLY 10 (Winter 1980): 51-62.

Shelley, Fred. "The Vice President Receives Bad News in Williamsburg: A Letter of James Lyons to John Tyler." VIRGINIA MAGAZINE OF HISTORY AND BIOGRAPHY 76 (July 1968): 337-39.

Siebeneck, Henry King. "John Tyler: Our First Accidental President." WESTERN PENNSYLVANIA HISTORICAL MAGAZINE 34 (March and June 1951): 35-50, 119-33.

Stathis, Stephen W. "John Tyler's Presidential Succession: A Reappraisal." PROLOGUE 8 (Winter 1976): 223-36.

Chapter 22

JAMES K. POLK, 1845-49

BIBLIOGRAPHY

Farrell, John J., ed. JAMES K. POLK, 1795-1849: CHRONOLOGY-DOCUMENTS-BIBLIOGRAPHICAL AIDS. Presidential Chronology Series. Dobbs Ferry, N.Y.: Oceana Publications, 1970. 92 p.

SOURCE MATERIALS

Polk, James Knox. CORRESPONDENCE OF JAMES K. POLK. 5 vols. Edited by Herbert Weaver et al. Nashville: Vanderbilt University Press, 1969-79.

Covers the period 1817-41.

______. THE DIARY OF JAMES K. POLK DURING HIS PRESIDENCY, 1845 TO 1849, NOW FIRST PRINTED FROM THE ORIGINAL MANUSCRIPT IN THE COLLECTIONS OF THE CHICAGO HISTORICAL SOCIETY. 4 vols. Edited and annotated by Milo Milton Quaife. Chicago: A.C. McClure and Co., 1910. Reprint. New York: Kraus Reprint Co., 1970.

BIOGRAPHIES

McCormac, Eugene Irving. JAMES K. POLK, A POLITICAL BIOGRAPHY. Berkeley: University of California Press, 1922. x, 746 p. Reprint. New York: Russell and Russell, 1965.

Standard work. Rates Polk highly.

Morrel, Martha McBride. "YOUNG HICKORY," THE LIFE AND TIMES OF PRESIDENT JAMES K. POLK. New York: E.P. Dutton, 1949. 381 p.

Sellers, Charles Grier. JAMES K. POLK, JACKSONIAN, 1794-1843. Princeton, N.J.: Princeton University Press, 1957. xiv, 526 p.

_____. JAMES K. POLK, CONTINENTALIST, 1843-1846. Princeton, N.J.: Princeton University Press, 1966. x, 513 p.

MONOGRAPHS

McCoy, Charles Allan. POLK AND THE PRESIDENCY. Austin: University of Texas Press, 1960. xiii, 238 p.

Sympathetic to Polk's use of presidential authority and direction regarding the Mexican war.

Schroeder, John H. MR. POLK'S WAR: AMERICAN OPPOSITION AND DISSENT, 1846-1848. Madison: University of Wisconsin Press, 1973. xvi, 184 p.

ARTICLES

Armistead, George H., Jr. "The Void Provision of a President's Will." TENNESSEE HISTORICAL QUARTERLY 15 (June 1956): 136-40.

Everett, Robert B. "James K. Polk and the Election of 1844 in Tennessee." WEST TENNESSEE HISTORICAL SOCIETY PAPERS 16 (1962): 5-28.

Gilley, B.H. "'Polk's War' and the Louisiana Press." LOUISIANA HISTORY 20 (Winter 1979): 5-23.

Graebner, Norman A. "James K. Polk: A Study in Federal Patronage." MISSISSIPPI VALLEY HISTORICAL REVIEW 38 (March 1952): 613-32.

Horn, James J. "Trends in Historical Interpretation: James K. Polk." NORTH CAROLINA HISTORICAL REVIEW 42 (October 1965): 454-64.

Nelson, Anna Kasten. "Secret Agents and Security Leaks: President Polk and the Mexican War." JOURNALISM QUARTERLY 52 (Spring 1975): 9-14.

Thurber, James. "Something about [James K.] Polk." WISCONSIN MAGAZINE OF HISTORY 50 (Winter 1967): 145-46.

Chapter 23

ZACHARY TAYLOR, 1849-50

BIBLIOGRAPHY

Farrell, John J., ed. ZACHARY TAYLOR, 1784-1850; MILLARD FILLMORE, 1800-1874: CHRONOLOGY-DOCUMENTS-BIBLIOGRAPHICAL AIDS. Presidential Chronologies Series. Dobbs Ferry, N.Y.: Oceana Publications, 1971. 118 p.

BIOGRAPHIES

Dyer, Brainerd. ZACHARY TAYLOR. Baton Rouge: Louisiana State University Press, 1946. xi, 455 p.

Especially good on Taylor's executive-legislative struggle.

Hamilton, Holman. ZACHARY TAYLOR. 2 vols. Indianapolis: Bobbs-Merrill, 1941-51.

Admirable, well-researched, and well-written study based upon twenty years' work.

Hoyt, Edwin P. ZACHARY TAYLOR. Chicago: Reilly and Lee, 1966. 162 p.

A brief biography for younger readers.

McKinley, Silas Bent, and Bent, Silas. OLD ROUGH AND READY: THE LIFE AND TIMES OF ZACHARY TAYLOR. New York: Vanguard Press, 1946. 329 p.

Contains some errors.

MONOGRAPHS

Hamilton, Holman. THE THREE KENTUCKY PRESIDENTS: LINCOLN, TAYLOR,

DAVIS. Lexington: University Press of Kentucky, 1978. xv, 69 p.

A bicentennial contribution by a well-known authority.

Rayback, Joseph G. FREE SOIL: THE ELECTION OF 1848. Lexington: University Press of Kentucky, 1970. ix, 326 p.

ARTICLES

Dewitt, D. "Medalets of the Presidential Campaign of 1848." NUMISMATIST 61 (November 1948): 726-44.

Hamilton, Holman. "Abraham Lincoln and Zachary Taylor." LINCOLN HERALD 53 (Fall 1951): 14-19.

_____. "'A Youth of Good Morals': Zachary Taylor Sends His Only Son to School." FILSON CLUB HISTORICAL QUARTERLY 27 (October 1953): 303-7.

Instructions as to the college preparation of Richard Taylor (1826-79).

_____. "Zachary Taylor: Resident or Fighter in 15 States." AMERICAN HERITAGE 4 (Summer 1953): 10-13.

_____. "Zachary Taylor and Minnesota." MINNESOTA HISTORY 30 (June 1949): 97-110.

On Lieutenant Colonel Taylor as commandant of Fort Snelling, 1828-29, and the aid of Minnesotans in his nomination and election as president.

Ketchum, Richard M. "Faces from the Past, XII." AMERICAN HERITAGE 14 (October 1963): 53.

Portrait and biographical sketch.

Lavender, David. "How to Make It to the White House without Really Trying." AMERICAN HERITAGE 18 (June 1967): 26-27, 80-86.

Murray, A.W. "Zachary Taylor for President: The Campaign of 1848." AMERICAN COLLECTOR 17 (November 1948): 15-17.

Spencer, Herbert R. "Explosion on the U.S.S. MICHIGAN." INLAND SEAS 16 (Spring 1960): 32-35.

On the visit of President Taylor and Vice President Fillmore to Erie, and the accidental death of two men on the MICHIGAN while firing a salute, August 1849.

Spurlin, Charles. "With Taylor and McCulloch through the Battle of Monterey." TEXAS MILITARY HISTORY [now titled MILITARY HISTORY OF TEXAS AND THE SOUTHWEST] 6 (Fall 1967).

Taylor, Zachary. "Zachary Taylor and Old Fort Snelling: A Letter." MINNESOTA HISTORY 28 (March 1947): 15-19.

_____. "Zachary Taylor on Jackson and the Military Establishment, 1835." Edited by W.D. Hoyt. AMERICAN HISTORICAL REVIEW 51 (April 1946): 480-84.

Walton, Brian G. "The Elections for the Thirtieth Congress and the Presidential Candidacy of Zachary Taylor." JOURNAL OF SOUTHERN HISTORY 35 (May 1969): 186-202.

Chapter 24

MILLARD FILLMORE, 1850-53

BIBLIOGRAPHY

Farrell, John J., ed. ZACHARY TAYLOR, 1784-1850; MILLARD FILLMORE, 1800-1874: CHRONOLOGY-DOCUMENTS-BIBLIOGRAPHICAL AIDS. Presidential Chronologies Series. Dobbs Ferry, N.Y.: Oceana Publications, 1971. 118 p.

SOURCE MATERIALS

Dix, Dorothea Lynde. THE LADY AND THE PRESIDENT: THE LETTERS OF DOROTHEA DIX & MILLARD FILLMORE. Edited by Charles M. Snyder. Lexington: University Press of Kentucky, 1975. 400 p.

Based upon correspondence opened in New York state in 1966.

Fillmore, Millard. MILLARD FILLMORE PAPERS. 2 vols. Edited by Frank H. Severance. Buffalo, N.Y.: Buffalo Historical Society, 1907. Reprint. New York: Kraus Reprint Co., 1970.

BIOGRAPHIES

Barre, W.L. THE LIFE AND PUBLIC SERVICES OF MILLARD FILLMORE. 1856. Reprint. New York: B. Franklin, 1971. 408 p.

Rayback, Robert J. MILLARD FILLMORE: BIOGRAPHY OF A PRESIDENT. Buffalo, N.Y.: H. Stewart, 1959. xv, 470 p. Bibliog.

Readable. Dispels image of Fillmore as an anti-Catholic bigot. Excellent bibliography.

Scarry, Robert J. MILLARD FILLMORE: THE MAN AND THE CABIN. Moravia, N.Y.: By the author, 1965. 37 p. Bibliog.

See also next entry.

_____. MILLARD FILLMORE, 13TH PRESIDENT. Moravia, N.Y.: By the author, 1970. 58 p.

Later edition of MILLARD FILLMORE, THE MAN AND THE CABIN (see entry above).

MONOGRAPHS

Grayson, Benson Lee. THE UNKNOWN PRESIDENT: THE ADMINISTRATION OF PRESIDENT MILLARD FILLMORE. Washington, D.C.: University Press of America, 1981. 179 p.

Hamilton, Holman. PROLOGUE TO CONFLICT: THE CRISIS AND COMPROMISE OF 1850. Lexington: University of Kentucky Press, 1964. viii, 236 p.

Merk, Frederick. MANIFEST DESTINY AND MISSION IN AMERICAN HISTORY: A REINTERPRETATION. New York: Knopf, 1963. ix, 265 p.

ARTICLES

Russel, Robert R. "What Was the Compromise of 1850?" JOURNAL OF SOUTHERN HISTORY 22 (August 1956): 292-309.

Snyder, Charles M. "Forgotten Fillmore Papers Examined: Sources for Reinterpretation of a Little-Known President." AMERICAN ARCHIVIST 32 (January 1969): 11-14.

Chapter 25

FRANKLIN PIERCE, 1853-57

BIBLIOGRAPHY

Sloan, Irving J., ed. FRANKLIN PIERCE, 1804-1869: CHRONOLOGY-DOCUMENTS-BIBLIOGRAPHICAL AIDS. Presidential Chronologies Series. Dobbs Ferry, N.Y.: Oceana Publications, 1968. v, 90 p.

BIOGRAPHIES

Hawthorne, Nathaniel. THE LIFE OF FRANKLIN PIERCE. Boston: Ticknor, Reed and Fields, 1852. Reprint. New York: Garrett Press, 1970. ix, 144 p.

A campaign biography by Pierce's college classmate at Bowdoin.

Hoyt, Edwin P. FRANKLIN PIERCE: THE FOURTEENTH PRESIDENT OF THE UNITED STATES. London: Abelard-Schuman, 1972. 157 p.

Intended for younger readers.

Nichols, Roy Franklin. FRANKLIN PIERCE, YOUNG HICKORY OF THE GRANITE HILLS. 2d ed., completely rev. Philadelphia: University of Pennsylvania Press, 1958. xvii, 625 p. Bibliog.

Excellent scholarship by one of the great masters of nineteenth-century American political history. A very good bibliography.

MONOGRAPH

Nevins, Allan. ORDEAL OF THE UNION. 2 vols. New York: Scribner, 1947.

Excellent political history through the Pierce administration.

ARTICLES

Anderson, Louise K. "Franklin Pierce and the Pierce Mansion." D.A.R. MAGAZINE 94 (May 1960): 374-75.

Klement, Frank L. "Franklin Pierce and the Treason Charges of 1861-1862." HISTORIAN 23 (August 1961): 436-48.

Nichols, Roy F. "The Kansas-Nebraska Act: A Century of Historiography." MISSISSIPPI VALLEY HISTORICAL REVIEW 43 (September 1956): 187-212.

Purcell, Richard J. "Franklin Pierce: A Forgotten President." CATHOLIC EDUCATIONAL REVIEW 31 (August 1933): 134-41.

Taylor, L.C. "Wife for Mr. Pierce." NEW ENGLAND QUARTERLY 28 (September 1955): 339-48

On Jane Appleton Pierce as the wife of Franklin Pierce, 1834-63.

Chapter 26

JAMES BUCHANAN, 1857-61

BIBLIOGRAPHY

Sloan, Irving J., ed. JAMES BUCHANAN, 1791-1868: CHRONOLOGY-DOCUMENTS-BIBLIOGRAPHICAL AIDS. Presidential Chronologies Series. Dobbs Ferry, N.Y.: Oceana Publications, 1968. v, 89 p.

SOURCE MATERIALS

Buchanan, James. THE WORKS OF JAMES BUCHANAN, COMPRISING HIS SPEECHES, STATE PAPERS, AND PRIVATE CORRESPONDENCE. 12 vols. Collected and edited by John Bassett Moore. Philadelphia: J.B. Lippincott, 1908-11.

Curtis, George Ticknor. LIFE OF JAMES BUCHANAN, FIFTEENTH PRESIDENT OF THE UNITED STATES. 2 vols. New York: Harper, 1883. Reprint. Freeport, N.Y.: Books for Libraries Press, 1969.

An early authorized biography based upon personal papers and access to Buchanan's family and friends. Contains personal correspondence.

Hoyt, Edwin Palmer. JAMES BUCHANAN. Chicago: Reilly and Lee, 1966. 150 p.

For young readers.

Klein, Philip Shriver. PRESIDENT JAMES BUCHANAN, A BIOGRAPHY. University Park: Pennsylvania State University, 1962. xviii, 506 p. Bibliog.

Definitive, yet very readable. Excellent bibliography.

MONOGRAPHS

Auchampaugh, Philip G. JAMES BUCHANAN AND HIS CABINET ON THE EVE OF

SECESSION. Lancaster, Pa.: Privately printed, 1926. ix, 224 p.

Favorable to Buchanan.

Nevins, Allan. THE EMERGENCE OF LINCOLN. 2 vols. New York: Scribner, 1950.

Covers the Buchanan administration, 1857-61.

Nichols, Roy F. THE DISRUPTION OF AMERICAN DEMOCRACY. New York: Macmillan, 1948. xviii, 612 p.

Pulitzer Prize winner. Excellent vignettes of major and minor political leaders. Outstanding analysis of the party process.

Smith, Elbert B. THE PRESIDENCY OF JAMES BUCHANAN. American Presidency Series. Lawrence: University Press of Kansas, 1975. xiii, 225 p.

ARTICLES

Auchampaugh, Philip G. "Political Techniques--1856 or Why the HERALD Went for Fremont." WESTERN POLITICAL QUARTERLY 1 (September 1948): 243-51.

Barondess, Benjamin. "Buchanan and the Dred Scott Justices." MANUSCRIPTS 10 (Winter 1958): 2-9.

Bóbr-Tylingo, Stanislaw. "James Buchanan and Poland in 1854." ANTEMURALE 23 (1979): 75-93.

Butler, Joseph T. "Two Documented Nineteenth-Century Rooms." ANTIQUES 73 (June 1949): 551-53.

Library at Buchanan's home, Wheatlands.

Carlson, Robert E. "James Buchanan and Public Office: An Appraisal." PENNSYLVANIA MAGAZINE OF HISTORY AND BIOGRAPHY 91 (July 1957): 255-79.

Davis, Robert Ralph, Jr. "James Buchanan and the Suppression of the Slave Trade, 1859-1861." PENNSYLVANIA HISTORY 33 (October 1966): 446-59.

_____, ed. "Buchanan Espionage: A Report on Illegal Slave Trading in the South in 1859." JOURNAL OF SOUTHERN HISTORY 37 (May 1971): 271-78.

Gates, Paul Wallace. "The Struggle for Land and the 'Irrepressible Conflict.'" POLITICAL SCIENCE QUARTERLY 66 (June 1951): 248-71.

On the political effects of the policies of James Buchanan regarding public lands in the West, 1857-61.

Johnson, Kenneth R., ed. "A Southern Student Describes the Inauguration of President James Buchanan." ALABAMA HISTORICAL QUARTERLY 31 (Fall-Winter 1969): 237-40.

Klein, Frederic S. "Wheatland: Home of James Buchanan." AMERICAN HERITAGE 5 (Spring 1954): 44-49.

Klein, Philip Shriver. "Bachelor Father: James Buchanan as a Family Man." WESTERN PENNSYLVANIA HISTORICAL MAGAZINE 50 (July 1967): 199-214.

______. "The Inauguration of President James Buchanan." JOURNAL OF THE LANCASTER COUNTY HISTORICAL SOCIETY 61 (October 1957): 145-68.

______. "James Buchanan: Selfish Politician or Christian Statesman?" JOURNAL OF PRESBYTERIAN HISTORY 42 (March 1964): 1-16.

______. "The Lost Love of a Bachelor President." AMERICAN HERITAGE 7 (December 1955): 20-21, 112-14.

______. "Patriotic Myths and Political Realities: Buchanan and the Origins of the Civil War." LOCK HAVEN REVIEW 15 (1974): 65-78.

Klingberg, Frank J. "James Buchanan and the Crises of the Union." JOURNAL OF SOUTHERN HISTORY 9 (November 1943): 455-74.

Meerse, David. "Buchanan, Corruption, and the Election of 1860." CIVIL WAR HISTORY 12 (June 1966): 116-31.

______. "Buchanan's Patronage Policy: An Attempt to Achieve Political Strength." PENNSYLVANIA HISTORY 40 (January 1973): 37-57.

Nevins, Allan. "The Needless Conflict: If Buchanan Had Met the Kansas Problem Firmly We Might Have Avoided Civil War." AMERICAN HERITAGE 7 (August 1955): 4-9, 88-90.

Rosenberger, Homer Tope. "Protecting the Buchanan Papers." JOURNAL OF THE LANCASTER COUNTY HISTORICAL SOCIETY 72 (1968): 137-69.

______. "To What Extent Did Harriet Lane Influence the Public Policies of James Buchanan?" JOURNAL OF THE LANCASTER COUNTY HISTORICAL SOCIETY 74 (1970): 1-22.

Russ, W.A., Jr. "Time Lag and Political Change as Seen in the Administrations of Buchanan and Hoover." SOUTH ATLANTIC QUARTERLY 46 (July 1947): 336-43.

Sceips, Paul J. "Buchanan and the Chiriqui Naval Station Sites." MILITARY AFFAIRS 18 (Summer 1954): 64-80.

Chapter 27

ABRAHAM LINCOLN, 1861-65

BIBLIOGRAPHIES

Angle, Paul McClelland. A SHELF OF LINCOLN BOOKS: A CRITICAL, SELECTIVE BIBLIOGRAPHY OF LINCOLNIANA. New Brunswick, N.J.: Rutgers University Press, 1946. Reprint. Westport, Conn.: Greenwood Press, 1972. xvii, 142 p.

Baker, Monty R. "Abraham Lincoln in Theses and Dissertations." LINCOLN HERALD 74 (Summer 1972): 107-11.

Elliot, Ian, ed. ABRAHAM LINCOLN, 1809-1865: CHRONOLOGY-DOCUMENTS-BIBLIOGRAPHICAL AIDS. Presidential Chronologies Series. Dobbs Ferry, N.Y.: Oceana Publications, 1970. vii, 144 p.

Gunderson, Robert G. "Another Shelf of Lincoln Books." QUARTERLY JOURNAL OF SPEECH 48 (October 1962): 308-13.

Searcher, Victor. LINCOLN TODAY: AN INTRODUCTION TO MODERN LINCOLNIANA. New York: T. Yoseloff, 1969. 342 p.

Well annotated.

SOURCE MATERIALS

Lincoln, Abraham. ABRAHAM LINCOLN: A DOCUMENTARY PORTRAIT THROUGH HIS SPEECHES AND WRITINGS. Edited and with an introduction by Don E. Fehrenbacher. New York: New American Library, 1964. xxix, 288 p.

_____. ABRAHAM LINCOLN: HIS AUTOBIOGRAPHICAL WRITINGS NOW BROUGHT TOGETHER FOR THE FIRST TIME AND PREFACED WITH AN INTRODUCTORY COMMENT BY PAUL M. ANGLE. New Brunswick, N.J.: Rutgers University Press, 1947. x, 62 p.

Writings dated, 1838–65.

______. ABRAHAM LINCOLN: HIS SPEECHES AND WRITINGS. Edited with critical and analytical notes by Roy P. Basler. Cleveland: World Publishing Co., 1946. 843 p.

______. ABRAHAM LINCOLN: SELECTED SPEECHES, MESSAGES, AND LETTERS. New York: Rinehart, 1957. xxi, 290 p.

______. ABRAHAM LINCOLN'S SPEECHES AND LETTERS, 1832–1865. New York: Dutton, 1957. xiii, 300 p.

______. THE COLLECTED WORKS OF ABRAHAM LINCOLN. 9 vols. Edited by Roy P. Basler. New Brunswick, N.J.: Rutgers University Press, 1953–55.

Covers the years, 1824–65. Volume 9 is a comprehensive index.

______. CREATED EQUAL? THE COMPLETE LINCOLN-DOUGLAS DEBATES OF 1858. Chicago: University of Chicago Press, 1958. xxxiii, 421 p.

______. IN THE NAME OF THE PEOPLE: SPEECHES AND WRITINGS OF LINCOLN AND DOUGLAS IN THE OHIO CAMPAIGN OF 1859. Columbus: Ohio State University Press for the Historical Society, 1959. x, 307 p.

______. THE LINCOLN-DOUGLAS DEBATES OF 1858. Edited by Robert W. Johannsen. New York: Oxford University Press, 1965. 330 p.

______. THE LINCOLN ENCYCLOPEDIA: THE SPOKEN AND WRITTEN WORDS OF A. LINCOLN ARRANGED FOR READY REFERENCE. Compiled and edited by Archer Hayes Shaw, with an introduction by David Chambers Mearns. New York: Macmillan, 1950. xii, 395 p.

Selections from about 1840 to 1865.

______. THE LITERARY WORKS OF ABRAHAM LINCOLN. Edited with an introduction by David D. Anderson. Columbus: Merrill, 1970. xiv, 274 p.

______. LIVING LINCOLN: THE MAN, HIS MIND, HIS TIMES, AND THE WAR HE FOUGHT RECONSTRUCTED FROM HIS OWN WRITINGS. Edited by Paul M. Angle and Earl Schenck Miers. New Brunswick, N.J.: Rutgers University Press, 1955. 673 p.

______. THE LIVING WORDS OF ABRAHAM LINCOLN: SELECTED WRITINGS OF A GREAT PRESIDENT. Edited by Edward Lewis and Jack Belck. Kansas City, Mo.: Hallmark Editions, 1967. 62 p.

_____. THE PHILOSOPHY OF ABRAHAM LINCOLN IN HIS OWN WORDS. Compiled by William E. Baringer. Indian Hills, Colo.: Falcon's Wing Press, 1959. xxxii, 167 p.

_____. QUOTATIONS FROM ABRAHAM LINCOLN. Edited Ralph Y. McGinnis. Chicago: Nelson-Hall, 1977. x, 134 p.

_____. A TREASURY OF LINCOLN QUOTATIONS. Compiled and edited by Fred Kerner. Garden City, N.Y.: Doubleday, 1965. ix, 320 p.

_____. UNCOLLECTED WORKS OF ABRAHAM LINCOLN: HIS LETTERS, ADDRESSES, AND OTHER PAPERS. Assembled and annotated by Rufus Rockwell Wilson et al. Elmira, N.Y.: Primavera Press, 1948. 693 p.

_____. THE WIT AND WISDOM OF ABRAHAM LINCOLN. New York: Pyramid Books, 1967. 63 p.

Lincoln, Robert Todd. A PORTRAIT OF ABRAHAM LINCOLN IN LETTERS BY HIS OLDEST SON. Edited by Paul M. Angle with the assistance of Richard G. Case. Chicago: Chicago Historical Society, 1968. xiii, 92 p.

Mearns, David C. THE LINCOLN PAPERS: THE STORY OF THE COLLECTION WITH SELECTIONS TO JULY 4, 1861. 2 vols. Garden City, N.Y.: Doubleday and Co., 1948.

Pratt, Harry Edward. ABRAHAM LINCOLN CHRONOLOGY, 1809-1865. Springfield: Illinois State Historical Library, 1955. 14 p.

BIOGRAPHIES

Agar, Herbert. ABRAHAM LINCOLN. Brief Lives Series. New York: Macmillan, 1952. 143 p.

Anderson, David D. ABRAHAM LINCOLN. New York: Twayne Publishers, 1970. 205 p.

Angle, Paul McClelland, ed. THE LINCOLN READER. New Brunswick, N.J.: Rutgers University Press, 1947. Reprint. Chicago: Rand, McNally, 1964. xii, 563 p.

A biography written by sixty-five authors.

Beveridge, Albert Jeremiah. ABRAHAM LINCOLN, 1809-1858. 2 vols. Boston: Houghton Mifflin, 1928.

Brogan, Denis W. ABRAHAM LINCOLN. New York: Schocken Books, 1963. 143 p.

Herndon, William Henry. HERNDON'S LINCOLN: THE TRUE STORY OF A GREAT LIFE. A selection, edited by David Freeman Hawke. Indianapolis: Bobbs-Merrill, 1970. xviii, 214 p.

Lincoln, Abraham. ABRAHAM LINCOLN: AN AUTOBIOGRAPHICAL NARRATIVE. Written and edited by Ralph Geoffrey Newman. Illustrated with 24 original drawings by Lloyd Ostendorf. Lincoln, Ill.: Lincoln College, 1971. 77 p.

> Two sketches by Lincoln combined into a single narrative, with minor changes, supplemented by autobiographical excerpts from Lincoln's letters and speeches, and editorial comments. The first sketch was originally prepared by him for J.W. Fell in 1859, and the second, written in the third person, for J.L. Scripps in 1860.

_____. ABRAHAM LINCOLN: HIS STORY IN HIS OWN WORDS. Edited with notes by Ralph Geoffrey Newman. Garden City, N.Y.: Doubleday, 1975. 117 p.

> An amalgamation of two autobiographical sketches written in 1859 and 1860, supplemented by autobiographical excerpts from Lincoln's letters and speeches.

Lorant, Stefan. LINCOLN: A PICTURE STORY OF HIS LIFE. Rev. and enl. ed. New York: Norton, 1969. 336 p.

Luthin, Reinhard Henry. THE REAL ABRAHAM LINCOLN: A COMPLETE ONE VOLUME HISTORY OF HIS LIFE AND TIMES. Englewood Cliffs, N.J.: Prentice-Hall, 1960. xviii, 778 p.

Mitgang, Herbert. ABRAHAM LINCOLN, A PRESS PORTRAIT: HIS LIFE AND TIMES FROM THE ORIGINAL NEWSPAPER DOCUMENTS OF THE UNION, THE CONFEDERACY, AND EUROPE. Chicago: Quadrangle Books, 1971. Reprint. New York: Octagon Books, 1980. xix, 519 p.

_____. THE FIERY TRAIL: A LIFE OF LINCOLN. New York: Viking Press, 1974. 207 p.

> Written for young readers.

Newman, Ralph G., ed. LINCOLN FOR THE AGES. Foreword by David C. Mearns. New York: Pyramid Books, 1964. 408 p.

Nicolay, John George, and Hay, John. ABRAHAM LINCOLN: A HISTORY. 10 vols. New York: Century Co., 1890. Reprint. Abr. and edited by Paul M. Angle. Chicago: University of Chicago Press, 1966. xix, 394 p.

Oates, Stephen B. WITH MALICE TOWARD NONE: THE LIFE OF ABRAHAM LINCOLN. New York: Harper and Row, 1977. xvii, 492 p.

Randall, James Garfield. LINCOLN, THE PRESIDENT. 4 vols. New York: Dodd, Mead, 1945-55.

Critical and yet sympathetic. Pictures Lincoln as a moderate liberal.

Sandburg, Carl. ABRAHAM LINCOLN: THE PRAIRIE YEARS AND THE WAR YEARS. Franklin Center, Pa.: Franklin Library, 1978. xiii, 1,086 p.

A limited edition of one of the great masterpieces of American literature.

_____. ABRAHAM LINCOLN: THE WAR YEARS. 4 vols. New York: Harcourt Brace, 1939.

Excellent. Stresses Lincoln's human qualities.

Thomas, Benjamin P. ABRAHAM LINCOLN, A BIOGRAPHY. New York: Knopf, 1952. xiv, 548 p.

A standard one-volume treatment.

MONOGRAPHS

A. LINCOLN, THE CIRCUIT LAWYER, 1839-1859, McLEAN COUNTY, ILLINOIS. Bloomington, Ill.: McLean County Historical Society, 1977. 34 p.

Angle, Paul McClelland. "HERE I HAVE LIVED": A HISTORY OF LINCOLN'S SPRINGFIELD, 1821-1865. Chicago: Abraham Lincoln Book Shop, 1971. xv, 313 p.

Armstrong, William Howard. THE EDUCATION OF ABRAHAM LINCOLN. New York: Coward, McCann and Geoghegan, 1974. 127 p.

For younger readers.

Baringer, William Eldon. LINCOLN'S RISE TO POWER. Boston: Little, Brown, 1937. xi, 373 p.

Barondess, Benjamin. THREE LINCOLN MASTERPIECES: COOPER INSTITUTE SPEECH, GETTYSBURG ADDRESS, SECOND INAUGURAL. Preface by David C. Mearns. Charleston: Education Foundation of West Virginia, 1954. ix, 156 p.

Basler, Roy Prentice. THE LINCOLN LEGEND: A STUDY IN CHANGING CONCEPTIONS. New York: Octagon Books, 1969. viii, 335 p.

_____. A TOUCHSTONE FOR GREATNESS: ESSAYS, ADDRESSES, AND OCCASIONAL PIECES ABOUT ABRAHAM LINCOLN. Westport, Conn.: Greenwood Press, 1973. ix, 257 p.

Bauer, Charles J. TAD'S SCRAPBOOK--LINCOLN'S BOY: 200 CARTOONS OF HIS FATHER'S DAY, COMMENTS AND POEMS, INCLUDING ALICE IN WONDERLAND! With Original Illustrations by John Tenniel. Silver Spring, Md.: Silver Spring Press, 1978. xii, 241 p.

Bernard, Kenneth A., comp. THE LINCOLN GROUP OF BOSTON: FORTY YEARS OF ITS HISTORY, 1938-1978. With the assistance of Grace N. Heron; with sections of Lincoln and New England by William F. Hanna III and Robert Larson and Sylvia Larson. Boston: The Group, 1978. 90 p.

Bishop, James Alonzo. THE DAY LINCOLN WAS SHOT. New York: Harper, 1955. viii, 304 p.

Bruce, Robert V. LINCOLN AND THE TOOLS OF WAR. Indianapolis: Bobbs-Merrill, 1956. xi, 368 p.

Cramer, John Henry. LINCOLN UNDER ENEMY FIRE. Baton Rouge: Louisiana University Press, 1948. 138 p.

The complete account of his experiences during General Early's attack on Washington.

Crissey, Elwell. LINCOLN'S LOST SPEECH: THE PIVOT OF HIS CAREER. New York: Hawthorn Books, 1967. 425 p.

Current, Richard N. LINCOLN AND THE FIRST SHOT. Philadelphia: J.B. Lippincott, 1963. 223 p.

_____. THE LINCOLN NOBODY KNOWS. New York: McGraw-Hill, 1958. x, 314 p.

Davis, Cullom, et al., eds. THE PUBLIC AND THE PRIVATE LINCOLN: CONTEMPORARY PERSPECTIVES. Carbondale: Southern Illinois University Press, 1979. x, 182 p.

Davis, Michael. THE IMAGE OF LINCOLN IN THE SOUTH. Knoxville: University of Tennessee Press, 1971. 205 p.

Dell, Christopher. LINCOLN AND THE WAR DEMOCRATS: THE GRAND EROSION OF CONSERVATIVE TRADITION. Rutherford, N.J.: Fairleigh Dickinson University Press, 1975. 455 p.

Dennis, Frank L. THE LINCOLN-DOUGLAS DEBATES. New York: Mason and Lipscomb Publishers, 1974. xi, 106 p.

Donald, David Herbert. LINCOLN RECONSIDERED: ESSAYS ON THE CIVIL WAR ERA. New York: Knopf, 1956. 200 p.

Dorris, Jonathan Truman. PARDON AND AMNESTY UNDER LINCOLN AND JOHNSON: THE RESTORATION OF THE CONFEDERATES TO THEIR RIGHTS AND PRIVILEGES, 1861-1898. Introduction by J.G. Randall. Chapel Hill: University of North Carolina, 1953. Reprint. Westport, Conn.: Greenwood Press, 1977. xxi, 459 p.

Duff, John J. A. LINCOLN, PRAIRIE LAWYER. New York: Rinehart, 1960. 433 p.

Dupuy, Trevor Nevitt. THE MILITARY LIFE OF ABRAHAM LINCOLN, COMMANDER IN CHIEF. New York: F. Watts, 1969. xii, 195 p.

Fehrenbacher, Don Edward. THE CHANGING IMAGE OF LINCOLN IN AMERICAN HISTORIOGRAPHY: AN INAUGURAL LECTURE DELIVERED BEFORE THE UNIVERSITY OF OXFORD ON 21 MAY 1968. Oxford: Clarendon Press, 1968. 24 p.

_____. THE LEADERSHIP OF ABRAHAM LINCOLN. New York: Wiley, 1970. 194 p.

Findley, Paul. A. LINCOLN, THE CRUCIBLE OF CONGRESS. New York: Crown Publishers, 1979. xvii, 270 p.

Forgie, George B. PATRICIDE IN THE HOUSE DIVIDED: A PSYCHOLOGICAL INTERPRETATION OF LINCOLN AND HIS AGE. New York: Norton, 1979. x, 308 p.

Frank, John Paul. LINCOLN AS A LAWYER. Urbana: University of Illinois Press, 1961. 190 p.

Graebner, Norman A., ed. THE ENDURING LINCOLN. Urbana: University of Illinois Press, 1959. viii, 129 p.

Lincoln sequicentennial lectures at the University of Illinois.

Hamilton, Charles, and Ostendorf, Lloyd. LINCOLN IN PHOTOGRAPHS: AN ALBUM OF EVERY KNOWN POSE. Norman: University Oklahoma Press, 1963. x, 409 p.

Harper, Robert S. LINCOLN AND THE PRESS. New York: McGraw-Hill, 1951. xii, 418 p.

Heckman, Richard Allen. LINCOLN VS. DOUGLAS: THE GREAT DEBATES CAMPAIGN. Washington, D.C.: Public Affairs Press, 1967. v, 192 p.

Hendrick, Burton Jesse. LINCOLN'S WAR CABINET. Boston: Little, Brown, 1946. 482 p.

Hesseltine, William Best. LINCOLN AND THE WAR GOVERNORS. New York: Knopf, 1948. x, 405 p.

_____. LINCOLN'S PLAN OF RECONSTRUCTION. Introduction by Richard N. Current. Chicago: Quadrangle Books, 1967. 154 p.

Hyman, Harold M. WITH MALICE TOWARD SOME: SCHOLARSHIP (OR SOMETHING LESS) ON THE LINCOLN MURDER. Springfield, Ill.: Abraham Lincoln Association, 1979. 23 p.

Keckley, Elizabeth. BEHIND THE SCENES: THIRTY YEARS A SLAVE AND FOUR YEARS IN THE WHITE HOUSE. New York: Arno Press, 1968. xvi, 371 p.

King, Willard L. LINCOLN'S MANAGER: DAVID DAVIS. Cambridge, Mass.: Harvard University Press, 1960. xiii, 383 p.

Kunhardt, Dorothy Meserve. TWENTY DAYS. New York: Harper and Row, 1965. 312 p.

A narrative in text and pictures of the assassination of Abraham Lincoln and the twenty days and nights that followed--the nation in mourning, the long trip home to Springfield.

Kunkel, Mabel. ABRAHAM LINCOLN, UNFORGETTABLE AMERICAN. Charlotte, N.C.: Delmar Co., 1976. xxiv, 448 p.

Lang, H. Jack. LINCOLN'S FIRESIDE READING: THE BOOKS THAT MADE THE MAN: THE STORY OF FIVE BASIC BOOKS WHICH SERVED AS THE FOUNDATION FOR ABRAHAM LINCOLN'S REMARKABLE SELF-EDUCATION. Cleveland: World Publishing Co., 1965. 111 p.

Defoe's ROBINSON CRUSOE, AESOP'S FABLES, Bunyan's PILGRIM'S PROGRESS, Weem's GEORGE WASHINGTON, and THE HOLY BIBLE.

Lewis, Lloyd. MYTHS AFTER LINCOLN. With an introduction by Carl Sandburg. New York: Grosset and Dunlap, 1929. xii, 367 p.

Lincoln, Abraham. ANECDOTES OF ABRAHAM LINCOLN AND LINCOLN'S STORIES. Edited by James B. McClure. Chicago: Rhodes and McClure Publishing Co., 1889. 246 p.

Including early life stories, professional life stories, White House stories, war stories, miscellaneous stories.

_____. THE POLITICAL THOUGHT OF ABRAHAM LINCOLN. Edited by Richard N. Current. Indianapolis: Bobbs-Merrill, 1967. xl, 340 p.

LINCOLN-LORE: LINCOLN IN THE POPULAR MIND. Edited by Ray B. Browne. Bowling Green, Ohio: Popular Press, 1974. xii, 510 p.

Luebke, Frederick C., comp. ETHNIC VOTERS AND THE ELECTION OF LINCOLN. Lincoln: University of Nebraska Press, 1971. xxxii, 226 p.

Luthin, Reinhard Henry. THE FIRST LINCOLN CAMPAIGN. Cambridge, Mass.: Harvard University Press, 1944. Reprint. Gloucester, Mass.: P. Smith, 1964. viii, 328 p.

McClure, Stanley W. THE LINCOLN MUSEUM AND THE HOUSE WHERE LINCOLN DIED. National Park Service Historical Handbook Series, no. 3. 2d rev. ed. Washington, D.C.: Government Printing Office, 1960. 42 p.

Mearns, David Chambers. LARGELY LINCOLN. New York: St. Martin's Press, 1961. xi, 227 p.

Monaghan, James. DIPLOMAT IN CARPET SLIPPERS: ABRAHAM LINCOLN DEALS WITH FOREIGN AFFAIRS. Indianapolis: Charter Books, 1962. 505 p.

Owen, George Frederick. A HEART THAT YEARNED FOR GOD: ABRAHAM LINCOLN, HIS LIFE AND FAITH. Washington, D.C.: Third Century Publishers, 1976. ix, 232 p.

Peterson, Gloria. AN ADMINISTRATIVE HISTORY OF ABRAHAM LINCOLN BIRTHPLACE NATIONAL HISTORIC SITE. Washington, D.C.: Division of

History, Office of Archaeology and Historic Preservation, 1968. 107 p.

Phelan, Mary Kay. MR. LINCOLN'S INAUGURAL JOURNEY. Drawings by Richard Cuffari. New York: Crowell, 1972. 211 p.

Potter, David Morris. THE LINCOLN THEME AND AMERICAN NATIONAL HISTORIOGRAPHY. Oxford: Clarendon Press, 1948. 24 p.

Pratt, Harry E. THE PERSONAL FINANCES OF ABRAHAM LINCOLN. Springfield, Ill.: Abraham Lincoln Association, 1943. xiii, 198 p.

Quarles, Benjamin. LINCOLN AND THE NEGRO. New York: Oxford University Press, 1962. 275 p.

Randall, James Garfield. CONSTITUTIONAL PROBLEMS UNDER LINCOLN. Rev. ed. Urbana: University of Illinois Press, 1951. xxxiii, 596 p.

_____. LINCOLN, THE LIBERAL STATESMAN. New York: Dodd, Mead, 1962. xv, 266 p.

_____. MR. LINCOLN. Edited by Richard N. Current. Apollo Editions. New York: Dodd, Mead, 1968. xi, 392 p.

Randall, Ruth Painter. THE COURTSHIP OF MR. LINCOLN. Boston: Little, Brown, 1957. xiv, 219 p.

Rawley, James A., comp. LINCOLN AND CIVIL WAR POLITICS. American Problem Studies. New York: Holt, Rinehart and Winston, 1969. Reprint. Huntington, N.Y.: R.E. Krieger Publishing Co., 1977. 129 p.

Riddle, Donald Wayne. CONGRESSMAN ABRAHAM LINCOLN. Urbana: University of Illinois Press, 1957. Reprint. Westport, Conn.: Greenwood Press, 1979. vii, 280 p.

Searcher, Victor. THE FAREWELL TO LINCOLN. New York: Abingdon Press, 1965. 320 p.

Silver, David Mayer. LINCOLN'S SUPREME COURT, 1861-66. Urbana: University of Illinois Press, 1956. ix, 272 p.

Thomas, Benjamin Platt. LINCOLN'S NEW SALEM. Drawings by Romaine Proctor. New and rev. ed. Introduction by Ralph G. Newman. Chicago: Abraham Lincoln Book Shop, 1966. xiv, 166 p.

_____. PORTRAIT FOR POSTERITY: LINCOLN AND HIS BIOGRAPHERS. New Brunswick, N.J.: Rutgers University Press, 1947. Reprint. Freeport, N.Y.: Books for Libraries Press, 1972. xvii, 329 p.

Viola, Herman J. LINCOLN AND THE INDIANS: ADDRESS AT ANNUAL MEETING, LINCOLN FELLOWSHIP OF WISCONSIN, MADISON, 1975. Historical Bulletin, no. 31. Madison: The Fellowship, 1976. 20 p.

Warren, Louis Austin. LINCOLN'S YOUTH: INDIANA YEARS, SEVEN TO TWENTY-ONE, 1816-1830. Indianapolis: Indiana Historical Society, 1959. Reprint. Westport, Conn.: Greenwood Press, 1976. xxii, 297 p.

_____, comp. A MAN FOR THE AGES: TRIBUTES TO ABRAHAM LINCOLN. Fort Wayne, Ind.: Louis A. Warren Lincoln Library and Museum, 1978. 87 p.

West, Richard S., Jr. MR. LINCOLN'S NAVY. New York: Longman's, Green and Co., 1957. xiii, 328 p.

Williams, Thomas Harry. LINCOLN AND HIS GENERALS. New York: Knopf, 1952. 363 p.

Wolf, William J. THE ALMOST CHOSEN PEOPLE: A STUDY OF THE RELIGION OF ABRAHAM LINCOLN. Garden City, N.Y.: Doubleday, 1959. 215 p.

Zornow, William Frank. LINCOLN AND THE PARTY DIVIDED. Norman: University of Oklahoma Press, 1954. Reprint. Westport, Conn.: Greenwood Press, 1972. xi, 264 p.

ARTICLES

Anderson, Ken. "The Role of Abraham Lincoln and Members of His Family in the Charleston Riot during the Civil War." LINCOLN HERALD 79 (Summer 1977): 53-60.

Andrews, Helen R. "President-Elect Abraham Lincoln's Inaugural Train Stop at Erie, Pa., Sat. Feb. 16, 1861." JOURNAL OF ERIE STUDIES 6 (Spring 1977): 41-43.

Angle, Paul M. "The Changing Lincoln." In THE JOHN H. HAUBERG HISTORICAL ESSAYS, edited by O. Fritiof Ander, pp. 1-17. Rock Island, Ill.: Augustana Book Concern, 1954.

Ashton, J. Hubley. "Lincolniana: A Glimpse of Lincoln in 1864." JOURNAL OF THE ILLINOIS STATE HISTORICAL SOCIETY 69 (February 1976): 67-69.

Barondess, Benjamin. "Lincoln's Trick Question." MANUSCRIPTS 10 (Summer 1958): 22-27, 57.

Lincoln-Douglas debates.

Bernard, Kenneth A. "Lincoln and the Civil War as Viewed by a Dissenting Yankee of Connecticut." LINCOLN HERALD 76 (Winter 1974): 208-15.

Borst, William A. "Lincoln's Historical Perspective." LINCOLN HERALD 76 (Winter 1974): 195-203.

Breiseth, Christopher N. "Lincoln and Frederick Douglass: Another Debate." JOURNAL OF THE ILLINOIS STATE HISTORICAL SOCIETY 68 (February 1975): 9-26.

Brumgardt, John R. "Overwhelmingly for 'Old Abe': Sherman's Soldiers and the Election of 1864." LINCOLN HERALD 78 (Winter 1976): 153-60.

Carleton, William G. "Sources of the Lincoln Legend, 1809-1865." PRAIRIE SCHOONER 25 (Summer 1951): 184-90.

Carson, Herbert L. "Nor Long Remember: Lincoln at Gettysburg." PENNSYLVANIA HISTORY 28 (October 1961): 365-71.

On the delivery and reception of the Gettysburg Address.

Catton, Bruce. "Lincoln's Difficult Decisions." CIVIL WAR HISTORY 2, no. 2 (1956): 5-12.

Chandler, A. "Lincoln and the Telegrapher." AMERICAN HERITAGE 12 (April 1961): 32-34.

Clark, Bayard S. "A Sermon by Phillips Brooks on the Death of Abraham Lincoln." HISTORICAL MAGAZINE OF THE PROTESTANT EPISCOPAL CHURCH 48 (March 1980): 37-49.

Croy, Homer. "A Lincoln Fingerprint." MANUSCRIPTS 10 (Winter 1958): 54-59.

Dorris, Jonathan T. "President Lincoln's Treatment of Confederates." FILSON CLUB HISTORICAL QUARTERLY 33 (April 1959): 139-60.

Eaton, Vincent L. "Abraham Lincoln, His Hand and Pen." MANUSCRIPTS 11 (Winter 1959): 5-12.

Eisendrath, Joseph L. "Lincoln's First Appearance on The National Scene, July, 1847." LINCOLN HERALD 76 (Summer 1974): 59-62.

Eisenschiml, Otto. "Addenda to Lincoln's Assassination." ILLINOIS STATE HISTORICAL SOCIETY JOURNAL 43 (Summer-Autumn 1950): 91-99, 204-9.

Endy, Melvin B., Jr. "Abraham Lincoln and American Civil Religion: A Reinterpretation." CHURCH HISTORY 44 (June 1975): 229-41.

Erickson, Gary Lee. "Lincoln's Civil Religion and the Lutheran Heritage." LINCOLN HERALD 75 (Winter 1973): 158-71.

Fehrenbacher, Don E. "The Historical Significance of the Lincoln-Douglas Debates." WISCONSIN MAGAZINE OF HISTORY 42 (Spring 1959): 193-99.

_____. "Lincoln and the Weight of Responsibility." JOURNAL OF THE ILLINOIS STATE HISTORICAL SOCIETY 68 (February 1975): 45-56.

_____. "Only His Stepchildren: Lincoln and the Negro." CIVIL WAR HISTORY 20 (December 1974): 293-310.

_____. "The Origins and Purpose of Lincoln's 'House-Divided' Speech." MISSISSIPPI VALLEY HISTORICAL REVIEW 46 (March 1960): 615-43.

Fischer, Leroy H. "Lincoln's Gadfly--Adam Gurowski." MISSISSIPPI VALLEY HISTORICAL REVIEW 36 (December 1949): 415-34.

Fries, Sylvia D. "Abraham Lincoln and the Language of Sectional Crisis." LINCOLN HERALD 79 (Summer and Fall 1977): 61-66; 104-9.

Glonek, James F. "Lincoln, Johnson, and the Baltimore Ticket." ABRAHAM LINCOLN QUARTERLY 6 (March 1951): 255-71.

Grob, Gerald N. "The Lincoln Legend." SOCIAL STUDIES 52 (January 1961): 3-8.

Gunderson, Robert G. "Lincoln and the Policy of Eloquent Silence: November 1860 to March 1861." QUARTERLY JOURNAL OF SPEECH 47 (February 1961): 1-9.

_____. "Reading Lincoln's Mail." INDIANA MAGAZINE OF HISTORY 55 (December 1959): 379-92.

Gurley, Phineas D. "The Funeral Sermon of Abraham Lincoln." JOURNAL OF THE PRESBYTERIAN HISTORICAL SOCIETY 39 (June 1961): 65-75.

Sermon by the pastor of the New York Avenue Presbyterian Church, delivered in the East Room of the White House, 19 April 1865.

Havighurst, Walter. "Journey's End." AMERICAN HERITAGE 13 (February 1962): 32-35.

Havlik, Robert J. "Abraham Lincoln and the Technology of 'Young America.'" LINCOLN HERALD 79 (Spring 1977): 3-11.

Hesseltine, William B. "Abraham Lincoln and the Politicians." CIVIL WAR HISTORY 6 (March 1960): 43-55.

Holzer, Harold. "The Imagemakers: Portraits of Lincoln in the 1860 Campaign." CHICAGO HISTORY 7 (Winter 1978-79): 198-207.

_____. "Lincoln and Washington: The Printmakers Blessed Their Union." REGISTER OF THE KENTUCKY HISTORICAL SOCIETY 75 (July 1977): 204-13.

Hyman, Harold M. "Lincoln and Congress: Why Not Congress and Lincoln?" JOURNAL OF THE ILLINOIS STATE HISTORICAL SOCIETY 68 (February 1975): 57-73.

Jaffa, Harry V. "Value Consensus in Democracy: The Issue in the Lincoln-Douglas Debates." AMERICAN POLITICAL SCIENCE REVIEW 52 (September 1958): 745-53.

Kelsey, Harry. "Abraham Lincoln and American Indian Policy." LINCOLN HERALD 77 (Fall 1975): 139-48.

Klement, Frank. "Jane Grey Swisshelm and Lincoln: A Feminist Fusses and Frets." ABRAHAM LINCOLN QUARTERLY 6 (December 1950): 227-38.

Krug, Mark M. "Lincoln, the Republican Party, and the Emancipation Proclamation." HISTORY TEACHER 7 (November 1973): 48-61.

Lewis, Lloyd. "Lincoln and Pinkerton." JOURNAL OF ILLINOIS STATE HISTORICAL SOCIETY 41 (December 1948): 367-82.

On Lincoln and the secret service.

Luthin, Reinhard H. "Lincoln and the American Tradition." MIDWEST JOURNAL 3 (Winter 1950-51): 1-10.

Deals particularly with his protection of civil liberties.

Lykes, Richard Wayne. "Teaching the Lincoln Legend." SOCIAL EDUCATION 23 (February 1959): 75-78.

McCorison, J.L., Jr. "The Great Lincoln Collections and What Became of Them." LINCOLN HERALD 50 (December 1948): 2-16; 51 (February 1949): 36.

McGinty, Brian. "'Castine' and Mr. Lincoln: A Reporter at the White House." CIVIL WAR TIMES ILLUSTRATED 16 (November 1977): 26-35.

Malone, Dumas. "Jefferson and Lincoln." ABRAHAM LINCOLN QUARTERLY 5 (June 1949): 327-47.

Monaghan, Jay. "The Growth of Abraham Lincoln's Influence in Literature since His Death." LINCOLN HERALD 51 (October 1949): 2-11.

Moulton, Gary E. "John Ross and W.P. Dole: A Case Study of Lincoln's Indian Policy." JOURNAL OF THE WEST 12 (July 1973): 414-23.

Neely, Mark E., Jr. "Abraham Lincoln and Black Colonization: Benjamin Butler's Spurious Testimony." CIVIL WAR HISTORY 25 (March 1979): 77-83.

Nevins, Allan. "Lincoln Takes Charge." AMERICAN HERITAGE 11 (October 1960): 42-47.

Nicolay, Helen. "The Writing of Abraham Lincoln: A History." JOURNAL OF THE ILLINOIS STATE HISTORICAL SOCIETY 42 (September 1949): 259-71.

> On the association of John G. Nicolay with Lincoln, about 1857-65, and the writing of ABRAHAM LINCOLN (10 vols.) between 1872 and 1890.

Oates, Stephen B. "'The Man of Our Redemption': Abraham Lincoln and the Emancipation of the Slaves." PRESIDENTIAL STUDIES QUARTERLY 9 (Winter 1979): 15-25.

Olsen, Otto H. "Abraham Lincoln as Revolutionary." CIVIL WAR HISTORY 24 (September 1978): 213-24.

Ostendorf, Lloyd. "Lincoln in Stereo." CIVIL WAR TIMES ILLUSTRATED 14 (February 1976): 4-9.

Parker, Owen W. "The Assassination and Gunshot Wound of President Abraham Lincoln, April 14, 1865." MINNESOTA MEDICINE 31 (February 1948): 147-49, 156.

Planck, Gary R. "Lincoln Assassination: The 'Forgotten' Litigation--*Shuey v. United States* (1875)." LINCOLN HERALD 75 (Fall 1973): 86-92.

______. "Lincoln's Assassination: More 'Forgotten' Litigation: Ex Parte Mudd (1868)." LINCOLN HERALD 76 (Summer 1974): 86-90.

Poland, Charles P., Jr. "Abraham Lincoln and Civil Liberties: A Reappraisal." LINCOLN HERALD 76 (Fall 1974): 119-32.

Rawley, James A. "The Nationalism of A. Lincoln." CIVIL WAR HISTORY 9 (September 1963): 283-98.

Read, Harry. "'A Hand to Hold While Dying': Dr. Charles A. Leale at Lincoln's Side." LINCOLN HERALD 79 (Spring 1977): 21-26.

Rietveld, Ronald D. "Lincoln and the Politics of Morality." JOURNAL OF THE ILLINOIS STATE HISTORICAL SOCIETY 68 (February 1975): 27-43.

______, ed. "An Eyewitness Account of Abraham Lincoln's Assassination." CIVIL WAR HISTORY 22 (March 1976): 60-69.

Robbins, Peggy. "The Lincolns and Spiritualism." CIVIL WAR TIMES ILLUSTRATED 15 (August 1976): 4-10, 46-47.

Rossiter, Clinton L. "Our Two Greatest Presidents." AMERICAN HERITAGE 10 (February 1959): 12-15, 100-101.

Russ, William A., Jr. "The Struggle between President Lincoln and Congress over Disfranchisement of Rebels." SUSQUEHANNA UNIVERSITY STUDIES 3 (March 1947): 221-43.

Schlesinger, Arthur M. "Lincoln and Lee." AMERICAN HERITAGE 4 (Winter 1953): 18-19, 70, 72.

Squires, J. Duane. "Some Enduring Achievements of the Lincoln Administration, 1861-1865." ABRAHAM LINCOLN QUARTERLY 5 (December 1948): 191-211.

Sweeney, Martin A. "The Personality of Lincoln the War President." SOCIAL STUDIES 65 (April 1974): 164-67.

Tegeder, V.G. "Lincoln and the Territorial Patronage: The Ascendancy of the Radicals in the West." MISSISSIPPI VALLEY HISTORICAL REVIEW 35 (June 1948): 77-90.

Theodore, Terry. "President Lincoln on the Confederate Stage." LINCOLN HERALD 78 (Winter 1976): 147-53.

Turner, John J., Jr., and D'Innocenzo, Michael. "The President and the Press: Lincoln, James Gordon Bennett and the Election of 1864." LINCOLN HERALD 76 (Summer 1974): 63-69.

Turner, Thomas R. "Public Opinion on the Assassination of Abraham Lincoln. Part 2." LINCOLN HERALD 78 (Summer 1976): 66-76.

Weisenburger, Francis P. "Lincoln and His Ohio Friends." OHIO HISTORICAL QUARTERLY 68 (July 1959): 223-56.

Wiley, Bell Irvin. ABRAHAM LINCOLN: A SOUTHERNER'S ESTIMATE AFTER 110 YEARS. New Orleans: Graduate School, Tulane University, 1976. 29 p.

Woody, R.H. "Inexhaustible Lincoln." SOUTH ATLANTIC QUARTERLY 52 (October 1953): 587-610.

Wright, Marcia. "The Growth of the Abraham Lincoln Papers." LIBRARY OF CONGRESS QUARTERLY JOURNAL OF CURRENT ACQUISITIONS 18 (November 1960): 5-9.

Zoellner, Robert H. "Negro Colonization: The Climate of Opinion Surrounding Lincoln, 1860-1865." MID-AMERICA 42 (July 1960): 131-50.

Zornow, William Frank. "Lincoln and Chase: Presidential Rivals." LINCOLN HERALD 52 (February 1950): 17-28; 52 (June 1950): 6-12.

______. "Treason as a Campaign Issue in the Re-Election of Lincoln." ABRAHAM LINCOLN QUARTERLY 5 (June 1949): 348-63.

Chapter 28

ANDREW JOHNSON, 1865-69

BIBLIOGRAPHY

Dickinson, John N., comp. ANDREW JOHNSON, 1808-1875: CHRONOLOGY-DOCUMENTS-BIBLIOGRAPHICAL AIDS. Presidential Chronologies Series. Dobbs Ferry, N.Y.: Oceana Publications, 1970. 84 p.

SOURCE MATERIALS

Johnson, Andrew. THE IMPEACHMENT AND TRIAL OF ANDREW JOHNSON, PRESIDENT OF THE UNITED STATES. By the United States Congress. 1868. Reprint. New York: Dover Publications, 1974. 289 p.

Johnson, Andrew. THE PAPERS OF ANDREW JOHNSON. Edited by LeRoy P. Graf and Ralph W. Haskins. 5 vols. Knoxville: University of Tennessee Press, 1967--.

Published volumes cover 1822-62.

______. SPEECHES OF ANDREW JOHNSON, PRESIDENT OF THE UNITED STATES. 1865. Reprint. With a biographical introduction by Frank Moore. New York: B. Franklin, 1970. xlviii, 494 p.

______. TRIAL OF ANDREW JOHNSON, PRESIDENT OF THE UNITED STATES, BEFORE THE SENATE OF THE UNITED STATES ON IMPEACHMENT BY THE HOUSE OF REPRESENTATIVES FOR HIGH CRIMES AND MISDEMEANORS. 3 vols. in 2. 1868. Reprint. New York: Da Capo Press, 1970.

Ross, Edmund Gibson. HISTORY OF THE IMPEACHMENT OF ANDREW JOHNSON, PRESIDENT OF THE UNITED STATES, BY THE HOUSE OF REPRESENTATIVES, AND HIS TRIAL BY THE SENATE FOR HIGH CRIMES AND MISDEMEANORS IN OFFICE. 1868. Reprint. New York: B. Franklin, 1965. 180 p.

BIOGRAPHIES

Brabson, Fay Warrington. ANDREW JOHNSON: A LIFE IN PURSUIT OF THE RIGHT COURSE, 1808-1875. Durham, N.C.: Seeman Printery, 1972. xv, 306 p.

Lomask, Milton. ANDREW JOHNSON: PRESIDENT ON TRIAL. New York: Farrar, Straus, and Giroux, 1960. Reprint. New York: Octagon Books, 1973. viii, 376 p.

McKitrick, Eric L., comp. ANDREW JOHNSON: A PROFILE. American Profiles Series. New York: Hill and Wang, 1969. xxvi, 224 p.

Steele, Robert V.P. THE FIRST PRESIDENT JOHNSON: THE THREE LIVES OF THE SEVENTEENTH PRESIDENT OF THE UNITED STATES OF AMERICA. New York: Morrow, 1968. x, 676 p.

Stryker, Lloyd Paul. ANDREW JOHNSON: A STUDY IN COURAGE. New York: Macmillan, 1929. Reprint. St. Clair Shores, Mich.: Scholarly Press, 1971. xvi, 881 p.

Winston, Robert Watson. ANDREW JOHNSON: PLEBEIAN AND PATRIOT. New York: Holt, 1928. Reprint. New York: Barnes and Noble, 1969. xvi, 549 p.

MONOGRAPHS

Baker, Gary G. ANDREW JOHNSON AND THE STRUGGLE FOR PRESIDENTIAL RECONSTRUCTION, 1865-1868. New Dimensions in American History. Boston: Heath, 1966. x, 178 p.

Beale, Howard K. THE CRITICAL YEAR: A STUDY OF ANDREW JOHNSON AND RECONSTRUCTION. New York: Harcourt, Brace, 1930. Reprint. New York: F. Ungar Publishing Co., 1958. xv, 454 p.

Benedict, Michael Les. A COMPROMISE OF PRINCIPLE: CONGRESSIONAL REPUBLICANS AND RECONSTRUCTION, 1863-1869. New York: Norton, 1974. 493 p.

_____. THE IMPEACHMENT AND TRIAL OF ANDREW JOHNSON. Norton Essays in American History. New York: Norton, 1973. x, 212 p.

Bond, John W. ANDREW JOHNSON HOUSE (1831-1851). Washington, D.C.: Division of History, Office of Archaeology and Historic Preservation, 1968. vii, 84 p.

Castel, Albert E. THE PRESIDENCY OF ANDREW JOHNSON. American Presidency Series. Lawrence: Regents Press of Kansas, 1979. viii, 262 p.

A revisionist study of Johnson's use of presidential power and his unsuccessful struggle against his party opponents.

Dewitt, David Miller. THE IMPEACHMENT AND TRIAL OF ANDREW JOHNSON. New York: Macmillan, 1903. Reprint. Madison: State Historical Society of Wisconsin, 1967. xiv, 646 p.

Foster, G. Allen. IMPEACHED: THE PRESIDENT WHO ALMOST LOST HIS JOB. New York: Criterion Books, 1964. 175 p.

McKitrick, Eric L. ANDREW JOHNSON AND RECONSTRUCTION. Chicago: University of Chicago, 1960. ix, 533 p.

The best account of President Johnson's struggles with the Radical Republicans and hostile Democrats.

Mantell, Martin E. JOHNSON, GRANT, AND THE POLITICS OF RECONSTRUCTION. New York: Columbia University Press, 1973. 209 p.

Milton, George Fort. THE AGE OF HATE: ANDREW JOHNSON AND THE RADICALS. New York: Coward-McCann, 1930. Reprint. Hampden, Conn.: Archon Books, 1965. xi, 788 p.

Nash, Howard Pervear. ANDREW JOHNSON: CONGRESS AND RECONSTRUCTION. Rutherford, N.J.: Fairleigh Dickinson University Press, 1972. 170 p.

Sefton, James E. ANDREW JOHNSON AND THE USES OF CONSTITUTIONAL POWER. Boston: Little, Brown, 1980. 212 p.

Smith, Gene. HIGH CRIMES AND MISDEMEANORS: THE IMPEACHMENT AND TRIAL OF ANDREW JOHNSON. New York: Morrow, 1977. 320 p.

Trefousse, Hans Louis. IMPEACHMENT OF A PRESIDENT: ANDREW JOHNSON, THE BLACKS, AND RECONSTRUCTION. Knoxville: University of Tennessee Press, 1975. xii, 252 p.

ARTICLES

Albright, Claude. "Dixon, Doolittle, and Norton: The Forgotten Republican Votes." WISCONSIN MAGAZINE OF HISTORY 59 (Winter 1975-76): 91-100.

Beale, Howard K. "On Rewriting Reconstruction History." AMERICAN HISTORICAL REVIEW 45 (July 1940): 807-27.

Benedict, Michael Les. "A New Look at the Impeachment of Andrew Johnson." POLITICAL SCIENCE QUARTERLY 88 (September 1973): 349-67.

Bowen, David W. "Andrew Johnson and the Negro." EAST TENNESSEE HISTORICAL SOCIETY PUBLICATIONS 40 (1968): 28-49.

Bridges, Roger D. "John Sherman and the Impeachment of Andrew Johnson." OHIO HISTORY 82 (Summer-Autumn 1973): 176-91.

Brownlow, Paul C. "The Northern Protestant Pulpit and Andrew Johnson." SOUTHERN SPEECH COMMUNICATION 39 (Spring 1974): 248-59.

Castel, Albert. "Andrew Johnson: His Historiographical Rise and Fall." MID-AMERICA 45 (July 1963): 175-84.

Connally, Ernest Allen. "The Andrew Johnson Homestead at Greenville, Tennessee." EAST TENNESSEE HISTORICAL SOCIETY PUBLICATIONS 29 (1957): 118-40.

On the home occupied by Johnson from 1851 to 1875, now restored.

Cox, John H., and Cox, Lawanda C. "Andrew Johnson and His Ghost Writers." MISSISSIPPI VALLEY HISTORICAL REVIEW 48 (December 1961): 460-79.

Concerning the Freedmen's Bureau and civil rights veto messages.

Donald, David Herbert. "Why They Impeached Andrew Johnson." AMERICAN HERITAGE 8 (December 1956): 20-25, 102-3.

Foner, Eric, ed. "Andrew Johnson and Reconstruction: A British View." JOURNAL OF SOCIAL HISTORY 41 (August 1975): 381-90.

Glonek, James F. "Lincoln, Johnson, and the Baltimore Ticket." LINCOLN QUARTERLY 6 (March 1951): 255-71.

Graf, Leroy P. "Editing the Andrew Johnson Papers." MISSISSIPPI QUARTERLY 15 (Summer 1962): 113-19.

Graf, Leroy P., and Haskins, Ralph W. "Work Begins on Johnson Papers." MANUSCRIPTS 9 (Spring 1957): 127.

Haskins, Ralph W. "Andrew Johnson and the Preservation of the Union." EAST TENNESSEE HISTORICAL SOCIETY PUBLICATIONS 33 (1961): 43-60.

Hays, Willard. "Andrew Johnson's Reputation." EAST TENNESSEE HISTORICAL SOCIETY PUBLICATIONS 31 (1959): 1-31; 32 (1960): 18-50.

Hyman, Harold Melvin. "Johnson, Stanton, and Grant: A Reconsideration of the Army's Role in the Events Leading to Impeachment." AMERICAN HISTORICAL REVIEW 66 (October 1960): 85-100.

Hyman, Harold Melvin, and Kinkaid, Larry George. "Victims of Circumstance: An Interpretation of Changing Attitudes toward Republican Policy Makers and Reconstruction." JOURNAL OF AMERICAN HISTORY 57 (June 1970): 48-66.

Kennedy, John F. "Ross of Kansas: The Man Who Saved a President." HARPER'S 211 (December 1955): 40-44.

Kurtz, Henry I. "The Impeachment of Andrew Johnson, 1868." HISTORY TODAY 24 (May 1974): 299-305; 24 (June 1974): 396-405.

Lawing, Hugh A. "Andrew Johnson National Monument." TENNESSEE HISTORICAL QUARTERLY 20 (June 1961): 103-19.

Lewis, H.H.W. "Impeachment of Andrew Johnson: A Political Tragedy." AMERICAN BAR ASSOCIATION JOURNAL 40 (January 1954): 15-18.

Lomask, Milton. "When Congress Tried to Rule." AMERICAN HERITAGE 11 (December 1959): 60-61, 109-12.

McDonough, James Lee, and Alderson, William T., eds. "Republican Politics and the Impeachment of Andrew Johnson." TENNESSEE HISTORICAL QUARTERLY 26 (Summer 1967): 177-83.

Mushkat, Jerome. "The Impeachment of Andrew Johnson: A Contemporary View." NEW YORK HISTORY 48 (July 1967): 275-86.

Nieman, Donald G. "Andrew Johnson, the Freedmen's Bureau, and the Problem of Equal Rights, 1865-1866." JOURNAL OF SOUTHERN HISTORY 44 (August 1978): 399-420.

Notaro, Carmen Anthony. "History of the Biographic Treatment of Andrew Johnson in the Twentieth Century." TENNESSEE HISTORICAL QUARTERLY 24 (Summer 1965): 143-55.

Perdue, M. Kathleen. "Salmon P. Chase and the Impeachment Trial of Andrew Johnson." HISTORIAN 27 (November 1964): 75-92.

Phifer, Gregg. "Andrew Johnson Loses His Battle." TENNESSEE HISTORICAL QUARTERLY 11 (December 1952): 291-328.

Rable, George C. "Anatomy of a Unionist: Andrew Johnson in the Secession Crisis." TENNESSEE HISTORICAL QUARTERLY 32 (Winter 1973): 332-54.

_____. "Forces of Darkness, Forces of Light: The Impeachment of Andrew Johnson and the Paranoid Style." SOUTHERN STUDIES 17 (Summer 1978): 151-73.

Roske, Ralph Joseph. "The Seven Martyrs." AMERICAN HISTORICAL REVIEW 64 (January 1959): 323-30.

On the legend that all of the radical Republicans who voted in 1868 for the acquittal of Andrew Johnson committed political suicide.

Schoonover, Thomas. "Mexican Affairs and the Impeachment of President Andrew Johnson." EAST TENNESSEE HISTORICAL SOCIETY PUBLICATIONS 46 (1974): 76-93.

Sefton, James E. "The Impeachment of Andrew Johnson: A Century of Writing." CIVIL WAR HISTORY 14 (June 1968): 120-47.

Shofner, Jerrell H. "Andrew Johnson and the Fernandina Unionists." PROLOGUE 10 (Winter 1978): 211-23.

Simkins, Francis B. "New Viewpoints of Southern Reconstruction." JOURNAL OF SOUTHERN HISTORY 5 (February 1939): 49-61.

Smith, Russell M. "The Andrew Johnson Papers." LIBRARY OF CONGRESS QUARTERLY JOURNAL OF CURRENT ACQUISITIONS 17 (November 1959): 13-16.

Thomas, Gordon L. "Benjamin F. Butler, Prosecutor." QUARTERLY JOURNAL OF SPEECH 45 (October 1959): 288-98.

Deals with Butler's opening argument in the impeachment trial of Johnson.

Trefousse, Hans L. "Ben Wade and the Failure of the Impeachment of Johnson." BULLETIN OF THE HISTORICAL AND PHILOSOPHICAL SOCIETY OF OHIO 18 (October 1960): 240-52.

On the reasons why many Republicans preferred Johnson to B.F. Wade of Ohio. Wade believed "that Negroes should vote in Ohio as well as in South Carolina" and that "the maldistribution of wealth called for relief."

Truman, Harry S. "The Most Mistreated of Presidents." NORTH CAROLINA HISTORICAL REVIEW 36 (April 1959): 197-204.

On the political career of Andrew Johnson, 1859-75.

Weaver, Bill. "That Brief but Pleasant Kentucky Interlude: Andrew Johnson's 'Swing Around the Circle,' 1866." FILSON CLUB HISTORICAL QUARTERLY 53, no. 3 (1979): 239-49.

Chapter 29

ULYSSES S. GRANT, 1869-77

BIBLIOGRAPHY

Moran, Philip R., ed. ULYSSES S. GRANT, 1822-1885: CHRONOLOGY-DOCUMENTS-BIBLIOGRAPHICAL AIDS. Presidential Chronologies Series. Dobbs Ferry, N.Y.: Oceana Publications, 1968. 114 p.

SOURCE MATERIALS

Grant, Ulysses Simpson. GENERAL GRANT'S LETTERS TO A FRIEND, 1861-1880. With introduction and notes by James Grant Wilson. New York: Crowell, 1897. Reprint. New York: AMS Press, 1973. x, 132 p.

______. THE PAPERS OF ULYSSES S. GRANT. 10 vols. Edited by John Y. Simon. Carbondale: Southern Illinois University Press, 1967--.

Volumes published to date cover the years 1837 to 1864.

______. PERSONAL MEMOIRS. Edited with notes and an introduction by E.B. Long. Cleveland: World Publishing Co., 1952. xxv, 608 p.

BIOGRAPHIES

Badeau, Adam. GRANT IN PEACE: FROM APPOMATTOX TO MOUNT McGREGOR, A PERSONAL MEMOIR. 1887. Reprint. Freeport, N.Y.: Books for Libraries Press, 1971. 591 p.

Carpenter, John Alcott. ULYSSES S. GRANT. Twayne's Rulers and Statesmen of the World Series. New York: Twayne Publishers, 1970. 217 p.

Catton, Bruce. U.S. GRANT AND THE AMERICAN MILITARY TRADITION. Library of American Biography. Boston: Little, Brown, 1954. x, 201 p.

Coolidge, Louis Arthur. ULYSSES S. GRANT. American Statesmen Series. Boston: Houghton Mifflin, 1917. Reprint. New York: AMS Press, 1972. xix, 596 p.

Frost, Lawrence A. U.S. GRANT ALBUM: A PICTORIAL BIOGRAPHY OF ULYSSES S. GRANT FROM LEATHER CLERK TO THE WHITE HOUSE. Seattle: Superior Publishing Co., 1966. 192 p.

Goldhurst, Richard. MANY ARE THE HEARTS: THE AGONY AND THE TRIUMPH OF ULYSSES S. GRANT. New York: Reader's Digest Press; distributed by Crowell, 1975. xxii, 297 p.

Hesseltine, William Best. ULYSSES S. GRANT, POLITICIAN. American Political Leaders Series. New York: Dodd, Mead and Co., 1935. Reprint. New York: F. Ungar Publishing Co, 1957. xiii, 480 p.

McFeely, William S. GRANT: A BIOGRAPHY. New York: W.W. Norton and Co., 1981. xiii, 592 p.

Todd, Helen. A MAN NAMED GRANT. Boston: Houghton Mifflin, 1940. 598 p.

Wister, Owen. ULYSSES S. GRANT. Beacon Biographies of Eminent Americans. Boston: Small, Maynard, 1900. xvii, 145 p.

Woodward, William E. MEET GENERAL GRANT. Foreword by James A. Rawley. New York: Liveright, 1965. 524 p.

MONOGRAPHS

Catton, Bruce. GRANT TAKES COMMAND. With maps by Samuel H. Bryant. Boston: Little, Brown, 1969. 556 p.

Conger, Arthur Latham. THE RISE OF U.S. GRANT. New York: Century, 1931. Reprint. Freeport, N.Y.: Books for Libraries Press, 1970. xi, 390 p.

Macartney, Clarence Edward Noble. GRANT AND HIS GENERALS. New York: McBride Co., 1953. Reprint. Freeport, N.Y.: Books for Libraries Press, 1971. xiv, 352 p.

Mantell, Martin E. JOHNSON, GRANT, AND THE POLITICS OF RECONSTRUCTION. New York: Columbia University Press, 1973. 209 p.

Nevins, Allan. HAMILTON FISH: THE INNER HISTORY OF THE GRANT ADMINISTRATION. New York: Dodd, Mead, 1936. Rev. ed. 2 vols. New York: F. Ungar Publishing Co., 1957. xxi, 932 p.

Solid political history from the vantage point of Grant's key cabinet officer and secretary of state for eight years.

Tatum, Lawrie. OUR RED BROTHERS AND THE PEACE POLICY OF PRESIDENT ULYSSES S. GRANT. Foreword by Richard N. Ellis. Lincoln: University of Nebraska Press, 1970. xx, 366 p.

Whitman, Walt. THE EIGHTEENTH PRESIDENCY. A Critical Text, edited by Edward F. Grier. Lawrence: University of Kansas Press, 1956. 47 p.

Williams, Thomas Harry. McCLELLAN, SHERMAN, AND GRANT. New Brunswick, N.J.: Rutgers University Press, 1962. Reprint. Westport, Conn.: Greenwood Press, 1976. 113 p.

ARTICLES

Catton, Bruce. "Grant and the Politicians." AMERICAN HERITAGE 19 (October 1968): 32-35, 81-87.

_____. "U.S. Grant: Man of Letters." AMERICAN HERITAGE 19 (June 1968): 97-100.

Dunne, Gerald T. "President Grant and Chief Justice Chase." ST. LOUIS UNIVERSITY LAW JOURNAL 5 (Fall 1959): 539-53.

Fritz, Henry E. "The Making of Grant's Peace Policy." CHRONICLES OF OKLAHOMA 37 (Winter 1959-60): 411-32.

Hardy, O. "Ulysses S. Grant, President of the Mexican Southern Railroad." PACIFIC HISTORICAL REVIEW 24 (May 1955): 111-20.

Hartje, Robert. "Grant and the Centennial of 1876." OCCASIONAL REVIEW 5 (Autumn 1976): 67-84.

Isaacs, Joakim. "Candidate Grant and the Jews." AMERICAN JEWISH ARCHIVES 17 (April 1965): 3-16.

Leiter, Kelly. "A President and One Newspaper: U.S. Grant and the Chicago TRIBUNE." JOURNALISM QUARTERLY 47 (Spring 1970): 71-80.

Leitman, Spencer L. "The Revival of an Image: Grant and the 1880 Republican Nominating Campaign." BULLETIN OF THE MISSOURI HISTORICAL SOCIETY 30 (April 1974): 196-204.

Monroe, Haskell. "The Grant Papers: A Review Article." JOURNAL OF THE ILLINOIS STATE HISTORICAL SOCIETY 61 (Winter 1968): 463-72.

Utley, Robert M. "The Celebrated Policy of General Grant." NORTH DAKOTA HISTORY 20 (July 1953): 121-42.

On his Indian policy, 1869-77.

Whitner, Robert Lee. "Grant's Indian Peace Policy on the Yakima Reservation, 1870-82." PACIFIC NORTHWEST QUARTERLY 5 (October 1959): 135-43.

Woodward, Comer Vann. "The Lowest Ebb." AMERICAN HERITAGE 8 (April 1957): 52-57, 106-9.

Chapter 30

RUTHERFORD B. HAYES, 1877-81

BIBLIOGRAPHY

Bishop, Arthur, ed. RUTHERFORD B. HAYES, 1822-1893: CHRONOLOGY-DOCUMENTS-BIBLIOGRAPHICAL AIDS. Presidential Chronologies Series. Dobbs Ferry, N.Y.: Oceana Publications, 1969. 90 p.

SOURCE MATERIALS

Cochrane, Elizabeth. "Nellie Bly Visits Spiegel Grove." Edited by Watt P. Marchman. HAYES HISTORICAL JOURNAL 1 (Fall 1976): 133-44.

Describes the house and house life of Lucy and Rutherford Hayes.

Davison, Kenneth E., comp. "Album: Political Cartoons of the Hayes Presidency." HAYES HISTORICAL JOURNAL 2 (Spring 1978): 38-45.

_____. "The Hayes Great Western Tour of 1880." HAYES HISTORICAL JOURNAL 3 (Spring-Fall 1980): 95-104.

Hayes was the first president to go to the West Coast while chief executive.

Davison, Kenneth E., and Marchman, Watt P., comps. "Contemporary Estimates of President Hayes." HAYES HISTORICAL JOURNAL 2 (Fall 1978): 132-38.

Excerpts from newspaper comments and editorials on Hayes.

Donaldson, Thomas. "The 'Memoirs' of Thomas Donaldson." Edited by Watt P. Marchman. HAYES HISTORICAL JOURNAL 2 (Spring-Fall 1979): 157-265.

Describes Washington politics including the Hayes era.

Hayes, Rutherford B. DIARY AND LETTERS OF RUTHERFORD B. HAYES. 5 vols. Edited by Charles R. Williams. Columbus: F.J. Heer Printing Co., 1922-26.

The only published version of Hayes's comprehensive diary which he kept intermittently throughout his life. A definitive edition of the diary is in progress at the Hayes Presidential Center in Fremont, Ohio.

______. HAYES, THE DIARY OF A PRESIDENT: 1875-1881. Edited by T. Harry Williams. New York: David McKay Co., 1964. xliv, 329 p.

One of the few diaries kept by a president in office. Complete for the years covered but only sparsely annotated.

______. "The Hayes-Bryan Correspondence." Edited by E.W. Winkler. SOUTHWESTERN HISTORICAL QUARTERLY (1921-26).

Twenty installments, beginning in October 1921 and lasting until July 1926, of Hayes's friendship with Guy Bryan, his classmate at Kenyon College, and later a Texas democratic congressman.

______. "President Hayes' Graduation Speeches." Edited by Wyman W. Parker. OHIO STATE ARCHAEOLOGICAL AND HISTORICAL QUARTERLY 63 (April 1954): 134-45.

Texts of the oration and valedictory delivered by Hayes at his graduation from Kenyon College in 1842.

______. TEACH THE FREEMAN: THE CORRESPONDENCE OF RUTHERFORD B. HAYES AND THE SLATER FUND FOR NEGRO EDUCATION, 1881-1893. 2 vols. Edited by Louis Decimus Rubin, Jr. Baton Rouge: Louisiana State University Press, 1959. Vol I, 1881-1887; Vol II, 1888-1893. Notes and index. 236; 302 p.

Representative of the president's humanitarian and philanthropic concerns.

Hayes, Webb C., and Marchman, Watt P., comps. "The First Days of the Hayes Administration: Inauguration to Easter Sunday, 1877." HAYES HISTORICAL JOURNAL 1 (Fall 1977): 230-62.

Keeler, Lucy Elliot. "Excursion to Baltimore, Md., and Washington, D.C., January 18-February 15, 1881." Edited by Watt P. Marchman. HAYES HISTORICAL JOURNAL 1 (Spring 1976): 6-21.

Marchman, Watt P. "Collections of the Rutherford B. Hayes State Memorial." OHIO HISTORY 71, no. 2 (July 1962): 151-57.

______, comp. "College Costs: What Rutherford B. Hayes Spent as a Student at Kenyon, 1838-1841." HAYES HISTORICAL JOURNAL 2 (Spring 1978): 14-20.

Palmer, Upton Sinclair. AN HISTORICAL AND CRITICAL STUDY OF THE SPEECHES OF RUTHERFORD B. HAYES. Ann Arbor, Mich.: University Microfilms, 1950.

BIOGRAPHIES

Barnard, Harry. RUTHERFORD B. HAYES AND HIS AMERICA. Indianapolis: Bobbs Merrill, 1954. 606 p. Reprint. New York: Russell and Russell, 1967.

Excellent on the disputed election of 1876 and the family background of President Hayes. Limited discussion of presidential period.

Davison, Kenneth E. THE PRESIDENCY OF RUTHERFORD B. HAYES. Contributions in American Studies, no. 3. Westport, Conn.: Greenwood Press, 1972. 266 p.

New material on Hayes's early life, nomination for president, White House staff, Indian policy, use of executive power, and travels.

Davison, Kenneth E., and Thurston, Helen M., eds. "Rutherford B. Hayes Special Edition." OHIO HISTORY 77 (Winter-Spring-Summer 1968): 1-208.

A significant collection of articles by specialists on Hayes as an attorney, as governor of Ohio, and president. Includes essays on Mrs. Hayes, John Sherman, and James Garfield, among others.

Eckenrode, Hamilton James. RUTHERFORD B. HAYES, STATESMAN OF REUNION. New York: Dodd, Mead, 1930. xii, 363 p. Bibliog.

Howells, William Dean. SKETCH OF THE LIFE AND CHARACTER OF RUTHERFORD B. HAYES: ALSO A BIOGRAPHICAL SKETCH OF WILLIAM A. WHEELER. New York: Hurd and Houghton, 1876. Reprint. Folcroft, Pa.: Folcroft Library Editions, 1977. vi, 195, 31 p.

Myers, Elisabeth P. RUTHERFORD B. HAYES. Chicago: Reilly and Lee, 1969. 121 p. Bibliog.

A biography of the man declared the nineteenth president of the United States by the electoral college in the disputed election of 1876.

Williams, Charles Richard. THE LIFE OF RUTHERFORD BIRCHARD HAYES. 2 vols. Boston: Houghton Mifflin Co., 1914. Index.

Still useful, especially volume 1. Valuable index.

MONOGRAPHS

Gonya, Gary Joseph. "Hayes and Unity (with a Travelogue of the Presidential Tour of 1880)." B.A. thesis, St. Meinrad Seminary, St. Meinrad, Indiana, May 1965.

Haworth, Paul Leland. THE HAYES-TILDEN DISPUTED PRESIDENTIAL ELECTION OF 1876. Cleveland: Burrows Brothers Co., 1906. Reprint. New York: Russell and Russell, 1966. xi, 365 p.

Pabst, Anna Catherine Smith. THE BIRTHPLACE OF R.B. HAYES. Delaware, Ohio: By the author, 1972. 128 p.

Price, Ruth P. "The Reform Activities of Rutherford B. Hayes." A thesis presented in partial fulfillment of the requirements for the degree of Master of Arts, University of Toledo, 1948. iii, 96 p.

Robinson, Lloyd. THE STOLEN ELECTION: HAYES VERSUS TILDEN, 1876. Garden City, N.Y.: Doubleday, 1968. 240 p. Bibliog.

Townsend, Samuel C. SPIEGEL GROVE; HOME OF RUTHERFORD BIRCHARD HAYES. Fremont, Ohio: Lesher Printers, 1965. 40 p.

A small booklet describing the property Hayes inherited in 1874 and how he gradually enlarged the house and developed the property.

Vaughan, Harold Cecil. THE HAYES-TILDEN ELECTION OF 1876: A DISPUTED PRESIDENTIAL ELECTION IN THE GILDED AGE. New York: Franklin Watts, 1972. 89 p. Bibliog.

Williams, Thomas Harry. HAYES OF THE TWENTY-THIRD: THE CIVIL WAR VOLUNTEER OFFICER. New York: Knopf, 1965. 324 p.

Woodward, Comer Vann. REUNION AND REACTION: THE COMPROMISE OF 1877 AND THE END OF RECONSTRUCTION. 2d rev. ed. Garden City, N.Y.: Doubleday and Co., 1956. 297 p.

A well-written detailed examination of the circumstances leading to the victory of Hayes over Tilden through the Electoral Commission.

ARTICLES

Baetzhold, Howard G. "Mark Twain Stumps for Hayes." HAYES HISTORICAL JOURNAL 1 (Fall 1976): 111-14.

Barnard, Harry. "Biographical Memories, _in re_ RBH." HAYES HISTORICAL JOURNAL 2 (Fall 1978): 89-96.

_____. "Essay Review: Gore Vidal, 1876, A NOVEL." HAYES HISTORICAL JOURNAL 1 (Spring 1977): 216-19.

Baur, John E. "A President Visits Los Angeles: Rutherford B. Hayes Tour of 1880." HISTORICAL SOCIETY OF SOUTHERN CALIFORNIA 37 (March 1955): 33-47.

Beeton, Beverly. "The Hayes Administration and the Woman Question." HAYES HISTORICAL JOURNAL 2 (Spring 1978): 52-56.

Blynn, William C. "An Unusual Indian Peace Medal of the Hayes Era." HAYES HISTORICAL JOURNAL 2 (Spring 1978): 33-37.

Clendenen, Clarence C. "President Hayes' 'Withdrawal' of the Troops--An Enduring Myth." SOUTH CAROLINA HISTORICAL MAGAZINE 70 (October 1969): 240-50.

Explains that Hayes simply sent the remaining occupation troops to nearby barracks rather than removing them from the states themselves.

Davison, Kenneth E. "The Nomination of Rutherford B. Hayes for the Presidency." OHIO HISTORY 77 (Winter-Spring-Summer 1968): 95-110.

______. "The Search for the Hayes Administration." HAYES HISTORICAL JOURNAL 2 (Fall 1978): 107-18.

Describes author's research experiences in preparing his book on the Hayes presidency.

______. "Travels of President Rutherford B. Hayes." OHIO HISTORY 80 (Winter 1971): 60-72.

De Santis, Vincent. "President Hayes' Southern Policy." JOURNAL OF SOUTHERN HISTORY 21 (November 1955): 476-91.

By a leading student of the Republican southern policy.

Garrison, Curtis W. "President Hayes: The Opponent of Prohibition." NORTHWEST OHIO QUARTERLY 16 (1944): 164-77.

Refutes the myth that Hayes stood for statutory prohibition.

Geer, Emily Apt. "Lucy Webb Hayes and Her Influence Upon Her Era." HAYES HISTORICAL JOURNAL 1, no. 1 (Spring 1976): 22-35.

______. "Lucy W. Hayes and the New Women of the 1880's." HAYES HISTORICAL JOURNAL 3 (Spring-Fall 1980): 18-26.

______. "The Rutherford B. Hayes Family." HAYES HISTORICAL JOURNAL 2 (Spring 1978): 46-51.

Gholson, Sam C. "The Artist as Biographer." HAYES HISTORICAL JOURNAL 2 (Fall 1978): 119-31.

Author relates his approach during the 1970s in painting portraits of Hayes.

HAYES HISTORICAL JOURNAL. Fremont, Ohio: Hayes Presidential Center, 1976-- . Semiannual.

Hendricks, Gordon. "Eakins Portrait of Rutherford B. Hayes." AMERICAN ART JOURNAL 1 (1969): 104-14.

An account of the famous missing portrait of Hayes by the well-known Philadelphia realist painter of the Gilded Age.

Hickerson, Frank R. "The Educational Contribution of Rutherford B. Hayes." NORTHWEST OHIO QUARTERLY 33 (Winter 1960-61): 46-53.

Howells, William Dean, and Hayes, Rutherford Birchard. "Howell's Campaign Biography of Rutherford B. Hayes: A Series of Letters." Edited by Leo P. Coyle. OHIO HISTORICAL QUARTERLY 66 (October 1957): 391-406. Notes.

McPherson, James M. "Coercion or Conciliation? Abolitionists Debate President Hayes's Southern Policy." NEW ENGLAND QUARTERLY 39 (December 1966): 474-97.

Marchman, Watt P. "The Hayes Memorial Library." AUTOGRAPH COLLECTOR'S JOURNAL 3 (October 1950): 8-10.

______. "Rutherford B. Hayes, Attorney at Law." OHIO HISTORY 77 (Winter-Spring-Summer 1968): 5-32.

______. "Rutherford B. Hayes in Lower Sandusky, 1845-1849." HAYES HISTORICAL JOURNAL 1 (Fall 1976): 122-32.

______. "The Washington Visits of Jenny Halstead, 1879-1881." BULLETIN OF THE HISTORICAL AND PHILOSOPHICAL SOCIETY OF OHIO 12 (July 1954): 179-93.

______, comp. "Rutherford B. Hayes as Painted by William Merritt Chase: The Documentary Story." HAYES HISTORICAL JOURNAL 1 (Spring 1976): 36-44.

______, ed. "Hayes Album: Fourteen Panels Depicting Scenes from the Life of President Hayes." Illustrated by William E. Turner. HAYES HISTORICAL JOURNAL 1 (Spring 1976): 45-59.

Myers, Elisabeth P. "Writing a Juvenile Biography of President Hayes." HAYES HISTORICAL JOURNAL 2 (Fall 1978): 97-101.

Nichols, Jeannette Paddock. "Rutherford B. Hayes and John Sherman." OHIO HISTORY 77 (Winter-Spring-Summer 1968): 125-38.

Parker, Wyman W. "The College Reading of a President." LIBRARY QUARTERLY 21 (April 1951): 107-12.

Hayes earned graduation honors at Kenyon College and was later elected to Phi Beta Kappa. As president, he owned an extensive library of Americana.

______. "Rutherford B. Hayes as a Student of Speech at Kenyon College." QUARTERLY JOURNAL OF SPEECH 39 (October 1953): 291-95.

Payne, Alma J. "William Dean Howells and Other Early Biographers of Rutherford B. Hayes." HAYES HISTORICAL JOURNAL 2 (Fall 1978): 78-88.

Peskin, Allan. "Garfield and Hayes: Political Leaders of the Gilded Age." OHIO HISTORY 77 (Winter-Spring-Summer 1968): 111-24.

Porter, Daniel R. "Governor Rutherford B. Hayes." OHIO HISTORY 77 (Winter-Spring-Summer 1968): 58-75.

Richardson, Lyon N. "Men of Letters and the Hayes Administration, with Text of the Letters." NEW ENGLAND QUARTERLY 15 (March 1942): 110-42.

President Hayes, a statesman with scholarly instincts, appointed a number of literary figures to positions in the government, including James R. Lowell and Bayard Taylor.

Sinkler, George. "Race: Principles and Policy of Rutherford B. Hayes." OHIO HISTORY 77 (Winter-Spring-Summer 1968): 149-67.

Smith, Thomas A. "Governor Hayes Visits the Centennial." HAYES HISTORICAL JOURNAL 1 (Spring 1977): 158-63.

Sternstein, Jerome L. "The Sickles Memorandum: Another Look at the Hayes-Tilden Election-Night Conspiracy." JOURNAL OF SOUTHERN HISTORY 32 (August 1966): 342-57.

Swift, Don C. "Ohio Republicans and the Hayes Administration Reforms: The Assault on the Spoils System." NORTHWEST OHIO QUARTERLY 42 (Fall 1970): 99-106; 43 (Winter 1971): 11-22.

Swint, Henry L. "Rutherford B. Hayes, Educator." MISSISSIPPI VALLEY HISTORICAL REVIEW 39 (June 1952): 45-60.

Describes Hayes's abiding interest in educational and humanitarian causes.

Thelen, David. "Rutherford B. Hayes and the Reform Tradition in the Gilded Age." AMERICAN QUARTERLY 22 (Summer 1970): 150-65.

One of the most significant articles on Hayes.

Van Sickle, Clifton E., and May, James T. "The Birthplace of President Hayes: A Study in Oral Tradition." OHIO STATE ARCHAEOLOGICAL AND HISTORICAL QUARTERLY 61 (April 1952): 167-72.

West, Richard Samuel. "The Kenyon Experience of R.B. Hayes." HAYES HISTORICAL JOURNAL 2 (Spring 1978): 6-13.

Wittke, Carl. "Carl Schurz and Rutherford B. Hayes." OHIO HISTORICAL QUARTERLY 65 (October 1956): 337-55.

Schurz was secretary of the interior in the Hayes Cabinet and a supporter of civil service reform.

Chapter 31

JAMES A. GARFIELD, 1881

BIBLIOGRAPHY

Furer, Howard B., ed. JAMES A. GARFIELD, 1831-1881; CHESTER A. ARTHUR, 1830-1886: CHRONOLOGY-DOCUMENTS-BIBLIOGRAPHICAL AIDS. Presidential Chronologies Series. Dobbs Ferry, N.Y.: Oceana Publications, 1970. v, 148 p.

SOURCE MATERIALS

Garfield, James Abram. THE DIARY OF JAMES A. GARFIELD. 4 vols. Edited by Harry James Brown and Frederick D. Williams. Vol. 1, 1884-1871; vol. 2, 1872-1874; vol. 3, 1875-1877; vol. 4, 1878-1881. East Lansing: Michigan State University Press, 1967-1981.

______. JAMES A. GARFIELD PAPERS. Washington, D.C.: Library of Congress, 1970. 177 reels.

______. THE WILD LIFE OF THE ARMY: CIVIL WAR LETTERS OF JAMES A. GARFIELD. Edited with an introduction by Frederick D. Williams. East Lansing: Michigan State University Press, 1964. xx, 325 p.

______. THE WORKS OF JAMES ABRAM GARFIELD. 2 vols. Edited by Burke A. Hinsdale. 1882-83. Reprint. Freeport, N.Y.: Books for Libraries Press, 1970.

Garfield, James Abram, and Henry, Charles E. POLITICS AND PATRONAGE IN THE GILDED AGE: THE CORRESPONDENCE OF JAMES A. GARFIELD AND CHARLES E. HENRY. Edited by James D. Norris and Arthur H. Shaffer. Madison: State Historical Society of Wisconsin, 1970. xxix, 304 p.

Garfield, James Abram, and Hinsdale, Burke Aaron. GARFIELD-HINSDALE LETTERS: CORRESPONDENCE BETWEEN JAMES ABRAM GARFIELD AND BURKE AARON HINSDALE. Edited by Mary Louise Hinsdale. Ann Arbor: University of Michigan Press, 1949. 556 p.

Smith, Thomas A. "A Pictorial Album: Garfield in Pen and Ink." HAYES HISTORICAL JOURNAL 3 (Fall 1981): 31-46.

BIOGRAPHIES

Bates, Richard O. THE GENTLEMAN FROM OHIO: AN INTRODUCTION TO GARFIELD. Durham, N.C.: Moore Publishing Co., 1973. xi, 375 p.

Caldwell, Robert G. JAMES A. GARFIELD, PARTY CHIEFTAIN. New York: Dodd, Mead, 1931. Reprint. Hamden, Conn.: Archon Books, 1965. xi, 383 p.

Conwell, Russell H. THE LIFE, SPEECHES, AND PUBLIC SERVICES OF GEN. JAMES A. GARFIELD. Boston: B.B. Russell and Co., 1880. 356 p.

Leech, Margaret, and Brown, Harry J. THE GARFIELD ORBIT. New York: Harper and Row, 1978. xi, 369 p.

Peskin, Allan. GARFIELD. Kent, Ohio: Kent State University Press, 1978. x, 716 p.

Shaw, John. "A Shooting Star: The Life and Achievements of James A. Garfield." A recital drama for five voices. HAYES HISTORICAL JOURNAL 3 (Spring 1982): 21-46.

Smith, Theodore Clarke. THE LIFE AND LETTERS OF JAMES ABRAM GARFIELD. 2 vols. New Haven, Conn.: Yale University Press, 1925. Reprint. Hamden, Conn.: Archon Books, 1968. ix, 1,283 p.

Taylor, John M. GARFIELD OF OHIO: THE AVAILABLE MAN. New York: Norton, 1970. 336 p.

MONOGRAPHS

Doenecke, Justus D. THE PRESIDENCIES OF JAMES A. GARFIELD & CHESTER A. ARTHUR. American Presidency Series. Lawrence: Regents Press of Kansas, 1981. xiii, 229 p.

Pletcher, David M. THE AWKWARD YEARS: AMERICAN FOREIGN RELATIONS UNDER GARFIELD AND ARTHUR. Columbia: University of Missouri Press, 1962. xvi, 381 p.

Rosenberg, Charles E. THE TRIAL OF THE ASSASSIN GUITEAU: PSYCHIATRY AND LAW IN THE GILDED AGE. Chicago: University of Chicago Press, 1968. xviii, 289 p.

Wasson, Woodrow W. JAMES A. GARFIELD: HIS RELIGION AND EDUCATION. A STUDY IN THE RELIGIOUS AND EDUCATIONAL THOUGHT AND ACTIVITY OF AN AMERICAN STATESMAN. Nashville: Tennessee Book Co., 1952. xi, 155 p.

ARTICLES

Brown, Harry James. "Garfield's Congress." HAYES HISTORICAL JOURNAL 3 (Fall 1981): 57-77.

Dawes, Charles Gates. "Young Charles Dawes Goes to the Garfield Inauguration: A Diary." Edited by Robert H. Ferrell. OHIO HISTORY QUARTERLY 70 (October 1961): 332-42.

De Santis, Vincent P. "President Garfield and the 'Solid South.'" NORTH CAROLINA HISTORICAL REVIEW 36 (October 1959): 422-65.

Evans, Frank B. "Wharton Barker and the Republican National Convention of 1880." PENNSYLVANIA HISTORY 27 (January 1960): 28-43.

Fish, Steward A. "The Death of President Garfield." BULLETIN OF THE HISTORY OF MEDICINE 24 (July-August 1950): 378-92. Ports., views., notes.

On his symptoms and treatment from a gunshot wound during the twelve weeks before his death.

Hatfield, Mark O. "James A. Garfield: A Man Called, A People Served." HAYES HISTORICAL JOURNAL 3 (Fall 1981): 21-30.

Peskin, Allan. "A Century of Garfield." HAYES HISTORICAL JOURNAL 3 (Fall 1981): 9-20.

_____. "Charles Guiteau of Illinois, President Garfield's Assassin." JOURNAL OF THE ILLINOIS STATE HISTORICAL SOCIETY 70 (May 1977): 130-39.

_____. "From Log Cabin to Oblivion." AMERICAN HISTORY ILLUSTRATED 11 (May 1976): 25-34.

_____. "Garfield and Hayes, Political Leaders of the Gilded Age." OHIO HISTORY 77 (Winter-Spring-Summer 1968): 111-24.

_____. "The 'Little Man on Horseback' and the 'Literary Fellow': Garfield's Opinions of Grant." MID-AMERICA 55 (October 1973): 271-82.

______. "President Garfield and the Rating Game: An Evaluation of a Brief Administration." SOUTH ATLANTIC QUARTERLY 76 (Winter 1977): 93-102.

______. "President Garfield and the Southern Question: The Making of a Policy that Never Was." SOUTH ATLANTIC QUARTERLY 16 (July 1978): 375-86.

______. "President Garfield Reconsidered." HAYES HISTORICAL JOURNAL 3 (Spring-Fall 1980): 35-40.

Robertson, A. "Murder Most Foul." AMERICAN HERITAGE 15 (August 1964): 91-104.

Roseberry, Cecil R. "The Letters of Garfield's Assassin." MANUSCRIPTS 7 (Winter 1955): 86-91.

Sawyer, Robert W. "James A. Garfield and the Classics." HAYES HISTORICAL JOURNAL 3 (Fall 1981): 47-56.

Stanley-Brown, Joseph. "My Friend Garfield." AMERICAN HERITAGE 22 (August 1971): 49-53, 100-101.

Starr, Michael E. "The Hiram College Garfield Commemoration Lectures." HAYES HISTORICAL JOURNAL 3 (Fall 1981): 5-7.

Temkin, Owsei, and Koudelka, Janet. "Simon Newcomb and the Location of President Garfield's Bullet." BULLETIN OF THE HISTORY OF MEDICINE 24 (July-August 1950): 393-97. Notes.

Chapter 32

CHESTER A. ARTHUR, 1881-85

BIBLIOGRAPHY

Furer, Howard B., ed. JAMES A. GARFIELD, 1831-1881; CHESTER A. ARTHUR, 1830-1886; CHRONOLOGY-DOCUMENTS-BIBLIOGRAPHICAL AIDS. Presidential Chronological Series. Dobbs Ferry, N.Y.: Oceana Publications, 1970. v, 148 p.

BIOGRAPHIES

Howe, George Frederick. CHESTER A. ARTHUR: A QUARTER-CENTURY OF MACHINE POLITICS. New York: Dodd, Mead, 1934. xi, 307 p.

Reeves, Thomas C. GENTLEMAN BOSS: THE LIFE OF CHESTER ALAN ARTHUR. New York: Alfred A. Knopf, 1975. xvii, 500 p.

The first full-scale biography, based on new manuscript finds.

Union College. Schenectady. CHESTER ALAN ARTHUR. Schenectady, N.Y.: Union College, 1948. 27 p.

MONOGRAPHS

Doenecke, Justus D. THE PRESIDENCIES OF JAMES A. GARFIELD & CHESTER A. ARTHUR. American Presidency Series. Lawrence: Regents Press of Kansas, 1981. xiii, 229 p.

Garraty, John A. THE NEW COMMONWEALTH: 1877-1890. New York: Harper and Row, 1968. xv, 364 p.

Hoogenboom, Ari. OUTLAWING THE SPOILS: A HISTORY OF THE CIVIL SERVICE REFORM MOVEMENT, 1865-1883. Urbana: University of Illinois Press, 1961. xiii, 306 p.

See especially pages 135-267 for a good account of Arthur's political career.

Pletcher, David M. THE AWKWARD YEARS: AMERICAN FOREIGN RELATIONS UNDER GARFIELD AND ARTHUR. Columbia: University of Missouri Press, 1962. xvi, 381 p.

ARTICLES

Bailey, Consuelo Northrop. "Our Horses and Chester A. Arthur." VERMONT LIFE 11 (Summer 1956): 10-11.

De Santis, Vincent P. "Negro Dissatisfaction with Republican Policy in the South, 1882-1884." JOURNAL OF NEGRO HISTORY 36 (April 1951): 148-59.

_____. "President Arthur and the Independent Movements in the South in 1882." JOURNAL OF SOUTHERN HISTORY 19 (August 1953): 346-63.

Doane, Gilbert H. "The Birthplace of Chester A. Arthur." PROCEEDINGS OF THE VERMONT HISTORICAL SOCIETY 9 (March 1941): 3-13.

Eidson, William G. "Who Were the Stalwarts?" MID-AMERICA 52 (October 1970): 235-61.

Goff, John S. "President Arthur's Domestic Legislative Program." NEW YORK HISTORICAL SOCIETY QUARTERLY 44 (April 1960): 166-77.

Newcomer, Lee. "Chester A. Arthur: The Factors Involved in His Removal from the New York Customhouse." NEW YORK HISTORY 18 (October 1937): 401-10.

Reeves, Thomas C. "Chester A. Arthur, Vermont Schoolmaster." VERMONT HISTORY 40 (Winter 1972): 43-46.

_____. "Chester A. Arthur and Campaign Assessments in the Election of 1880." HISTORIAN 31 (August 1969): 573-82.

_____. "Chester A. Arthur and the Campaign of 1880." POLITICAL SCIENCE QUARTERLY 84 (December 1969): 628-37.

______. "The Diaries of Malvina Arthur: Windows into the Past of Our 21st President." VERMONT HISTORY 38 (Summer 1970): 177-88.

______. "The Mystery of Chester Alan Arthur's Birthplace." VERMONT HISTORY 38 (Autumn 1970): 291-304.

______. "President Arthur in Yellowstone National Park." MONTANA THE MAGAZINE OF WESTERN HISTORY 19 (July 1969): 18-29.

______. "The Search for the Chester Alan Arthur Papers." WISCONSIN MAGAZINE OF HISTORY 55 (Summer 1972): 310-19.

______. "Silas Burt and Chester Arthur: A Reformer's View of the Twenty-First President." NEW YORK HISTORICAL SOCIETY QUARTERLY 54 (October 1970): 318-37.

Richardson, Joe M. "The Florida Excursion of President Chester A. Arthur." TEQUESTA: THE JOURNAL OF THE HISTORICAL ASSOCIATION OF SOUTHERN FLORIDA 24 (1964): 41-47.

Shelley, Fred. "The Chester A. Arthur Papers." LIBRARY OF CONGRESS QUARTERLY JOURNAL OF CURRENT ACQUISITIONS 16 (May 1959): 115-21.

"Vermont Remembers President Arthur." VERMONT HISTORICAL SOCIETY NEWS AND NOTES 6 (October 1954): 9-12.

Chapter 33

GROVER CLEVELAND, 1885-89; 1893-97

BIBLIOGRAPHY

Vexler, Robert I., ed. GROVER CLEVELAND, 1837-1908: CHRONOLOGY-DOCUMENTS-BIBLIOGRAPHICAL AIDS. Presidential Chronologies Series. Dobbs Ferry, N.Y.: Oceana Publications, 1968. 118 p.

SOURCE MATERIALS

Cleveland, Grover. GOOD CITIZENSHIP. Philadelphia: H. Alternus, 1908. 78 p.

______. LETTERS OF GROVER CLEVELAND, 1850-1908. Selected and edited by Allan Nevins. Boston and New York: Houghton Mifflin Co., 1933. xix, 640 p.

______. PRESIDENTIAL PROBLEMS. New York: Century Co., 1904. xi, 281 p.

______. PRINCIPLES AND PURPOSES OF OUR FORM OF GOVERNMENT AS SET FORTH IN PUBLIC PAPERS OF GROVER CLEVELAND. Compiled by Francis Gottsberger. New York: G.G. Peck, 1892. 187 p.

______. THE WRITINGS AND SPEECHES OF GROVER CLEVELAND. Edited by George F. Parker. New York: Cassell Publishing Co., 1892. xxvii, 571 p.

Parker, George F. RECOLLECTIONS OF GROVER CLEVELAND. New York: Century Co., 1909. xv, 427 p.

Wilson, William Lyne. THE CABINET DIARY OF WILLIAM L. WILSON, 1896-1897. With an introduction by Newton D. Baker. Edited by Festus P. Summers. Chapel Hill: University of North Carolina Press, 1957. vii, 276 p.

Grover Cleveland

BIOGRAPHIES

De Santis, Vincent P. "Grover Cleveland." In AMERICA'S ELEVEN GREATEST PRESIDENTS, 2d ed., edited by Morton Borden, pp. 156-79. Chicago: Rand, McNally and Co., 1971.

Lynch, Denis T. GROVER CLEVELAND, A MAN FOUR SQUARE. New York: H. Liveright, 1932. 581 p.

McElroy, Robert McNutt. GROVER CLEVELAND, THE MAN AND THE STATESMAN. 2 vols. New York: Harper and Brothers, 1923.

Merrill, Horace Samuel. BOURBON LEADER: GROVER CLEVELAND AND THE DEMOCRATIC PARTY. Boston: Little, Brown, 1957. viii, 224 p.

A well-written brief biography.

Nevins, Allan. GROVER CLEVELAND, A STUDY IN COURAGE. New York: Dodd, Mead, 1932. xiii, 832 p.

Pulitzer Prize winner. Definitive.

Tugwell, Rexford G. GROVER CLEVELAND. New York: Macmillan, 1968. xviii, 298 p.

MONOGRAPHS

Faulkner, Harold U. POLITICS, REFORM AND EXPANSION, 1890-1900. New York: Harper and Brothers, 1959. 312 p.

Ford, Henry Jones. THE CLEVELAND ERA: A CHRONICLE OF THE NEW ORDER IN POLITICS. New Haven, Conn.: Yale University Press, 1919. ix, 232 p.

Hollingsworth, J. Rogers. THE WHIRLIGIG OF POLITICS: THE DEMOCRACY OF CLEVELAND AND BRYAN. Chicago: University of Chicago Press, 1963. xii, 263 p.

Knoles, George H. THE PRESIDENTIAL CAMPAIGN AND ELECTION OF 1892. Palo Alto, Calif.: Stanford University Press, 1942. 268 p.

LaFeber, Walter Frederick. THE LATIN AMERICAN POLICY OF THE SECOND CLEVELAND ADMINISTRATION. Ann Arbor, Mich.: University Microfilms, 1959. 351 p.

Thomas, Harrison C. THE RETURN OF THE DEMOCRATIC PARTY TO POWER IN 1884. New York: Columbia University, 1919. 263 p.

ARTICLES

Bolt, Robert. "Donald M. Dickinson and the Second Election of Grover Cleveland, 1892." MICHIGAN HISTORY 49 (March 1965): 28-39.

Coletta, Paolo E. "Bryan, Cleveland, and the Disrupted Democracy, 1890-1896." NEBRASKA HISTORY 41 (March 1960): 1-27.

DeSantis, Vincent P. "Grover Cleveland--Another Look." HAYES HISTORICAL JOURNAL 3 (Spring-Fall 1980): 41-50.

Durden, Robert F. "Grover Cleveland and the Bourbon Democracy." SOUTH ATLANTIC QUARTERLY 57 (Summer 1958): 333-38.

Hammett, Hugh B. "The Cleveland Administration and Anglo-American Naval Friction in Hawaii, 1893-1894." MILITARY AFFAIRS 40 (February 1976): 27-32.

Kelley, Robert. "Presbyterianism, Jacksonianism and Grover Cleveland." AMERICAN QUARTERLY 18 (Winter 1966): 615-36.

Knoles, George H., ed. "Grover Cleveland on Imperialism." MISSISSIPPI VALLEY HISTORICAL REVIEW 37 (September 1950): 303-4.

With text of Cleveland's letter, 9 November 1898.

LaFeber, Walter Frederick. "The American Business Community and Cleveland's Venezuela Message." BUSINESS HISTORY REVIEW 34 (Winter 1969): 393-402. Port., notes.

______. "The Background of Cleveland's Venezuelan Policy: A Reinterpretation." AMERICAN HISTORICAL REVIEW 66 (July 1961): 947-67.

Martin, John Stuart. "When the President Disappeared." AMERICAN HERITAGE 8 (October 1957): 10-13, 102-3.

O'Brien, Robert Lincoln. "Grover Cleveland as Seen by His Stenographers, July 1892-November 1895." MASSACHUSETTS HISTORICAL SOCIETY PROCEEDINGS 70 (1957): 128-43.

Robertson, P.L. "Cleveland's Constructive Use of the Pension Vetoes." MID-AMERICA 44 (January 1962): 33-45.

Rosenberg, Marvin, and Rosenberg, Dorothy. "The Dirtiest Election." AMERICAN HERITAGE 13 (August 1962): 4-9.

Stewart, Kate MacLean. "The Daniel Scott Lamont Papers." LIBRARY OF CONGRESS QUARTERLY JOURNAL 17 (February 1960): 63-83.

Includes many communications from and to Cleveland, related mainly to his service as Cleveland's private secretary.

Wickser, P.J. "Grover Cleveland: His Character, Background and Legal Career." AMERICAN BAR ASSOCIATION JOURNAL 33 (April 1947): 327-30.

Workmaster, Wallace F. "Grover Cleveland: American Victorian." HISTORIAN 22 (February 1960): 185-96.

On the "Victorian" quality of his personal habits and ethical standards, 1855-93.

Chapter 34

BENJAMIN HARRISON, 1889-93

BIBLIOGRAPHY

Sievers, Harry J., S.J., ed. BENJAMIN HARRISON, 1833-1901: CHRONOLOGY-DOCUMENTS-BIBLIOGRAPHICAL AIDS. Presidential Chronologies Series. Dobbs Ferry, N.Y.: Oceana Publications, 1969. 89 p.

SOURCE MATERIALS

Harrison, Benjamin. "Letters of Benjamin Harrison." Edited by William B. Miller. PRESBYTERIAN HISTORICAL SOCIETY JOURNAL 37 (September 1959): 143-54.

_____. PUBLIC PAPERS AND ADDRESSES OF BENJAMIN HARRISON, TWENTY-THIRD PRESIDENT OF THE U.S. Washington, D.C.: Government Printing Office, 1893. 302 p.

_____. SPEECHES OF BENJAMIN HARRISON, TWENTY-THIRD PRESIDENT OF THE U.S. Compiled by Charles Hedges. New York: United States Book Co., 1892. 580 p.

> A complete collection of his public addresses from February 1888 to February 1892.

_____. THIS COUNTRY OF OURS. New York: Charles Scribner's Sons, 1897. xxiv, 360 p.

_____. VIEWS OF AN EX-PRESIDENT. Compiled by Mary Lord Harrison. Indianapolis: Bobbs-Merrill, 1901. 532 p.

> Addresses and writings on subjects of public interest after the close of his presidential administration.

Harrison, Benjamin, and Blaine, James G. THE CORRESPONDENCE BETWEEN BENJAMIN HARRISON AND JAMES G. BLAINE, 1882-1893. Edited by Albert T. Volwiler. Philadelphia: American Philosophical Society, 1940. xii, 314 p.

BIOGRAPHIES

Sievers, Harry J. BENJAMIN HARRISON: HOOSIER WARRIOR, 1833-1865. Chicago: Henry Regnery Co., 1952. xxi, 334 p.

_____. BENJAMIN HARRISON: HOOSIER STATESMAN, 1865-1888. New York: University Publishers, 1959. xxi, 502 p.

_____. BENJAMIN HARRISON, HOOSIER PRESIDENT, 1888-1901. Indianapolis: Bobbs Merrill, 1968. xviii, 319 p.

> The first comprehensive biography based upon intensive use of the Harrison Papers.

ARTICLES

"Addition to Benjamin Harrison Papers in Library of Congress." MANUSCRIPTS 12 (Summer 1960): 54.

Baker, G.W., Jr. "Benjamin Harrison and Hawaiian Annexation: A Reinterpretation." PACIFIC HISTORICAL REVIEW 33 (August 1964): 295-309.

De Santis, Vincent P. "Benjamin Harrison and the Republican Party in the South, 1889-1893." INDIANA MAGAZINE OF HISTORY 51 (December 1955): 279-302.

Dozer, Donald M. "Benjamin Harrison and the Presidential Campaign of 1892." AMERICAN HISTORICAL REVIEW 53 (October 1948): 49-77.

Hinckley, Ted C. "Sheldon Jackson and Benjamin Harrison: Presbyterians and the Administration of Alaska." PACIFIC NORTHWEST QUARTERLY 54 (April 1963): 66-74.

Hirshon, Stanley P. "James S. Clarkson Versus Benjamin Harrison, 1891-1893: A Political Saga." IOWA JOURNAL OF HISTORY 58 (July 1960): 219-27.

> On the efforts of Clarkson, first assistant postmaster general and chairman of the Republican National Committee, and others, to obtain the Republican nomination for James G. Blaine and their attacks upon Harrison before and after his renomination and after the victory of Grover Cleveland.

Sinkler, George. "Benjamin Harrison and the Matter of Race." INDIANA MAGAZINE OF HISTORY 65 (September 1969): 197-214.

Spetter, Allan. "Harrison and Blaine: Foreign Policy, 1889-1893." INDIANA MAGAZINE OF HISTORY 65 (September 1969): 215-28.

Volwiler, Albert T. "The Early Empire Days of the United States." WEST VIRGINIA HISTORY 18 (January 1957): 116-27.

Wright, Marcia. "The Benjamin Harrison Papers." LIBRARY OF CONGRESS QUARTERLY JOURNAL OF CURRENT ACQUISITIONS 18 (May 1961): 121-25.

Chapter 35

WILLIAM McKINLEY, 1897-1901

BIBLIOGRAPHY

Sievers, Harry J., ed. WILLIAM McKINLEY, 1843-1901: CHRONOLOGY-DOCUMENTS-BIBLIOGRAPHY. Presidential Chronologies Series. Dobbs Ferry, N.Y.: Oceana Publications, 1970. 83 p.

SOURCE MATERIAL

Dawes, Charles G. A JOURNAL OF THE McKINLEY YEARS. Edited by Bascom N. Timmons. Chicago: Lakeside Press, 1950. xxiv, 458 p.

BIOGRAPHIES

Heald, Edward Thornton. WILLIAM McKINLEY STORY. Canton, Ohio: Stark County Historical Society, 1964. 125 p.

Leech, Margaret. IN THE DAYS OF McKINLEY. New York: Harper, 1959. Reprint. Westport, Conn.: Greenwood Press, 1975. viii, 686 p.

> Pulitzer Prize winner. Gives a balanced view of McKinley's presidency. Excellent personal vignettes, especially of Mrs. McKinley.

Morgan, H. Wayne. WILLIAM McKINLEY AND HIS AMERICA. Syracuse, N.Y.: Syracuse University Press, 1963. xi, 595 p.

> Particularly strong on McKinley as a political leader and president.

Olcott, Charles Summer. THE LIFE OF WILLIAM McKINLEY. 2 vols. Boston: Houghton Mifflin Co., 1911.

Rhodes, James Ford. THE McKINLEY AND ROOSEVELT ADMINISTRATIONS, 1897-1909. New York: Macmillan, 1922. 418 p.

Spielman, William Carl. WILLIAM McKINLEY, STALWART REPUBLICAN: A BIOGRAPHICAL STUDY. New York: Exposition, 1954. 215 p.

MONOGRAPHS

Gould, Lewis L. THE PRESIDENCY OF WILLIAM McKINLEY. American Presidency Series. Lawrence: Regents Press of Kansas, 1980. xi, 294 p.

McCormick, Thomas Joseph. "A FAIR FIELD AND NO FAVOR": AMERICAN CHINA POLICY DURING THE McKINLEY ADMINISTRATIONS, 1897-1901. Ann Arbor, Mich.: University Microfilms, 1960. 426 l.

Offner, John Layser. PRESIDENT McKINLEY AND THE ORIGINS OF THE SPANISH-AMERICAN WAR. Ann Arbor, Mich.: University Microfilms, 1957. 395 l.

Stern, Clarence Ames. RESURGENT REPUBLICANISM: THE HANDIWORK OF HANNA. Ann Arbor, Mich.: Edwards Brothers, 1968. xi, 96 p.

ARTICLES

Adler, Selig. "The Operation on President McKinley." SCIENTIFIC AMERICAN 208 (March 1963): 118-30.

Bacote, Clarence A. "Negro Officeholders in Georgia under President McKinley." JOURNAL OF NEGRO HISTORY 44 (July 1959): 217-39.

Coletta, Paolo Enrico. "Bryan, McKinley, and the Treaty of Paris [1899]." PACIFIC HISTORICAL REVIEW 26 (November 1961): 131-46.

______. "McKinley, the Peace Negotiations, and the Acquisition of the Philippines." PACIFIC HISTORICAL REVIEW 30 (November 1961): 341-50.

Fine, Sidney. "Anarchism and the Assassination of McKinley." AMERICAN HISTORICAL REVIEW 60 (July 1955): 777-99.

Fry, Joseph A. "William McKinley and the Coming of the Spanish-American War: A Study of the Besmirching and Redemption of an Historical Image." DIPLOMATIC HISTORY 3 (Winter 1979): 77-89.

Gould, Lewis L. "William McKinley and the Expansion of Presidential Power." OHIO HISTORY 87 (Winter 1978): 5-20.

McDonald, Timothy G. "McKinley and the Coming of the War with Spain." MIDWEST QUARTERLY 7 (April 1966): 225-38.

Morgan, H. Wayne. "William McKinley as a Political Leader." REVIEW OF POLITICS 28 (October 1966): 417-32.

Nichols, Jeannette P. "The Monetary Problems of William McKinley." OHIO HISTORY 72 (October 1963): 263-92.

Waksmundski, John. "William McKinley and the Railway Workers: Insight into Political Strategy." WEST VIRGINIA HISTORY 36 (October 1974): 37-39.

Walker, Kenneth. "The Third Assassination." NEW YORK HISTORICAL SOCIETY QUARTERLY 41 (October 1957): 407-22.

Chapter 36

THEODORE ROOSEVELT, 1901-09

BIBLIOGRAPHIES

Black, Gilbert J., ed. THEODORE ROOSEVELT, 1858-1919: CHRONOLOGY-DOCUMENTS-BIBLIOGRAPHICAL AIDS. Presidential Chronologies Series. Dobbs Ferry, N.Y.: Oceana Publications, 1969. 120 p.

Grantham, Dewey W., Jr. "Theodore Roosevelt in American Historical Writing, 1945-1960." MID-AMERICA 43 (January 1961): 3-35.

Topical and evaluative summary of articles, books, and unpublished theses.

SOURCE MATERIALS

Butt, Archibald W. THE LETTERS OF ARCHIE BUTT, PERSONAL AIDE TO PRESIDENT ROOSEVELT. Edited by Lawrence W. Abbott. Garden City, N.Y.: Doubleday, Page, 1924. xxviii, 395 p.

_____. TAFT AND ROOSEVELT: THE INTIMATE LETTERS OF ARCHIE BUTT, MILITARY AIDE. 2 vols. Garden City, N.Y.: Doubleday, Doran and Co., 1930. 862 p.

Hart, Albert Bushnell, and Ferleger, Herbert R.,eds. THEODORE ROOSEVELT CYCLOPEDIA. New York: Roosevelt Memorial Association, 1941. 674 p.

Morison, Elting E., ed. THE LETTERS OF THEODORE ROOSEVELT. 8 vols. Cambridge: Harvard University Press, 1951-54.

Roosevelt, Theodore. AMERICAN IDEALS, AND OTHER ESSAYS, SOCIAL AND POLITICAL. New York: Putnam, 1897. Reprint. St. Clair Shores, Mich.: Scholarly Press, 1970. viii, 354 p.

_____. AN AUTOBIOGRAPHY. New York: Charles Scribner's 1958. xi, 372 p.

Completed by Roosevelt in 1913, it covers his views and actions through his presidency.

_____. LETTERS TO HIS CHILDREN. Edited by Joseph Bocklin Bishop. With an epilogue and prologue by Elting E. Morison. Signet Classics. New York: New American Library, 1964. 159 p. Bibliog., illus.

_____. THE STRENUOUS LIFE: ESSAYS AND ADDRESSES. New York: Century, 1902. Reprint. St. Clair Shores, Mich.: Scholarly Press, 1970. 332 p. port.

_____. "The Theodore Roosevelt Letters to Cardinal Gibbons [1901-18]." Edited by John Joseph Gallagher. CATHOLIC HISTORICAL REVIEW 44 (January 1959): 440-56.

Documents from the Archives of the Archdiocese of Baltimore.

_____. THEODORE ROOSEVELT ON RACE, RIOTS, REDS, CRIME. Compiled by Archibald B. Roosevelt. West Sayville, N.Y.: Probe, 1968. xiv, 101 p.

_____. THE THEODORE ROOSEVELT TREASURY: A SELF-PORTRAIT FROM HIS WRITINGS. Compiled by Hermann Hagedorn. New York: Putnam, 1957. 342 p.

_____. THE WRITINGS OF THEODORE ROOSEVELT. Edited by William H. Harbaugh. Indianapolis: Bobbs-Merrill, 1967. liii, 407 p.

_____. THE WORKS OF THEODORE ROOSEVELT. 20 vols. Edited by Hermann Hagedorn. New York: Memorial Edition, Scribner's, 1926.

U.S. Library of Congress. "Catalog of the Theodore Roosevelt Centennial Exhibit." Prepared by Kate MacLean Stewart and Arthur G. Burton. LIBRARY OF CONGRESS QUARTERLY JOURNAL OF CURRENT ACQUISITIONS 15 (May 1958): 106-64.

U.S. Theodore Roosevelt Centennial Commission. FINAL REPORT RELATING TO A CELEBRATION OF THE HUNDREDTH ANNIVERSARY OF THEODORE ROOSEVELT, 1858-1958. Washington, D.C.: Government Printing Office, 1959. 219 p.

BIOGRAPHIES

Bishop, Joseph Bucklin. THEODORE ROOSEVELT AND HIS TIME SHOWN IN HIS OWN LETTERS. 2 vols. New York: C. Scribner's Sons, 1920.

Blum, John Morton. THE REPUBLICAN ROOSEVELT. 2d ed. Cambridge, Mass.: Harvard University Press, 1977. xix, 170 p.

A very good brief political biography.

Burton, David Henry. THEODORE ROOSEVELT. New York: Twayne Publishers, 1972. 236 p.

______. THEODORE ROOSEVELT: CONFIDENT IMPERIALIST. Philadelphia: University of Pennsylvania Press, 1968. ix, 203 p.

Egloff, Franklin R. THEODORE ROOSEVELT, AN AMERICAN PORTRAIT. New York: Vantage Press, 1980. 186 p.

Garraty, John Arthur. THEODORE ROOSEVELT: THE STRENUOUS LIFE. By the editors of AMERICAN HERITAGE. New York: American Heritage Publishing Co., 1967. 153 p.

Harbaugh, William Henry. THE LIFE AND TIMES OF THEODORE ROOSEVELT. Rev. ed. New York: Oxford University Press, 1975. xiv, 542. Bibliog. refs., index.

First published in 1961 under title POWER AND RESPONSIBILITY. A solid book, emphasizing Roosevelt the man and the political leader.

______. POWER AND RESPONSIBILITY: THE LIFE AND TIMES OF THEODORE ROOSEVELT. New York: Farrar, Straus and Cudahy, 1963. Reprint. New rev. ed. New York: Octagon Books, 1975. 540 p.

Johnston, William Davison. T.R.: CHAMPION OF THE STRENUOUS LIFE: A PHOTOGRAPHIC BIOGRAPHY OF THEODORE ROOSEVELT. New York: Farrar, Straus, and Cudahy, 1958. 141 p.

Keller, Morton, ed. THEODORE ROOSEVELT: A PROFILE. American Profiles Series. New York: Hill and Wang, 1967. xix, 554 p.

Lorant, Stefan. THE LIFE AND TIMES OF THEODORE ROOSEVELT. Garden City, N.Y.: Doubleday, 1959. 604 p.

A superb pictorial biography, seventeen years in the making.

Morris, Edmund. THE RISE OF THEODORE ROOSEVELT. New York: Coward, McCann and Geoghegan, 1979. 886 p.

Pringle, Henry F. THEODORE ROOSEVELT, A BIOGRAPHY. Rev. ed. New York: Harcourt, Brace, 1956. x, 435 p.

Pulitzer Prize winner. Well grounded in the sources.

Putnam, Carleton. THEODORE ROOSEVELT: A BIOGRAPHY. Vol. 1, THE FORMATIVE YEARS, 1858-1886. New York: Charles Scribner's Sons, 1958. xiii, 626 p.

Thayer, William Roscoe. THEODORE ROOSEVELT: AN INTIMATE BIOGRAPHY. New York: Grosset and Dunlap, 1919. xiii, 474 p.

Wagenknecht, Edward Charles. THE SEVEN WORLDS OF THEODORE ROOSEVELT. New York: Longmans, Green, 1958. xvii, 325 p.

MONOGRAPHS

Beale, Howard Kennedy. THEODORE ROOSEVELT AND THE RISE OF AMERICA TO WORLD POWER. Baltimore: Johns Hopkins Press, 1956. xxi, 579 p.

Chessman, George Wallace. GOVERNOR THEODORE ROOSEVELT: THE ALBANY APPRENTICESHIP, 1898-1900. Cambridge, Mass.: Harvard University Press, 1965. ix, 335 p.

Based on thesis, Harvard University.

______. THEODORE ROOSEVELT AND THE POLITICS OF POWER. Edited by Oscar Handlin. Boston: G.K. Hall, 1976. xiii, 306 p.

Cutright, Paul Russell. THEODORE ROOSEVELT, THE NATURALIST. New York: Harper, 1956. xiv, 297 p.

Gable, John Allen. THE BULL MOOSE YEARS: THEODORE ROOSEVELT AND THE PROGRESSIVE PARTY. Series in American Studies. Port Washington, N.Y.: Kennikat Press, 1978. xi, 302 p.

Gardner, Joseph Lawrence. DEPARTING GLORY: THEODORE ROOSEVELT AS EX-PRESIDENT. New York: Scribner, 1973. xv, 432 p.

Gatewood, Willard B., Jr. THEODORE ROOSEVELT AND THE ART OF CONTROVERSY. Baton Rouge: Louisiana State University Press, 1970. vii, 294 p.

An examination of seven episodes from the Roosevelt years in the White House.

Hagedorn, Hermann. GUIDE TO SAGAMORE HILL: THE PLACE, THE PEOPLE, THE LIFE, THE MEANING. New York: Theodore Roosevelt Association, 1953. 74 p.

______. THE ROOSEVELT FAMILY OF SAGAMORE HILL. New York: Macmillan, 1954. 435 p.

McKee, Delber L. CHINESE EXCLUSION VERSUS THE OPEN DOOR POLICY, 1900-1906: CLASHES OVER CHINA POLICY IN THE ROOSEVELT ERA. Detroit: Wayne State University Press, 1977. 292 p.

Manners, William. TR AND WILL: A FRIENDSHIP THAT SPLIT THE REPUBLICAN PARTY. New York: Harcourt, Brace and World, 1969. xiv, 335 p.

Marks, Frederick W. III. VELVET ON IRON: THE DIPLOMACY OF THEODORE ROOSEVELT. Lincoln: University of Nebraska Press, 1979. xiv, 247 p.

Mowry, George E. THE ERA OF THEODORE ROOSEVELT, 1900-1912. New York: Harper, 1958. xvi, 330 p.

Excellent treatment of Roosevelt's philosophy and policies as a national leader.

______. THEODORE ROOSEVELT AND THE PROGRESSIVE MOVEMENT. Madison: University of Wisconsin Press, 1946. viii, 405 p. Bibliog.

Neu, Charles E. AN UNCERTAIN FRIENDSHIP: THEODORE ROOSEVELT AND JAPAN, 1906-1909. Cambridge, Mass.: Harvard University Press, 1967. x, 347 p.

O'Gara, Gordon Carpenter. THEODORE ROOSEVELT AND THE RISE OF THE MODERN NAVY. Westport, Conn.: Greenwood Press, 1969. 138 p.

Riis, Jacob August. THEODORE ROOSEVELT, THE CITIZEN. New York: Outlook Co., 1918. Reprint. St. Clair Shores, Mich.: Scholarly Press, 1970. vii, 471 p.

Roosevelt, Thomas A. THEODORE ROOSEVELT AND THE JAPANESE-AMERICAN CRISES. Gloucester, Mass.: P. Smith, 1964. ix, 353 p.

An account of the international complications arising from the race problem on the Pacific coast.

THEODORE ROOSEVELT ASSOCIATION JOURNAL. Oyster Bay, N.Y.: Theodore Roosevelt Association, 1975--. Semiannual.

White, G. Edward. THE EASTERN ESTABLISHMENT AND THE WESTERN EXPERIENCE: THE WEST OF FREDERIC REMINGTON, THEODORE ROOSEVELT, AND OWEN WISTER. New Haven, Conn.: Yale University Press, 1968. 238 p.

ARTICLES

Andrews, Avery Delano. "Theodore Roosevelt as Police Commissioner." NEW YORK HISTORICAL SOCIETY QUARTERLY 42 (April 1958): 116-41.

> Reminiscences by another member of the Board of Police Commissioners. Covers New York City, 1895-98.

Blackorby, Edward C. "Theodore Roosevelt's Conservation Policies and Their Impact upon America and the American West." NORTH DAKOTA HISTORY 25 (October 1958): 105-17.

Blum, John M. "Editor's Camera: 'The Letters of Theodore Roosevelt.'" AMERICAN DOCUMENTATION 1 (October 1950): 181-84.

> On the use of microfilm in the collection of historical materials.

Cane, Guy. "Sea Power--Teddy's 'Big Stick' [Roosevelt and Mahan]." UNITED STATES NAVAL INSTITUTE PROCEEDINGS 102 (August 1976): 40-48.

Conrad, David E. "Creating the Nation's Largest Forest Reserve: Roosevelt, Emmons and the Tongass National Forest." PACIFIC HISTORICAL REVIEW 46 (February 1977): 65-83.

Ellsworth, Clayton S. "Theodore Roosevelt's County Life Commission." AGRICULTURAL HISTORY 34 (October 1960): 155-72.

Fenton, Charles. "Theodore Roosevelt as an American Man of Letters." WESTERN HUMANITIES REVIEW 13 (Autumn 1959): 369-74.

Fischer, Robert, and Gay, James T. "A Post-Mortem of Theodore Roosevelt in Historical Writings, 1919-1929." MID-AMERICA 56 (July 1974): 139-59.

Garraty, John A., ed. "Theodore Roosevelt on the Telephone." AMERICAN HERITAGE 9 (December 1957): 99-108.

Gordon, Donald C. "Roosevelt's 'Smart Yankee Trick.'" PACIFIC HISTORICAL REVIEW 30 (November 1961): 351-58.

Concerns his diplomatic manuevers of 1908 involving the British Empire and Japanese migration into the United States.

Gores, Stan. "The Attempted Assassination of Teddy Roosevelt." WISCONSIN MAGAZINE OF HISTORY 53 (Summer 1970): 269-77.

Gow, Douglas R. "How Did the Roosevelt Corollary Become Linked to the Dominican Republic?" MID-AMERICA 58 (October 1976): 159-65.

Grantham, Dewey W., Jr. "Dinner at the White House: Theodore Roosevelt, Booker T. Washington, and the South." TENNESSEE HISTORICAL QUARTERLY 17 (June 1958): 112-30.

Johnson, Arthur Menzies. "Theodore Roosevelt and the Navy." U.S. NAVAL INSTITUTE PROCEEDINGS 84 (October 1958): 76-86.

Covers period, 1887-1909.

Kitchens, Joseph. "Theodore Roosevelt and the Politics of War 1914-1918." INTERNATIONAL REVIEW OF HISTORY AND POLITICAL SCIENCE 13 (May 1976): 1-16.

Lucas, Stephen E. "Theodore Roosevelt's 'The Man with the Muck-Rake': A Reinterpretation." QUARTERLY JOURNAL OF SPEECH 59 (December 1973): 452-62.

Morison, Elting Elmore. "The Letters of Theodore Roosevelt." HARVARD LIBRARY BULLETIN 5 (Autumn 1951): 378-81.

______. "Some Thoughts on the Roosevelt Papers." QUARTERLY JOURNAL OF THE LIBRARY OF CONGRESS 15 (May 1958): 101-5.

______. "The Uneasy Chair: Selecting and Editing the Letters of Theodore Roosevelt." HARVARD ALUMNI BULLETIN 60 (3 May 1958): 598-601.

Parsons, Edward B. "Roosevelt's Containment of the Russo-Japanese War." PACIFIC HISTORICAL REVIEW 38 (February 1969): 21-43.

Quinlan, J. "Theodore Roosevelt: A Centenary Tribute." CONTEMPORARY REVIEW 195 (February 1959): 108-10.

Robinson, Elwyn B. "Theodore Roosevelt: Amateur Historian." NORTH DAKOTA HISTORY 25 (January 1959): 4-13.

Scheinberg, Stephen J. "Theodore Roosevelt and the A.F of L's Entry into Politics, 1906-1908." LABOR HISTORY 3 (Spring 1962): 131-48.

Scheiner, Seth M. "President Theodore Roosevelt and the Negro, 1901-1908." JOURNAL OF NEGRO HISTORY 47 (July 1962): 169-82.

> This examination of Theodore Roosevelt's statements and actions on the question of Negro rights demonstrates he gave up his fight for Negro rights, which was incidental to his political policy, by mid-1903, not in 1905 or 1906 as some historians contend.

Sellen, Robert W. "Theodore Roosevelt: Historian with a Moral." MID-AMERICA 41 (October 1959): 223-40.

Stillson, Albert C. "Military Policy without Political Guidance: Theodore Roosevelt's Navy." MILITARY AFFAIRS 25 (Spring 1961): 18-31.

Tinsley, James A. "Roosevelt, Foraker, and the Brownsville Affair." JOURNAL OF NEGRO HISTORY 41 (January 1956): 43-65.

Tuchman, Barbara; McCullough, David; and Morris, Edmund. Harvard Theodore Roosevelt Centennial Symposium. THEODORE ROOSEVELT ASSOCIATION JOURNAL 6 (Summer 1980): 10-17.

> Three short speeches at Harvard's Houghton Library on the occasion of the one hundredth anniversary of Theodore Roosevelt's graduation from Harvard College in 1880.

Watson, Richard L., Jr. "Theodore Roosevelt: The Years of Preparation, 1868-1900." SOUTH ATLANTIC QUARTERLY 51 (April 1952): 301-15.

_____. "Theodore Roosevelt and Herbert Hoover." SOUTH ATLANTIC QUARTERLY 53 (January 1954): 109-29.

White, Leonard D. "Public Life of T.R." PUBLIC ADMINISTRATION REVIEW 14, no. 4 (1954): 278-82.

Woods, Randall B. "Terrorism in the Age of Roosevelt: The Miss Stone Affair, 1901-1902." AMERICAN QUARTERLY 31 (Fall 1979): 478-95.

Chapter 37

WILLIAM HOWARD TAFT, 1909-13

BIBLIOGRAPHY

Black, Gilbert J., ed. WILLIAM HOWARD TAFT, 1857-1930: CHRONOLOGY, DOCUMENTS-BIBLIOGRAPHICAL AIDS. Presidential Chronologies Series. Dobbs Ferry, N.Y.: Oceana Publications, 1970. 89 p.

SOURCE MATERIALS

Butt, Archibald. TAFT AND ROOSEVELT: THE INTIMATE LETTERS OF ARCHIE BUTT, MILITARY AIDE. 2 vols. Garden City, N.Y.: Doubleday, Doran and Co., 1930. 862 p.

Schlup, Leonard, comp. and ann. "Selected Letters of Senator McCumbert to Former President Taft Concerning the League of Nations." NORTH DAKOTA HISTORY 46 (Summer 1979): 15-23.

Taft, William Howard. THE PRESIDENT AND HIS POWERS. Introduction by Nicholas Murray Butler. New York: Columbia University Press, 1967. 165 p.

Taft, William Howard, and Edwards, George B. "Letters of Roommates: William H. Taft and George B. Edwards." Edited by Walter P. Armstrong. AMERICAN BAR ASSOCIATION JOURNAL 34 (May 1948): 383-85.

U.S. Library of Congress. Manuscript Division. INDEX TO THE WILLIAM HOWARD TAFT PAPERS. 6 vols. Washington, D.C.: Government Printing Office, 1972.

BIOGRAPHIES

Duffy, Herbert Smith. WILLIAM HOWARD TAFT. New York: Minton, Balch and Co., 1930. x, 345 p.

Myers, Elisabeth P. WILLIAM HOWARD TAFT. Chicago: Reilly and Lee, 1970. 168 p.

Pringle, Henry F. THE LIFE AND TIMES OF WILLIAM HOWARD TAFT, A BIOGRAPHY. 2 vols. New York: Farrar and Rinehart, 1939.

___ Definitive. Based on Taft Papers in the Library of Congress.

MONOGRAPHS

Anderson, Donald F. WILLIAM HOWARD TAFT: A CONSERVATIVE'S CONCEPTION OF THE PRESIDENCY. Ithaca, N.Y.: Cornell University Press, 1973. ix, 355 p. Illus.

Coletta, Paolo E. THE PRESIDENCY OF WILLIAM HOWARD TAFT. American Presidency Series. Lawrence: University Press of Kansas, 1973. ix, 306 p.

Haley, P. Edward. REVOLUTION AND INTERVENTION: THE DIPLOMACY OF TAFT AND WILSON WITH MEXICO, 1910-1917. Cambridge: MIT Press, 1970. 294 p.

Kutler, Stanley Ira. THE JUDICIAL PHILOSOPHY OF CHIEF JUSTICE TAFT AND ORGANIZED LABOR, 1921-1930. Ann Arbor, Mich.: University Microfilms, 1960. 265 l.

Manners, William. TR AND WILL: A FRIENDSHIP THAT SPLIT THE REPUBLICAN PARTY. New York: Harcourt, Brace and World, 1969. xiv, 335 p.

Mason, Alpheus Thomas. WILLIAM HOWARD TAFT: CHIEF JUSTICE. New York: Simon and Schuster, 1965. 354 p.

Ross, Ishbel. AN AMERICAN FAMILY: THE TAFTS, 1678 TO 1964. 2d ed. Cleveland: World Publishing Co., 1964. vii, 468 p. Bibliog., illus.

Scholes, Walter Vinton. FOREIGN POLICIES OF THE TAFT ADMINISTRATION. Columbia: University of Missouri Press, 1970. 259 p.

Wilensky, Norman M. CONSERVATIVES IN THE PROGRESSIVE ERA: THE TAFT REPUBLICANS OF 1912. Gainesville: University of Florida Press, 1965. 75 p.

ARTICLES

Alderson, William T., ed. "Taft, Roosevelt, and the U.S. Steel Case: A

Letter of Jacob McGavock Dickinson." TENNESSEE HISTORICAL QUARTERLY 18 (September 1959): 266-72.

Ballard, Rene N. "The Administrative Theory of William Howard Taft." WESTERN POLITICAL QUARTERLY 7 (March 1954): 65-74.

Bates, James Leonard. "The Midwest Decision, 1915, a Landmark in Conservation History." PACIFIC NORTHWEST QUARTERLY 51 (January 1960): 26-34.

Bennett, A.L. "Profile of a Year: 1910." AMERICAN FORESTS 66 (September 1960): 30-33.

Campbell, John P. "Taft, Roosevelt, and the Arbitration Treaties of 1911." JOURNAL OF AMERICAN HISTORY 53 (September 1966): 279-98.

Chay, Jongsuk. "The Taft-Katsura Memorandum Reconsidered." PACIFIC HISTORICAL REVIEW 37 (August 1968): 321-26.

Clark, T.R. "President Taft and the Puerto Rican Appropriation Crisis of 1909." AMERICAS 26 (October 1969): 152-70.

Coulter, E. Merton. "Presidential Visits to Georgia during Ante-Bellum Times." GEORGIA HISTORICAL QUARTERLY 55 (Fall 1971): 329-64.

_____. "William Howard Taft's Visit to Athens." GEORGIA HISTORICAL QUARTERLY 52 (December 1968): 388-97.

Crawford, Charlotte. "The Border Meeting of Presidents Taft and Diaz." PASSWORD 3 (July 1958): 86-96.

Dick, Charles W.F. "Organizing a National Convention: a Lesson from Senator Dick." Edited by Thomas E. Felt. OHIO HISTORICAL QUARTERLY 67 (January 1958): 50-62.

Detailed instructions to friends of President Taft, 28 May 1912, for insuring his nomination at the Republican Convention in Chicago and preventing that of Theodore Roosevelt.

Esthus, Raymond A. "The Taft-Katsura Agreement--Reality or Myth?" JOURNAL OF MODERN HISTORY 31 (March 1959): 46-51.

Farrell, John T. "Background of the 1902 Taft Mission to Rome." CATHOLIC HISTORICAL REVIEW 36 (April 1950): 1-32.

On the status of Catholic friars in the Philippines, 1898-1902, and the policies of Taft.

German, James C., Jr. "The Taft Administration and Sherman Antitrust Act." MID-AMERICA 54 (July 1972): 172-86.

______. "Taft, [Theodore] Roosevelt, and United States Steel." HISTORIAN 34 (August 1972): 598-613.

Hahn, Harlan. "President Taft and the Discipline of Patronage." JOURNAL OF POLITICS 28 (May 1966): 368-90.

Hess, Stephen. "Big Bill Taft." AMERICAN HERITAGE 17 (October 1966): 33-37, 82-86.

Kutler, Stanley I. "Chief Justice Taft, National Regulation, and the Commerce Power." JOURNAL OF AMERICAN HISTORY 51 (March 1965): 651-68.

Larson, Robert W. "Taft, Roosevelt, and New Mexico Statehood." MID-AMERICA 45 (April 1963): 99-114.

McHargue, Daniel S. "President Taft's Appointments to the Supreme Court." JOURNAL OF POLITICS 12 (August 1950): 478-510.

Minger, Ralph Eldin. "Taft, MacArthur, and the Establishment of Civil Government in the Philippines." OHIO HISTORY QUARTERLY 70 (October 1961): 308-31.

______. "Taft's Missions to Japan: A Study in Personal Diplomacy." PACIFIC HISTORICAL REVIEW 30 (August 1961): 279-94.

______. "William H. Taft and the U.S. Intervention in Cuba in 1906." HISPANIC AMERICAN HISTORICAL REVIEW 41 (February 1961): 75-89.

______. "William Howard Taft's Forgotten Visit to Russia." RUSSIAN REVIEW 22 (April 1963): 149-56.

Ness, Gary. "William Howard Taft and the Great War." CINCINNATI HISTORICAL SOCIETY BULLETIN 34 (Spring 1976): 7-24.

North, Gene. "The Tafts Went to Texas." BULLETIN OF THE HISTORICAL AND PHILOSOPHICAL SOCIETY OF OHIO 15 (October 1957): 290-301.

> On the visit of William Howard Taft to the ranch of his half-brother, Charles P. Taft, near Gregory, Texas, 1909.

Parsons, Elsie Worthington [Clews]. "Congressional Junket in Japan: The Taft Party of 1905 Meets the Mikado." Edited by John E. Parsons. NEW YORK HISTORICAL SOCIETY QUARTERLY 41 (October 1957): 382-406.

Rosenthal, Herbert H. "The Cruise of the Tarpon [Taft-Roosevelt conference, Sept. 1910]." NEW YORK HISTORY 39 (October 1958): 303-20.

On a brief secret meeting between Roosevelt and Taft at New Haven to confer on the affairs of the Republican Party, 19 September 1910.

Schultz, L. Peter. "William Howard Taft: A Constitutionalist's View of the Presidency." PRESIDENTIAL STUDIES QUARTERLY 9 (Fall 1979): 402-14.

Scribner, Robert Leslie. "Now About This Football Situation. . ." VIRGINIA CAVALCADE 6 (Autumn 1956): 30-33.

On the unofficial intervention of Taft in disciplinary measures applied by the faculty of Randolph-Macon College to its football team, 1910.

Shriver, Phillip R., ed. "William Howard Taft and Myron T. Herrick: Selected Letters, 1912-1916." BULLETIN OF THE HISTORICAL AND PHILOSOPHICAL SOCIETY OF OHIO 14 (October 1956): 221-31.

Solvick, Stanley D. "The Conservative as Progressive: William Howard Taft and the Politics of the Square Deal." NORTHWEST OHIO QUARTERLY 39 (Summer 1967): 38-48.

_____. "The Pre-Presidential Political and Economic Thought of William Howard Taft." NORTHWEST OHIO QUARTERLY 43 (Fall 1971): 87 ff.

_____. "William Howard Taft and Cannonism." WISCONSIN MAGAZINE OF HISTORY 48 (Autumn 1964): 48-58.

_____. "William Howard Taft and the Payne-Aldrich Tariff." MISSISSIPPI VALLEY HISTORICAL REVIEW 50 (December 1963): 424-42.

Stewart, Kate MacLean. "The William Howard Taft Papers." LIBRARY OF CONGRESS QUARTERLY JOURNAL OF CURRENT ACQUISITIONS 15 (November 1957): 1-11.

Chapter 38

WOODROW WILSON, 1913-21

BIBLIOGRAPHIES

Turnbull, Laura Shearer, comp. WOODROW WILSON: A SELECTED BIBLIOGRAPHY OF HIS PUBLISHED WRITINGS, ADDRESSES, AND PUBLIC PAPERS. Princeton, N.J.: University Press, 1948. vi, 173 p.

Vexler, Robert I., ed. WOODROW WILSON, 1856-1924: CHRONOLOGY-DOCUMENTS-BIBLIOGRAPHICAL AIDS. Presidential Chronologies Series. Dobbs Ferry, N.Y.: Oceana Publications, 1969. 123 p.

SOURCE MATERIALS

Hoover, Herbert. THE HOOVER-WILSON WARTIME CORRESPONDENCE. Edited and with commentaries by Francis William O'Brien. Ames: Iowa State University Press, 1974. xxvi, 297 p.

______. TWO PEACEMAKERS IN PARIS: THE HOOVER-WILSON POST-ARMISTICE LETTERS, 1918-1920. Edited by Francis William O'Brien. College Station: Texas A & M University Press, 1978. xlix, 254 p.

House, Edward Mandell. THE INTIMATE PAPERS OF COLONEL HOUSE. 4 vols. Edited by Charles Seymour. Boston: Houghton Mifflin, 1926-28.

Houston, David Franklin. EIGHT YEARS WITH WILSON'S CABINET, 1913 TO 1920; WITH A PERSONAL ESTIMATE OF THE PRESIDENT. 2 vols. Garden City, N.Y.: Doubleday, Page, 1926.

Wilson, Edith Bolling Galt. MY MEMOIR. Indianapolis: Bobbs-Merrill, 1939. 386 p.

Wilson, Woodrow. A DAY OF DEDICATION: THE ESSENTIAL WRITINGS AND SPEECHES OF WOODROW WILSON. Edited by Albert Fried. New York: Macmillan, 1965. 478 p.

_____. THE PAPERS OF WOODROW WILSON. Edited by Arthur S. Link. 40 vols. Princeton, N.J.: Princeton University Press, 1966-82.

_____. THE POLITICAL THOUGHT OF WOODROW WILSON. Edited by E. David Cronon. American Heritage Series. Indianapolis: Bobbs-Merrill, 1965. xcv, 559 p.

_____. THE POLITICS OF WOODROW WILSON. SELECTIONS FROM HIS SPEECHES AND WRITINGS. Edited with an introduction by August Heckscher. New York: Harper, 1956. xxvi, 389 p.

_____. THE PRICELESS GIFT: THE LOVE LETTERS OF WOODROW WILSON AND ELLEN AXSON WILSON. Edited by Eleanor Wilson McAdoo. New York: McGraw-Hill, 1962. x, 324 p.

_____. THE WILSON READER. Edited by Francis Farmer. Docket Series, no. 4. New York: Oceana Publications, 1956. 286 p.

BIOGRAPHIES

Baker, Ray Stannard. WOODROW WILSON: LIFE AND LETTERS. 8 vols. Garden City, N.Y.: Doubleday, Doran and Co., 1927-39.

> Authorized biography. Very informative firsthand volumes by Wilson's literary executor.

Blum, John Morton. WOODROW WILSON AND THE POLITICS OF MORALITY. Library of American Biography. Boston: Little, Brown, 1956. vi, 215 p.

Bragdon, Henry Wilkinson. WOODROW WILSON: THE ACADEMIC YEARS. Cambridge, Mass.: Belknap Press of Harvard University Press, 1967. xiii, 519 p.

Daniels, Josephus. THE LIFE OF WOODROW WILSON, 1856-1924. Chicago: J.C. Winston Co., 1924. 381 p.

Garraty, John Arthur. WOODROW WILSON: A GREAT LIFE IN BRIEF. New York: Knopf, 1956. Reprint. Westport, Conn.: Greenwood Press, 1977. 206 p.

Grayson, Cary Travers. WOODROW WILSON: AN INTIMATE MEMOIR. New York: Holt, Rinehart and Winston, 1960. xi, 143 p.

Hoover, Herbert Clark. THE ORDEAL OF WOODROW WILSON. New York: McGraw-Hill, 1958. xiii, 318 p.

Link, Arthur Stanley. WOODROW WILSON. 5 vols. Princeton, N.J.: Princeton University Press, 1947--.

Critical, but far from hostile biography, destined to be the definitive account when the series, now up to 1917, is completed.

______. WOODROW WILSON: A BRIEF BIOGRAPHY. Cleveland: World Publishing Co., 1963. 191 p.

______, ed. WOODROW WILSON: A PROFILE. American Profiles. New York: Hill and Wang, 1968. viii, 197 p.

Loth, David. THE STORY OF WOODROW WILSON. New York: Woodrow Wilson Foundation, 1957. 56 p.

McAdoo, Eleanor Randolph Wilson. THE WOODROW WILSONS. New York: Macmillan Co., 1937. x, 301 p.

Mulder, John M. WOODROW WILSON: THE YEARS OF PREPARATION. Princeton, N.J.: Princeton University Press, 1977. xv, 304 p.

Supplementary volume to THE PAPERS OF WOODROW WILSON ______ (1966-82).

Osborn, George C. WOODROW WILSON: THE EARLY YEARS. Baton Rouge: Louisiana State University Press, 1968. ix, 345 p.

Pisney, Raymond F., ed. WOODROW WILSON IN RETROSPECT. Verona, Va.: McClure Press, 1978. 144 p.

A publication of the Woodrow Wilson Birthplace Foundation, including addresses sponsored by the organization from 1940 to 1959 and some of the papers presented during the centennial of Wilson's birth in Staunton, Virginia.

Walworth, Arthur Clarence. WOODROW WILSON. 2d ed., rev. Boston: Houghton Mifflin, 1965. xiv, 436 p.

Weinstein, Edwin A. WOODROW WILSON: A MEDICAL AND PSYCHOLOGICAL BIOGRAPHY. Princeton, N.J.: Princeton University Press, 1981. xi, 399 p.

MONOGRAPHS

Alsop, E.B., ed. THE GREATNESS OF WOODROW WILSON, 1856-1956. New York: Rinehart, 1956. xiv, 268 p.

Bailey, Thomas A. WOODROW WILSON AND THE LOST PEACE. New York: Macmillan, 1944. xii, 381 p.

For annotation, see next entry.

_____. WOODROW WILSON AND THE GREAT BETRAYAL. New York: Macmillan, 1945. xii, 429 p.

Highly readable accounts of Wilson's inflexibility at the time of the fight for the League of Nations.

Blum, John Morton. JOE TUMULTY AND THE WILSON ERA. Boston: Houghton Mifflin, 1951. Reprint. Hamden, Conn.: Archon Books, 1969. ix, 337 p.

Buehrig, Edward Henry. WOODROW WILSON AND THE BALANCE OF POWER. Bloomington: Indiana University Press, 1955. Reprint. Gloucester, Mass.: P. Smith, 1968. x, 325 p.

_____, ed. WILSON'S FOREIGN POLICY IN PERSPECTIVE. Bloomington: Indiana University Press, 1957. 176 p.

Carter, Purvis M. CONGRESSIONAL AND PUBLIC REACTION TO WILSON'S CARIBBEAN POLICY, 1913-1917. New York: Vantage Press, 1977. 164 p.

Craig, Hardin. WOODROW WILSON AT PRINCETON. Norman: University of Oklahoma Press, 1960. 175 p.

Creel, George. THE WAR, THE WORLD AND WILSON. New York: Harper, 1920. 366 p.

Curry, Roy Watson. WOODROW WILSON AND FAR EASTERN POLICY, 1913-1921. New York: Octagon Books, 1968. 411 p.

Daniels, Josephus. WILSON ERA: YEARS OF WAR AND AFTER, 1917-1923. Chapel Hill: University of North Carolina Press, 1946. 654 p.

Devlin, Patrick. TOO PROUD TO FIGHT: WOODROW WILSON'S NEUTRALITY. New York: Oxford University Press, 1975. xviii, 731 p.

Dudden, Arthur Power, ed. WOODROW WILSON AND THE WORLD OF TODAY. Philadelphia: University of Pennsylvania Press, 1957. 96 p.

Fifield, Russell Hunt. WOODROW WILSON AND THE FAR EAST: THE DIPLOMACY OF THE SHANTUNG QUESTION. New York: Crowell, 1952. Reprint. Hamden, Conn.: Archon Books, 1965. xv, 383 p.

Freud, Sigmund, and Bullitt, William C. THOMAS WOODROW WILSON: TWENTY-EIGHTH PRESIDENT OF THE UNITED STATES: A PSYCHOLOGICAL STUDY. Boston: Houghton Mifflin, 1967. 307 p.

George, Alexander L., and George, Juliette L. WOODROW WILSON AND COLONEL HOUSE: A PERSONALITY STUDY. New York: J. Day Co., 1956. xvii, 362 p.

Gilderhus, Mark T. DIPLOMACY AND REVOLUTION: U.S.-MEXICAN RELATIONS UNDER WILSON AND CARRANZA. Tucson: University of Arizona Press, 1977. xiv, 159 p.

Hirst, David W. WOODROW WILSON, REFORM GOVERNOR: A DOCUMENTARY NARRATIVE. Princeton, N.J.: Van Nostrand, 1965. xv, 256 p.

Jennings, David Henry. PRESIDENT WILSON'S TOUR IN SEPTEMBER 1919: A STUDY OF FORCES OPERATING DURING THE LEAGUE OF NATIONS FIGHT. Ann Arbor, Mich.: University Microfilms, 1958. 226 p.

Latham, Earl, ed. THE PHILOSOPHY AND POLICIES OF WOODROW WILSON. Prepared for the American Political Science Association. Chicago: University of Chicago Press, 1958. xv, 266 p.

Link, Arthur Stanley. WILSON THE DIPLOMATIST: A LOOK AT HIS MAJOR FOREIGN POLICIES [1913-20]. New York: New Viewpoints, 1974. xvi, 165 p.

_____. WOODROW WILSON AND THE PROGRESSIVE ERA, 1910-1917. New American Nation Series. New York: Harper and Brothers, 1954. xvii, 331 p.

Livermore, Seward W. POLITICS IS ADJOURNED: WOODROW WILSON AND THE WAR CONGRESS, 1916-1918. Middletown, Conn.: Wesleyan University Press, 1966. 324 p.

Maddox, Robert James. THE UNKNOWN WAR WITH RUSSIA: WILSON'S SIBERIAN INTERVENTION. San Rafael, Calif.: Presidio Press, 1977. ix, 156 p.

Mamatey, Victor S. THE UNITED STATES AND EAST CENTRAL EUROPE, 1914-1918: A STUDY IN WILSONIAN DIPLOMACY AND PROPAGANDA. Princeton, N.J.: Princeton University Press, 1957. xi, 431 p.

Parsons, Edward B. WILSONIAN DIPLOMACY: ALLIED-AMERICAN RIVALRIES IN WAR AND PEACE. St. Louis: Forum Press, 1978. ix, 213 p.

Safford, Jeffrey J. WILSONIAN MARITIME DIPLOMACY, 1913-1921. New Brunswick, N.J.: Rutgers University Press, 1978. xii, 282 p.

Scheiber, Harry N. THE WILSON ADMINISTRATION AND CIVIL LIBERTIES, 1917-1921. Cornell Studies in American History, Literature, and Folklore. Ithaca, N.Y.: Cornell University Press, 1960. ix, 69 p.

Seymour, Charles. AMERICAN DIPLOMACY DURING THE WORLD WAR. Baltimore: Johns Hopkins Press, 1934. Reprint. Hamden, Conn.: Archon Books, 1964. xviii, 427 p.

Smith, Gene. WHEN THE CHEERING STOPPED: THE LAST YEARS OF WOODROW WILSON. New York: William Morrow and Co., 1964. xi, 307 p.

Fascinating account of Wilson's last years and crippling illness. Based upon documents found after his widow's death.

Tumulty, Joseph Patrick. WOODROW WILSON AS I KNOW HIM. Garden City, N.Y.: Doubleday, Page, 1921. 553 p.

Walworth, Arthur Clarence. AMERICA'S MOMENT, 1918: AMERICAN DIPLOMACY AT THE END OF WORLD WAR I. New York: Norton, 1977. vii, 309 p.

WOODROW WILSON: IDEALISM AND REALITY. Edited by Raymond F. Pisney. Verona, Va.: McClure Press, 1977. 83 p.

Woodrow Wilson Centennial Celebration Commission. FINAL REPORT OF THE WOODROW WILSON CENTENNIAL CELEBRATION COMMISSION. Washington, D.C.: 1958. x, 253 p.

ARTICLES

Abrams, Richard M. "Woodrow Wilson and the Southern Congressmen, 1913-1916." JOURNAL OF SOUTHERN HISTORY 22 (November 1956): 417-37.

Ambrosious, Lloyd E. "Wilson, Clemenceau and the German Problem at the

Paris Peace Conference of 1919." ROCKY MOUNTAIN SOCIAL SCIENCE JOURNAL 12 (April 1975): 69-79.

Bailey, Thomas Andrew. "Woodrow Wilson Wouldn't Yield [1919]." AMERICAN HERITAGE 8 (June 1957): 20-25, 105-6.

Best, Gary Dean. "President Wilson's Second Industrial Conference, 1919-1920." LABOR HISTORY 16 (Fall 1975): 505-20.

Blumenthal, Henry. "Woodrow Wilson and the Race Question." JOURNAL OF NEGRO HISTORY 48 (January 1963): 1-21.

Brand, Katherine E. "The Woodrow Wilson Collection." LIBRARY OF CONGRESS QUARTERLY JOURNAL 2 (February 1945): 3-10.

_____. "Woodrow Wilson in His Own Time." LIBRARY OF CONGRESS QUARTERLY JOURNAL 13 (February 1956): 61-72.

Brodie, Bernard. "A Psychoanalytic Interpretation of Woodrow Wilson." WORLD POLITICS 9 (April 1957): 413-22.

Brownlow, Louis. "Woodrow Wilson and Public Administration." PUBLIC ADMINISTRATION REVIEW 16 (Spring 1956): 77-81.

Burner, David. "The Breakup of the Wilson Coalition of 1916." MID-AMERICA 45 (January 1963): 18-35.

Carleton, William G. "A New Look at Woodrow Wilson." VIRGINIA QUARTERLY REVIEW 38 (Autumn 1962): 545-66.

Chan, Loran B. "Fighting for the League: President Wilson in Nevada: 1919." NEVADA HISTORICAL SOCIETY QUARTERLY 22 (Summer 1979): 115-27.

Childs, R.S. "Woodrow Wilson Legacy." NATIONAL MUNCIPAL REVIEW 46 (January 1957): 14-19.

Cornwell, Elmer E., Jr. "The Press Conferences of Woodrow Wilson." JOURNALISM QUARTERLY 39 (Summer 1962): 292-300.

Craig, H. "Woodrow Wilson as an Orator." QUARTERLY JOURNAL OF SPEECH 38 (April 1952): 145-48.

Cuff, Robert D. "We Band of Brothers--Woodrow Wilson's War Managers." CANADIAN REVIEW OF AMERICAN STUDIES 5 (Fall 1974): 135-48.

Curti, Merle. "Woodrow Wilson's Concept of Human Nature." MIDWEST JOURNAL OF POLITICAL SCEINCE 1 (May 1957): 1-19.

Dabney, Virginius. "The Human Side of Woodrow Wilson." VIRGINIA QUARTERLY REVIEW 32 (Autumn 1956): 508-23.

Daniels, Jonathan Worth. "The Long Shadow of Woodrow Wilson." VIRGINIA QUARTERLY REVIEW 32 (Autumn 1956): 481-93.

_____, et al. "Woodrow Wilson 1856-1924." [Symposium]. VIRGINIA QUARTERLY 32 (Autumn 1956): 481-610.

Davidson, John Wells. "Wilson as Presidential Leader." CURRENT HISTORY 39 (October 1960): 198-202.

Dayer, Roberta A. "Strange Bedfellows: J.P. Morgan and Co., Whitehall and the Wilson Administration during World War I." BUSINESS HISTORY 18 (July 1976): 127-51.

Dimock, Marshall Edward. "Wilson the Domestic Reformer." VIRGINIA QUARTERLY REVIEW 32 (Autumn 1956): 546-65.

_____. "Woodrow Wilson as Legislative Leader." JOURNAL OF POLITICS 19 (February 1957): 3-19.

Durden, Robert F. "Woodrow Wilson and His New Biographers." SOUTH ATLANTIC QUARTERLY 56 (Autumn 1957): 500-505.

Ezell, John S. "Woodrow Wilson as Southerner, 1856-1885: A Review Essay." CIVIL WAR HISTORY 15 (June 1969): 160-67.

Ferrell, Robert H. "Woodrow Wilson: Man and Statesman." REVIEW OF POLITICS 18 (April 1956): 131-56.

Gaines, William Harris, Jr. "A House on 'Gospel Hill': Woodrow Wilson's Birthplace Becomes a Shrine." VIRGINIA CAVALCADE 6 (Winter 1956): 12-19.

On "The Manse," Staunton, Virginia, where Wilson was born in 1856. Established as a national shrine in 1941.

_____. "A House on 'Gospel Hill': Woodrow Wilson's Homecoming to the Manse, 1912." VIRGINIA CAVALCADE 6 (Autumn 1956): 42-47.

On a visit of Woodrow Wilson, president-elect of the United States, to his birthplace in Staunton, 1912.

Garraty, John Arthur. "The Training of Woodrow Wilson: His Career at Princeton Prepared Him for a Larger Role, but Also Showed His Strange Blend of Strength and Weakness [1902-1910]." AMERICAN HERITAGE 7 (August 1956): 24-27, 94.

_____. "Woodrow Wilson: A Study in Personality." SOUTH ATLANTIC QUARTERLY 56 (April 1957): 176-85.

Gatewood, Willard B. "Woodrow Wilson: The Formative Years, 1856-1880: An Essay Review." GEORGIA REVIEW 21 (Spring 1967): 3-13.

_____. "Woodrow Wilson: Years of Trial and Decision, 1881-1885." GEORGIA REVIEW 22 (Fall 1968): 306-15.

George, Alexander L., and George, Juliette L. "Dr. Weinstein's Interpretation of Woodrow Wilson: Some Preliminary Observations." PSYCHO-HISTORY REVIEW 8 (Summer-Fall 1979): 72.

Glazier, Kenneth M. "W.E.B. Du Bois' Impressions of Woodrow Wilson." JOURNAL OF NEGRO HISTORY 58 (October 1973): 452-59.

Grant, Philip A., Jr. "World War I: Wilson and Southern Leadership." PRESIDENTIAL STUDIES QUARTERLY 6 (Winter-Spring 1976): 44-49.

Grayson, Cary T. "The Colonel's Folly and the President's Distress." AMERICAN HERITAGE 15 (October 1964): 4-7, 94-101.

_____. "Memories of Woodrow Wilson." ATLANTIC 204 (November 1959): 65-74.

Hansen, Alvin Harvey. "Woodrow Wilson as an Economic Reformer." VIRGINIA QUARTERLY REVIEW 32 (Autumn 1956): 566-77.

Herring, Pendleton. "Woodrow Wilson--Then and Now." PS 7 (Summer 1974): 256-59.

Hitchens, Keith. "Woodrow Wilson and the Union of Transylvania with Rumania, 1917-1918." REVIEW ROUMAINE D'HISTOIRE 18 (October-December 1979): 803-10.

Holt, W. Stull. "What Wilson Sent and What House Received: Or Scholars Need to Check Carefully." AMERICAN HISTORICAL REVIEW 65 (April 1960): 569-71.

Jensen, Billie Barnes. "Woodrow Wilson's Intervention in the Coal Strike of 1914." LABOR HISTORY 43 (Summer 1973): 199-212.

Johnson, Donald. "Wilson, Burleson, and Censorship in the First World War." JOURNAL OF SOUTHERN HISTORY 28 (February 1962): 46-58.

Johnson, Gerald White. "Wilson the Man." VIRGINIA QUARTERLY REVIEW 32 (Autumn 1956): 494-507.

Johnson, James P. "The Wilsonians as War Managers: Coal and the 1917-18 Winter Crisis." PROLOGUE 9 (Winter 1977): 193-208.

Kirwan, Kent Aiken. "The Crisis of Identity in the Study of Public Administration: Woodrow Wilson." POLITY 9 (Spring 1977): 321-43.

Le Pore, Herbert P. "Prelude to Prejudice: Hiram Johnson, Woodrow Wilson, and the California Alien Land Law Controversy of 1913." SOUTHERN CALIFORNIA QUARTERLY 61 (Spring 1979): 99-110.

Link, Arthur Stanley. "The Case for Woodrow Wilson [Refutation of Freud-Bullitt Interpretation]." HARPER'S 234 (April 1967): 85-93.

_____. "A Portrait of Wilson." VIRGINIA QUARTERLY REVIEW 32 (Autumn 1956): 524-40.

_____. "Woodrow Wilson: The American as Southerner." JOURNAL OF SOUTHERN HISTORY 36 (February 1970): 3-17.

_____. "Woodrow Wilson and the Study of Administration." PROCEEDINGS OF THE AMERICAN PHILOSOPHICAL SOCIETY 112 (December 1968): 431-34.

McFarland, C.K., and Neal, Nevin E. "The Reluctant Reformer: Woodrow Wilson and Woman Suffrage, 1913-1920." ROCKY MOUNTAIN SOCIAL SCIENCE JOURNAL 11 (April 1947): 33-43.

MacMahon, Arthur W. "Woodrow Wilson as Legislative Leader and Administrator." AMERICAN POLITICAL SCIENCE REVIEW 50 (September 1956): 641-75.

Moynihan, Daniel P. "Was Woodrow Wilson Right?" COMMENTARY 57 (May 1974): 25-31.

Noble, Ransom E., Jr. "Woodrow Wilson: Centennial Interpretations." PROCEEDINGS OF NEW JERSEY HISTORICAL SOCIETY 75 (April 1957): 79-95.

Commentary on seven books published in 1956.

Noggle, Burl. "A Note on Historical Editing: The Wilson Papers in Perspective." LOUISIANA HISTORY 8 (Summer 1967): 281-97.

Osborn, George C. "The Influence of Joseph Ruggles Wilson on His Son Woodrow Wilson." NORTH CAROLINA HISTORICAL REVIEW 32 (October 1955): 519-43.

_____. "Pass Christian, The Winter White House, Christmas 1913." JOURNAL OF MISSISSIPPI HISTORY 22 (January 1960): 1-26.

Good social history.

_____. "Woodrow Wilson as a Speaker." SOUTHERN SPEECH JOURNAL 22 (Winter 1956): 61-72.

_____. "Woodrow Wilson as a Young Lawyer, 1882-1883." GEORGIA HISTORICAL QUARTERLY 41 (June 1957): 126-42.

Phifer, Gregg. "Woodrow Wilson's Swing Around the Circle in Defense of His League, September 3-28, 1919." FLORIDA STATE UNIVERSITY STUDIES, no. 23 (1956): 65-102.

Piccard, Paul J. "The Electoral Colleges of President Woodrow Wilson." FLORIDA STATE UNIVERSITY STUDIES, no. 23 (1956): 29-64.

Pomeroy, Earl. "Woodrow Wilson: The End of His First Century." OREGON HISTORICAL QUARTERLY 57 (December 1956): 315-32.

Roberts, George C. "Woodrow Wilson, John W. Kern and the 1916 Indiana Election: Defeat of a Senate Majority Leader." PRESIDENTIAL STUDIES QUARTERLY 10 (Winter 1980): 63-73.

Rogin, Michael. "Max Weber and Woodrow Wilson: The Iron Cage in Germany and America." POLITY 3 (Summer 1971): 557-73.

Safford, Jeffrey J. "Edward Hurley and American Shipping Policy: An Elaboration on Wilsonian Diplomacy, 1918-1919." HISTORIAN 35 (August 1973): 568-86.

Schwabe, Klaus. "Woodrow Wilson and Germany's Membership in the League of Nations, 1918-1919." CENTRAL EUROPEAN HISTORY 8 (March 1975): 3-22.

Seltzer, Alan L. "Woodrow Wilson as 'Corporate Liberal': Toward a Reconsideration of Left Revisionist Historiography." WESTERN POLITICAL QUARTERLY 30 (June 1977): 183-212.

Seymour, Charles. "Woodrow Wilson: A Political Balance Sheet." PROCEEDINGS OF THE AMERICAN PHILOSOPHICAL SOCIETY 101 (April 1957): 135-41.

_____. "Woodrow Wilson in Perspective." FOREIGN AFFAIRS 34 (January 1956): 175-86.

Shannon, David A. "Woodrow Wilson's Youth and Personality: An Essay Review." PACIFIC NORTHWEST QUARTERLY 58 (October 1967): 205-7.

Shotwell, James T. "The Leadership of Wilson." CURRENT HISTORY 21 (November 1951): 263-68.

Smith, Daniel M. "Robert Lansing and the Wilson Interregnum, 1919-1920." HISTORIAN 21 (February 1959): 135-61.

A study in "presidential incapacitation."

Stillman, Richard J. II. "Woodrow Wilson and the Study of Administration: A New Look at an Old Essay." AMERICAN POLITICAL SCIENCE REVIEW 67 (June 1973): 582-88.

Trani, Eugene P. "Woodrow Wilson and the Decision to Intervene in Russia: A Reconsideration." JOURNAL OF MODERN HISTORY 48 (September 1976): 440-61.

Tuchman, Barbara W. "Can History Use Freud? The Case of Woodrow Wilson." ATLANTIC 219 (February 1967): 19-44.

Turner, Henry A. "Woodrow Wilson and Public Opinion." PUBLIC OPINION QUARTERLY 21 (Winter 1958): 505-20.

_____. "Woodrow Wilson as Administrator." PUBLIC ADMINISTRATION REVIEW 16 (Autumn 1956): 249-57.

Veysey, Laurence R. "The Academic Mind of Woodrow Wilson." MISSISSIPPI VALLEY HISTORICAL REVIEW 49 (March 1963): 613-34.

Ward, Robert D., and Brogdon, Frederick W. "The Revolt against Wilson: Southern Leadership and the Democratic Caucus of 1920." ALABAMA HISTORICAL QUARTERLY 38 (Summer 1976): 144-57.

Watson, Richard L., Jr. "Woodrow Wilson and His Interpreters, 1947-1957." MISSISSIPPI VALLEY HISTORICAL REVIEW 44 (September 1957): 207-36.

Weinstein, Edwin A. "Woodrow Wilson's Neurological Illness." JOURNAL OF AMERICAN HISTORY 57 (September 1970): 324-51.

Weinstein, Edwin A.; Anderson, James William; and Link, Arthur S. "Woodrow Wilson's Political Personality: A Reappraisal." POLITICAL SCIENCE QUARTERLY 93 (Winter 1978): 585-98.

Wilmer, Kurt. "Woodrow Wilson Tries Conciliation: An Effort That Failed." HISTORIAN 25 (August 1963): 419-38.

"Wilson Centennial Number." VIRGINIA QUARTERLY REVIEW 32 (Fall 1956): 481-540.

Wolfe, Christopher. "Woodrow Wilson: Interpreting the Constitution." REVIEW OF POLITICS 41 (January 1979): 121-42.

Wolgemuth, Kathlene L. "Woodrow Wilson and Federal Segregation." JOURNAL OF NEGRO HISTORY 44 (April 1959): 158-73.

_____. "Woodrow Wilson's Appointment Policy and the Negro." JOURNAL OF SOUTHERN HISTORY 24 (November 1958): 457-71.

Younger, Edward. "Woodrow Wilson: The Making of a Leader." VIRGINIA MAGAZINE OF HISTORY AND BIOGRAPHY 64 (October 1956): 387-401.

Chapter 39

WARREN G. HARDING, 1921-23

BIBLIOGRAPHY

Moran, Philip R., ed. WARREN G. HARDING, 1865-1923: CHRONOLOGY-DOCUMENTS-BIBLIOGRAPHICAL AIDS. Presidential Chronologies Series. Dobbs Ferry, N.Y.: Oceana Publications, 1970. 120 p.

SOURCE MATERIALS

Harding, Warren Gamaliel. WARREN G. HARDING PAPERS: A MICROFILM EDITION. Columbus: Manuscripts Department, Ohio Historical Society, 1969.

Approximately 350,000 papers including the executive office files from his presidential years as well as private, political, and business correspondence from the 1890s through 1923.

______. THE WARREN G. HARDING PAPERS: AN INVENTORY TO THE MICROFILM EDITION. Edited by Andrea D. Lentz. Columbus: Ohio Historical Society, 1970. 283 p.

Shortemeier, Frederick E., ed. REDEDICATING AMERICA: LIFE AND RECENT SPEECHES OF WARREN G. HARDING. Indianapolis: Bobbs-Merrill, 1920. 256 p.

BIOGRAPHIES

Downes, Randolph C. THE RISE OF WARREN GAMALIEL HARDING, 1865-1920. Columbus: Ohio State University Press, 1970. x, 734 p.

The best account of Harding's career before he became president. Based upon the extensive Harding papers in the Ohio Historical Society, opened in 1964.

Russell, Francis. THE SHADOW OF BLOOMING GROVE: WARREN G. HARDING IN HIS TIMES. New York: McGraw-Hill, 1968. xvi, 691 p.

A highly controversial book which became a best seller. Interesting for Russell's account of his search for additional Harding documents and the difficulties he encountered in publishing his findings.

Sinclair, Andrew. THE AVAILABLE MAN: THE LIFE BEHIND THE MASKS OF WARREN GAMALIEL HARDING. New York: Macmillan, 1965. viii, 344 p.

The first major study based upon the newly opened Harding Papers in 1964. Gives a mixed interpretation of Harding's ability and record.

MONOGRAPHS

Adams, Samuel Hopkins. INCREDIBLE ERA. Boston: Houghton Mifflin Co., 1939. vii, 456 p.

A lively book based upon oral interviews, newspaper reports, and an unpublished thesis from Syracuse University. Gives a portrait of Harding as weak and subservient to his ambitious wife, conservative Republican leaders, and Harry Daugherty, his campaign manager. Typical of the older interpretations of Harding.

Bagby, Wesley M. THE ROAD TO NORMALCY: THE PRESIDENTIAL CAMPAIGN AND ELECTION OF 1920. Baltimore: Johns Hopkins Press, 1962. 206 p.

Cottrill, Dale E. THE CONCILIATOR. Philadelphia: Dorrance, 1969. xix, 343 p.

Contains Harding speeches and a helpful list of Harding addresses on pages 259-301.

Daugherty, Harry M. THE INSIDE STORY OF THE HARDING TRAGEDY. New York: Churchill, 1932. Reprint. Freeport, N.Y.: Books for Libraries Press, 1971. viii, 323 p.

Grieb, Kenneth J. THE LATIN AMERICAN POLICY OF WARREN G. HARDING. Texas Christian University Monographs in History and Culture, no. 13. Fort Worth: Texas Christian University Press, 1976. viii, 223 p.

Mee, Charles L., Jr. THE OHIO GANG: THE WORLD OF WARREN G. HARDING. New York: M. Evans, 1981. 248 p.

Murray, Robert. THE HARDING ERA: WARREN G. HARDING AND HIS ADMINISTRATION. Minneapolis: University of Minnesota Press, 1969. ix, 626 p.

The most up-to-date and scholarly account of the Harding presidency.

Noggle, Burl. TEAPOT DOME: OIL AND POLITICS IN THE 1920S. Baton Rouge: Louisiana State University Press, 1962. 234 p.

The story of the principal scandal in the Harding administration.

Trani, Eugene P., and Wilson, David L. THE PRESIDENCY OF WARREN G. HARDING. American Presidency Series. Lawrence: Regents Press of Kansas, 1977. ix, 232 p.

ARTICLES

Accinelli, Robert D. "Was There a 'New' Harding? Warren G. Harding and the World Court Issue, 1920-1923." OHIO HISTORY 84 (Autumn 1975): 168-81.

Bagby, Wesley M., Jr. "The 'Smoke Filled Room' and the Nomination of Warren G. Harding." MISSISSIPPI VALLEY HISTORICAL REVIEW 41 (March 1955): 657-74.

Discounts the older interpretation of Harding's nomination as being dictated by a cabal in a "smoke-filled room."

Coren, Robert W. "Samuel Hopkins Adams, His Novel [REVELRY], and the Reputation of Warren G. Harding." COURIER [Syracuse], 11 (Spring 1974): 3-10.

Dewitt, Howard A. "The 'New' Harding and American Foreign Policy: Warren G. Harding, Hiram W. Johnson, and Pragmatic Diplomacy." OHIO HISTORY 86 (Spring 1977): 96-114.

Downes, Randolph C. "The Harding Muckfest: Warren G. Harding--Chief Victim of the Muck-For-Muck's Sake Writers and Readers." NORTHWEST OHIO QUARTERLY 39 (Summer 1967): 5-37.

______. "Some Correspondence between Warren G. Harding and William Allen White during the Presidential Campaign of 1920." NORTHWEST OHIO QUARTERLY 37 (Autumn 1965): 121-32.

______. "Wanted: A Scholarly Appraisal of Warren G. Harding." OHIOANA QUARTERLY 2, no. 1 (1959): 18-22.

Downes is one of the leading revisionists who has attempted to rehabilitate Harding's reputation.

______, ed. "President Making: The Influence of Newton H. Fairbanks and Harry M. Daugherty on the Nomination of Warren G. Harding for the Presidency." NORTHWEST OHIO QUARTERLY 31 (Fall 1959): 170-78.

Duckett, Kenneth W., and Russell, Francis. "Harding Papers: How Some Were Burned; and Some Were Saved." AMERICAN HERITAGE 16 (February 1965): 24-31, 102-10.

A fascinating pair of articles describing the history of the main body of the Harding Papers now in the Ohio Historical Society; and the discovery of the Harding-Phillips love letters in 1963.

Ficken, Robert E. "President Harding Visits Seattle." PACIFIC NORTHWEST QUARTERLY 66 (July 1975): 105-14.

Grieb, Kenneth J. "Warren G. Harding and the Dominican Republic: U.S. Withdrawal, 1921-1923." JOURNAL OF INTERAMERICAN STUDIES AND WORLD AFFAIRS 11 (July 1969): 425-39.

Hard, Charles E. "The Man Who Did Not Want to Become President." NORTHWEST OHIO QUARTERLY 31, no. 3 (1959): 120-25.

Harris, Ray Baker. "Background and Youth of the Seventh Ohio President." OHIO STATE ARCHAEOLOGICAL AND HISTORICAL QUARTERLY 52, no. 3 (1943): 260-75.

Harris had hoped to write a Harding biography based on his belief in the man and his place in history.

Jennings, David H. "Historiography and Warren Harding." OHIO HISTORY 78 (Winter 1969): 46-49.

A critical review of Francis Russell's biography of Harding (see p. 286) with comment on Russell's use of sources and predilection toward the sensational.

_____. "President Harding and International Organization." OHIO HISTORY 75 (Spring-Summer 1966): 149-65.

Johnson, Evans C. "Underwood and Harding: A Bipartisan Friendship." ALABAMA HISTORICAL QUARTERLY 30 (Spring 1968): 65-78.

Murray, Robert K. "Harding on History." JOURNAL OF AMERICAN HISTORY 53 (March 1967): 781-84.

_____. "How Harding Saved the Versailles Treaty." AMERICAN HERITAGE 20 (December 1968): 66-67, 111.

_____. "President Harding and His Cabinet." OHIO HISTORY 75 (Spring-Summer 1966): 108-25.

_____. "The President under Fire." AMERICAN HISTORY ILLUSTRATED 9 (August 1974): 32-40.

OHIO HISTORY 75 (Spring-Summer 1966): 75-165. Edited by David H. Jennings.

A special issue devoted to a vital reassessment of the 1920s which centers around the presidential campaign of 1920 and the 1920-23 era in the life of President Harding. Includes articles on the "Harding Papers," "Negro Rights," and the "Campaign of 1920," "Harding's Cabinet," "Mexican Relations," and "Harding and International Organization."

Pitzer, Donald E. "An Introduction to the Harding Papers." OHIO HISTORY 75 (Spring-Summer 1966): 76-84.

Potts, Louis W. "Who Was Warren G. Harding?" HISTORIAN 36 (August 1974): 621-45.

An excellent survey of the Harding literature. Summarizes two decades of revisionism.

Russell, Francis. "The Four Mysteries of Warren Harding." AMERICAN HERITAGE 14 (April 1963): 5-9, 81-86.

A popular treatment of the circumstances surrounding Harding's alleged Negro ancestry; affair with Nan Britton; strange death; and the burning of his papers by Mrs. Harding.

_____. "The Shadow of Warren Harding." ANTIOCH REVIEW 36 (Winter 1978): 57-76.

Schapsmeier, Edward L., and Schapsmeier, Frederick H. "Disharmony in the Harding Cabinet: Hoover-Wallace Conflict." OHIO HISTORY 75 (Spring-Summer 1966): 126-36.

Schruben, Francis W. "An Even Stranger Death of President Harding." SOUTHERN CALIFORNIA QUARTERLY 48 (March 1966): 57-78.

Sherman, Richard B. "The Harding Administration and the Negro: An Opportunity Lost." JOURNAL OF NEGRO HISTORY 49 (July 1964): 151-68.

Walker, Kenneth R., and Downes, Randolph C. "The Death of Warren G. Harding." NORTHWEST OHIO QUARTERLY 35 (Winter 1962-63): 7-17.

Warren, Sidney. "Harding's Abdication from Leadership." CURRENT HISTORY 39 (October 1960): 203-7.

Whitaker, W. Richard. "Harding: First Radio President." NORTHWEST OHIO QUARTERLY 45 (Summer 1973): 75-86.

_____. "The Working Press and the Harding Myth." JOURNALISM HISTORY 2 (Autumn 1975): 90-97.

Wimer, Kurt, and Wimer, Sarah. "The Harding Administration, the League of Nations, and the Separate Peace Treaty." REVIEW OF POLITICS 29 (1967): 13-24.

Chapter 40

CALVIN COOLIDGE, 1923-29

BIBLIOGRAPHY

Moran, Philip R., ed. CALVIN COOLIDGE, 1872-1933: CHRONOLOGY-DOCUMENTS-BIBLIOGRAPHICAL AIDS. Presidential Chronologies Series. Dobbs Ferry, N.Y.: Oceana Publications, 1970. 144 p.

SOURCE MATERIALS

Coolidge, Calvin. THE AUTOBIOGRAPHY OF CALVIN COOLIDGE. New York: Cosmopolitan Book Corp., 1929. 247 p.

Quint, Howard H., and Ferrell, Robert H., eds. TALKATIVE PRESIDENT: THE OFF-THE-RECORD PRESS CONFERENCES OF CALVIN COOLIDGE. Amherst: University of Massachusetts Press, 1964. 276 p.

BIOGRAPHIES

Fuess, Claude Moore. CALVIN COOLIDGE, THE MAN FROM VERMONT. Boston: Little, Brown, 1940. Reprint. Westport, Conn.: Greenwood Press, 1976. xii, 522 p.

Interesting and well written, but uncritical.

McCoy, Donald R. CALVIN COOLIDGE: THE QUIET PRESIDENT. New York: Macmillan, 1967. viii, 472 p.

A reassessment well researched and presented.

Ross, Ishbel. GRACE COOLIDGE AND HER ERA. New York: Dodd, Mead and Co., 1962. xiii, 370 p.

White, William Allen. A PURITAN IN BABYLON: THE STORY OF CALVIN COOLIDGE. New York: Macmillan, 1938. Reprint. Gloucester, Mass.: Patterson Smith, 1973. xvi, 460 p.

A sardonic view of Coolidge's shortcomings.

MONOGRAPHS

Lathem, Edward Connery, ed. MEET CALVIN COOLIDGE: THE MAN BEHIND THE MYTH. Brattleboro, Vt.: Stephen Greene Press, 1960. 223 p.

Rofinot, Henry Louis. NORMALCY AND THE FARMER: AGRICULTURAL POLICY UNDER HARDING AND COOLIDGE, 1920-1928. Ann Arbor, Mich.: University Microfilms, 1958. vii, 246 p.

ARTICLES

Barber, James David. "Classifying and Predicting Presidential Styles: Two 'Weak' Presidents." JOURNAL OF SOCIAL ISSUES 24 (July 1968): 51-80.

Blair, John L. "Calvin Coolidge and the Advent of Radio Politics." VERMONT HISTORY 44 (Winter 1976): 28-37.

_____. "The Clark-Coolidge Correspondence and the Election of 1932." VERMONT HISTORY 34 (April 1966): 83-114.

_____. "I Do Not Choose to Run for President in Nineteen Twenty Eight." VERMONT HISTORY 30 (July 1962): 177-94.

Cornwell, Elmer E., Jr. "Coolidge and Presidential Leadership." PUBLIC OPINION QUARTERLY 21 (Summer 1957): 265-78.

Fenno, R.F. "Coolidge: Representative of the People." CURRENT HISTORY 39 (October 1960): 208-12.

Fleser, Arthur F. "Coolidge's Delivery: Everybody Liked It." VERMONT HISTORY 38 (Autumn 1970): 320-25.

_____. "A New England Education: The Early Career and Rhetorical Training of Calvin Coolidge." VERMONT HISTORY 35 (July 1967): 151-59.

Fountain, Joe Harry. "Presidential Oath." VERMONT LIFE 3 (Autumn 1948): 4-7, 55.

Eyewitness account of Coolidge taking presidential oath of office from his father Col. John Coolidge, at Plymouth, Vermont, 3 August 1923.

Fuess, Claude M. "Calvin Coolidge [1872-1933]." VERMONT LIFE 3 (Autumn 1948): 3, 54.

On Coolidge as a product of Vermont.

_____. "Calvin Coolidge: Twenty Years After." AMERICAN ANTIQUARIAN SOCIETY PROCEEDINGS 63 (October 1953): 351-69.

Lockwood, C. "President Calvin Coolidge, b. July 4, 1872." ANTIQUES 102 (July 1972): 109-12.

Maddox, Robert James. "Keeping Cool with Coolidge." JOURNAL OF AMERICAN HISTORY 53 (March 1967): 772-80.

Meredith, H.L. "Beyond Humor: Will Rogers and Calvin Coolidge." VERMONT HISTORY 40 (Summer 1972): 178-84.

O'Connor, Richard. "Mr. Coolidge's Jungle War in Nicaragua, 1927-1933." AMERICAN HERITAGE 19 (December 1967): 36-39, 89-93.

Russell, Francis. "Coolidge and the Boston Police Strike." ANTIOCH REVIEW 16 (December 1956): 403-15.

_____. "Strike that Made a President." AMERICAN HERITAGE 14 (October 1963): 44-47, 90-94.

Scandrett, Richard. "Remembering Calvin Coolidge: An Oral History Memoir." VERMONT HISTORY 40 (Summer 1972): 190-215.

Soule, Harris W. "The White House Calling: A Reminiscence of Calvin Coolidge at Plymouth, Vermont." VERMONT HISTORY 37 (Winter 1969): 49-51.

Wilson, C.M. "Lamplight Inauguration." AMERICAN HERITAGE 15 (December 1963): 80-86.

Zieger, Robert H. "Pinchot and Coolidge: The Politics of the 1923 Anthracite Crisis." JOURNAL OF AMERICAN HISTORY 52 (December 1965): 566-81.

Chapter 41

HERBERT HOOVER, 1929-33

BIBLIOGRAPHIES

Herbert Hoover Presidential Library. West Branch, Iowa. BIBLIOGRAPHICAL GUIDE TO THE LIFE AND INTERESTS OF HERBERT CLARK HOOVER. West Branch, Iowa: Hoover Presidential Library, n.d.

A compilation of over two thousand entries available on request at the Hoover Presidential Library in West Branch, Iowa.

_____. HISTORICAL MATERIALS IN THE HERBERT HOOVER PRESIDENTIAL LIBRARY. West Branch, Iowa: Herbert Hoover Presidential Library, National Archives and Records Service, General Services Administration, 1977. vii, 51 p.

Rice, Arnold S., ed. HERBERT HOOVER, 1874-1964: CHRONOLOGY-DOCUMENTS-BIBLIOGRAPHICAL AIDS. Presidential Chronologies Series. Dobbs Ferry, N.Y.: Oceana Publications, 1971. 114 p.

Tracey, Kathleen, comp. HERBERT HOOVER--A BIBLIOGRAPHY: HIS WRITINGS AND ADDRESSES. Hoover Bibliographical Series, no. 58. Stanford, Calif.: Hoover Institution Press, 1977. xiii, 202 p.

SOURCE MATERIALS

Hoover, Herbert Clark. A BOYHOOD IN IOWA. New York: Aventine Press, 1931. 64 p.

_____. CAMPAIGN SPEECHES OF 1932, BY PRESIDENT HOOVER AND EX-PRESIDENT COOLIDGE. Garden City, N.Y.: Doubleday, Doran, 1933. vi, 329 p.

_____. A CAUSE TO WIN: FIVE SPEECHES BY HERBERT HOOVER ON AMERICAN FOREIGN POLICY IN RELATION TO SOVIET RUSSIA. Concord, N.H.: Rumford Press, 1951. 32 p.

______. ADDRESSES UPON THE AMERICAN ROAD, 1933-1938. New York: Charles Scribner's Sons, 1938. viii, 390 p.

______. ADDRESSES UPON THE AMERICAN ROAD, 1940-1941. New York: Charles Scribner's Sons, 1941. vii, 272 p.

______. ADDRESSES UPON THE AMERICAN ROAD, 1941-1945. New York: D. Van Nostrand Co., 1946. xi, 442 p.

______. ADDRESSES UPON THE AMERICAN ROAD, 1945-1948. New York: D. Van Nostrand Co., 1949. xii, 319 p.

______. ADDRESSES UPON THE AMERICAN ROAD, 1948-1950. Stanford, Calif.: Stanford University Press, 1951. xi, 221 p.

______. ADDRESSES UPON THE AMERICAN ROAD, 1950-1955. Stanford, Calif.: Stanford University Press, 1955. 365 p.

______. ADDRESSES UPON THE AMERICAN ROAD, 1955-1960. Caldwell, Idaho: Caxton Printer, 1961. 415 p.

______. AN AMERICAN EPIC. 4 vols. Chicago: Henry Regnery Co., 1959-64.

______. AMERICAN IDEALS VERSUS THE NEW DEAL. New York: Scribner Press, 1936. ix, 89 p.

______. AMERICAN INDIVIDUALISM. Garden City, N.Y.: Doubleday, Page and Co., 1922. 81 p.

______. AMERICA'S FIRST CRUSADE. New York: Charles Scribner's Sons, 1942. 81 p.

______. AMERICA'S WAY FORWARD. New York: Scribner Press, 1939. 83 p.

______. THE CHALLENGE TO LIBERTY. New York: Random House, 1963. Reprint. Rockford, Ill.: Herbert Hoover Presidential Library Association, 1971. 212 p.

______. FISHING FOR FUN--AND WASH YOUR SOUL. New York: Random House, 1963. 86 p.

_____. FORTY KEY QUESTIONS ABOUT OUR FOREIGN POLICY. Scarsdale, N.Y.: Updegraff Press, 1952. 102 p.

_____. FURTHER ADDRESSES UPON THE AMERICAN ROAD, 1938-1940. New York: Charles Scribner's Sons, 1940. vii, 265 p.

_____. HERBERT HOOVER: PROCLAMATIONS AND EXECUTIVE ORDERS, MARCH 4, 1929 TO MARCH 4, 1933. 2 vols. Washington, D.C.: Government Printing Office, 1974. iii, 1,566 p.

_____. HERBERT HOOVER'S CHALLENGE TO AMERICA: HIS LIFE AND WORDS. Waukesha, Wis.: Country Beautiful Foundation, 1965. 82 p.

_____. HOOVER AFTER DINNER: ADDRESSES BY HERBERT HOOVER BEFORE THE GRIDIRON CLUB OF WASHINGTON, D.C., WITH OTHER INFORMAL SPEECHES. New York: Charles Scribner's Sons, 1933. xii, 144 p.

_____. THE HOOVER-WILSON WARTIME CORRESPONDENCE, SEPTEMBER 24, 1914 TO NOVEMBER 11, 1918. Edited and with commentaries by Francis William O'Brien. Ames: Iowa State University Press, 1974. xxvi, 297 p.

_____. THE MEMOIRS OF HERBERT HOOVER. 3 vols. New York: Macmillan Co., 1951-52.

Volume 2 deals with his cabinet and presidential years.

_____. THE NEW DAY: CAMPAIGN SPEECHES OF HERBERT HOOVER, 1928. Stanford, Calif.: Stanford University Press, 1928. xiv, 230 p.

_____. ON GROWING UP: LETTERS TO AMERICAN BOYS AND GIRLS INCLUDING THE UNCOMMON MAN, AND OTHER SELECTIONS. Edited by William Nichols. New York: William Morrow and Co., 1962. 160 p.

_____. PUBLIC PAPERS OF THE PRESIDENTS OF THE UNITED STATES: HERBERT HOOVER, 1929-1933. 4 vols. Washington, D.C.: Office of the Federal Register, National Archives and Records Service, 1974-77.

_____. THE REMINISCENCES OF HERBERT CLARK HOOVER. Glen Rock, N.J.: Microfilming Corporation of America, 1975. 22 p.

_____. THE STATE PAPERS AND OTHER PUBLIC WRITINGS OF HERBERT HOOVER. 2 vols. Collected and edited by William Starr Myers. Garden City, N.Y.: Doubleday, Doran, 1934.

The best published source for Hoover's public statements in the period of his presidency [1929-33].

_____. TWO PEACEMAKERS IN PARIS: THE HOOVER-WILSON POST-ARMISTICE LETTERS, 1918-1920. Edited and with commentaries by Francis William O'Brien. College Station: Texas A & M University Press, 1978. xlix, 254 p.

Hoover, Herbert, and Gibson, Hugh. THE BASIS OF A LASTING PEACE. New York: D. Van Nostrand Co., 1945. 44 p.

_____. THE PROBLEMS OF LASTING PEACE. Garden City, N.Y.: Doubleday, Doran and Co., 1942. ix, 303 p.

Joslin, Theodore G. HOOVER OFF THE RECORD. Garden City, N.Y.: Doubleday, Doran, 1934. vi, 367 p.

By Hoover's press secretary, 1931-33.

Myers, William S., and Newton, Walter H. THE HOOVER ADMINISTRATION, A DOCUMENTED NARRATIVE. New York: Charles Scribner's Sons, 1936. Reprint. St. Clair Shores, Mich.: Scholarly Press, 1971. viii, 553 p.

Includes edited versions of Hoover speeches, statements and conversations. Limited to domestic policies.

O'Brien, Francis W., ed. THE HOOVER-WILSON WARTIME CORRESPONDENCE. Ames: Iowa State University Press, 1974. xxvi, 297 p.

U.S. Commission on Organization of the Executive Branch of the Government. THE HOOVER COMMISSION REPORT ON ORGANIZATION OF THE EXECUTIVE BRANCH OF THE GOVERNMENT. Washington, D.C.: Government Printing Office, 1955.

A series of nineteen reports on different agencies of the government.

Wilbur, Ray Lyman, and Hyde, Arthur M. THE HOOVER POLICIES. New York: Charles Scribner's Sons, 1937. x, 667 p.

BIOGRAPHIES

Burner, David. HERBERT HOOVER: A PUBLIC LIFE. New York: Knopf, 1979. xii, 433 p.

Darling, Jay Norwood. AS DING SAW HOOVER. Edited by John M. Henry. Ames: Iowa State College Press, 1954. 138 p.

Hinshaw, David. HERBERT HOOVER: AMERICAN QUAKER. New York: Farrar, Straus and Co., 1950. 469 p.

Friendly to Hoover.

Hoover Presidential Library Association. West Branch, Iowa. HERBERT HOOVER THE UNCOMMON MAN. West Branch, Iowa: Hoover Presidential Library Association, 1974. 59 p.

Liggett, Walter W. THE RISE OF HERBERT HOOVER. New York: H.K. Fly Co., 1932. 400 p.

An early critical account of Hoover.

Lyons, Eugene. OUR UNKNOWN EX-PRESIDENT: A PORTRAIT OF HERBERT HOOVER. New York: Doubleday, 1948. Rev. ed. Garden City, N.Y.: Doubleday, 1964. 444 p.

First edition more critical than the 1964 revision.

McGee, Dorothy Horton. HERBERT HOOVER: ENGINEER, HUMANITARIAN, STATESMAN. New York: Dodd, Mead, 1965. x, 325 p.

McLean, Hulda Hoover. THE GENEALOGY OF THE HERBERT HOOVER FAMILY. Stanford, Calif.: Hoover Institution of War, Revolution and Peace, 1967. 486 p.

Written by Hoover's niece.

Nash, George H. THE LIFE OF HERBERT HOOVER: THE ENGINEER, 1874-1914. New York: W.W. Norton and Co., 1983.

Pryor, Helen B. LOU HENRY HOOVER: GALLANT FIRST LADY. New York: Dodd, Mead and Co., 1969. 271 p.

Contains interesting personal sidelights about the Hoovers. Pryor used the now closed Lou Henry Hoover Papers.

Robinson, Edgar Eugene, and Bornet, Vaughn Davis. HERBERT HOOVER, PRESIDENT OF THE UNITED STATES. Hoover Institution Publications, no. 149. Stanford, Calif.: Hoover Institution Press, 1975. xii, 398 p.

Steinberg, Alfred. HERBERT HOOVER. The Lives to Remember Series. New York: Putnam, 1967. 255 p.

Wilson, Carol Green. HERBERT HOOVER: A CHALLENGE FOR TODAY. New York: Evans Publishing Co., 1968. xiv, 338 p.

Wilson, Joan Hoff. HERBERT HOOVER: FORGOTTEN PROGRESSIVE. Library of American Biography. Boston: Little, Brown, 1975. viii, 307 p.

An excellent interpretive biography based upon considerable research in the Hoover Papers by one of the leading young scholars of the Hoover period. Contains a good bibliographical essay on the Hoover sources and secondary literature including a valuable list of papers read at professional meetings and dissertations on Hoover.

Wolfe, Harold. HERBERT HOOVER: PUBLIC SERVANT AND LEADER OF THE LOYAL OPPOSITION. New York: Exposition Press, 1956. 507 p.

Best of the earlier biographies written before the opening of the Hoover Library.

MONOGRAPHS

Bearss, Edwin C. HISTORICAL BASE MAP AND GROUND STUDY: HERBERT HOOVER NATIONAL HISTORIC SITE, WEST BRANCH, IOWA. Washington, D.C.: Division of History, Office of Archeology and Historic Preservation, 1968. x, 148 p.

Best, Gary Dean. THE POLITICS OF AMERICAN INDIVIDUALISM: HERBERT HOOVER IN TRANSITION, 1918-1921. Westport, Conn.: Greenwood Press, 1975. vi, 202 p.

Brandes, Joseph. HERBERT HOOVER AND ECONOMIC DIPLOMACY: DEPARTMENT OF COMMERCE POLICY, 1921-1928. Foreword by Lewis Strauss. Pittsburgh: University of Pittsburgh Press, 1962. Reprint. Westport, Conn.: Greenwood Press, 1975. xiv, 237 p.

Details Hoover's outstanding record as Secretary of Commerce.

Curry, Earl R. HOOVER'S DOMINICAN DIPLOMACY AND THE ORIGINS OF THE GOOD NEIGHBOR POLICY. Modern American History. New York: Garland Publishers, 1979. iii, 277 p.

De Conde, Alexander. HERBERT HOOVER'S LATIN-AMERICAN POLICY. Stanford, Calif.: Stanford University Press, 1951. Reprint. New York: Octagon Books, 1970. xiii, 154 p.

Fausold, Martin L., ed. THE HOOVER PRESIDENCY: REAPPRAISAL. Albany: State University of New York Press, 1974. vi, 224 p.

Nine persuasive essays, plus an introductory chapter and bibliographical note, based on a conference held 27-28 April 1973 at State University College, Geneseo, New York. Offers a major reevaluation of the Hoover era.

Ferrell, Robert H. AMERICAN DIPLOMACY IN THE GREAT DEPRESSION: HOOVER-STIMSON FOREIGN POLICY, 1929-1933. New Haven, Conn.: Yale University Press, 1957. 319 p.

Lerski, George Jan, comp. HERBERT HOOVER AND POLAND: DOCUMENTARY HISTORY OF A FRIENDSHIP. Foreword by Mark O. Hatfield. Hoover Archival Documentaries. Hoover Institution Publication, no. 174. Stanford, Calif.: Hoover Institution Press, 1977. xvi, 124 p.

Lloyd, Craig. AGGRESSIVE INTROVERT: A STUDY OF HERBERT HOOVER AND PUBLIC RELATIONS MANAGEMENT, 1912-1932. Columbus: Ohio State University Press, 1972. xiv, 206 p.

Myers, William Starr. THE FOREIGN POLICIES OF HERBERT HOOVER, 1929-1933. New York: Charles Scribner's Sons, 1940. 259 p.

> A companion study to the earlier work by Myers and Newton (see p. 298) which covered the domestic policies of the Hoover administration.

Nelsen, Clair Everet. THE IMAGE OF HERBERT HOOVER AS REFLECTED IN THE AMERICAN PRESS [1917-1955]. Ann Arbor, Mich.: University Microfilms, 1956. ix, 220 l.

Olson, James Stuart. HERBERT HOOVER AND THE RECONSTRUCTION FINANCE CORPORATION, 1931-1933. Ames: Iowa State University Press, 1977. xi, 155 p.

Peel, Roy V., and Donnelly, Thomas C. THE 1928 CAMPAIGN: AN ANALYSIS. New York: R.R. Smith, 1931. xii, 129 p.

______. THE 1932 CAMPAIGN: AN ANALYSIS. New York: Farrar and Rinehart, 1935. viii, 242 p.

Romasco, Albert U. THE POVERTY OF ABUNDANCE: HOOVER, THE NATION, THE DEPRESSION. New York: Oxford University Press, 1965. x, 282 p.

> A revisionist view of what happened between 1929 and 1933; sympathetic to Hoover and more critical of the nation's institutional leadership.

Schwarz, Jordan A. INTERREGNUM OF DESPAIR: HOOVER'S CONGRESS AND THE DEPRESSION. Urbana: University of Illinois Press, 1970. ix, 281 p.

> Pictures Hoover as a spokesman for a frightened, cautious consensus which included the congressional democratic leadership.

Silva, Ruth C. RUM, RELIGION, AND VOTES: 1928. RE-EXAMINED. University Park: Pennsylvania State University Press, 1962. ix, 76 p.

Smith, Gene. THE SHATTERED DREAM: HERBERT HOOVER AND THE GREAT DEPRESSION. New York: William Morrow and Co., 1970. 278 p.

Sobel, Robert. HERBERT HOOVER AT THE ONSET OF THE GREAT DEPRESSION, 1929-1930. America's Alternatives Series. Philadelphia: J.B. Lippincott, 1975. xiii, 113 p.

Warren, Harris G. HERBERT HOOVER AND THE GREAT DEPRESSION. New York: Oxford University Press, 1959. x, 372 p.

A good secondary account, but written without access to the Hoover papers.

ARTICLES

Albjerg, V.L. "Hoover: The Presidency in Transition." CURRENT HISTORY 39 (October 1960): 213-19.

Aoki, Reiko. "Prospect and Limitation of Reevaluating Herbert Hoover." AMERICAN REVIEW 12 (1978): 201-4.

Barber, J.D. "Classifying and Predicting Presidential Styles: Two 'Weak' Presidents." JOURNAL OF SOCIAL ISSUES 24 (July 1968): 51-80.

Coolidge and Hoover.

Best, Gary Dean. "Herbert Hoover as Titular Leader of the GOP, 1933-35." MID-AMERICA 61 (April-July 1979): 81-97.

_____. "The Hoover-for-President Boom." MID-AMERICA 53 (October 1971): 227-44.

_____. "Totalitarianism or Peace: Herbert Hoover and the Road to War, 1939-1941." ANNALS OF IOWA 44 (Winter 1979): 516-29.

Cowley, Robert. "The Drought and the Dole: Herbert Hoover's Dismal Dilemma." AMERICAN HERITAGE 23 (February 1972): 16-19, 92-99.

Davis, Joseph H. "Herbert Hoover, 1874-1964: Another Appraisal." SOUTH ATLANTIC QUARTERLY 68 (Summer 1969): 295-318.

De Conde, Alexander. "Herbert Hoover's Good Will Tour." HISTORIAN 12 (Spring 1950): 167-81.

Degler, Carl N. "The Ordeal of Herbert Hoover." YALE REVIEW 52 (Summer 1963): 563-83.

Drake, Douglas C. "Herbert Hoover, Ecologist: The Politics of Oil Pollution Control, 1921-1926." MID-AMERICA 55 (July 1973): 207-28.

Edwards, John Carver. "Herbert Hoover's Public Lands Policy: A Struggle for Control of the Western Domain." PACIFIC HISTORIAN 20 (Spring 1976): 34-45.

Fausold, Martin L. "President Hoover's Farm Policies, 1929-1933." AGRICULTURAL HISTORY 51 (April 1977): 362-77.

Fite, G.C. "Agricultural Issue in the Presidential Campaign of 1928." MISSISSIPPI VALLEY HISTORICAL REVIEW 37 (March 1951): 653-72.

Garcia, George F. "Herbert Hoover and the Issue of Race." ANNALS OF IOWA 44 (Winter 1979): 507-15.

Hawley, Ellis W. "Herbert Hoover, the Commerce Secretariat, and the Vision of an 'Associative State,' 1921-1928." JOURNAL OF AMERICAN HISTORY 61 (June 1974): 116-40.

Hoxie, R. Gordon. "Herbert Hoover: Multi-National Man." PRESIDENTIAL STUDIES QUARTERLY 7 (Winter 1977): 49-52.

_____. "Hoover and the Banking Crisis." PRESIDENTIAL STUDIES QUARTERLY 4 (Summer-Fall 1974): 25-28.

Jansky, Cyril Monroe, Jr. "The Contribution of Herbert Hoover to Broadcasting." JOURNAL OF BROADCASTING 1 (Summer 1957): 241-49.

Karl, Barry D. "Presidential Planning and Social Science Research: Mr. Hoover's Experts." PERSPECTIVES IN AMERICAN HISTORY 3 (1969): 347-409.

Kottman, Richard N. "Herbert Hoover and the St. Lawrence Seaway Treaty of 1932." NEW YORK HISTORY 56 (July 1975): 314-46.

_____. "Herbert Hoover and the Smoot-Hawley Tariff: Canada, A Case Study." JOURNAL OF AMERICAN HISTORY 62 (December 1975): 609-35.

_____. "The Hoover-Bennett Meeting of 1931: Mismanaged Summitry." ANNALS OF IOWA 42 (Winter 1974): 205-21.

Lambert, Roger. "Hoover, the Red Cross, and Food for the Hungry." ANNALS OF IOWA 44 (Winter 1979): 530-40.

_____. "Hoover and the Red Cross in the Arkansas Drought of 1930." ARKANSAS HISTORICAL QUARTERLY 29 (Spring 1970): 3-19.

Lohof, Bruce A. "Herbert Hoover, Spokesman of Humane Efficiency: The Mississippi Flood of 1927." AMERICAN QUARTERLY 22 (Fall 1970): 690-700.

_____. "Herbert Hoover's Mississippi Valley Reform Memorandum: A Document." ARKANSAS HISTORICAL QUARTERLY 29 (Summer 1970): 112-18.

Metcalf, Evan B. "Secretary Hoover and the Emergence of Macroeconomic Management." BUSINESS HISTORY REVIEW 49 (Spring 1975): 60-80.

Nash, Gerald D. "Herbert Hoover and the Origins of the Reconstruction Finance Corporation." MISSISSIPPI VALLEY HISTORICAL REVIEW 46 (December 1959): 455-68.

Olson, James S. "Herbert Hoover and 'War' on the Depression." PALIMPSEST 54 (July-August 1973): 26-31.

_____. "The Philosophy of Herbert Hoover: A Contemporary Perspective." ANNALS OF IOWA 43 (Winter 1976): 181-91.

_____. "Rehearsal for Disaster: Hoover, the R.F.C. and the Banking Crisis in Nevada, 1932-1933." WESTERN HISTORICAL QUARTERLY 6 (April 1975): 149-61.

Ortquist, Richard T. "Unemployment and Relief: Michigan's Response to the Depression during the Hoover Years." MICHIGAN HISTORY 57 (Fall 1973): 209-36.

Philip, Kenneth. "Herbert Hoover's New Era: A False Dawn for the American Indian, 1929-1932." ROCKY MOUNTAIN SOCIAL SCIENCE JOURNAL 9 (April 1972): 53-60.

Pryor, Helen B. "Lou Henry Hoover." PALIMPSEST 52 (July 1971): 353-400.

Rhodes, Benjamin D. "Herbert Hoover and the War Debts, 1919-33." PROLOGUE 6 (Summer 1974): 130-44.

Rogers, Benjamin. "'Dear Mr. President': The Hoover-Truman Correspondence." PALIMPSEST 55 (September-October 1974): 152-58.

Russ, W.A., Jr. "Time Lag and Political Change as Seen in the Administrations of Buchanan and Hoover." SOUTH ATLANTIC QUARTERLY 46 (July 1947): 336-43.

Shideler, James H. "Herbert Hoover and the Federal Farm Board Project, 1921-1925." MISSISSIPPI VALLEY HISTORICAL REVIEW 42 (March 1956): 710-29.

Snyder, J. Richard. "Hoover and the Hawley-Smoot Tariff: A View of Executive Leadership." ANNALS OF IOWA 38 (Winter 1973): 1173-89.

Tugwell, Rexford G. "Protagonists: Roosevelt and Hoover." ANTIOCH REVIEW 13 (December 1953): 419-42.

______. "Transition: Hoover to Roosevelt, 1932-1933." CENTENNIAL REVIEW 9 (Spring 1965): 160-91.

Watson, Richard L., Jr. "Theodore Roosevelt and Herbert Hoover." SOUTH ATLANTIC QUARTERLY 53 (January 1954): 109-29.

Williams, William Appelman. "What This Country Needs." NEW YORK REVIEW OF BOOKS 15 (5 November 1970): 7-11.

Williams offers a controversial reevaluation of Hoover's philosophy.

Wilson, Joan Hoff. "Herbert Hoover's Plan for Ending the Second World War." INTERNATIONAL HISTORY REVIEW 1 (January 1979): 84-102.

______. "Hoover's Agricultural Policies, 1921-1929." AGRICULTURAL HISTORY 51 (April 1977): 335-61.

Wilson, John R.M. "The Quaker and the Sword: Herbert Hoover's Relations with the Military." MILITARY AFFAIRS 38 (April 1974): 41-47.

Zieger, Robert H. "Herbert Hoover: A Reinterpretation." AMERICAN HISTORICAL REVIEW 81 (October 1976): 800-810.

______. "Labor, Progressivism, and Herbert Hoover in the 1920s." WISCONSIN MAGAZINE OF HISTORY 58 (Spring 1975): 196-208.

Chapter 42

FRANKLIN D. ROOSEVELT, 1933-45

BIBLIOGRAPHIES

Bremer, Howard F., ed. FRANKLIN DELANO ROOSEVELT, 1882-1945: CHRONOLOGY-DOCUMENTS-BIBLIOGRAPHICAL AIDS. Presidential Chronologies Series. Dobbs Ferry, N.Y.: Oceana Publications, 1971. 220 p.

Chambers, Clarke A. "FDR, Pragmatist-Idealist: An Essay in Historiography." PACIFIC NORTHWEST QUARTERLY 52 (April 1961): 50-55.

Franklin D. Roosevelt Library. Hyde Park, New York. HISTORICAL MATERIALS IN THE FRANKLIN D. ROOSEVELT LIBRARY. Hyde Park, N.Y.: Franklin D. Roosevelt Library, National Archives and Records Service, General Services Administration, 1974. 16 p.

Rosen, Elliot A. "Roosevelt and the Brains Trust: An Historiographical Overview." POLITICAL SCIENCE QUARTERLY 87 (December 1972): 531-63.

Stewart, William James, comp., with the assistance of Jeanne Schauble. THE ERA OF FRANKLIN D. ROOSEVELT: A SELECTED BIBLIOGRAPHY OF PERIODICAL, ESSAY, AND DISSERTATION LITERATURE, 1945-1971. 2nd ed. Hyde Park, N.Y.: Franklin D. Roosevelt Library, National Archives and Records Service, General Services Administration, 1974. 360 p.

> An excellent annotated guide documenting 2,603 articles covering FDR, the New Deal, and World War II. A basic introduction to a large quantity of writing on the Roosevelt era. Does not include books.

Watson, Richard L., Jr. "Franklin D. Roosevelt in Historical Writing, 1950-1957." SOUTH ATLANTIC QUARTERLY 57 (Winter 1958): 104-26.

SOURCE MATERIALS

Asbell, Bernard. F.D.R.: THE MEMOIRS. Introduction by Anna Roosevelt Halsted. Garden City, N.Y.: Doubleday, 1973. xvii, 461 p.

Center for Cassette Studies. INDEX TO THE COMPLETE RECORDED SPEECHES OF FRANKLIN DELANO ROOSEVELT: 278 SPEECHES DATING FROM 1920 TO 1945. The Presidents Speak, vol. 1. North Hollywood, Calif.: 1974.

Hassett, William D. OFF THE RECORD WITH F.D.R., 1942-1945. New Brunswick, N.J.: Rutgers University Press, 1958. 366 p.

By Roosevelt's aide.

Leuchtenburg, William E., ed. THE NEW DEAL: A DOCUMENTARY HISTORY. Columbia: University of South Carolina Press, 1968. 263 p.

NEW DEAL MOSAIC; ROOSEVELT CONFERS WITH HIS NATIONAL EMERGENCY COUNCIL, 1933-1936. Edited by Lester G. Seligman and Elmer E. Cornwell, Jr. Eugene: University of Oregon Books, 1965. xxix, 578 p.

Nixon, Edgar B., ed. FRANKLIN D. ROOSEVELT AND CONSERVATION, 1911-1945. 2 vols. Hyde Park, N.Y.: Franklin D. Roosevelt Library, 1957. xiv, 614 p. Illus., notes, index.

Roosevelt, Franklin Delano. AH THAT VOICE: THE FIRESIDE CHATS OF FRANKLIN DELANO ROOSEVELT. Compiled by Kenneth D. Yielding and Paul H. Carlson. Odessa, Tex.: John Ben Shepperd, Jr., Library of the Presidents, Presidential Museum, 1974. xxi 248 p.

_____. AS F.D.R. SAID: A TREASURY OF HIS SPEECHES, CONVERSATIONS, AND WRITINGS. Edited by Frank Kindon. New York: Duell, Sloan and Pearce, 1950. 256 p.

_____. COMPLETE PRESIDENTIAL PRESS CONFERENCES OF FRANKLIN D. ROOSEVELT. Introduction by Jonathan Daniels. 12 vols. New York: Da Capo Press, 1973. 7,000 p.

_____. F.D.R.: HIS PERSONAL LETTERS, 1905-1945. 4 vols. Edited by Elliott Roosevelt. New York: Duell, Sloan and Pearce, 1947-50.

_____. FOR THE PRESIDENT--PERSONAL AND SECRET: CORRESPONDENCE BETWEEN FRANKLIN D. ROOSEVELT AND WILLIAM C. BULLITT. Edited by Orville H. Bullitt. Introduction by George Kennan. Boston: Houghton Mifflin, 1972. xlvi, 655 p.

Bullitt was ambassador to Russia, 1933-36, and to France, 1936-40.

_____. FRANKLIN D. ROOSEVELT AND CONSERVATION, 1911-1945. 2 vols. Compiled and edited by Edgar B. Nixon. New York: Arno Press, 1972. Reprint. Hyde Park, N.Y.: Franklin D. Roosevelt Library, 1957. 700 p.

_____. FRANKLIN D. ROOSEVELT AND FOREIGN AFFAIRS. 3 vols. Edited by Edgar B. Nixon. Cambridge, Mass.: Belknap Press of Harvard University Press, 1969.

_____. FRANKLIN D. ROOSEVELT'S OWN STORY, TOLD IN HIS OWN WORDS FROM HIS PRIVATE AND PUBLIC PAPERS. Compiled by Donald Day. Boston: Little, Brown, 1951. 14 p.

_____. MEMORABLE QUOTATIONS OF FRANKLIN D. ROOSEVELT. Compiled by E. Taylor Parks and Lois F. Parks. New York: Crowell, 1965. Var. pag.

_____. NOTHING TO FEAR: THE SELECTED ADDRESSES OF FRANKLIN DELANO ROOSEVELT, 1932-1945. Edited, with an introduction and historical notes by B.D. Zevin. Foreword by Harry L. Hopkins. Essay Index Reprint Series. Freeport, N.Y.: Books for Libraries Press, 1970. xxi, 470 p.

_____. ON OUR WAY. New York: Da Capo Press, 1973. xiv, 300 p.

_____. THE PUBLIC PAPERS AND ADDRESSES OF FRANKLIN D. ROOSEVELT, WITH A SPECIAL INTRODUCTION AND EXPLANATORY NOTES BY PRESIDENT ROOSEVELT. 13 vols. Compiled by Samuel I. Rosenman. New York: Russell and Russell, 1969.

_____. QUOTATIONS FROM ADDRESSES, MESSAGES AND STATEMENTS OF FRANKLIN D. ROOSEVELT. N.p.: 193[?]. Var. pag.

_____. ROOSEVELT AND CHURCHILL: THEIR SECRET WARTIME CORRESPONDENCE. Edited by Francis L. Lowenheim, Harold D. Langley, and Manfred Jonas. New York: Saturday Review Press, 1975. xvi, 805 p.

Includes most of the vital personal correspondence between the two leaders from 1939 to 1945.

_____. ROOSEVELT AND DANIELS: A FRIENDSHIP IN POLITICS. Edited with an introduction by Carroll Kilpatrick. Chapel Hill: University of North Carolina Press, 1952. xvi, 226 p.

Covers their exchange of correspondence from 1913 to 1945.

Daniels was secretary of the navy in World War I while FDR served as his assistant.

_____. ROOSEVELT AND FRANKFURTER: THEIR CORRESPONDENCE, 1928-1945. Annotated by Max Freedman. Boston: Little, Brown 1968. xiv, 772 p.

Justice Frankfurter was one of the most trusted advisers of Roosevelt.

_____. THE ROOSEVELT READER: SELECTED SPEECHES, MESSAGES, PRESS CONFERENCES, AND LETTERS OF FRANKLIN D. ROOSEVELT. Edited by Basil Rauch. New York: Rinehart, 1957. xxiv, 391 p.

_____. THE SUNNY SIDE OF FDR. Compiled and edited by M.S. Venkataramani. Athens: Ohio University Press, 1973. 292 p.

_____. WARTIME CORRESPONDENCE BETWEEN PRESIDENT ROOSEVELT AND POPE PIUS XII. With an introduction and explanatory notes by Myron C. Taylor. New York: Macmillan, 1947. xiii, 127 p. Reprint. New York: Da Capo Press, 1975.

Illustrates Roosevelt's concern for the importance of moral and spiritual values.

BIOGRAPHIES

Burns, James MacGregor. ROOSEVELT: THE LION AND THE FOX. New York: Harcourt, Brace and Co., 1956. xvi, 553 p. Bibliog., cartoons, ports.

_____. ROOSEVELT: THE SOLDIER OF FREEDOM. New York: Harcourt Brace Jovanovich, 1970. xiv, 722 p.

The first scholarly biography, informative and critical, of President Roosevelt. Excellent descriptions of the political scene.

Butterfield, Roger. FDR. New York: Harper and Row, 1963. 255 p.

A pictorial biography.

Davis, Kenneth Sydney. FDR: THE BECKONING OF DESTINY, 1882-1928; A HISTORY. New York: Putnam, 1972. 936 p. Bibliog.

Places Roosevelt against the background and happenings of almost half a century and shows how the man and his career were shaped and influenced by the world in which he lived.

_____. INVINCIBLE SUMMER: AN INTIMATE PORTRAIT OF THE ROOSEVELTS, BASED ON THE RECOLLECTIONS OF MARION DICKERMAN. New York: Atheneum, 1974. ix, 176 p.

Marion Dickerman was a close friend of Franklin and Eleanor Roosevelt for nearly twenty-five years.

Freidel, Frank. FRANKLIN D. ROOSEVELT. 4 vols. Boston: Little, Brown, 1952-73.

Excellent biography.

Lash, Joseph. ELEANOR AND FRANKLIN: THE STORY OF THEIR RELATIONSHIP. Based on Eleanor Roosevelt's Private Papers. Foreword by Arthur M. Schlesinger, Jr. Introduction by Franklin D. Roosevelt, Jr. New York: W.W. Norton and Co., 1971. 765 p.

Personal and family history.

Leuchtenburg, William E., ed. FRANKLIN D. ROOSEVELT: A PROFILE. American Profiles Series. New York: Hill and Wang, 1967. xxi, 257 p.

A collection of sixteen essays by fifteen experts representing some of the best biographical and interpretive writing on FDR.

Lorant, Stefan. FDR: A PICTORIAL BIOGRAPHY. New York: Simon and Schuster, 1950. 159 p.

Nash, Gerald D., ed. FRANKLIN DELANO ROOSEVELT. Great Lives Observed Series. Englewood Cliffs, N.J.: Prentice-Hall, 1967. vi, 182 p.

Roosevelt, Eleanor. FRANKLIN D. ROOSEVELT AND HYDE PARK: PERSONAL RECOLLECTIONS. Washington, D.C.: Government Printing Office, 1949. 18 p.

Roosevelt, Elliott, and Brough, James. MOTHER R.: ELEANOR ROOSEVELT'S UNTOLD STORY. New York: Putnam, 1977. 288 p.

_____. A RENDEZVOUS WITH DESTINY: THE ROOSEVELTS OF THE WHITE HOUSE. New York: Putnam, 1975. 446 p.

_____. AN UNTOLD STORY: THE ROOSEVELTS OF HYDE PARK. New York: Putnam Sons, 1973. 318 p.

Roosevelt, James, with assistance of Bill Libby. MY PARENTS: A DIFFERING VIEW. Chicago: Playboy Press, 1976. xi, 369 p.

Roosevelt, James, and Shalett, Sidney. AFFECTIONATELY, F.D.R.: A SON'S STORY OF A COURAGEOUS MAN. Westport, Conn.: Greenwood Press, 1975. Reprint. New York: Harcourt, Brace and Co., 1959. xii, 394 p.

Schlesinger, Arthur M., Jr. THE AGE OF ROOSEVELT. 3 vols. Cambridge, Mass.: Houghton Mifflin, 1957-60.

An exciting series which carries the account to 1936.

Schoor, Gene. THE PICTURE STORY OF FDR [1882-1945]. New York: Fell, 1950. 94 p. Facsims., ports., views.

Photographs and attached text.

Sullivan, Wilson. FRANKLIN DELANO ROOSEVELT. By the editors of American Heritage. Consultant, Frank Freidel. New York: American Heritage Publishing Co., 1970. 153 p.

Tugwell, Rexford Guy. THE DEMOCRATIC ROOSEVELT: A BIOGRAPHY OF FRANKLIN D. ROOSEVELT. Garden City, N.Y.: Doubleday, 1957. 712 p.

Tugwell was a member of the original brain trust.

MONOGRAPHS

Alsop, Joseph. FDR: A CENTENARY REMEMBRANCE. New York: Viking, 1981. 256 p.

Asbell, Bernard. WHEN F.D.R. DIED. New York: Holt, Rinehart and Winston, 1961. xi, 211 p.

A journalistic account of events surrounding the president's death.

Bailey, Thomas Andrew, and Ryan, Paul B. HITLER VS. ROOSEVELT: THE UNDECLARED NAVAL WAR. New York: Free Press, 1979. xi, 303 p.

Beard, Charles Austin. PRESIDENT ROOSEVELT AND THE COMING OF THE WAR, 1941: A STUDY IN APPEARANCES AND REALITIES. New Haven, Conn.: Yale University Press, 1948. vi, 614 p.

A vigorous indictment of the Roosevelt foreign policy.

Bellush, Bernard. FRANKLIN D. ROOSEVELT AS GOVERNOR OF NEW YORK. Columbia University Studies in the Social Sciences, no. 585. New York: Columbia University Press, 1955. 338 p.

Helpful in understanding Roosevelt's earlier social and economic ideas.

Bishop, James Alonzo. FDR'S LAST YEAR: APRIL 1944-APRIL 1945. London: Hart-Davis MacGibbon, 1975. xiv, 690 p.

Blum, John Morton. ROOSEVELT AND MORGANTHAU. Boston: Houghton Mifflin, 1970. xvi, 686 p.

A revision and condensation of the author's FROM THE MORGANTHAU DIARIES (1959-67). Based upon an eight hundred-volume set of records kept by the secretary of the treasury.

Brogan, Denis W. THE ERA OF FRANKLIN D. ROOSEVELT: A CHRONICLE OF THE NEW DEAL AND THE GLOBAL WAR. Chronicles of America Series, vol. 52. New Haven, Conn.: Yale University Press, 1950. ix, 382 p.

Carlson, Earland Irving. FRANKLIN D. ROOSEVELT'S FIGHT FOR THE PRESIDENTIAL NOMINATION, 1928-1932. Ann Arbor, Mich.: University Microfilms, 1955. vii, 462 p. Bibliogs.

Shows Roosevelt's technique of seeking the presidency and the work of his managers behind the scenes: Louis Howe, James Farley, and Edward Flynn.

Conkin, Paul K. FDR AND THE ORIGINS OF THE WELFARE STATE. New York: Thomas Y. Crowell, 1967. x, 118 p.

Dallek, Robert. FRANKLIN D. ROOSEVELT AND AMERICAN FOREIGN POLICY, 1932-1945. New York: Oxford University Press, 1979. xii, 657 p.

The first full-scale history of Roosevelt's foreign policy.

Divine, Robert A. ROOSEVELT AND WORLD WAR II. Baltimore: Johns Hopkins Press, 1969. x, 107 p.

A reappraisal of Roosevelt's foreign policy. Omits Latin America and the Far East. Deals with the coming of the war, founding of the United Nations, and Soviet policy.

Dorsett, Lyle W. FRANKLIN D. ROOSEVELT AND THE CITY BOSSES. Interdisciplinary Urban Series. Port Washington, N.Y.: Kennikat Press, 1977. x, 134 p.

Einaudi, Mario. THE ROOSEVELT REVOLUTION. London: Constable, 1960. Reprint. Westport, Conn.: Greenwood Press, 1977. x, 372 p.

Ekirch, Arthur A., Jr. IDEOLOGIES AND UTOPIAS: THE IMPACT OF THE NEW DEAL ON AMERICAN THOUGHT. Chicago: Quadrangle Books, 1969. ix, 307 p.

An account of the relationship between the New Deal and its intellectual supporters and critics.

Farley, James A. JIM FARLEY'S STORY: THE ROOSEVELT YEARS. New York: Whittlesey House, 1948. x, 388 p.

An inside story by Roosevelt's famous campaign manager.

Feis, Herbert. CHURCHILL, ROOSEVELT, AND STALIN: THE WAR THEY WAGED AND THE PEACE THEY SOUGHT. Princeton, N.J.: Princeton University Press, 1957. xi, 692 p.

_____. 1933: CHARACTERS IN CRISIS. Boston: Little, Brown, 1966. 366 p.

Freidel, Frank. F.D.R. AND THE SOUTH. Baton Rouge: Louisiana State University Press, 1965. x, 102 p.

A series of three lectures by an eminent scholar.

Frisch, Morton J. FRANKLIN D. ROOSEVELT; THE CONTRIBUTION OF THE NEW DEAL TO AMERICAN POLITICAL THOUGHT AND PRACTICE. Twayne's World Leaders Series. New York: Twayne Publishers, 1975. 165 p. Bibliog.

Fusfeld, Daniel R. THE ECONOMIC THOUGHT OF FRANKLIN D. ROOSEVELT AND THE ORIGINS OF THE NEW DEAL. New York: Columbia University Press, 1956. 337 p. Bibliog.

Covers Roosevelt's pre-presidential years.

Greer, Thomas H. WHAT ROOSEVELT THOUGHT: THE SOCIAL AND POLITICAL IDEAS OF FRANKLIN D. ROOSEVELT. East Lansing: Michigan State University Press, 1958. xv, 244 p.

Claims the New Deal had intelligible and consistent objectives. Shows Roosevelt's thought was informed and solidly based in his education, reading, love of history, and experience.

Guerrant, Edward O. ROOSEVELT'S GOOD NEIGHBOR POLICY, 1933-1945. Inter-Americana Studies, 5. Albuquerque: University of New Mexico Press, 1950. x, 235 p.

Gurney, Gene, and Gurney, Clare. FDR AND HYDE PARK. New York: Franklin Watts, 1970. 65 p.

Jackson, Robert H. THE STRUGGLE FOR JUDICIAL SUPREMACY: A STUDY OF A CRISIS IN AMERICAN POWER POLITICS. New York: Alfred A. Knopf, 1941. xx, 361 p.

A study of Roosevelt's proposal to reorganize the judiciary.

Karl, Barry Dean. EXECUTIVE REORGANIZATION AND REFORM IN THE NEW DEAL. Cambridge, Mass.: Harvard University Press, 1963. xv, 292 p.

The story of the reorganization of the executive branch based on the work of the Brownlow Commission.

Kimball, Warren F., ed. FRANKLIN D. ROOSEVELT AND THE WORLD CRISIS, 1937-1945. Lexington, Mass.: D.C. Heath and Co., 1973. xxii, 297 p.

A collection of articles representing the competing interpretations of Roosevelt's foreign policy held by twenty authors.

Kirkendall, Richard S. SOCIAL SCIENTISTS AND FARM POLITICS IN THE AGE OF ROOSEVELT. Columbia: University of Missouri Press, 1966. xi, 358 p.

Lash, Joseph P. ROOSEVELT AND CHURCHILL, 1939-1941: THE PARTNERSHIP THAT SAVED THE WEST. New York: Norton, 1976. 528 p.

Leuchtenburg, William E. FRANKLIN D. ROOSEVELT AND THE NEW DEAL, 1932-1940. The New American Nation Series. New York: Harper and Row, 1963. xvii, 393 p.

The best short account of the New Deal.

Lippman, Theo, Jr. THE SQUIRE OF WARM SPRINGS: F.D.R. IN GEORGIA, 1924-1945. Chicago: Playboy Press; New York: trade distribution by Simon and Schuster, 1977. 248 p.

Moley, Raymond, with the assistance of Elliot A. Rosen. THE FIRST NEW DEAL. Foreword by Frank Freidel. New York: Harcourt, Brace and World, 1966. 577 p.

An excellent account of Roosevelt's first term by one of his closest advisors and leader of the brain trust.

Mooney, Booth. ROOSEVELT AND RAYBURN: A POLITICAL PARTNERSHIP. Philadelphia: J.B. Lippincott, 1971. x, 228 p.

Moscow, Warren. ROOSEVELT AND WILLKIE. Englewood Cliffs, N.J.: Prentice-Hall, 1968. xi, 210 p.

A study of the 1940 campaign.

Nesbitt, Victoria Henrietta [Kugler]. WHITE HOUSE DIARY BY HENRIETTA NESBITT, F.D.R.'S HOUSEKEEPER. Garden City, N.Y.: Doubleday, 1948. 314 p.

On housekeeping in the White House, 1933-45.

Neumann, William Louis. AFTER VICTORY: CHURCHILL, ROOSEVELT, STALIN AND THE MAKING OF THE PEACE. New York: Harper and Row, 1967. xii, 212 p.

Nevins, Allan. THE PLACE OF FRANKLIN D. ROOSEVELT IN HISTORY. New York: Humanities Press, 1965. 20 p.

Praises Roosevelt as an innovator who reinforced old ideas while transforming American life and goals.

Parmet, Herbert S., and Hecht, Marie B. NEVER AGAIN: A PRESIDENT RUNS FOR A THIRD TERM. New York: Macmillan, 1968. xii, 306 p.

Patterson, James T. CONGRESSIONAL CONSERVATISM AND THE NEW DEAL: THE GROWTH OF THE CONSERVATIVE COALITION IN CONGRESS, 1933-1939. Lexington: University of Kentucky Press for the Organization of American Historians, 1967. ix, 369 p.

Perkins, Dexter. THE NEW AGE OF FRANKLIN ROOSEVELT, 1932-45. Chicago: University of Chicago Press, 1957. ix, 193 p.

Perkins, Frances. THE ROOSEVELT I KNEW. New York: Harper and Row, 1946. vii, 408 p.

An excellent memoir by Roosevelt's secretary of labor.

Polenberg, Richard. REORGANIZING ROOSEVELT'S GOVERNMENT: THE CONTROVERSY OVER EXECUTIVE REORGANIZATION, 1936-1939. Cambridge, Mass.: Harvard University Press, 1966. viii, 275 p.

Analyzes the administrative reform effort of 1937 and the opposition to it.

Pritchett, C. Herman. THE ROOSEVELT COURT: A STUDY IN JUDICIAL POLITICS AND VALUES, 1937-1947. New York: Macmillan, 1948. xvi, 314 p.

Ramsay, Marion Livingston. PYRAMIDS OF POWER: THE STORY OF ROOSEVELT, INSULL AND THE UTILITY WARS. Indianapolis: Bobbs-Merrill, 1937. Reprint. New York: Da Capo Press, 1975. 342 p.

Rauch, Basil. ROOSEVELT, FROM MUNICH TO PEARL HARBOR: A STUDY IN THE CREATION OF A FOREIGN POLICY. New York: Barnes and Noble, 1967. Reprint. New York: Da Capo Press, 1975. xvi, 527 p.

Robinson, Edgar Eugene. THE ROOSEVELT LEADERSHIP, 1933-1945. Philadelphia: J.B. Lippincott, 1955. Reprint. New York: Da Capo Press, 1972. 491 p.

Very critical of Roosevelt's pragmatism.

______. THEY VOTED FOR ROOSEVELT: THE PRESIDENTIAL VOTE, 1932-1944. New York: Octagon Books, 1970. x, 207 p.

Rollins, Alfred B., Jr. ROOSEVELT AND HOWE. New York: Alfred A. Knopf, 1962. xii, 479 p.

A first-rate dual biography which traces Roosevelt's rise from state assembly to the presidency.

Rosen, Elliot A. HOOVER, ROOSEVELT, AND THE BRAINS TRUST: FROM DEPRESSION TO NEW DEAL. New York: Columbia University Press, 1977. x, 446 p.

Rosenman, Samuel I. WORKING WITH ROOSEVELT. New York: Harper and Brothers, 1952. Reprint. New York: Da Capo Press, 1972. xiv, 560 p.

Rosenman was a speechwriter and principal aide to FDR.

Seligman, Lester G., and Cornwell, Elmer E., Jr. NEW DEAL MOSAIC: ROOSEVELT CONFERS WITH HIS NATIONAL EMERGENCY COUNCIL, 1933-1936. Eugene: University of Oregon Books, 1965. xxix, 578 p.

Sherwood, Robert Emmet. ROOSEVELT AND HOPKINS: AN INTIMATE HISTORY. Rev. ed. New York: Harper and Brothers, 1950. xix, 1,002 p.

An excellent account of the war years.

Stettinius, Edward, Jr. ROOSEVELT AND THE RUSSIANS: THE YALTA CONFERENCE. Garden City, N.Y.: Doubleday and Co., 1949. Reprint. Westport, Conn.: Greenwood Press, 1970. xvi, 367 p.

Stiles, Lela. THE MAN BEHIND ROOSEVELT: THE STORY OF LOUIS McHENRY HOWE. Cleveland: World Publishing Co., 1954. 311 p.

Sutton, Anthony C. WALL STREET AND FDR. New Rochelle, N.Y.: Arlington House Publishers, 1975. 200 p.

Tansill, Charles Callan. BACK DOOR TO WAR: THE ROOSEVELT FOREIGN POLICY, 1933-1941. Chicago: Henry Regnery, 1952. xxi, 690 p.

Very critical of Roosevelt.

Tugwell, Rexford Guy. THE BRAINS TRUST. New York: Viking Press, 1968. xxxii, 538 p.

A detailed account of FDR as a candidate and campaigner for the presidency in 1932.

______. FDR: ARCHITECT OF AN ERA. New York: Macmillan, 1967. xvii, 270 p.

______. IN SEARCH OF ROOSEVELT. Cambridge, Mass.: Harvard University Press, 1972. ix, 313 p.

______. ROOSEVELT'S REVOLUTION: THE FIRST YEAR, A PERSONAL PERSPECTIVE. New York: Macmillan, 1977. xix, 327 p.

Tully, Grace George. F.D.R.: MY BOSS. Foreword by William O. Douglas. New York: Scribner, 1949. xiii, 391 p.

Wann, A.J. THE PRESIDENT AS CHIEF ADMINISTRATOR: A STUDY OF FRANKLIN D. ROOSEVELT. Washington, D.C.: Public Affairs Press, 1968. v, 219 p.

Wolf, Ann M. THE LONG SHADOW OF FRANKLIN D. ROOSEVELT. Philadelphia: Dorrance, 1974. 81 p.

Wolfskill, George, and Hudson, John A. ALL BUT THE PEOPLE: ROOSEVELT AND HIS CRITICS, 1933-1939. New York: Macmillan, 1969. xii, 386 p.

A view of FDR through the eyes of his detractors.

Zinn, Howard, ed. NEW DEAL THOUGHT. The American Heritage Series. Indianapolis: Bobbs-Merrill, 1966. xlvii, 431 p.

ARTICLES

Adler, Selig. "Franklin D. Roosevelt Foreign Policy: An Assessment." INTERNATIONAL REVIEW OF HISTORY AND POLITICAL SCIENCE 15 (May 1978): 1-17.

Appleby, Paul H. "Roosevelt's Third-Term Decision." AMERICAN POLITICAL SCIENCE REVIEW 46 (September 1952): 754-65.

Says FDR did not make his decision until after the convention delegates voted.

Armstrong, W.M. "Franklin D. Roosevelt's Economic Thought." AMERICAN JOURNAL OF ECONOMICS 17 (April 1958): 329-31.

Arnold, Thurman. "Roosevelt's Contribution to the American Competitive Ideal." CENTENNIAL REVIEW 9 (Spring 1965): 192-208.

Discusses the National Industrial Recovery Administration and the court-packing proposal.

Asbell, Bernard. "F.D.R.'s Extra Burden: What Poliomyelitis Meant to a Political Career." AMERICAN HERITAGE 24 (June 1973): 21-25.

Bateman, Herman E. "Observations on President Roosevelt's Health during World War II." MISSISSIPPI VALLEY HISTORICAL REVIEW 43 (June 1956): 82-102.

Roosevelt's associates did not regard his physical or mental capabilities as impaired even in the winter of 1944-45.

Bellush, Jewel. "Old and New Left Reappraisals of the New Deal and Roosevelt's Presidency." PRESIDENTIAL STUDIES QUARTERLY 9 (Summer 1979): 243-65.

Berlin, Isaiah. "President Franklin Delano Roosevelt." POLITICAL QUARTERLY 26 (December 1955): 336-44.

Praises Roosevelt's imagination, sense of history, and political skill.

Bernstein, Barton J. "Roosevelt, Truman, and the Atomic Bomb, 1941-1945: A Reinterpretation." POLITICAL SCIENCE QUARTERLY 90 (Spring 1975): 23-69.

_____. "The Uneasy Alliance: Roosevelt, Churchill, and the Atomic Bomb, 1940-1945." WESTERN POLITICAL QUARTERLY 29 (June 1976): 202-30.

Bhana, Surendra. "An Attempt by the Roosevelt Administration to 'Reinforce' Self-Government in Puerto Rico: The Elective Government Bill of 1943." REVISTA INTERAMERICANA 2 (Winter 1973): 558-73.

Blum, John M. "That Kind of Liberal: Franklin D. Roosevelt after Twenty-Five Years." YALE REVIEW 60 (Autumn 1970): 14-23.

Bruenn, Howard G. "Clinical Notes on the Illness and Death of President Franklin D. Roosevelt." ANNALS OF INTERNAL MEDICINE 72 (April 1970): 579-91.

By Roosevelt's cardiologist and his physician during 1944-45. Explains medical history, diagnosis, and treatment.

Burns, James MacGregor. "F.D.R.: The Last Journey." AMERICAN HERITAGE 21 (August 1970): 8-11, 78-85.

_____. "FDR: The Untold Story of His Last Year." SATURDAY REVIEW OF LITERATURE 53 (11 April 1970): 12-15, 39.

Indicates Roosevelt was an effective leader despite health problems in 1944-45.

Cowperthwaite, L.L. "Franklin D. Roosevelt at Harvard." QUARTERLY JOURNAL OF SPEECH 38 (February 1952): 37-41.

Traces the development of Roosevelt as a speaker and the Harvard teachers who influenced him most.

Cross, Whitney R. "Ideas in Politics: The Conservation Policies of the Two Roosevelts." JOURNAL OF THE HISTORY OF IDEAS 14 (June 1953): 421-38.

Dallek, Robert. "Franklin Roosevelt as World Leader." AMERICAN HISTORICAL REVIEW 76 (December 1971): 1503-13.

A double review article of ROOSEVELT: THE SOLDIER OF FREEDOM (1970) by J.M. Burns and THE POLITICS OF RESCUE (1970) by Henry Feingold. Dallek prefers the Feingold book because it puts the president's actions in a more realistic context.

Daniels, Jonathan. "Franklin Delano Roosevelt and Books." In THREE PRESIDENTS AND THEIR BOOKS, edited by Robert B. Downs, pp. 89-105. Fifth Annual Windsor Lectures. Urbana: University of Illinois Press, 1955.

Dorsett, Lyle W. "Frank Hague, Franklin Roosevelt, and the Politics of the New Deal." NEW JERSEY HISTORY 94 (Spring 1976): 23-35.

Emerson, William. "Franklin Roosevelt as Commander-in-Chief in World War II." MILITARY AFFAIRS 22 (Winter 1958): 181-207.

Feis, Herbert. "When Roosevelt Died." VIRGINIA QUARTERLY REVIEW 46 (Autumn 1970): 576-89.

Thinks Roosevelt postponed the problems of peacemaking too long.

Ficken, Robert E. "Political Leadership in Wartime: Franklin D. Roosevelt and the Elections of 1942." MID-AMERICA 57 (January 1975): 20-37.

Haines, Gerald K. "The Roosevelt Administration Interprets the Monroe Doctrine." AUSTRALIAN JOURNAL OF POLITICS AND HISTORY 24 (December 1978): 322-45.

______. "Under the Eagle's Wing: The Franklin Roosevelt Administration Forges an American Hemisphere." DIPLOMATIC HISTORY 1 (Fall 1977): 373-88.

Hamby, Alonzo L. "The Liberals, Truman and FDR as Symbol and Myth." JOURNAL OF AMERICAN HISTORY 56 (March 1970): 856-67.

Shows the influence of FDR's prestige in postwar liberal politics.

Hammersmith, Jack L. "Franklin Roosevelt, the Polish Question and the Election of 1944." MID-AMERICA 59 (January 1977): 5-17.

Hand, Samuel B. "Al Smith, Franklin D. Roosevelt and the New Deal: Some Comments on Perspective." HISTORIAN 27 (May 1965): 366-81.

Says Smith opposed the New Deal because of his deep respect for the institutions and traditions of society.

Kahn, Herman. "The Long-Range Implications for Historians and Archivists of the Charges against the Franklin D. Roosevelt Library." AMERICAN ARCHIVIST 34 (July 1971): 265-75.

______. "World War II and Its Background: Research Materials at the Franklin D. Roosevelt Library and Policies Concerning Their Use." AMERICAN ARCHIVIST 17 (April 1954): 149-62.

Katterjohn, Monte M. "FDR Folklore." HOOSIER FOLKLORE 7 (March 1948): 22-23.

Legends concerning the death of FDR.

Kimball, Warren F. "Churchill and Roosevelt: The Personal Equation." PROLOGUE 6 (Fall 1974): 169-82.

Kirkendall, Richard S. "Franklin D. Roosevelt and the Service Intellectual." MISSISSIPPI VALLEY HISTORICAL REVIEW 49 (December 1962): 456-71.

Discusses Roosevelt's use of academicians in helping to form the New Deal.

______. "The New Deal as Watershed: The Recent Literature." JOURNAL OF AMERICAN HISTORY 54 (March 1968): 839-52.

A survey of about one hundred publications from 1962 to 1966 on the New Deal.

Leiter, William M. "The Presidency and Non-Federal Government: FDR and the Promotion of State Legislative Action." PRESIDENTIAL STUDIES QUARTERLY 9 (Spring 1979): 101-21.

Leland, Waldo G. "The Creation of the Franklin D. Roosevelt Library: A Personal Narrative." AMERICAN ARCHIVIST 18 (January 1955): 11-29.

Lowitt, Richard. "'Present at the Creation': George W. Norris, Franklin D. Roosevelt and the TVA Enabling Act." EAST TENNESSEE HISTORICAL SOCIETY'S PUBLICATIONS 48 (1976): 116-26.

Morrison, Rodney J. "Franklin D. Roosevelt and the Supreme Court: An Example of the Use of Probability Theory in Political History." HISTORY AND THEORY 16, no. 2 (1977): 137-46.

Neustadt, Richard E. "Approaches to Staffing the Presidency: Notes on FDR and JFK." AMERICAN POLITICAL SCIENCE REVIEW 57 (December 1963): 855-64.

Niedziela, Theresa A. "Franklin D. Roosevelt and the Supreme Court." PRESIDENTIAL STUDIES QUARTERLY 6 (Fall 1976): 51-57.

Partin, John W. "Roosevelt, Byrnes and the 1944 Vice-Presidential Nomination." HISTORIAN 42 (November 1979): 85-100.

Parzen, Herbert. "The Roosevelt Palestine Policy, 1943-1945: An Exercise in Dual Diplomacy." AMERICAN JEWISH ARCHIVES 26 (April 1974): 31-65.

Polenberg, Richard. "Historians and the Liberal Presidency: Recent Appraisals of Roosevelt and Truman." SOUTH ATLANTIC QUARTERLY 75 (Winter 1976): 20-35.

_____. "The Roosevelt Library Case: A Review Article." AMERICAN ARCHIVIST 34 (July 1971): 277-84.

Pusey, Merlo J. "FDR vs. the Supreme Court." AMERICAN HERITAGE 9 (April 1958): 24-27, 105-7.

> Claims the justices did not adjust their views to save the court after the fight to enlarge its membership.

Rossiter, Clinton L. "The Political Philosophy of F.D. Roosevelt: A Challenge to Scholarship." REVIEW OF POLITICS 11 (January 1949): 87-95.

> Suggests the problem requires the combined talents of the historian and the psychoanalyst.

Ryan, Halford Ross. "Roosevelt's First Inaugural: A Study of Technique." QUARTERLY JOURNAL OF SPEECH 65 (April 1979): 137-49.

Sargent, James E. "FDR and Lewis W. Douglas: Budget Balancing and the Early New Deal." PROLOGUE 6 (Spring 1974): 33-43.

_____. "Oral History, Franklin D. Roosevelt, and the New Deal: Some Recollections of Adolph A. Berle, Jr., Lewis W. Douglas, and Raymond Moley." ORAL HISTORY REVIEW 1 (1973): 92-109.

Sargent, James E. "Roosevelt's Economy Act: Fiscal Conservatism and the Early New Deal." CONGRESSIONAL STUDIES 7 (Winter 1980): 33-51.

Schlesinger, Arthur M., Jr. "A Comment on 'Roosevelt and His Foreign Policy Critics.'" POLITICAL SCIENCE QUARTERLY 94 (Spring 1979): 33-36.

His view of an article by Richard W. Steele appearing on pages 15-32 of the same issue of this journal.

_____. "Roosevelt and His Detractors." HARPER'S 200 (June 1950): 62-68.

On Roosevelt's foreign policy and several new books dealing with it. The revisionists criticize Roosevelt not for intervening, but for doing it unwisely and ineffectively.

Shappee, Nathan D. "Zangara's Attempted Assassination of Franklin D. Roosevelt." FLORIDA HISTORICAL QUARTERLY 37 (October 1958): 101-10.

Critical of Zangara's execution. Zangara was electrocuted just thirty-three days after his attack on Roosevelt and murder of Mayor Cermak of Chicago.

Skau, George H. "Franklin D. Roosevelt and the Expansion of Presidential Power." CURRENT HISTORY 66 (June 1974): 246-48, 274-75.

Sterling, Kier B. "Roosevelt and Garner, 1933-1941." TEXANA 10, no. 2 (1972): 129-49.

Sternsher, Bernard. "Tugwell's Appraisal of F.D.R." WESTERN POLITICAL QUARTERLY 15 (March 1962): 67-79.

Tugwell rates Roosevelt high for his achievements in the face of formidable obstacles.

Sussman, Leila Aline. "FDR and the White House Mail." PUBLIC OPINION QUARTERLY 20 (Spring 1956): 3-16.

Roosevelt used mail as a way of gaining support for a program. He also arranged to have all letters answered.

Theoharis, Athan. "Roosevelt and Truman on Yalta: The Origins of the Cold War." POLITICAL SCIENCE QUARTERLY 87 (June 1972): 210-11.

Tugwell, Rexford Guy. "The Fallow Years of Franklin D. Roosevelt." ETHICS 66 (January 1956): 98-116.

Covers the period between the polio attack and the beginning of the governorship.

______. "Franklin D. Roosevelt on the Verge of the Presidency." ANTIOCH REVIEW 16 (March 1956): 46-79.

The author's recollections of the inauguration, selection of cabinet officials, and the first few days FDR was president.

______. "The Preparation of a President." WESTERN POLITICAL QUARTERLY 1 (June 1948): 131-53.

On Roosevelt as governor and presidential candidate and what he learned from his advisers as well as his own experience.

______. "The Protagonists: Roosevelt and Hoover." ANTIOCH REVIEW 13 (December 1953): 419-42.

Points up the differences on means and ends between the two rivals.

______. "Roosevelt and Frankfurter: An Essay Review." POLITICAL SCIENCE QUARTERLY 85 (March 1970): 99-114.

______. "Roosevelt and Howe." ANTIOCH REVIEW 14 (September 1954): 367-73.

Winfield, B.H. "Franklin D. Roosevelt's Efforts to Influence the News During His Term Press Conferences." PRESIDENTIAL STUDIES QUARTERLY 11 (Spring 1981): 189-99.

Young, Lowell T. "Franklin D. Roosevelt and the Expansion of the Monroe Doctrine." NORTH DAKOTA QUARTERLY 42 (Winter 1974): 23-32.

Chapter 43

HARRY S. TRUMAN, 1945-53

BIBLIOGRAPHIES

Furer, Howard B., ed. HARRY S. TRUMAN, 1884-1972: CHRONOLOGY-DOCUMENTS-BIBLIOGRAPHICAL AIDS. Presidential Chronologies Series. Dobbs Ferry, N.Y.: Oceana Publications, 1970. iv, 155 p.

Harry S. Truman Library. Independence, Missouri. HISTORICAL MATERIALS IN THE HARRY S. TRUMAN LIBRARY. Independence: Harry S. Truman Library, 1982. v, 65 p.

Stapleton, Margaret L. THE TRUMAN AND EISENHOWER YEARS, 1945-1960: A SELECTIVE BIBLIOGRAPHY. Metuchen, N.J.: Scarecrow Press, 1973. vii, 221 p.

SOURCE MATERIALS

Bernstein, Barton J., and Matusow, Allen J., eds. THE TRUMAN ADMINISTRATION: A DOCUMENTARY HISTORY. New York: Harper and Row, 1966. viii, 518 p.

Weaves together a narrative history from transcripts of hearings, correspondence, diaries, and other sources.

Republican National Committee, 1948. THE TRUMAN CHRONOLOGY: A DAY-BY-DAY RECORD OF THE PRESIDENCY OF HARRY S. TRUMAN. Washington, D.C.: Research Division, Republican National Committee, 1948.

Truman, Harry S. FREEDOM AND EQUALITY: ADDRESSES. Edited by David S. Horton. Columbia: University of Missouri Press, 1960. 85 p.

______. THE MAN FROM MISSOURI: THE MEMORABLE WORDS OF THE THIRTY-THIRD PRESIDENT. Selected and arranged by Ted Sheldon. Kansas City, Mo.: Hallmark Editions, 1970. 61 p.

_____. MEMOIRS BY HARRY S. TRUMAN. 2 vols. Garden City, N.Y.: Doubleday and Co., 1955-56. xi, 596; xi, 594 p.

_____. MR. CITIZEN. New York: Bernard Geis Associates, 1960. 315 p.

_____. PUBLIC PAPERS OF THE PRESIDENTS OF THE UNITED STATES, HARRY S. TRUMAN, 1945-1953. 8 vols. Washington, D.C.: Government Printing Office, 1961-67.

_____. THE TRUMAN ADMINISTRATION, ITS PRINCIPLES AND PRACTICE. Edited by Louis W. Koenig. New York: New York University Press, 1956. xii, 394 p.

_____. TRUMAN PROGRAM: ADDRESSES AND MESSAGES. Edited by M.B. Schnapper. Washington, D.C.: Public Affairs Press, 1949. x, 261 p.

_____. THE TRUMAN WIT. Edited by Alex J. Goldman. New York: Citadel Press, 1966. 88 p.

_____. THE TRUMAN YEARS: THE WORDS AND TIMES OF HARRY S. TRUMAN. By the editors of Country Beautiful; editorial direction, Michael P. Dineen; edited by Robert L. Polley; art direction, Buford Nixon. Waukesha, Wis.: Country Beautiful, 1976. 111 p.

_____. THE WIT AND WISDOM OF HARRY S. TRUMAN. Compiled by George S. Caldwell. Reprint of the edition published by Hawthorn Books, New York, 1966, under the title GOOD OLD HARRY. New York: Stein and Day, 1973. 96 p.

Truman, Margaret, ed. LETTERS FROM FATHER: THE TRUMAN FAMILY'S PERSONAL CORRESPONDENCE. New York: Pinnacle Books, 1982. 255 p.

U.S. Congress. Senate. Committee on Armed Services and Committee on Foreign Relations. HEARINGS: MILITARY SITUATION IN THE FAR EAST. 82d Cong., 1st sess., 1973. Washington, D.C.: Government Printing Office, 1951. 3,691 p.

BIOGRAPHIES

Cochran, Bert. HARRY TRUMAN AND THE CRISIS PRESIDENCY. New York: Funk and Wagnalls, 1973. 432 p.

Critical of Truman.

Daniels, Jonathan. THE MAN OF INDEPENDENCE. Philadelphia: J.B. Lippincott, 1950. 384 p.

Early life of Truman in Missouri, his army service in France, and his experience in Missouri and national politics. The best work on Truman's pre-presidential career.

Donovan, Robert J. CONFLICT AND CRISIS: THE PRESIDENCY OF HARRY S. TRUMAN, 1945-1948. New York: W.W. Norton and Co., 1977. xvii, 473 p.

_____. TUMULTUOUS YEARS: THE PRESIDENCY OF HARRY S. TRUMAN, 1949-53. New York: W.W. Norton and Co., 1982. 444 p.

Faber, Doris. HARRY TRUMAN. New York: Abelard-Schuman, 1973. 96 p. Photos.

Gies, Joseph. HARRY S. TRUMAN, A PICTORIAL BIOGRAPHY. Garden City, N.Y.: Doubleday, 1968. ix, 178 p.

Gosnell, Harold F. TRUMAN'S CRISES: A POLITICAL BIOGRAPHY OF HARRY S. TRUMAN. Westport, Conn.: Greenwood Press, 1980. xv, 656 p.

A scholarly study of Truman's career. Makes use of manuscript sources, social science analysis, and new monographs.

Hillman, William. MR. PRESIDENT. New York: Farrar, Straus and Young, 1952. 253 p.

Important for the illustrations; and excerpts from Truman's private papers.

Phillips, Cabell. THE TRUMAN PRESIDENCY. New York: Macmillan, 1966. xiii, 463 p.

Robbins, Jhan. BESS AND HARRY: AN AMERICAN LOVE STORY. New York: G.P. Putnam's Sons, 1980. ix, 194 p.

Steinberg, Alfred. THE MAN FROM MISSOURI: THE LIFE AND TIMES OF HARRY S. TRUMAN. New York: Putnam, 1962. 447 p.

The best of the earlier books on Truman.

Truman, Harry S. HARRY TRUMAN: MR. CITIZEN. Photographs by C.H. Schrepfer. Independence, Mo.: Independence Press, 1972. 33 p.

Chiefly illustrations.

Truman, Margaret. HARRY S. TRUMAN. New York: William Morrow and Co., 1972. 602 p.

Interesting for its personal history and the Truman-Roosevelt relationship.

_____. SOUVENIR, MARGARET TRUMAN'S OWN STORY. New York: McGraw-Hill, 1956. 365 p.

Much of the book covers the presidential years of the Trumans.

U.S. Congress. House. MEMORIAL SERVICES IN THE CONGRESS OF THE UNITED STATES AND TRIBUTES IN EULOGY OF HARRY S. TRUMAN. 93d Cong., 1st sess., 1973. Washington, D.C.: Government Printing Office, 1973. xxxiv, 196 p.

MONOGRAPHS

Berman, William C. THE POLITICS OF CIVIL RIGHTS IN THE TRUMAN ADMINISTRATION. Columbus: Ohio State University Press, 1970. xi, 261 p.

Bernstein, Barton J., ed. POLITICS AND POLICIES OF THE TRUMAN ADMINISTRATION. Chicago: Quadrangle Books, 1970. 330 p.

A collection of seven essays by younger historians who are sharply critical of Truman's foreign and domestic policies.

Caute, David. THE GREAT FEAR: THE ANTI-COMMUNIST PURGE UNDER TRUMAN AND EISENHOWER. New York: Simon and Schuster, 1978. 697 p.

Dalfiume, Richard M. DESEGREGATION OF THE UNITED STATES ARMED FORCES: FIGHTING ON TWO FRONTS, 1939-1953. Columbia: University of Missouri Press, 1969. viii, 252 p.

Davies, Richard O. HOUSING REFORM DURING THE TRUMAN ADMINISTRATION. Columbia: University of Missouri Press, 1966. xiv, 197 p.

Druks, Herbert. HARRY S. TRUMAN AND THE RUSSIANS, 1945-1953. New York: Robert Speller and Sons, 1966. viii, 291 p.

Freeland, Richard M. THE TRUMAN DOCTRINE AND THE ORIGINS OF McCARTHYISM. New York: Alfred A. Knopf, 1972. xii, 419 p.

Argues that the McCarthy hysteria was a direct result of the

Truman administration's deliberate campaign to exaggerate the Communist issue. Also says anticommunism was a device to get congressional and popular support for unpopular foreign policies.

Hamby, Alonzo L. BEYOND THE NEW DEAL: HARRY S. TRUMAN AND AMERICAN LIBERALISM. New York: Columbia University Press, 1973. xx, 635 p.

The most complete scholarly account of the Truman administration to date.

_____, ed. HARRY S. TRUMAN AND THE FAIR DEAL. Lexington, Mass.: D.C. Heath and Co., 1974. xv, 233 p.

A reader which concentrates on conflicting interpretations of President Truman's domestic program.

Harper, Alan. THE POLITICS OF LOYALTY. Westport, Conn.: Greenwood Press, 1969. xii, 318 p.

A study of the White House and the Communist issue, 1946-1952, with emphasis upon the Truman administration's effort to create a loyalty program which would satisfy the need for security and yet protect the rights of the individual.

Hartmann, Susan M. TRUMAN AND THE 80TH CONGRESS. Columbia: University of Missouri Press, 1971. viii, 241 p.

Haynes, Richard F. THE AWESOME POWER: HARRY S. TRUMAN AS COMMANDER IN CHIEF. Baton Rouge: Louisiana State University Press, 1973. vii, 359 p.

Hechler, Ken. WORKING WITH TRUMAN: A PERSONAL MEMOIR OF THE WHITE HOUSE YEARS. New York: G.P. Putnam's Sons, 1982. 320 p.

Heller, Francis H., ed. ECONOMICS AND THE TRUMAN ADMINISTRATION. Lawrence: Regent's Press of Kansas, 1981. xviii, 193 p.

_____. THE KOREAN WAR: A 25-YEAR PERSPECTIVE. Lawrence: Regents Press of Kansas, 1977. xxii, 251 p.

Huthmacher, J. Joseph, ed. THE TRUMAN YEARS: THE RECONSTRUCTION OF POSTWAR AMERICA. Hinsdale, Ill.: Dryden Press, 1972. 236 p.

A collection of essays which survey the changing interpretations of Truman's foreign and domestic policies.

Kirkendall, Richard Stewart. HARRY S. TRUMAN, KOREA, AND THE IMPERIAL PRESIDENCY. The Forum Series in American History. Saint Charles, Mo.: Forum Press, 1975. 36 p.

_____, ed. THE TRUMAN PERIOD AS A RESEARCH FIELD. Columbia: University of Missouri Press, 1967. v, 284 p.

Four essays touching upon aspects of domestic politics.

_____. THE TRUMAN PERIOD AS A RESEARCH FIELD: A REAPPRAISAL, 1972. Columbia: University of Missouri Press, 1974. 246 p.

Contains additional essays to those above, commentaries by the first-edition authors, and an up-to-date comprehensive bibliography.

Lee, R. Alton. TRUMAN AND TAFT-HARTLEY: A QUESTION OF MANDATE. Lexington: University of Kentucky Press, 1966. vii, 254 p.

McClure, Arthur F. THE TRUMAN ADMINISTRATION AND THE PROBLEMS OF POSTWAR LABOR, 1945-1948. Rutherford, N.J.: Fairleigh Dickinson University Press, 1969. 267 p.

McCoy, Donald R., and Ruetten, Richard T. QUEST AND RESPONSE: MINORITY RIGHTS AND THE TRUMAN ADMINISTRATION. Lawrence: University Press of Kansas, 1973. ix, 427 p.

The best study of civil rights and minority problems under Truman.

Marcus, Maeva. TRUMAN AND THE STEEL SEIZURE CASE: THE LIMITS OF PRESIDENTIAL POWER. New York: Columbia University Press, 1977. xiv, 390 p.

Matusow, Allan J. FARM POLICIES AND POLITICS IN THE TRUMAN YEARS. Cambridge, Mass.: Harvard University Press, 1967. 267 p.

Paterson, Thomas G., ed. COLD WAR CRITICS: ALTERNATIVES TO AMERICAN FOREIGN POLICY IN THE TRUMAN YEARS. Chicago: Quadrangle Books, 1971. 313 p.

Riddle, Donald H. THE TRUMAN COMMITTEE: A STUDY IN CONGRESSIONAL MILITARY RELATIONS. Ann Arbor, Mich.: University Microfilms, 1956. 323 p.

Rogge, Edward Alexander. THE SPEECHMAKING OF HARRY S. TRUMAN, 1934 TO 1953. Ann Arbor, Mich.: University Microfilms, 1958. 584 p.

Ross, Irwin. THE LONELIEST CAMPAIGN: THE TRUMAN VICTORY OF 1948. New York: New American Library, 1968. Reprint. Westport, Conn.: Greenwood Press, 1977. viii, 304 p.

A detailed account of the most dramatic upset in modern American political history.

Rudoni, Dorothy June. HARRY S. TRUMAN: A STUDY IN PRESIDENTIAL PERSPECTIVE. Ann Arbor, Mich.: University Microfilms, 1969. vi, 586 l.

An examination of the ideas and forces which shaped President Truman's concept of the presidential office.

Schmidtlein, Eugene F. "Truman the Senator." Ph.D. dissertation, University of Missouri, 1961.

Snetsinger, John. TRUMAN, THE JEWISH VOTE, AND THE CREATION OF ISRAEL. Stanford, Calif.: Hoover Institution Press, 1974. xv, 208 p.

Spanier, John W. THE TRUMAN-MacARTHUR CONTROVERSY AND THE KOREAN WAR. Cambridge, Mass.: Belknap Press of Harvard University, 1959. xi, 311 p.

Theoharis, Athan G. SEEDS OF REPRESSION: HARRY S. TRUMAN AND THE ORIGINS OF McCARTHYISM. Chicago: Quadrangle Books, 1971. xi, 238 p.

Says McCarthyism gained effect because of the intensification of the cold war and President Truman's loss of credibility.

Thomson, David S. A PICTORIAL BIOGRAPHY: HST. New York: Grosset and Dunlap, 1973. 152 p.

THE TRUMAN WHITE HOUSE: THE ADMINISTRATION OF THE PRESIDENCY, 1945-1953. Edited for the Harry S. Truman Library Institute for National and International Affairs by Francis H. Heller. Lawrence: Regents Press of Kansas, 1980. xxiii, 247 p. Bibliog., index.

See pages 237-39 for a list of primary sources on the Truman White House.

Walton, Richard J. HENRY WALLACE, HARRY TRUMAN, AND THE COLD WAR. New York: Viking, 1976. x, 388 p.

A study of the 1948 campaign and the Wallace-Truman debate over the origins and intentions of the cold war.

Westin, Alan Furman, ed. THE ANATOMY OF A CONSTITUTIONAL LAW CASE: YOUNGSTOWN SHEET AND TUBE CO. V. SAWYER, THE STEEL SEIZURE DECISION. New York: Macmillan, 1958. viii, 183 p.

On seizure by order of President Truman.

Yarnell, Allen. DEMOCRATS AND PROGRESSIVES: THE 1948 PRESIDENTIAL ELECTION AS A TEST OF POSTWAR LIBERALISM. Berkeley and Los Angeles: University of California Press, 1974. xii, 155 p.

Argues that the Wallace Progressives made it easier for Truman to take tough stands on foreign policy issues, thus aiding the Democrats in their 1948 victory.

ARTICLES

Acheson, Dean. "The Truman Years." FOREIGN SERVICE JOURNAL 42 (August 1965): 22-24.

Albjerg, Victor. "Truman and Eisenhower: Their Administrations and Campaigns." CURRENT HISTORY 47 (October 1964): 221-28.

Berger, Henry W. "Bipartisanship, Senator Taft, and the Truman Administration." POLITICAL SCIENCE QUARTERLY 90 (Summer 1975): 221-37.

Bernstein, Barton J. "The Truman Administration and Its Reconversion Wage Policy." LABOR HISTORY 6 (Fall 1965): 214-31.

______. "The Truman Administration and the Steel Strike of 1946." JOURNAL OF AMERICAN HISTORY 52 (March 1966): 791-803.

Bhana, Surendra. "Puerto Rico and the Truman Administration, 1945-47: Self-Government 'Little by Little.'" PROLOGUE 5 (Fall 1973): 155-65.

Bickerton, Ian. "President Truman's Recognition of Israel." AMERICAN JEWISH HISTORICAL QUARTERLY 58 (December 1968): 173-240.

Billington, Monroe. "Civil Rights, President Truman and the South." JOURNAL OF NEGRO HISTORY 58 (April 1973): 127-39.

Brembeck, Cole S. "Harry Truman at the Whistle Stops." QUARTERLY JOURNAL OF SPEECH 38 (February 1952): 42-50.

Brooks, Phillip C. "The Harry S. Truman Library: Plans and Reality." AMERICAN ARCHIVIST 25 (January 1962): 25-37.

______. "Understanding the Presidency: The Harry S. Truman Library." PROLOGUE 1 (Winter 1969): 3-12.

Dalfiume, Richard M. "The 'Forgotten Years' of the Negro Revolution." JOURNAL OF AMERICAN HISTORY 55 (June 1968): 90-106.

Davies, Richard O. "Whistle-Stopping through Ohio." OHIO HISTORY 71 (July 1962): 113-23.

Divine, Robert A. "The Cold War and the Election of 1948." JOURNAL OF AMERICAN HISTORY 59 (June 1972): 90-110.

Dorsett, Lyle W. "Truman and the Pendergast Machine." MIDCONTINENT AMERICAN STUDIES JOURNAL 7 (Fall 1966): 16-39.

Feis, Herbert. "The Secret that Traveled to Potsdam." FOREIGN AFFAIRS 38 (January 1960): 300-317.

Fink, Gary M., and Hilty, James W. "Prologue: The Senate Voting Record of Harry S. Truman." JOURNAL OF INTERDISCIPLINARY HISTORY 4 (Autumn 1973): 207-35.

Garson, Robert A. "The Alienation of the South: A Crisis for Harry S. Truman and the Democratic Party, 1945-1948." MISSOURI HISTORICAL REVIEW 64 (July 1970): 448-71.

Graber, Doris A. "The Truman and Eisenhower Doctrines in the Light of the Doctrine of Non-Intervention." POLITICAL SCIENCE QUARTERLY 73 (September 1958): 321-34.

Graebner, Norman. "The Truman Administration and the Cold War." CURRENT HISTORY 35 (October 1958): 223-28.

Grant, Philip A., Jr. "The Election of Harry S. Truman to the United States Senate." BULLETIN OF THE MISSOURI HISTORICAL SOCIETY 36 (January 1980): 103-9.

Griffith, Robert. "Truman and the Historians: The Reconstruction of Postwar American History." WISCONSIN MAGAZINE OF HISTORY 59 (Autumn 1975): 20-50.

Gustafson, Merlin. "The Church, the State, and the Military in the Truman Administration." ROCKY MOUNTAIN SOCIAL SCIENCE JOURNAL 2 (October 1965): 2-10.

______. "Religion and Politics in the Truman Administration." ROCKY MOUNTAIN SOCIAL SCIENCE JOURNAL 3 (October 1966): 125-34.

______. "The Religion of a President." JOURNAL OF CHURCH AND STATE 10 (Autumn 1968): 379-87.

Hamby, Alonzo L. "The Liberals, Truman, and FDR as Symbol and Myth." JOURNAL OF AMERICAN HISTORY 56 (March 1970): 859-67.

Hensley, Carl Wayne. "Harry S. Truman: Fundamental Americanism in Foreign Policy Speechmaking, 1945-1946." SOUTHERN SPEECH COMMUNICATION JOURNAL 40 (Winter 1975): 180-90.

Herring, George C. "The Truman Administration and the Restoration of French Sovereignty in Indochina." DIPLOMATIC HISTORY 1 (Spring 1977): 97-177.

Iselin, John Jay. "The Truman Doctrine: Its Passage through Congress and the Aftermath." FOREIGN SERVICE JOURNAL 44 (May 1967): 19-22.

Kahana, Yoram. "Captain Harry: The Cussing Doughboy of Battery D." MANKIND 5, no. 11 (1977): 37-40.

Truman and World War I.

Kaiser, Robert G. "The Truman Doctrine: How It All Began." FOREIGN SERVICE JOURNAL 44 (May 1967): 17-18.

Kirkendall, Richard S. "Election of 1948." In A HISTORY OF AMERICAN PRESIDENTIAL ELECTIONS, 1789-1968, vol. 4, edited by Fred R. Israel and Arthur M. Schlesinger, Jr., pp. 3099-145. New York: Chelsea House Publishers, 1971.

______. "Harry S. Truman: A Missouri Farmer in the Golden Age." AGRICULTURAL HISTORY 48 (October 1974): 467-83.

______. "Harry Truman." In AMERICA'S ELEVEN GREATEST PRESIDENTS, edited by Morton Borden, pp. 225-88. Chicago: Rand McNally and Co., 1971.

______. "Truman's Path to Power." SOCIAL SCIENCE 43 (April 1968): 67-73.

Argues Truman reached the presidency because of his gregarious and pragmatic personality.

Kish, Major Francis B. "Citizen-Soldier: Harry S. Truman, 1884-1972." MILITARY REVIEW 53 (February 1973): 30-44.

Lagerquist, P.D. "Harry S. Truman Library." LIBRARY JOURNAL 83 (15 January 1958): 144-47.

Lee, R. Alton. "The Truman-80th Congress Struggle over Tax Policy." HISTORIAN 33 (November 1970): 68-82.

_____. "The Turnip Session of the Do-Nothing Congress: Presidential Campaign Strategy." SOUTHWESTERN SOCIAL SCIENCE QUARTERLY 43 (December 1963): 256-67.

Lorenz, A.L., Jr. "Truman and the Press Conference." JOURNALISM QUARTERLY 43 (Winter 1966): 671-79, 708.

McClure, Arthur F., and Costigan, Donna. "The Truman Vice Presidency: Constructive Apprenticeship or Brief Interlude?" MISSOURI HISTORICAL REVIEW 65 (April 1971): 318-41.

Mitchell, Franklin D., et al. "Truman and the Pendergast Machine." MID-CONTINENT AMERICAN STUDIES JOURNAL 7 (Fall 1966): 3-39.

Morgan, H. Wayne. "History and the Presidency: Harry S. Truman." PHYLON QUARTERLY 19 (Summer 1958): 162-70.

Morrissey, Charles T. "Truman and the Presidency--Records and Oral Recollections." AMERICAN ARCHIVIST 28 (January 1965): 53-61.

Mrozek, Donald J. "The Truman Administration and the Enlistment of the Aviation Industry in Postwar Defense." BUSINESS HISTORY REVIEW 48 (Spring 1974): 73-94.

Parzen, Herbert. "President Truman and the Palestine Quandary: His Initial Experience, April-December, 1945." JEWISH SOCIAL STUDIES 35 (January 1973): 42-72.

Paterson, Thomas G. "Presidential Foreign Policy, Public Opinion, and Congress: The Truman Years." DIPLOMATIC HISTORY 3 (Winter 1979): 1-18.

Peterson, Frank Ross. "Harry S. Truman and His Critics: The 1948 Progressives and the Origins of the Cold War." In ESSAYS ON RADICALISM IN CONTEMPORARY AMERICA, edited by Leon Borden Blair, pp. 32-62. Austin: University of Texas Press, 1972.

Pollard, James E. "Truman and the Press: Final Phase, 1951-1953." JOURNALISM QUARTERLY 30 (Summer 1953): 273-86.

Quade, Quentin L. "The Truman Administration and the Separation of Powers: The Case of the Marshall Plan." REVIEW OF POLITICS 27 (January 1965): 58-77.

Ryan, Henry Butterfield, Jr. "The American Intellectual Tradition Reflected in the Truman Doctrine." AMERICAN SCHOLAR 42 (Spring 1973): 294-307.

Salant, Walter S. "Some Intellectual Contributions of the Truman Council of Economic Advisers to Policy-Making." HISTORY OF POLITICAL ECONOMY 5 (Spring 1973): 36-49.

Sander, Alfred D. "Truman and the National Security Council, 1945-1947." JOURNAL OF AMERICAN HISTORY 59 (September 1972): 369-88.

Schmidtlein, Gene. "Truman's First Senatorial Election." MISSOURI HISTORICAL REVIEW 57 (January 1963): 128-55.

Sherwin, Martin. "The Atomic Bomb as History: An Essay Review." WISCONSIN MAGAZINE OF HISTORY 53 (Winter 1969-70): 128-34.

Sitkoff, Harvard. "Harry Truman and the Election of 1948: The Coming of Age of Civil Rights in American Politics." JOURNAL OF SOUTHERN HISTORY 37 (November 1971): 597-616.

Smith, Geoffrey S. "'Harry, We Hardly Know You': Revisionism, Politics and Diplomacy, 1945-1954." AMERICAN POLITICAL SCIENCE REVIEW 70 (June 1976): 560-82.

Snowman, Daniel. "President Truman's Decision to Drop the First Atomic Bomb." POLITICAL STUDIES 14 (October 1966): 365-73.

Stebbins, Phillip E. "Truman and the Seizure of Steel: A Failure in Communication." HISTORIAN 34 (November 1971): 1-21.

Stutesman, John H., Jr. "The Architecture of a Decision." FOREIGN SERVICE JOURNAL 43 (July 1966): 19-20.

How the Truman Doctrine evolved.

Theoharis, Athan. "Roosevelt and Truman on Yalta: The Origins of the Cold War." POLITICAL SCIENCE QUARTERLY 87 (June 1972): 210-41.

_____. "The Truman Presidency: Trial and Error." WISCONSIN MAGAZINE OF HISTORY 55 (Autumn 1971): 49-58.

Thorpe, James A. "Truman's Ultimatum to Stalin on the 1946 Azerbaijan Crisis: The Making of a Myth." JOURNAL OF POLITICS 40 (February 1978): 188-95.

Vaughan, Philip H. "The Truman Administration's Fair Deal for Black America." MISSOURI HISTORICAL REVIEW 70 (April 1976): 291-305.

Williams, Robert J. "Harry S. Truman and the American Presidency." JOURNAL OF AMERICAN STUDIES 13 (December 1979): 393-74.

Chapter 44

DWIGHT D. EISENHOWER, 1953-61

BIBLIOGRAPHIES

Bohanan, Robert D., comp. DWIGHT D. EISENHOWER: A SELECTED BIBLIOGRAPHY OF PERIODICAL AND DISSERTATION LITERATURE. Abilene, Kans.: Dwight D. Eisenhower Library, 1981. iv, 162 p.

Dwight D. Eisenhower Library. Abilene, Kansas. HISTORICAL MATERIALS IN THE DWIGHT D. EISENHOWER LIBRARY. Abilene: 1981. v, 62 p.

Stapleton, Margaret L. THE TRUMAN AND EISENHOWER YEARS, 1945-1960: A SELECTIVE BIBLIOGRAPHY. Metuchen, N.J.: Scarecrow Press, 1973. vii, 221 p.

Vexler, Robert I., ed. DWIGHT D. EISENHOWER, 1890-1969: CHRONOLOGY-DOCUMENTS-BIBLIOGRAPHICAL AIDS. Presidential Chronologies Series. Dobbs Ferry, N.Y.: Oceana Publications, 1970. 150 p.

SOURCE MATERIALS

Eisenhower, Dwight David. AT EASE: STORIES I TELL TO FRIENDS. London: Hale, 1968. 400 p.

______. THE EISENHOWER ADMINISTRATION, 1953-1961: A DOCUMENTARY HISTORY. Compiled by Robert L. Branyan and Lawrence H. Larsen. 2 vols. New York: Random House, 1971. 1,414 p.

______. THE EISENHOWER DIARIES. Edited by Robert H. Ferrell. New York: W.W. Norton, 1981. xvii, 445 p.

______. GENERAL DWIGHT D. EISENHOWER: REMARKS AT FREEDOMS FOUNDATION AT VALLEY FORGE, 1948-1969. Compiled by Edward Salt. Valley Forge, Pa.: Freedoms Foundation, 1969. 92 p.

_____. MANDATE FOR CHANGE, 1953-56. Garden City, N.Y.: Doubleday, 1963. 650 p.

_____. WAGING PEACE: WHITE HOUSE YEARS, 1956-1961. Garden City, N.Y.: Doubleday, 1965. 741 p.

_____. THE PAPERS OF DWIGHT DAVID EISENHOWER: THE WAR YEARS. 5 vols. Edited by Alfred D. Chandler, Jr. Baltimore: Johns Hopkins Press, 1970.

_____. PEACE WITH JUSTICE: SELECTED ADDRESSES OF DWIGHT D. EISENHOWER. New York: Columbia University Press, 1961. vii, 273 p.

_____. PUBLIC PAPERS OF THE PRESIDENTS OF THE UNITED STATES, DWIGHT D. EISENHOWER, 1953-61. 8 vols. Washington, D.C.: Government Printing Office, 1958-61.

_____. THE QUOTABLE DWIGHT D. EISENHOWER. Compiled and edited by Elsie Gollagher and the staff of Quote. Anderson, S.C.: Droke House; distributed by Grosset and Dunlap, 1967. vii, 242 p.

_____. SELECTED SPEECHES OF DWIGHT DAVID EISENHOWER, 34TH PRESIDENT OF THE UNITED STATES. Washington, D.C.: Government Printing Office, 1970. x, 158 p.

BIOGRAPHIES

Hagerty, James C. THE DIARY OF JAMES C. HAGERTY: EISENHOWER IN MID-COURSE, 1954-1955. Bloomington: Indiana University Press, 1983.

Childs, Marquis William. EISENHOWER, CAPTIVE HERO: A CRITICAL STUDY OF THE GENERAL AND THE PRESIDENT. New York: Harcourt, Brace, 1958. 310 p.

Eisenhower, Dwight David. AMERICAN HERO, THE HISTORICAL RECORD OF HIS LIFE. Introduction by Bruce Catton. New York: American Heritage Publishing Co., 1969. 144 p.

_____. IN REVIEW: PICTURES I'VE KEPT; A CONCISE PICTORIAL AUTOBIOGRAPHY. Garden City, N.Y.: Doubleday, 1969. 237 p.

IKE, A PICTORIAL BIOGRAPHY. Text by William F. Longgood. New York: Time-Life Books, 1969. 144 p.

Larson, Arthur. EISENHOWER: THE PRESIDENT NOBODY KNEW. New York: Scribner, 1968. xii, 210 p.

Morin, Relman. DWIGHT D. EISENHOWER: A GAUGE OF GREATNESS. New York: Simon and Schuster, 1969. 256 p.

Parmet, Herbert S. EISENHOWER AND THE AMERICAN CRUSADES. New York: Macmillan, 1972. xi, 660 p.

First major assessment of the Eisenhower administrations based on interviews, oral history recordings, and manuscript sources.

Steinberg, Alfred. DWIGHT DAVID EISENHOWER. New York: Putnam, 1968. 223 p.

U.S. Congress. House. MEMORIAL SERVICES IN THE CONGRESS OF THE UNITED STATES AND TRIBUTES IN EULOGY OF DWIGHT DAVID EISENHOWER, LATE PRESIDENT OF THE UNITED STATES. 91st Cong., 1st sess., 1969. Compiled under direction of the Joint Committee on Printing. Washington, D.C.: Government Printing Office, 1970. xxxi, 226 p.

Whitney, David C. THE PICTURE LIFE OF DWIGHT D. EISENHOWER. New York: F. Watts, 1968. 56 p.

MONOGRAPHS

Adams, Sherman. FIRSTHAND REPORT: THE STORY OF THE EISENHOWER ADMINISTRATION. New York: Harper and Row, 1961. xvi, 481 p.

Adams served as Eisenhower's chief of staff in the White House until forced to resign for accepting gifts.

Albertson, Dean, ed. EISENHOWER AS PRESIDENT. New York: Hill and Wang, 1963. xxi, 169 p.

Ten essays which evaluate various aspects of the Eisenhower administrations in foreign and domestic affairs.

Ambrose, Stephen E. EISENHOWER AND BERLIN, 1945: THE DECISION TO HALT AT THE ELBE. New York: W.W. Norton, 1967. 119 p.

Ambrose, Stephen E., and Immerman, Richard H. IKE'S SPIES: EISENHOWER AND THE ESPIONAGE ESTABLISHMENT. Garden City, N.Y.: Doubleday, 1981. x, 368 p.

_____. THE SUPREME COMMANDER. Garden City, N.Y.: Doubleday, 1970. ix, 732 p.

A careful study of Eisenhower's military leadership in World War II by one of the editors of Eisenhower's papers.

Anderson, John Weir. EISENHOWER, BROWNELL, AND THE CONGRESS. University: University of Alabama Press, for the Inter-University Case Program, 1964. viii, 139 p.

Origins of the Civil Rights Bill of 1956-57.

Bearss, Edwin C. EISENHOWER NATIONAL HISTORIC SITE. Washington, D.C.: Office of History and Historic Architecture, Eastern Service Center, National Park Service, 1970. xiv, 196 p.

Bragg, William, Jr. EISENHOWER THE PRESIDENT: CRUCIAL DAYS: 1951-1960. Englewood Cliffs, N.J.: Prentice-Hall, 1981. 336 p.

Capitanchik, David Bernard. THE EISENHOWER PRESIDENCY AND AMERICAN FOREIGN POLICY. New York: Humanities Press, 1969. xi, 80 p.

Cook, Blanche Wiesen. THE DECLASSIFIED EISENHOWER: A DIVIDED LEGACY OF PEACE AND POLITICAL WARFARE. Garden City, N.Y.: Doubleday, 1981. xxiv, 432 p.

Donovan, Robert J. EISENHOWER: THE INSIDE STORY. New York: Harper, 1956. xviii, 423 p.

Greenstein, Fred I. THE HIDDEN-HAND PRESIDENCY: EISENHOWER AS LEADER. New York: Basic Books, Inc., 1982. x, 286 p.

Hughes, Emmet John. THE ORDEAL OF POWER: A POLITICAL MEMOIR OF THE EISENHOWER YEARS. New York: Atheneum, 1963. vii, 372 p.

Plischke, Elmer. SUMMIT DIPLOMACY OF THE PRESIDENT OF THE UNITED STATES. College Park: University of Maryland, 1958. Reprint. Westport, Conn.: Greenwood Press, 1974. viii, 125 p.

Pusey, Merlo J. EISENHOWER THE PRESIDENT. New York: Macmillan, 1956. 300 p.

Richardson, Elmo. THE PRESIDENCY OF DWIGHT D. EISENHOWER. American Presidency Series. Lawrence: Regents Press of Kansas, 1979. x, 218 p.

Smith, A. Merriman. A PRESIDENT'S ODYSSEY. New York: Harper, 1961. Reprint. Westport, Conn.: Greenwood Press, 1975. xii, 272 p.

Deals with Eisenhower's good-will tours in search of world peace.

Summersby, Kathleen [McCarthy-Morrogh]. EISENHOWER WAS MY BOSS. Edited by Michael Kearns. Englewood Cliffs, N.J.: Prentice-Hall, 1948. 302 p.

Memoir by Eisenhower's driver during World War II.

ARTICLES

Brown, Stuart Gerry. "Eisenhower and Stevenson in the McCarthy Era: A Study in Leadership (1950-54)." ETHICS 69 (July): 233-54.

De Santis, Vincent P. "Eisenhower Revisionism." REVIEW OF POLITICS 38 (April 1976): 190-207.

DiBacco, Thomas V. "American Business and Foreign Aid: The Eisenhower Years." BUSINESS HISTORY REVIEW 41 (Spring 1967): 21-35.

Duram, James C. "'A Good Growl': The Eisenhower Cabinet's January 16, 1959 Discussion of Federal Aid to Education." PRESIDENTIAL STUDIES QUARTERLY 8 (Fall 1978): 434-44.

Ekirch, Arthur A., Jr. "Eisenhower and Kennedy: The Rhetoric and the Reality." MIDWEST QUARTERLY 17 (Spring 1976): 279-90.

Graber, Doris Appel. "The Truman and Eisenhower Doctrines [1947-57] in the Light of the Doctrine of Non-Intervention." POLITICAL SCIENCE QUARTERLY 73 (September 1958): 321-34.

Greenstein, Fred I. "Eisenhower,as an Activist President: A Look at New Evidence." PRESIDENTIAL STUDIES QUARTERLY 94 (Winter 1979-80): 575-99.

Griffith, Robert. "The General and the Senator: Republican Politics and the 1952 Campaign in Wisconsin." WISCONSIN MAGAZINE OF HISTORY 54 (Autumn 1970): 23-29.

Hobbs, E.H. "President and Administration--Eisenhower." PUBLIC ADMINISTRATION REVIEW 18 (Fall 1958): 306-13.

Hyman, H.H., and Sheatsley, P.B. "Political Appeal of President Eisenhower." PUBLIC OPINION QUARTERLY 17, no. 4. (1953): 443-60.

Kinnard, Douglas. "President Eisenhower and the Defense Budget." JOURNAL OF POLITICS 39 (August 1977): 596-623.

Leo, J. "Dwight David Eisenhower: Ranking an Ex-President." COMMONWEAL 90 (11 April 1969): 95-96.

Mitchell, James. "Government and Labor in the Eisenhower Administration." CURRENT HISTORY 37 (September 1959): 129-32, 145.

Pear, R.H. "American Presidency under Eisenhower." POLITICAL QUARTERLY 28 (January 1957): 5-12.

Plischke, Elmer. "Eisenhower's 'Correspondence Diplomacy' with the Kremlin: Case Study in Summit Diplomatics." JOURNAL OF POLITICS 30 (February 1968): 137-59.

Pollard, James E. "Eisenhower and the Press: The First Two Years." JOURNALISM QUARTERLY 32 (Summer 1955): 285-300.

Also discusses the extension of the presidential news conference to include television cameras.

_____. "Eisenhower and the Press: The Final Phase." JOURNALISM QUARTERLY 38 (Spring 1961): 181-86.

Reichard, Gary W. "Eisenhower and the Bricker Amendment." PROLOGUE 6 (Summer 1974): 88-99.

_____. "Eisenhower as President: The Changing View." SOUTH ATLANTIC QUARTERLY 77 (Summer 1978): 265-81.

Rovere, Richard H. "Eisenhower over the Shoulder." AMERICAN SCHOLAR 31 (Spring 1962): 176-79.

An appraisal of his two terms in office.

Saulnier, Raymond J. "The Eisenhower Economic Policies: Policies that Succeeded in Ending Inflation, 1956-61." PRESIDENTIAL STUDIES QUARTERLY 4 (Summer and Fall 1974): 28-34.

Shannon, W.V. "Eisenhower as President: A Critical Appraisal of the Record." COMMENTARY 26 (November 1958): 390-98.

Yarnell, Allen. "Eisenhower and McCarthy: An Appraisal of Presidential Strategy." PRESIDENTIAL STUDIES QUARTERLY 10 (Winter 1980): 90-98.

Chapter 45

JOHN F. KENNEDY, 1961-63

BIBLIOGRAPHIES

Crown, James Tracy. THE KENNEDY LITERATURE: A BIBLIOGRAPHICAL ESSAY ON JOHN F. KENNEDY. New York: New York University Press; London: University of London Press, 1968. viii, 181 p.

A basic introduction to the Kennedy era. Written as a connective narrative, Crown's work is highly readable, informative, and comprehensive up to 1968.

John Fitzgerald Kennedy Library. Waltham, Massachusetts. ARCHIVAL RESOURCES OF THE JOHN F. KENNEDY LIBRARY. Waltham, Mass.: 1971.

______. HISTORICAL MATERIALS IN THE JOHN F. KENNEDY LIBRARY. Waltham, Mass.: 1975. iii, 64 p.

______. THE KENNEDY COLLECTION: A SUBJECT GUIDE. Waltham, Mass.: 1976. ix, 299 p.

Newcomb, Joan I. JOHN F. KENNEDY: AN ANNOTATED BIBLIOGRAPHY. Metuchen, N.J.: Scarecrow Press, 1977. 143 p.

Stone, Ralph A., ed. JOHN F. KENNEDY, 1917-1963: CHRONOLOGY-DOCUMENTS-BIBLIOGRAPHICAL AIDS. Presidential Chronologies Series. Dobbs Ferry, N.Y.: Oceana Publications, 1971. 110 p.

U.S. Library of Congress. JOHN FITZGERALD KENNEDY, 1917-1963; A CHRONOLOGICAL LIST OF REFERENCES. Washington, D.C.: General Reference and Bibliography Division, Reference Department, Library of Congress, 1964. viii, 68 p.

SOURCE MATERIALS

Kennedy, John Fitzgerald. THE BURDEN AND THE GLORY; THE HOPES AND PURPOSES OF PRESIDENT KENNEDY'S SECOND AND THIRD YEARS IN OFFICE AS REVEALED IN HIS PUBLIC STATEMENTS AND ADDRESSES. Edited by Allan Nevins. New York: Harper and Row, 1964. xvii, 293 p.

_____. THE COMPLETE KENNEDY WIT. Edited by Bill Adler. New York: Citadel Press, 1967. 203 p.

_____. THE HUMOR OF JFK. Compiled by Booton Herndon. Greenwich, Conn.: Fawcett Publications, 1964. 127 p.

_____. A JOHN F. KENNEDY MEMORIAL MINIATURE. 4 vols. New York: Random House, 1966.

_____. JOHN F. KENNEDY ON EDUCATION. Selected and edited by William T. O'Hara. Foreword by John Brademas. New York: Teachers College Press, Columbia University, 1966. xi, 305 p.

_____. JOHN F. KENNEDY ON ISRAEL, ZIONISM, AND JEWISH ISSUES. Compiled by Ernest E. Barbarash. New York: Herzl Press for the Zionist Organization of America, 1965. 69 p.

_____. JOHN F. KENNEDY SPEAKS: THE TEXTS OF ELEVEN MAJOR SPEECHES BY THE LATE PRESIDENT TOGETHER WITH A SELECTION OF PHOTOGRAPHS. Manila, Philippines: Regional Service Center, 1964. 75 p.

_____. JOHN FITZGERALD KENNEDY: A COMPILATION OF STATEMENTS AND SPEECHES MADE DURING HIS SERVICE IN THE UNITED STATES SENATE AND HOUSE OF REPRESENTATIVES. Washington, D.C.: Government Printing Office, 1964. xvii, 1,143 p.

Kennedy served in the House of Representatives from 1947 to 1953 and in the Senate from 1953 to 1961.

_____. KENNEDY AND THE PRESS: THE NEWS CONFERENCES. Edited and annotated by Harold W. Chase and Allen H. Lerman. New York: Thomas Y. Crowell, 1965. 555 p.

_____. THE KENNEDY PRESIDENTIAL PRESS CONFERENCES. Introduction by David Halberstam. New York: E.M. Coleman Enterprises, 1978. vii, 640 p.

______. THE KENNEDY READER. Compiled by Jay David. Indianapolis: Bobbs-Merrill, 1967. xi, 428 p.

______. PUBLIC PAPERS OF THE PRESIDENTS OF THE UNITED STATES, JOHN F. KENNEDY. 3 vols. Washington, D.C.: Government Printing Office, 1962-64.

> The authoritative source for Kennedy's news conferences and prepared addresses. Notable for their literary style and grace.

______. RELIGIOUS VIEWS OF PRESIDENT JOHN F. KENNEDY IN HIS OWN WORDS. Compiled by Nicholas A. Schneider. St. Louis: Herder, 1965. xv, 125 p.

______. TO TURN THE TIDE; A SELECTION FROM PRESIDENT KENNEDY'S PUBLIC STATEMENTS FROM HIS ELECTION THROUGH THE 1961 ADJOURNMENT OF CONGRESS, SETTING FORTH THE GOALS OF HIS FIRST LEGISLATIVE YEAR. Edited by John W. Gardner. New York: Harper, 1962. xvii, 235 p.

______. WORDS TO REMEMBER. Foreword by Robert F. Kennedy. Color illustrations by Frank V. Szasz. Kansas City, Mo.: Hallmark Cards, 1967. 59 p.

Kraus, Sidney, ed. THE GREAT DEBATES: BACKGROUND, PERSPECTIVE, EFFECTS. Bloomington: Indiana University Press, 1962. 439 p.

> Contains the texts of the four famous Kennedy-Nixon television debates of the 1960 campaign. Comments on the effect of the debates on the election are given by various experts.

Mansfield, Michael Joseph. SUMMARY OF THE THREE-YEAR KENNEDY RECORD, AND DIGEST OF MAJOR ACCOMPLISHMENTS OF THE EIGHTY-SEVENTH AND THE EIGHTY-EIGHTH CONGRESS, 1961-1963. Washington, D.C.: Government Printing Office, 1964. xii, 303 p.

> Senator Mansfield of Montana served as Senate majority leader during the Kennedy presidency.

Stewart, Charles J., and Kendall, Bruce, eds. A MAN NAMED JOHN F. KENNEDY; SERMONS ON HIS ASSASSINATION. Glen Rock, N.J.: Paulist Press, 1964. 208 p.

SELECTED BOOKS BY KENNEDY

Kennedy, John Fitzgerald. A NATION OF IMMIGRANTS. Rev. and enl. ed. New York: Harper and Row, 1964. xi, 111 p.

A brief survey of American immigration history with a suggestion for changes in immigration policy.

_____. PROFILES IN COURAGE. Memorial ed. New York: Harper and Row, 1964. xvi, 238 p.

A study of eight U.S. senators who risked their careers by supporting causes opposed by their constituents. Written by Kennedy while convalescing from a back operation. The book earned him a Pulitzer Prize in 1957.

_____. WHY ENGLAND SLEPT. New York: Wilfred Funk, 1940. xxx, 252 p.

A revision of Kennedy's honors' thesis at Harvard. Discusses England's unpreparedness for war.

BIOGRAPHIES

Barnes, Clare. JOHN F. KENNEDY: SCRIMSHAW COLLECTOR. Photographs by Alan Fontaine. Boston: Little, Brown, 1969. 129 p. Illus.

Beautifully illustrated volume on one of the president's favorite hobbies.

Blair, Joan, and Blair, Clay, Jr. THE SEARCH FOR JFK. New York: Berkley Publishing Corp.; distributed by Putnam, 1976. 608 p.

Burns, James MacGregor. JOHN KENNEDY: A POLITICAL PROFILE. New York: Harcourt, Brace and World, 1960. xxiii, 309 p.

The best account of Kennedy's life before he became president. Based upon interviews and family papers.

Damore, Leo. THE CAPE COD YEARS OF JOHN FITZGERALD KENNEDY. Englewood Cliffs, N.J.: Prentice-Hall, 1967. vii, 262 p.

Details the Hyannis Port life of Kennedy and his family.

Donald, Aida Dipace, ed. JOHN F. KENNEDY AND THE NEW FRONTIER. New York: Hill and Wang, 1966. xx, 264 p.

A collection of essays and early appraisals of Kennedy.

Donovan, Robert J. PT-109: JOHN F. KENNEDY IN WORLD WAR II. New York: McGraw-Hill, 1961. 247 p.

Tells how Kennedy became a war hero: "It was easy. They sunk my boat."

Exner, Judith, as told to Ovid Demaris. MY STORY. New York: Grove Press, 1977. 299 p.

Memoir of her alleged affair with Kennedy.

Lane, Thomas A. THE LEADERSHIP OF PRESIDENT KENNEDY. Introduction by Ben Moreell. Caxton Libertarian Books. Caldwell, Idaho: Caxton Printers, 1964. xiv, 114 p.

Latham, Earl, comp. J.F. KENNEDY AND PRESIDENTIAL POWER. Edited and with an introduction by Earl Latham. Lexington, Mass: Heath, 1972. xxiv, 296 p.

Levine, Israel E. YOUNG MAN IN THE WHITE HOUSE: JOHN FITZGERALD KENNEDY. New York: Messner, 1964. 192 p.

Lincoln, Evelyn. MY TWELVE YEARS WITH JOHN F. KENNEDY. New York: David McKay, 1965. 371 p.

Based upon a well-kept diary by Kennedy's personal secretary. Provides an intimate glimpse of Kennedy's personal life and rise to the presidency.

Longford, Frank Pakenham, 7th Earl of. KENNEDY. London: Weidenfeld and Nicholson, 1976. x, 223 p.

LOOK, editorial staff. JFK MEMORIAL BOOK: NEW COLOR PICTURES OF HIS FAMILY, A COLOR VISIT TO HIS IRELAND, PAGES FROM A FAMILY ALBUM, THE UNKNOWN JFK. New York: 1964. 64 p.

Manchester, William R. PORTRAIT OF A PRESIDENT: JOHN F. KENNEDY IN PROFILE. Rev. ed. Boston: Little, Brown, 1967. xxii, 266 p.

The 1962 edition of this book led to the choice of Manchester by the Kennedy family to write the account of Kennedy's assassination.

Meyers, Joan Simpson, ed. JOHN FITZGERALD KENNEDY AS WE REMEMBER HIM. New York: Atheneum, 1965. ix, 241 p.

A superb collection of interviews, documents, and pictures.

New York Times. THE KENNEDY YEARS. Text prepared under the direction of Harold Faber, with contributions by John Corry et al. Introduction by Tom Wicker. Photographs by Jacques Lowe et al. Contributing photographer, George Tames. New York: Viking Press, 1964. 327 p.

O'Donnell, Kenneth P. JOHNNY, WE HARDLY KNEW YE. Boston: Little, Brown, 1972. ix, 434 p.

Parmet, Herbert S. JACK: THE STRUGGLES OF JOHN F. KENNEDY. New York: Dial Press, 1980. xvii, 586 p.

Schlesinger, Arthur M., Jr. A THOUSAND DAYS: JOHN F. KENNEDY IN THE WHITE HOUSE. Cambridge, Mass.: Houghton Mifflin, 1965. 1,087 p.

An important memoir by a distinguished historian and Kennedy special assistant, 1961-63. The best work on Kennedy as president.

Schwab, Peter, and Shneidman, J. Lee. JOHN F. KENNEDY. Twayne's World Leaders Series. New York: Twayne Publishers, 1974. 173 p. Bibliog.

Sidey, Hugh. JOHN F. KENNEDY, PRESIDENT. New York: Atheneum, 1964. 434 p.

Sorensen, Theodore C. KENNEDY. New York: Harper and Row, 1965. viii, 783 p.

A superb account of decision making by Kennedy as senator (1953-61) and president (1961-63). Written by his closest assistant and speech writer.

Stoughton, Cecil. THE MEMORIES--JFK, 1961-1963 OF CECIL STOUGHTON, THE PRESIDENT'S PHOTOGRAPHER, AND MAJOR GENERAL CHESTER V. CLIFTON, THE PRESIDENT'S MILITARY AIDE. New York: W.W. Norton, 1973. 200 p.

U.S. Congress. Senate. MEMORIAL ADDRESSES IN THE CONGRESS OF THE UNITED STATES AND TRIBUTES IN EULOGY OF JOHN FITZGERALD KENNEDY. 88th Cong., 2d sess., 1964. Washington, D.C.: Government Printing Office, 1964. 911 p.

THE ASSASSINATION

Associated Press. THE TORCH IS PASSED: THE ASSOCIATED PRESS STORY OF THE DEATH OF A PRESIDENT. New York: 1963. 99 p.

Baker, Dean C. THE ASSASSINATION OF PRESIDENT KENNEDY; A STUDY OF THE PRESS COVERAGE. Ann Arbor: Department of Journalism, University of Michigan, 1965. 55, 45 p.

Bishop, Jim. THE DAY KENNEDY WAS SHOT. New York: Funk and Wagnalls, 1968. xvii, 713 p. Bibliog.

Epstein, Edward J. INQUEST: THE WARREN COMMISSION AND THE ESTABLISHMENT OF TRUTH. New York: Viking Press, 1966. xix, 224 p.

A concise criticism of the Warren Commission's findings.

FOUR DARK DAYS IN HISTORY: NOVEMBER 22, 23, 24, 25, 1963. A PHOTO HISTORY OF PRESIDENT KENNEDY'S ASSASSINATION. Los Angeles: J. Matthews, 1963. 68 p.

Guth, DeLloyd J., and Wrone, David R., comps. THE ASSASSINATION OF JOHN F. KENNEDY: A COMPREHENSIVE HISTORICAL AND LEGAL BIBLIOGRAPHY, 1963-1979. Westport, Conn.: Greenwood Press, 1980. 500 p.

Organizes the many references to the historical evidence in published and unpublished form. An invaluable guide to the Kennedy tragedy.

Irwin, Thomas Henry, and Hale, Hazel, comps. A BIBLIOGRAPHY OF BOOKS, NEWSPAPER AND MAGAZINE ARTICLES, PUBLISHED OUTSIDE THE UNITED STATES OF AMERICA, RELATED TO THE ASSASSINATION OF JOHN F. KENNEDY. Belfast: The authors, 1975. 19 p.

Knight, Janet M., ed. THREE ASSASSINATIONS: THE DEATHS OF JOHN AND ROBERT KENNEDY AND MARTIN LUTHER KING. New York: Facts on File, 1971. iii, 266 p.

Lane, Mark. A CITIZEN'S DISSENT; MARK LANE REPLIES. New York: Holt, Rinehart and Winston, 1968. xiii, 290 p.

______. RUSH TO JUDGMENT: A CRITIQUE OF THE WARREN COMMISSION'S INQUIRY INTO THE MURDERS OF PRESIDENT JOHN F. KENNEDY, OFFICER J.D. TIPPIT, AND LEE HARVEY OSWALD. Introduction by Hugh Trevor-Roper. New York: Holt, Rinehart and Winston, 1966. 478 p.

Very critical of the evidence used to support the commission's findings, and of Chief Justice Warren's handling of the inquiry.

Lattimer, John K.; Schlesinger, Edward B.; and Merritt, H. Houston. "President Kennedy's Spine Hit by First Bullet." BULLETIN OF THE NEW ACADEMY OF MEDICINE 53 (April 1977): 280-91.

Lifton, David S. BEST EVIDENCE: DISGUISE AND DECEPTION IN THE ASSASSINATION OF JOHN F. KENNEDY. New York: Macmillan, 1980. xix, 747 p.

Manchester, William Raymond. THE DEATH OF A PRESIDENT, NOVEMBER 20-NOVEMBER 25, 1963. New York: Harper and Row, 1967. xvi, 710 p.

Mayo, John B., Jr. BULLETIN FROM DALLAS: THE PRESIDENT IS DEAD; THE STORY OF JOHN F. KENNEDY'S ASSASSINATION AS COVERED BY RADIO AND TV. New York: Exposition Press, 1967. 157 p.

Meagher, Sylvia. ACCESSORIES AFTER THE FACT: THE WARREN COMMISSION, THE AUTHORITIES, AND THE REPORT. Indianapolis: Bobbs-Merrill, 1967. xxxiii, 477 p.

One of the best books on the assassination although seldom cited.

National Broadcasting Co. THERE WAS A PRESIDENT. Prepared and produced by the Ridge Press. New York: Ridge Press, 1966. 158 p. Illus.

O'Toole, George. THE ASSASSINATION TAPES: AN ELECTRONIC PROBE INTO THE MURDER OF JOHN F. KENNEDY AND THE DALLAS COVERUP. New York: Penthouse Press, 1975. 265 p.

Payne, Darwin. THE PRESS CORPS AND THE KENNEDY ASSASSINATION. Journalism Monographs, no. 15. Lexington, Ky.: Association for Education in Journalism, 1970. xi, 53 p.

Rice, William R., comp. JOHN F. KENNEDY-ROBERT F. KENNEDY: ASSASSINATION BIBLIOGRAPHY. Orangevale, Calif.: Rice, 1975. 62 p.

Roffman, Howard. PRESUMED GUILTY: LEE HARVEY OSWALD IN THE ASSASSINATION OF PRESIDENT KENNEDY. Rutherford, N.J.: Fairleigh Dickinson University Press, 1975. 297 p.

Thompson, Josiah. SIX SECONDS IN DALLAS: A MICRO-STUDY OF THE KENNEDY ASSASSINATION. New York: B. Geis Associates, distributed by Random House, 1968. xviii, 323 p.

Concludes at least three gunmen participated in the assassination.

Thompson, William Clifton. A BIBLIOGRAPHY OF LITERATURE RELATING TO THE ASSASSINATION OF PRESIDENT JOHN F. KENNEDY. Rev. ed. San Antonio, Tex.: Carleton Printing Co., 1968. 40 p.

An extremely comprehensive and detailed list of 283 entries, excluding magazine and newspaper articles, by a private citizen. Lists distributors and prices of several sources of movie film and still photographs on the assassination.

Toscano, Vincent L. SINCE DALLAS: IMAGES OF JOHN F. KENNEDY IN POPULAR AND SCHOLARLY LITERATURE, 1963-1973. San Francisco: R and E Research Associates, 1978. ix, 102 p.

United Press International. FOUR DAYS: THE HISTORICAL RECORD OF THE DEATH OF PRESIDENT KENNEDY. Compiled by United Press International and American Heritage Magazine. New York: American Heritage Publishing Co., 1964. 143 p.

U.S. President's Commission on the Assassination of President Kennedy. INVESTIGATION OF THE ASSASSINATION OF PRESIDENT JOHN F. KENNEDY. 26 vols. Washington, D.C.: Government Printing Office, 1964.

A random selection of twenty thousand pages of unpublished evidence collected by the Warren Commission staff. Lacks a subject index. For this purpose see: Meagher, Sylvia. SUBJECT INDEX TO THE WARREN REPORT AND HEARINGS & EXHIBITS. New York: Scarecrow Press, 1966. 150 p.

_____. REPORT OF THE PRESIDENT'S COMMISSION ON THE ASSASSINATION OF PRESIDENT JOHN F. KENNEDY. Washington, D.C.: Government Printing Office, 1964. xxiv, 888 p.

A condensation prepared by clerks and staff of the Warren Commission.

_____. THE WITNESSES. Selected and edited from the Warren Commission's hearings by the New York Times. Introduction by Anthony Lewis. New York: McGraw-Hill, 1965. xiii, 634 p.

Weisberg, Harold. POST MORTEM: JFK ASSASSINATION COVER-UP SMASHED! Frederick, Md.: Weisberg, 1975. x, 650 p.

_____. WHITEWASH: THE REPORT ON THE WARREN REPORT. Hyattstown, Md.: the author, 1966. xvi, 224 p.

The first book to reject the conclusions of the Warren Commission.

Wrone, David R. "The Assassination of John Fitzgerald Kennedy: An Annotated Bibliography." WISCONSIN MAGAZINE OF HISTORY 56 (1972): 21-36.

An excellent introduction to the subject.

MONOGRAPHS

Allison, Graham T. ESSENCE OF DECISION: EXPLAINING THE CUBAN MISSILE CRISIS. Boston: Little, Brown, 1971. xii, 388 p.

Contains an overview of the methods used by analysts in explaining government actions, plus two alternate approaches to viewing the Cuban crisis.

Bishop, Jim. A DAY IN THE LIFE OF PRESIDENT KENNEDY. New York: Random House, 1964. 108 p.

An hour-by-hour account of the president at work and with his family.

Bradlee, Benjamin. CONVERSATIONS WITH KENNEDY. New York: W.W. Norton, 1975. 251 p.

Based on private notes kept by Kennedy's neighbor and WASHINGTON POST editor.

Brauer, Carl M. JOHN F. KENNEDY AND THE SECOND RECONSTRUCTION. Contemporary American History Series. New York: Columbia University Press, 1977. xi, 396 p.

Crown, James T. KENNEDY IN POWER. New York: Ballantine, 1961. 192 p.

A shrewd thoughtful analysis of Kennedy's first year as president.

David, Paul T., ed. THE PRESIDENTIAL ELECTION AND TRANSITION, 1960-1961. Washington, D.C.: Brookings Institution, 1961. ix, 353 p.

A thorough analysis by ten experts.

Fairlie, Henry. THE KENNEDY PROMISE: THE POLITICS OF EXPECTATION. Garden City, N.Y.: Doubleday, 1973. 376 p.

Argues that Kennedy, by his speeches and actions, raised American hopes beyond reasonable expectations.

Fanta, J. Julius. SAILING WITH PRESIDENT KENNEDY: THE WHITE HOUSE YACHTSMAN. New York: Sea Lore Publishing Co., 1968. 101 p.

Details President Kennedy's love of sailing.

Freed, Donald, and Lane, Mark. EXECUTIVE ACTION: ASSASSINATION OF A HEAD OF STATE. With special material by Stephen Jaffe; introduction by Richard H. Popkin. New York: Dell Publishing, 1976. 251 p.

Fuchs, Lawrence H. JOHN F. KENNEDY AND AMERICAN CATHOLICISM. New York: Meredith Press, 1967. xiv, 271 p.

Relates Kennedy's family, campaigns, and presidency to the changing American attitude toward Catholicism.

Golden, Harry. MR. KENNEDY AND THE NEGROES. Cleveland: World Publishing Co., 1964. 319 p.

A sympathetic view by a southern editor of Kennedy's relationship with blacks and white officials in the South.

Gromyko, Anatolii Andreevich. THROUGH RUSSIAN EYES: PRESIDENT KENNEDY'S 1036 DAYS. Washington, D.C.: International Library, 1973. xviii, 239 p.

Professor Gromyko, son of Soviet Foreign Minister Andrei Gromyko, headed the Foreign Policy Section in the USA Institute of the USSR Academy of Sciences and is considered one of Russia's leading "Americanists."

Hamilton, Charles. THE ROBOT THAT HELPED TO MAKE A PRESIDENT: A RECONNAISSANCE INTO THE MYSTERIES OF JOHN F. KENNEDY'S SIGNATURE. New York: The Author, 1965. xiv, 63 p.

An account of the Autopen device used to sign Kennedy's name.

Heath, Jim F. DECADE OF DISILLUSIONMENT: THE KENNEDY-JOHNSON YEARS. Bloomington: Indiana University Press, 1975. xvi, 332 p.

The first balanced survey of the period. Portrays Kennedy as a cautious leader despite his bold rhetoric.

Hilsman, Roger. TO MOVE A NATION: THE POLITICS OF FOREIGN POLICY IN THE ADMINISTRATION OF JOHN F. KENNEDY. New York: Doubleday, 1967. xxii, 602 p.

Hilsman writes well, understands the operation of the presidential bureaucracy from his experience in the State Department, and is especially good on Asian policy.

Kennedy, Robert F. THIRTEEN DAYS: A MEMOIR OF THE CUBAN MISSILE CRISIS. New York: W.W. Norton, 1969. 224 p.

An inside view--by the president's brother and attorney general--of the events surrounding the 1962 Russian challenge to the United States in Cuba.

Lincoln, Evelyn. KENNEDY AND JOHNSON. New York: Holt, Rinehart and Winston, 1968. xi, 207 p.

Lord, Donald C., and Cadenhead, I.E., eds. JOHN F. KENNEDY: THE POLITICS OF CONFRONTATION AND CONCILIATION. Woodbury, N.Y.: Barron's, 1977. x, 458 p.

McQuain, Thomas J., Jr. AN ANALYSIS OF THE INAUGURAL ADDRESS OF JOHN F. KENNEDY. Parsons, W.Va.: McClain Printing Co., 1977. v, 78 p.

Miroff, Bruce. PRAGMATIC ILLUSIONS: THE PRESIDENTIAL POLITICS OF JOHN F. KENNEDY. New York: McKay, 1976. xvii, 334 p.

Paper, Lewis J. JOHN F. KENNEDY: THE PROMISE AND THE PERFORMANCE. Foreword by James MacGregor Burns. New York: Crown Publishers, 1975. Reprint. New Introduction by Bill Bradley. New York: Da Capo Press, 1980. xv, 408 p.

Rollins, Alfred B. THE ORAL HISTORY PROJECT OF THE JOHN FITZGERALD KENNEDY LIBRARY. Cambridge, Mass.: Harvard University, 1965. iii, 195 p.

Salinger, Pierre. WITH KENNEDY. New York: Doubleday, 1966. xvi, 391 p.

Salinger was Kennedy's press secretary from 1959 to 1963. His inside view of news management is very revealing.

Saunders, Doris E., ed. THE KENNEDY YEARS AND THE NEGRO, A PHOTOGRAPHIC RECORD. Chicago: Johnson Publishing Co., 1964. xiii, 143 p.

Sorensen, Theodore C. DECISION MAKING IN THE WHITE HOUSE: THE OLIVE BRANCH OR THE ARROWS. New York: Columbia University Press, 1963. xvi, 94 p.

A series of lectures delivered at Columbia University on the differences between a president's hopes and actions.

______. THE KENNEDY LEGACY. New York: Macmillan, 1969. 414 p.

Walton, Richard J. COLD WAR AND COUNTERREVOLUTION: THE FOREIGN POLICY OF JOHN F. KENNEDY. New York: Viking Press, 1972. 250 p.

White, Theodore H. THE MAKING OF A PRESIDENT, 1960. New York: Atheneum Publishers, 1961. 400 p.

The first and best of White's four detailed accounts of presidential campaigns from 1960 to 1972.

ARTICLES

Beck, Kent M. "The Kennedy Image: Politics, Camelot, and Vietnam." WISCONSIN MAGAZINE OF HISTORY 58 (Autumn 1974): 45-55.

Bradford, Richard H. "John F. Kennedy and the 1960 Presidential Primary in West Virginia." SOUTH ATLANTIC QUARTERLY 75 (Spring 1976): 161-72.

Chai, Jae Hyung. "Presidential Control of the Foreign Policy Bureaucracy: The Kennedy Case." PRESIDENTIAL STUDIES QUARTERLY 8 (Fall 1978): 391-403.

Dector, Midge. "Kennedyism." COMMENTARY 49 (January 1970): 19-27.

A discussion of the assertion of the right of those properly endowed by education, upbringing, leisured high purpose, and birth to rule; and its relationship to the new politics of the 1970s.

Ecroyd, Donald H. "Recording the President." QUARTERLY JOURNAL OF SPEECH 48 (October 1962): 336-40.

Discusses the career of Jack Romagna of the White House staff who served as a shorthand reporter for Presidents Roosevelt, Truman, Eisenhower, and Kennedy.

Erskine, H.G. "Polls: Kennedy as President." PUBLIC OPINION QUARTERLY 28 (Summer 1964): 334-42.

Golden, James L. "John F. Kennedy and the 'Ghosts.'" QUARTERLY JOURNAL OF SPEECH 52 (December 1966): 348-57.

Pictures Kennedy as the principal architect of his own speeches, although he received help from others at times.

Hart, John. "Kennedy, Congress, and Civil Rights." JOURNAL OF AMERICAN STUDIES 13 (August 1979): 165-78.

Kraft, Joseph. "Kennedy's Working Staff." HARPER'S 225 (December 1962): 29-36.

Lewis, Eleanor G. "The House Committee on Rules and the Legislative Program of the Kennedy and Johnson Administrations." CAPITOL STUDIES 6 (Fall 1978): 27-38.

Lord, Donald C. "JFK and Civil Rights." PRESIDENTIAL STUDIES QUARTERLY 8 (Spring 1978): 151-63.

Mongar, Thomas M. "Personality and Decision-Making: John F. Kennedy in Four Crisis Decisions." CANADIAN JOURNAL OF POLITICAL SCIENCE 2 (1969): 200-225.

A study of the role of Kennedy's personality in shaping decisions in the Cuban missile crisis, the Bay of Pigs affair, the steel seizure case, and the James Meredith episode.

Neustadt, Richard E. "Approaches to Staffing the Presidency: Notes on FDR and JFK." AMERICAN POLITICAL SCIENCE REVIEW 57 (December 1963): 855-64.

Neustadt prepared a paper on staffing problems for President Kennedy who tried to follow FDR's system.

Nurse, Ronald J. "Critic of Colonialism: JFK and Algerian Independence." HISTORIAN 39 (February 1977): 307-26.

Pelz, Stephen E. "'When Do I Have Time to Think?' John F. Kennedy, Roger Hilsman, and the Laotian Crisis of 1962." DIPLOMATIC HISTORY 3 (Spring 1979): 215-30.

Pollard, James E. "The Kennedy Administration and the Press." JOURNALISM QUARTERLY 41 (1964): 3-14.

Good analysis by the author of THE PRESIDENTS AND THE PRESS (1964).

Polsby, Nelson W. "JFK through Russian Eyes." POLITICAL SCIENCE QUARTERLY 90 (Spring 1975): 117-26.

Shannon, William V. "The Kennedy Administration: The Early Months." AMERICAN SCHOLAR 30 (Autumn 1961): 481-88.

Discusses the intense loyalty of the Kennedy staff to their leader.

Sorensen, Theodore C. "The Election of 1960." In HISTORY OF AMERICAN PRESIDENTIAL ELECTIONS, 1789-1968, vol. 4, edited by Arthur Schlesinger, Jr., pp. 3449-562. New York: Chelsea House, 1971.

Chapter 46

LYNDON B. JOHNSON, 1963-69

BIBLIOGRAPHY

Furer, Howard B., ed. LYNDON B. JOHNSON, 1908-1973: CHRONOLOGY-DOCUMENTS-BIBLIOGRAPHICAL AIDS. Presidential Chronologies Series. Dobbs Ferry, N.Y.: Oceana Publications, 1971. 154 p.

SOURCE MATERIALS

Burns, James MacGregor, ed. TO HEAL AND TO BUILD: THE PROGRAMS OF PRESIDENT LYNDON B. JOHNSON. New York: McGraw-Hill, 1968. xiv, 506 p.

Johnson, Claudia T. A WHITE HOUSE DIARY. New York: Holt, Rinehart and Winston, 1970. ix, 806 p.

Primarily important for social and family history.

Johnson, Lyndon Baines. THE JOHNSON HUMOR. Edited by Bill Adler. New York: Simon and Schuster, 1965. 124 p.

______. THE JOHNSON WIT. Edited by Francis Spatz Leighton. New York: Citadel Press, 1965. 94 p.

______. MY HOPE FOR AMERICA. New York: Random House, 1964. 127 p.

______. THE QUOTABLE LYNDON B. JOHNSON. Compiled and edited by Sarah H. Hayes and the staff of Quote. Anderson, S.C.: Droke House; distributed by Grosset and Dunlap, New York, 1968. vi, 311 p.

______. ORAL HISTORY INTERVIEW WITH LYNDON B. JOHNSON BY RAYMOND HENLE, DIRECTOR, JANUARY 8, 1971 AT LBJ RANCH, JOHNSON CITY, TEXAS. N.p., 1972.

For the Hoover Presidential Library, West Branch, Iowa, and the Hoover Institution on War, Revolution and Peace, Stanford, California.

_____. PUBLIC PAPERS OF THE PRESIDENTS OF THE UNITED STATES, LYNDON B. JOHNSON, 1963-1969. 10 vols. Washington, D.C.: Government Printing Office, 1965-76.

_____. A TIME FOR ACTION: A SELECTION FROM THE SPEECHES AND WRITINGS OF LYNDON B. JOHNSON, 1953-1964. New York: Atheneum Publishers, 1964. xv, 183 p.

_____. THE VANTAGE POINT: PERSPECTIVES OF THE PRESIDENCY, 1963-1969. New York: Holt, Rinehart and Winston, 1971. x, 636 p.

BIOGRAPHIES

Bard, Bernard. LBJ: THE PICTURE STORY OF LYNDON BAINES JOHNSON. New York: Lion Press, 1966. 90 p.

Bishop, James Alonzo. A DAY IN THE LIFE OF PRESIDENT JOHNSON. New York: Random House, 1967. 274 p.

Caro, Robert A. THE YEARS OF LYNDON JOHNSON: THE PATH TO POWER. New York: Alfred A. Knopf, 1982. xxiii, 882 p.

Johnson, Sam Houston. MY BROTHER, LYNDON. New York: Cowles Book Co., 1970. 278 p.

Kearns, Doris. LYNDON JOHNSON AND THE AMERICAN DREAM. New York: Harper and Row, 1976. xii, 432 p.

Miller, Merle, ed. LYNDON: AN ORAL BIOGRAPHY. New York: G.P. Putnam's Sons, 1980. xix, 645 p.

Mooney, Booth. THE LYNDON JOHNSON STORY. New York: Farrar, Straus and Co., 1964. xxii, 198 p.

Pool, William C., et al. LYNDON BAINES JOHNSON: THE FORMATIVE YEARS. San Marcos: Southwest Texas State College Press, 1965. 185 p.

Discusses the youth and early career of Johnson to the 1930s.

Rulon, Philip Reed. THE COMPASSIONATE SAMARITAN: THE LIFE OF LYNDON BAINES JOHNSON. Chicago: Nelson-Hall, 1981. xv, 348 p.

Deals especially with Johnson's ideas on public education.

Steinberg, Alfred. SAM JOHNSON'S BOY: A CLOSE-UP OF THE PRESIDENT FROM TEXAS. New York: Macmillan, 1968. 871 p.

Uncomplimentary, but exhaustively researched and well written. Based to a large degree upon interviews with contemporaries and associates of Johnson.

U.S. Congress. Senate. TRIBUTES TO THE PRESIDENT AND MRS. LYNDON BAINES JOHNSON IN THE CONGRESS OF THE UNITED STATES. 91st Cong., 1st sess., 1969. Washington, D.C.: Government Printing Office, 1969. 185 p.

Valenti, Jack. A VERY HUMAN PRESIDENT. New York: Norton, 1975. xii, 402 p.

White, William S. THE PROFESSIONAL: LYNDON B. JOHNSON. Cambridge, Mass.: Houghton Mifflin, 1964. 273 p.

Favorable brief biography.

Yager, Thomas C. PRESIDENTS, PRIME MINISTERS, AND PREMIERS. Vol. 1, PRESIDENT LYNDON B. JOHNSON. Los Angeles: American Institute, 1969.

MONOGRAPHS

Amrine, Michael. THIS AWESOME CHALLENGE, THE HUNDRED DAYS OF LYNDON JOHNSON. New York: Putnam, 1964. 283 p.

Covers Johnson's first three months in office and the difficulties of assuming leadership.

Baker, Leonard. THE JOHNSON ECLIPSE: A PRESIDENT'S VICE PRESIDENCY. New York: Macmillan, 1966. 280 p.

Focuses on the three years Johnson spent as vice president.

Bearss, Edwin C. LYNDON B. JOHNSON NATIONAL HISTORIC SITE. Washington, D.C.: U.S. National Park Service, 1971. xii, 200 p.

Historic resource study, including base maps and historic structure report.

Bell, Jack. THE JOHNSON TREATMENT; HOW LYNDON B. JOHNSON TOOK OVER THE PRESIDENCY AND MADE IT HIS OWN. New York: Harper and Row, 1965. 305 p.

Berman, Larry. PLANNING A TRAGEDY: THE AMERICANIZATION OF THE WAR IN VIETNAM. New York: W. W. Norton and Co., 1982. 192 p.

Califano, Joseph. A PRESIDENTIAL NATION. New York: W.W. Norton, 1975. xii, 338 p.

A key Johnson aide describes the LBJ White House with emphasis on domestic operations.

Carpenter, Liz. RUFFLES AND FLOURISHES: THE WARM AND TENDER STORY OF A SIMPLE GIRL WHO FOUND ADVENTURE IN THE WHITE HOUSE. Garden City, N.Y.: Doubleday, 1970. xv, 341 p.

Memoir by Lady Bird Johnson's staff director and press secretary.

Christian, George. THE PRESIDENT STEPS DOWN: A PERSONAL MEMOIR OF THE TRANSFER OF POWER. New York: Macmillan, 1970. 282 p.

An inside view by Johnson's press secretary.

Cummings, Milton C., Jr. THE NATIONAL ELECTION OF 1964. Washington, D.C.: Brookings Institution, 1966. xi, 295 p.

A detailed analysis by seven experts covering the conventions, campaign, media strategy, finances, House and Senate contests, and the meaning of the election of Lyndon Johnson.

Deakin, James. LYNDON JOHNSON'S CREDIBILITY GAP. Washington, D.C.: Public Affairs Press, 1968. 65 p.

By the White House correspondent for the ST. LOUIS POST DISPATCH, a recognized authority on the presidency and the truth.

Divine, Robert A., ed. EXPLORING THE JOHNSON YEARS. Austin: University of Texas Press, 1981. viii, 280 p.

Evans, Rowland, and Novak, Robert. LYNDON B. JOHNSON: THE EXERCISE OF POWER. New York: New American Library, 1966. viii, 597 p.

Most of the book deals with Johnson's Senate career.

Faber, Harold, ed. THE ROAD TO THE WHITE HOUSE. New York: McGraw-Hill, 1965. xvi, 305 p.

The story of the 1964 election by the staff of the NEW YORK TIMES.

Geyelin, Philip L. LYNDON B. JOHNSON AND THE WORLD. New York: F.A. Praeger, 1966. viii, 309 p.

By the diplomatic correspondent of WALL STREET JOURNAL. Good for the early years of Johnson's administration.

Goldman, Eric. THE TRAGEDY OF LYNDON JOHNSON. New York: Knopf, 1969. xii, 531 p.

A memoir by Johnson's disillusioned "intellectual-in-residence."

Graff, Henry Franklin. THE TUESDAY CABINET: DELIBERATION AND DECISION ON PEACE AND WAR UNDER LYNDON B. JOHNSON. Englewood Cliffs, N.J.: Prentice-Hall, 1970. 200 p.

Graff regularly interviewed Johnson and other key persons in the government about their views on the Vietnam war.

Halberstam, David. THE BEST AND THE BRIGHTEST. New York: Random House, 1972. 831 p.

The detailed story of how America became involved in Vietnam.

Heren, Louis. NO HAIL, NO FAREWELL. New York: Harper and Row, 1970. 275 p.

Journalistic view of the Johnson era.

Hoopes, Townsend. THE LIMITS OF INTERVENTION. New York: David McKay Co., 1969. ix, 245 p.

Written by the under secretary of the Air Force. Good on the decision of March 1968 not to escalate American involvement.

Inaugural Committee. 1965. THRESHOLD OF TOMORROW: THE GREAT SOCIETY. Washington, D.C., 1965. 107 p.

A combination essay-pictorial volume designed as a lasting memento of the 1964 inaugural festivities.

Kearns, Doris. LYNDON JOHNSON AND THE AMERICAN DREAM. New York: Harper and Row, 1976. xii, 432 p.

A psychological analysis of Johnson's career.

Lamb, Karl A., and Smith, Paul A. CAMPAIGN DECISION-MAKING: THE PRESIDENTIAL ELECTION OF 1964. Belmont, Calif.: Wadsworth Publishing Co., 1968. 238 p.

Lincoln, Evelyn. KENNEDY AND JOHNSON. New York: Holt, Rinehart and Winston, 1968. xi, 207 p.

Kennedy's secretary gives her impressions of the relationship between Kennedy and Johnson. Based on diary notes kept by Mrs. Lincoln.

McPherson, Harry. A POLITICAL EDUCATION. Boston: Little, Brown, 1972. 467 p.

Written by one of Johnson's key aides.

Maguire, Jack R., ed. A PRESIDENT'S COUNTRY; A GUIDE TO THE LBJ COUNTRY OF TEXAS. Drawings by Mac Tatchell. 2d ed. Austin, Tex.: Shoal Creek Publishers, 1973. 84 p.

Pollard, James E. THE PRESIDENTS AND THE PRESS: TRUMAN TO JOHNSON. Washington, D.C.: Public Affairs Press, 1964. 125 p.

An updated supplement to Pollard's standard history of the subject.

Reedy, George. LYNDON B. JOHNSON: A MEMOIR. New York: Andrews and McMeel, Inc., 1982. xvi, 159 p.

Roberts, Charles Wesley. LBJ'S INNER CIRCLE. New York: Delacorte Press, 1965. 223 p.

A study of Johnson's closest advisers, assistants, and confidantes.

Rostow, Walt W. THE DIFFUSION OF POWER. New York: Macmillan, 1972. xx, 739 p.

The best single volume on foreign affairs during the 1960s.

Schandler, Herbert Y. THE UNMAKING OF A PRESIDENT: LYNDON JOHNSON AND VIETNAM. Princeton, N.J.: Princeton University Press, 1977. xx, 419 p.

Sherrill, Robert. THE ACCIDENTAL PRESIDENT. New York: Grossman Publishers, 1967. vi, 282 p.

A witty, journalistic version of the Johnson years.

Sidey, Hugh. A VERY PERSONAL PRESIDENCY: LYNDON JOHNSON IN THE WHITE HOUSE. New York: Atheneum, 1968. ix, 305 p.

Slater, Jerome. INTERVENTION AND NEGOTIATION: THE UNITED STATES AND THE DOMINICAN REVOLUTION. New York: Harper and Row, 1970. 254

Sundquist, James L. POLITICS AND POLICY: THE EISENHOWER, KENNEDY, AND JOHNSON YEARS. Washington, D.C.: Brookings Institution, 1968. viii, 560 p.

Good study of domestic policy.

White, J. Roy. THE RESTORATION OF THE BIRTHPLACE OF PRESIDENT LYNDON B. JOHNSON. Austin, Tex.: n.p., 1965. Unpaged.

White, Theodore H. THE MAKING OF THE PRESIDENT, 1964. New York: Atheneum, 1965. xiii, 460 p.

Wicker, Tom. JFK AND LBJ: THE INFLUENCE OF PERSONALITY UPON POLITICS. New York: Morrow, 1968. 297 p.

Shows the connection between Vietnam and domestic affairs in the Johnson administration.

Williams, William Appelman. SOME PRESIDENTS: WILSON TO NIXON. New York: New York Review, 1972. 122 p.

See chapter on Johnson.

ARTICLES

Baker, James T. "Lyndon Johnson: America's Oedipus?" SOUTHERN HUMANITIES REVIEW 8 (Spring 1974): 127-39.

Billington, Monroe. "Lyndon B. Johnson and Blacks: The Early Years." JOURNAL OF NEGRO HISTORY 62 (January 1977): 26-42.

Branyan, Robert L., and Lee, R. Alton. "Lyndon B. Johnson and the Art of the Possible." SOUTHWESTERN SOCIAL SCIENCE QUARTERLY 45 (December 1964): 213-25.

On Johnson's skill as a congressional politician.

Bunge, Walter, et al. "Johnson's Information Strategy for Vietnam: An Evaluation." JOURNALISM QUARTERLY 45 (Autumn 1968): 419-25.

Conkin, Paul K. "The Johnson Years: An Essay Review." WISCONSIN MAGAZINE OF HISTORY 56 (Autumn 1972): 59-64.

A double review of THE PENTAGON PAPERS (1972) and Johnson's memoirs, THE VANTAGE POINT (1971).

Dyer, Stanford P., and Knighten, Merrell A. "Discrimination after Death: Lyndon Johnson and Felix Longoria." SOCIAL STUDIES 17 (Winter 1978): 411-26.

Fairlie, Henry. "Johnson and the Intellectuals." COMMENTARY 40 (October 1965): 49-55.

Argues that attacks by intellectuals on Johnson were unwarranted.

Frantz, Joe B. "The Lyndon Baines Johnson Library." STIRPES: TEXAS STATE GENEALOGICAL SOCIETY QUARTERLY 10 (March-June 1970): 3-6, 45-46.

______. "Opening a Curtain: The Metamorphosis of Lyndon B. Johnson." JOURNAL OF SOUTHERN HISTORY 45 (February 1979): 3-26.

Frantz, Joe B. "Why London?" WESTERN HISTORICAL QUARTERLY 11 (January 1980): 5-15.

Huitt, R.K. "Democratic Party Leadership in the Senate: Leadership of Senator Johnson." AMERICAN POLITICAL SCIENCE REVIEW 55 (June 1961): 337-41.

Janos, L. "Last Days of the President." ATLANTIC 232 (July 1973): 35-41.

Kearns, Doris. "Lyndon Johnson's Political Personality." POLITICAL SCIENCE QUARTERLY 91 (Fall 1976): 385-409.

Lawson, Steven F., and Gelfand, Mark I. "Consensus and Civil Rights: Lyndon B. Johnson and the Black Franchise." PROLOGUE 8 (Summer 1976): 65-76.

Lekachman, Robert. "Death of a Slogan--The Great Society, 1967." COMMENTARY 43 (January 1967): 56-61.

Leuchtenburg, William. "The Genesis of the Great Society." REPORTER 34, no. 8 (21 April 1966): 36-39.

McNaught, Kenneth. "American Progressives and the Great Society." JOURNAL OF AMERICAN HISTORY 53 (December 1966): 504-20.

Moyers, Bill. "Bill Moyers Talks about LBJ, Power, Poverty, War and the Young: An Interview." ATLANTIC MONTHLY 222 (July 1968): 29-37.

Sellen, Robert W. "Old Assumptions Versus New Realities: Lyndon Johnson and Foreign Policy." INTERNATIONAL JOURNAL 28 (Spring 1973): 205-29.

Sigelman, Lee. "Rallying to the President's [Johnson's] Support: A Reappraisal of the Evidence." POLITY 11 (Summer 1979): 542-61.

Williams, T. Harry. "Huey, Lyndon, and Southern Radicalism." JOURNAL OF AMERICAN HISTORY 60 (September 1973): 267-93.

Chapter 47

RICHARD M. NIXON, 1969-74

BIBLIOGRAPHY

Bremer, Howard F., ed. RICHARD M. NIXON, 1913--: CHRONOLOGY-DOCUMENTS-BIBLIOGRAPHICAL AIDS. Presidential Chronologies Series. Dobbs Ferry, N.Y.: Oceana Publications, 1975. v, 250 p.

SOURCE MATERIALS

Nixon, Richard Milhous. THE CLEAREST CHOICE. N.p.: 1972. 90 p.

Contains the fourteen radio and two television speeches delivered during the 1972 presidential campaign.

______. A CONVERSATION WITH THE PRESIDENT. Department of State Publication, 8545, General Foreign Policy Series, 248. Washington, D.C.: Government Printing Office, 1970. 34 p.

______. EDUCATION FOR THE 1970'S: RENEWAL AND REFORM; MESSAGES TO THE CONGRESS. Washington, D.C.: For sale by the Superintendent of Documents, Government Printing Office, 1970. 33 p.

______. THE MEMOIRS OF RICHARD NIXON. New York: Grosset and Dunlap, 1978. xii, 1,120 p.

______. NIXON: THE FIRST YEAR OF HIS PRESIDENCY. Washington, D.C.: Congressional Quarterly, 1970. 92, 128A p.

______. NIXON: THE SECOND YEAR OF HIS PRESIDENCY. Washington, D.C.: Congressional Quarterly, 1971. 80, 166A p.

______. NIXON: THE THIRD YEAR OF HIS PRESIDENCY. Washington, D.C.: Congressional Quarterly, 1972. 78, 159A p.

_____. NIXON: THE FOURTH YEAR OF HIS PRESIDENCY. Washington, D.C.: Congressional Quarterly, 1973. 46, 146A p.

_____. NIXON: THE FIFTH YEAR OF HIS PRESIDENCY. Washington, D.C.: Congressional Quarterly, 1974. 74, 191A p.

_____. PUBLIC PAPERS OF THE PRESIDENTS OF THE UNITED STATES, RICHARD M. NIXON, 1969-74. 6 vols. Washington, D.C.: Government Printing Office, 1971-75.

_____. THE REAL WAR. New York: Warner Books, 1980. 341 p.

_____. SETTING THE COURSE, THE FIRST YEAR: MAJOR POLICY STATEMENTS. New York: Funk and Wagnalls, 1970. xix, 500 p.

_____. UNITED STATES FOREIGN POLICY FOR THE 1970'S; BUILDING FOR PEACE. A REPORT BY PRESIDENT RICHARD NIXON TO THE CONGRESS, FEBRUARY 25, 1971. New York: Harper and Row, 1971. xiii, 193 p.

_____. THE YOUNG NIXON: AN ORAL INQUIRY. Edited by Renée K. Schulte. Fullerton: California State University, Fullerton, Oral History Program, Richard M. Nixon Project, 1978. xxxvi, 279 p.

U.S. Office of Management and Budget. PAPERS RELATING TO THE PRESIDENT'S DEPARTMENTAL REORGANIZATION PROGRAM: A REFERENCE COMPILATION. Rev. ed. Washington, D.C.: For sale by the Superintendent of Documents, Government Printing Office, 1972. xiv, 311 p.

BIOGRAPHIES

Alsop, Stewart. NIXON AND ROCKEFELLER: A DOUBLE PORTRAIT. Garden City, N.Y.: Doubleday, 1960. 240 p.

Arnold, William A. BACK WHEN IT ALL BEGAN: THE EARLY NIXON YEARS: BEING SOME REMINISCENCES OF PRESIDENT NIXON'S EARLY POLITICAL CAREER BY HIS FIRST ADMINISTRATIVE ASSISTANT AND PRESS SECRETARY. New York: Vantage Press, 1975. 45 p.

Bell, Raymond Martin. THE ANCESTRY OF RICHARD MILHOUS NIXON. 3d ed. Washington, Pa.: n.p., 1971. 75 l.

Brodie, Fawn M. RICHARD NIXON: THE SHAPING OF HIS CHARACTER. New York: W.W. Norton, 1981. 574 p.

Campbell, Ann Raymond. THE PICTURE LIFE OF RICHARD MILHOUS NIXON. New York: F. Watts, 1969. 57 p.

Describes briefly in text and photograph the life of Richard M. Nixon.

Cavan, Sherri. 20TH CENTURY GOTHIC: AMERICA'S NIXON. San Francisco: Wigan Pier Press, 1979. ix, 330 p.

David, Lester. THE LONELY LADY OF SAN CLEMENTE: THE STORY OF PAT NIXON. New York: Crowell, 1978. 235 p.

De Toledano, Ralph. ONE MAN ALONE: RICHARD NIXON. New York: Funk and Wagnalls, 1969. 386 p.

Eisenhower, Julie Nixon, comp. EYE ON NIXON; A PHOTOGRAPHIC STUDY OF THE PRESIDENT AND THE MAN. Text by William Safire. Art director, Byron Schumaker. New York: Hawthorn Books, 1972. 128 p.

Mazlish, Bruce. IN SEARCH OF NIXON: A PSYCHOHISTORICAL INQUIRY. Baltimore: Penquin Books, 1972. x, 187 p.

A fascinating effort to probe President Nixon's personality.

Mazo, Earl. RICHARD [MILHOUS] NIXON [BORN 1913]: A POLITICAL AND PERSONAL PORTRAIT. New York: Harper, 1959. viii, 309 p.

Mazo, Earl, and Hess, Stephen. NIXON: A POLITICAL PORTRAIT. New York: Harper and Row, 1968. 326 p.

MONOGRAPHS

Atkins, Ollie. THE WHITE HOUSE YEARS: TRIUMPH AND TRAGEDY. Chicago: Playboy Press, 1977. 244 p.

Burke, Vincent J., and Burke, Vee. NIXON'S GOOD DEED: WELFARE REFORM. New York: Columbia University Press, 1974. xxi, 243 p.

Evans, Rowland, Jr., and Novak, Robert D. NIXON IN THE WHITE HOUSE: THE FRUSTRATION OF POWER. New York: Random House, 1971. xiii, 431 p.

A journalistic account of the first Nixon administration.

Frost, David. "I GAVE THEM A SWORD": BEHIND THE SCENES OF THE NIXON INTERVIEWS. Photographs by John Bryson. New York: Morrow, 1978. 320 p.

Gardner, Lloyd C. THE NIXON TURNAROUND: AMERICA'S NEW FOREIGN POLICY IN THE POST-LIBERAL ERA (HOW A COLD WARRIOR CLIMBED CLEAN OUT OF HIS SKIN); ESSAYS AND ARTICLES. Introductory statement by Lloyd C. Gardner. New York: New Viewpoints, 1973. xii, 350 p.

THE INAUGURAL STORY, 1789-1969. Created and produced by the editors of American Heritage magazine and the 1969 Inaugural Book Committee. New York: American Heritage Publishing Co., 1969. 175 p.

Jones, Alan M., Jr., ed. UNITED STATES FOREIGN POLICY IN A CHANGING WORLD: THE NIXON ADMINISTRATION, 1969-1973. New York: David McKay, 1973. xvi, 379 p.

Keogh, James. PRESIDENT NIXON AND THE PRESS. New York: Funk and Wagnalls, 1972. 212 p.

Kintner, William Roscoe. THE IMPACT OF PRESIDENT NIXON'S VISIT TO PEKING ON INTERNATIONAL POLITICS. Research Monograph Series, no. 13. Philadelphia: Foreign Policy Research Institute, 1972. viii, 65 p.

Kissinger, Henry Alfred. WHITE HOUSE YEARS. Boston: Little, Brown, 1979. xxiv, 1,521 p.

Klein, Herbert G. MAKING IT PERFECTLY CLEAR. Garden City, N.Y.: Doubleday, 1980. xiii, 464 p.

Laird, Melvin R., et al. THE NIXON DOCTRINE. Washington, D.C.: American Enterprise Institute for Public Policy Research, 1972. 79 p.

Lurie, Ranan R. NIXON RATED CARTOONS. Foreword by Thomas Griffith. Rev. ed. New York: Quadrangle, 1974. 320 p.

McGinniss, Joe. THE SELLING OF THE PRESIDENT 1968. New York: Trident Press, 1969. 253 p.

Morrison, Rodney J. EXPECTATIONS AND INFLATION: NIXON, POLITICS, AND ECONOMICS. Lexington, Mass.: Lexington Books, 1973. xi, 167 p.

Moynihan, Daniel Patrick. THE POLITICS OF A GUARANTEED INCOME; THE NIXON ADMINISTRATION AND THE FAMILY ASSISTANCE PLAN. New York: Vintage Books, 1973. xiii, 579 p.

Murphy, Reg, and Gulliver, Hal. THE SOUTHERN STRATEGY. New York: Scribner, 1971. 273 p.

Osborne, John THE NIXON WATCH. [A Series]. New York: Liverright, 1970-75.

Consists of articles that appeared in the NEW REPUBLIC from October 1968 to September 1974.

Panetta, Leon E., and Gall, Peter. BRING US TOGETHER: THE NIXON TEAM AND THE CIVIL RIGHTS RETREAT. Philadelphia: J.B. Lippincott, 1971. xii, 380 p.

Porter, William Earl. ASSAULT ON THE MEDIA: THE NIXON YEARS. Ann Arbor: University of Michigan Press, 1976. x, 320 p.

THE PRESIDENT'S TRIP TO CHINA: A PICTORIAL RECORD OF THE HISTORIC JOURNEY TO THE PEOPLE'S REPUBLIC OF CHINA WITH TEXT BY MEMBERS OF THE AMERICAN PRESS CORPS. Edited by Richard Wilson. New York: Bantam Books, 1972. 159 p.

Price, Raymond. WITH NIXON. New York: Viking Press, 1977. x, 398 p.

Rather, Dan, and Gates, Gary Paul. THE PALACE GUARD. New York: Harper and Row, 1974. ix, 326 p.

Safire, William L. BEFORE THE FALL: AN INSIDE VIEW OF THE PRE-WATERGATE WHITE HOUSE. Garden City, N.Y.: Doubleday, 1975. xii, 704 p.

Szulc, Tad. THE ILLUSION OF PEACE: FOREIGN POLICY IN THE NIXON YEARS. New York: Viking Press, 1978. xii, 822 p.

Van der Linden, Frank. NIXON'S QUEST FOR PEACE. Washington, D.C.: R.B Luce, 1972. 247 p.

White, Theodore H. THE MAKING OF THE PRESIDENT, 1968. New York: Atheneum, 1969. xii, 459 p.

Whitney, David C. THE WEEK THAT CHANGED THE WORLD: PRESIDENT RICHARD M. NIXON'S HISTORIC VISIT TO COMMUNIST CHINA, FEBRUARY 21-28, 1972. Chicago: J.G. Ferguson Publishing Co., 1972. 32 p.

Wills, Garry. NIXON AGONISTES: THE CRISIS OF THE SELF-MADE MAN. Boston: Houghton Mifflin, 1970. 617 p.

An analysis of President Nixon's methods and ideology.

Witcover, Jules. THE RESURRECTION OF RICHARD NIXON. New York: Putnam, 1970, 479 p.

WATERGATE

Ball, Howard. NO PLEDGE OF PRIVACY: THE WATERGATE TAPES LITIGATION. Multi-Disciplinary Studies in the Law. Port Washington, N.Y.: Kennikat Press, 1977. xi, 144 p.

Breslin, Jimmy. HOW THE GOOD GUYS FINALLY WON: NOTES FROM AN IMPEACHMENT SUMMER. New York: Viking Press, 1975. 192 p.

CONSTITUTIONAL ASPECTS OF WATERGATE: DOCUMENTS AND MATERIALS. Compiled and edited by A. Stephen Boyan, Jr. Dobbs Ferry, N.Y.: Oceana Publications, 1976. 587 p.

Drew, Elizabeth. WASHINGTON JOURNAL: THE EVENTS OF 1973-1974. New York: Vintage Books, 1976. xvii, 428 p.

THE END OF A PRESIDENCY. By the staff of the New York Times. New York: Holt, Rinehart and Winston, 1974. ix, 353 p.

Evans, Les, and Myers, Allen. WATERGATE AND THE MYTH OF AMERICAN DEMOCRACY. New York: Pathfinder Press, 1974. 206 p.

THE FALL OF A PRESIDENT. By the staff of the Washington Post. New York: Delacorte Press, 1974. xxi, 232 p.

Jaworski, Leon. THE RIGHT AND THE POWER: THE PROSECUTION OF WATERGATE. New York: Reader's Digest Press, distributed by Crowell, 1976. 305 p.

McGuckin, Henry E. "A Value Analysis of Richard Nixon's 1952 Campaign-Fund Speech." SOUTHERN SPEECH JOURNAL, Summer 1968.

Nixon, Richard Milhous. THE PRESIDENTIAL TRANSCRIPTS. Written in conjunction with the staff of the WASHINGTON POST. New York: Delacorte Press, 1974. xl, 693 p.

_____. THE WHITE HOUSE TRANSCRIPTS: SUBMISSION OF RECORDED PRESIDENTIAL CONVERSATIONS TO THE COMMITTEE ON THE JUDICIARY OF THE HOUSE OF REPRESENTATIVES BY PRESIDENT RICHARD NIXON. Introduction by R.W. Apple, Jr. Chronology by Linda Amster. General editor, Gerald Gold. New York: Viking Press, 1974. ix, 877 p.

Osborne, J. "Summing Up of a Nixon-Watcher." NEW REPUBLIC 159 (26 October 1968): 15-17.

Sorensen, Theodore C. WATCHMEN IN THE NIGHT: PRESIDENTIAL ACCOUNTABILITY AFTER WATERGATE. Cambridge: MIT Press, 1975. xviii, 178 p.

Tretick, Stanley. THEY COULD NOT TRUST THE KING: NIXON, WATERGATE, AND THE AMERICAN PEOPLE. Photographs by Stanley Tretick. Text by William V. Shannon. Foreword by Barbara W. Tuchman. New York: Macmillan, 1974. 197 p. Illus.

U.S. Congress. House. Committee on the Judiciary. IMPEACHMENT OF RICHARD M. NIXON, PRESIDENT OF THE UNITED STATES: THE FINAL REPORT OF THE COMMITTEE ON THE JUDICIARY, HOUSE OF REPRESENTATIVES, PETER W. RODINO, JR., CHAIRMAN. 93d Cong., 2d sess., 1974. Introduction by R.W. Apple, Jr. New York: Viking Press, 1975. xxvi, 755 p.

WATERGATE, POLITICS, AND THE LEGAL PROCESS. Washington, D.C.: American Enterprise Institute for Public Policy Research, 1974. 89 p.

White, Theodore Harold. BREACH OF FAITH: THE FALL OF RICHARD NIXON. New York: Atheneum Publishers, 1975. 373 p.

WHY WATERGATE? Edited by Paul J. Halpern. Pacific Palisades, Calif.: Palisades Publishers, 1975. viii, 233 p.

Woodward, Bob, and Bernstein, Carl. THE FINAL DAYS. New York: Simon and Schuster, 1976. 476 p.

ARTICLES

Aberback, Joel D., and Rockman, Bert A. "Clashing Beliefs within the Executive Branch: The Nixon Administration Bureaucracy." AMERICAN POLITICAL SCIENCE REVIEW 70 (June 1976): 456-68.

Barber, James David. "The Nixon Brush with Tyranny." POLITICAL SCIENCE QUARTERLY 92 (Winter 1977-78): 581-606.

Brown, Steven R. "Richard Nixon and the Public Conscience: The Struggle for Authenticity." JOURNAL OF PSYCHOHISTORY 6 (Summer 1978): 93-111.

Cameron, J. "Richard Nixon's Very Personal White House." FORTUNE, July 1970, pp. 57-59.

Cole, Richard L., and Caputo, David A. "Presidential Control of the Senior Civil Service: Assessing the Strategies of the Nixon Years." AMERICAN POLITICAL SCIENCE REVIEW 73 (June 1979): 399-412.

Garrett, Stephen A. "Nixonian Foreign Policy: A New Balance of Power or a Revived Concert?" POLITY 8 (Spring 1976): 389-421.

Graber, Doris A. "Press Coverage and Voter Reaction in the 1968 Presidential Election." POLITICAL SCIENCE QUARTERLY 89 (March 1974): 68-100.

Harrell, Jackson; Ware, B.L.; and Linkugel, Wil A. "Failure of Apology in American Politics: Nixon on Watergate." SPEECH MONOGRAPHS 42 (November 1975): 245-61.

Hershey, Marjorie Randon, and Hill, David B. "Watergate and Pre-Adults' Attitudes toward the President." AMERICAN JOURNAL OF POLITICAL SCIENCE 19 (November 1975): 703-26.

Hofstetter, C. Richard, and Zukin, Cliff. "TV Network News and Advertising in the Nixon and McGovern Campaigns." JOURNALISM QUARTERLY 56 (Spring 1979): 106-15, 152.

James, Judson Lehman, and James, Dorothy Buckton. "Lessons of Watergate: The Nixon Campaigns." CURRENT HISTORY 67 (July 1974): 31-33, 38.

Kohl, Wilfred L. "The Nixon-Kissinger Foreign Policy System and U.S.-European Relations: Patterns of Policy Making." WORLD POLITICS 28 (October 1975): 1-43.

Kolodziej, Edward A. "Congress and Foreign Policy: The Nixon Years." PROCEEDINGS OF THE ACADEMY OF POLITICAL SCIENCE 32, no.1 (1975): 167-79.

Laing, Robert B., and Stevenson, Robert L. "Public Opinion Trends in the Last Days of the Nixon Administration." JOURNALISM QUARTERLY 53 (Summer 1976): 294-302.

Mazon, Mauricio. "Young Richard Nixon: A Study in Political Precocity." HISTORIAN 41 (November 1978): 21-40.

Morton, Rogers C.B. "The Nixon Administration Energy Policy." ANNALS OF THE AMERICAN ACADEMY OF POLITICAL AND SOCIAL SCIENCES 410 (November 1973): 65-74.

Osborne, John. "Summing Up of a Nixon-Watcher." NEW REPUBLIC 159 (26 October 1968): 15-17.

Pipes, Richard. "America, Russia and Europe in the Light of the Nixon Doctrine." SURVEY 19 (Summer 1973): 30-40.

Randall, Ronald. "Presidential Power versus Bureaucratic Intransigence: The Influence of the Nixon Administration on Welfare Policy." AMERICAN POLITICAL SCIENCE REVIEW 73 (September 1979): 795-810.

Seelye, John. "The Measure of His Company: Richard M. Nixon in Amber." VIRGINIA QUARTERLY REVIEW 53 (Autumn 1977): 585-606.

Sorensen, Theodore C. "First Hundred Days of Richard M. Nixon." SATURDAY REVIEW, 17 May 1969, pp. 17-19.

Summers, Laura. "Cambodia: Model of the Nixon Doctrine." CURRENT HISTORY HISTORY 65 (December 1973): 252-56, 276.

Chapter 48

GERALD R. FORD, 1974-77

BIBLIOGRAPHIES

Horrocks, David A., and McNitt, William H., comps. HISTORICAL MATERIALS IN THE GERALD R. FORD LIBRARY. Ann Arbor, Mich.: Gerald R. Ford Library, 1982. iii, 43 p.

Lankevich, George J., ed. GERALD R. FORD, 1913--: CHRONOLOGY-DOCUMENTS-BIBLIOGRAPHICAL AIDS. Presidential Chronologies Series. Dobbs Ferry, N.Y.: Oceana Publications, 1977. 183 p.

SOURCE MATERIALS

Congressional Quarterly. PRESIDENCY, 1974. Washington, D.C.: 1975. 144 p. Appendix.

> Review of 1974; messages to Congress, vetoes, news conferences, and major statements.

______. PRESIDENCY, 1975. Washington, D.C.: 1976. 60 p. Appendix.

> Summarizes the main issues of 1975. Also includes Ford's messages to Congress, veto messages, news conferences, and major statements.

______. PRESIDENCY, 1976. Washington, D.C.: 1977. 118 p. Appendix.

> An overview of Ford's last year in office.

______. PRESIDENT FORD: THE MAN AND HIS RECORD. Washington, D.C.: 1974. 79 p. Ports.

> A convenient overview of Ford's political career and legislative record to August 1974 when he assumed the leadership of the nation. Includes a personal and political profile along with his statements on major issues, 1964-74.

THE CUMULATED INDEXES TO THE PUBLIC PAPERS OF THE PRESIDENTS OF THE UNITED STATES: GERALD R. FORD, 1974-1977. Millwood, N.Y.: Kraus International Publications, 1980. 111 p.

Ford, Betty. THE TIMES OF MY LIFE. New York: Harper and Row, 1978. xi, 302 p.

A candid autobiography emphasizing the personal and family experiences of the Fords rather than political events.

Ford, Gerald R. THE CHALLENGES THAT FACE AMERICA. Sound Recording. New York: Encyclopedia Americana/CBS News Audio Resource Library, 1975. 25 min. and 17 secs. Vital History Cassettes, April 1975, No. 2. "The Tulane Speech on America's New Agenda after 'A War That is Finished.'" Recorded April 23, 1975 in New Orleans.

_____. CONGRESSIONAL TESTIMONY ON THE PARDON OF FORMER PRESIDENT NIXON. Sound Recording. New York: Encyclopedia Americana/CBS News Audio Resource Library, 1974. Vital History Cassettes, October 1974, No. 1. 42 min. and 31 secs. Recorded October 17, 1974 in Washington, D.C.

_____. "A Conversation with Gerald R. Ford: Thoughts on Economics and Politics in the 1980's." AEI Studies, no. 279. Washington, D.C.: American Enterprise Institute, 1980. 19 p.

_____. A DISCUSSION WITH GERALD R. FORD: THE AMERICAN PRESIDENCY. Washington, D.C.: American Enterprise Institute for Public Policy Research, 1977. 21 p.

Transcript of an interview conducted in Washington on March 25, 1977.

_____. "Exercise and Sports." JOURNAL OF HEALTH, PHYSICAL EDUCATION AND RECREATION 45 (April 1974): 10-11.

Interview.

_____. "Impeachment: A Mace for the Federal Judiciary." NOTRE DAME LAWYER 46 (Summer 1971): 669-77.

_____. "In Defense of the Competitive Urge." SPORTS ILLUSTRATED 8 July 1974, pp. 16-23.

_____. "On the Threshold of the White House." ATLANTIC MONTHLY 234 (July 1974): 63-65.

Gives Ford's view of the role of vice president.

______. PUBLIC PAPERS OF THE PRESIDENTS OF THE UNITED STATES, GERALD R. FORD, 1974-1977. 6 vols. Washington, D.C.: Government Printing Office, 1975-79.

______. "The Rule of Law: Equal Justice for All." VITAL SPEECHES 40 (15 December 1973): 149.

Delivered before U.S. Congress on 6 December 1973.

______. "Science and Technology and Presidential Science and Technology Advice." TECHNOLOGY IN SOCIETY 2, nos. 1 and 2 (1980): 77-78.

______. SELECTED SPEECHES BY GERALD R. FORD. Edited by Michael V. Doyle. Arlington, Va.: R.W. Beatty, 1973. xiv, 246 p.

______. "Seminar in Economic Policy with Gerald R. Ford." AEI Studies, No. 186. Washington, D.C.: American Enterprise Institute, 1978. 14 p.

______. A TIME TO HEAL: THE AUTOBIOGRAPHY OF GERALD R. FORD. New York: Harper and Row, 1979. 454 p.

There is a 1980 paperback edition by Berkley Books with a new introduction by Ford.

______. "Towards a Healthy Economy." Francis Boyer Lectures on Public Policy. Washington, D.C.: American Enterprise Institute, 1978. 14 p.

______. THE WAR POWERS RESOLUTION: STRIKING A BALANCE BETWEEN THE EXECUTIVE AND LEGISLATIVE BRANCHES. Washington, D.C.: American Enterprise Institute, 1977. 7 p.

______. "Why I Will Not Run in '76." U.S. NEWS AND WORLD REPORT, 17 December 1973, pp. 24-30.

Interview.

______. "The World is Choice." VITAL SPEECHES 34 (1 September 1968): 685-87.

Speech to Republican National Convention, 8 August 1968.

Ford, Gerald R., and Stiles, John R. PORTRAIT OF THE ASSASSIN. New York: Simon and Schuster, 1965. 508 p.

Based on hearings of the President's Commission on the Assassination of President Kennedy.

THE GREAT DEBATES: CARTER VS. FORD, 1976. Edited by Sidney Kraus. Bloomington: Indiana University Press, 1979. xi, 553 p.

Includes the text of the three televised debates between Jimmy Carter and Gerald R. Ford, and of the vice-presidential debate between Robert Dole and Walter F. Mondale, in the 1976 presidential campaign.

THE PRESIDENTIAL CAMPAIGN, 1976. 3 vols. in 5. Washington, D.C.: Government Printing Office, under the direction of the Committee on House Administration, U.S. House of Representatives, 1978-79.

U.S. Congress. House. IMPRESSIONS OF NEW CHINA: JOINT REPORT TO THE HOUSE OF REPRESENTATIVES BY MAJORITY LEADER HALE BOGGS AND MINORITY LEADER GERALD R. FORD ON THEIR MISSION TO THE PEOPLE'S REPUBLIC OF CHINA, JUNE 23 TO JULY 7, 1972. 92d Cong., 2d sess., 1973. House Document 92-337. Washington, D.C.: Government Printing Office, 1972. v, 27 p.

______. TRIBUTES TO HONORABLE GERALD R. FORD, PRESIDENT OF THE UNITED STATES, TO COMMEMORATE HIM FOR HIS YEARS OF SERVICE TO THE NATION, FEBRUARY 1, 1977: DELIVERED IN THE HOUSE OF REPRESENTATIVES OF THE UNITED STATES. 95th Cong., 1st sess., 1977. Washington, D.C.: Government Printing Office, 1977. xii, 221 p.

U.S. Congress. House. Committee on the Judiciary. PARDON OF RICHARD M. NIXON AND RELATED MATTERS. Hearings before the Subcommittee on Criminal Justice. 93d Cong., 2d sess., 1974. Washington, D.C.: Government Printing Office, 1975. iv, 271 p.

U.S. Congress. Senate. Committee of Rules and Administration. NOMINATION OF GERALD R. FORD TO BE VICE PRESIDENT OF THE UNITED STATES. Hearings. 93d Cong., 1st sess., 1973. Washington, D.C.: Government Printing Office, 1973. vi, 373 p.

U.S. Library of Congress. Congressional Research Service. ANALYSIS OF THE PHILOSOPHY OF VOTING RECORD OF GERALD R. FORD, NOMINEE FOR VICE PRESIDENT OF THE UNITED STATES. Washington, D.C.: 1973. Typescript.

BIOGRAPHIES

LeRoy, Dave. GERALD FORD: UNTOLD STORY. Arlington, Va.: R.W. Beatty, 1974. viii, 128 p.

Sidey, Hugh. PORTRAIT OF A PRESIDENT. Photographs by Fred Ward. New York: Harper and Row, 1975. 189 p. Illus.

A pictorial biography of the first few months of the Ford administration.

terHorst, Jerald F. GERALD FORD AND THE FUTURE OF THE PRESIDENCY. New York: Third Press, 1974. xiv, 245 p.

A brief biography based upon the author's twenty-five year friendship with the president. Included is a discussion of the first thirty days of the Ford administration, the Nixon pardon, and the events surrounding the author's resignation as Ford's first press secretary.

Vestal, Bud. JERRY FORD, UP CLOSE: AN INVESTIGATIVE BIOGRAPHY. New York: Coward, McCann and Geoghegan, 1974. ix, 214 p.

Superficial and uncritical treatment written by Vestal and researched by seven Michigan journalists.

Watson, Christopher, ed. GERALD R. FORD: OUR 38TH PRESIDENT. New York: Mayfair Publications, 1974.

MONOGRAPHS

Barber, James David. THE PRESIDENTIAL CHARACTER: PREDICTING PERFORMANCE IN THE WHITE HOUSE. 2d ed. Englewood Cliffs, N.J.: Prentice-Hall, 1977. xi, 576 p.

See chapter 15, "The Crucial Ford Transistion," pp. 485-97, in which Barber characterizes Ford as an active-positive type of president.

Bitzer, Lloyd, and Rueter, Theodore. CARTER VS. FORD: THE COUNTERFEIT DEBATES OF 1976. Madison: University of Wisconsin Press, 1980. xii, 428 p.

Bonafede, Dom, and Cohen, R., eds. "The Ford Presidency." Introduction by Thomas E. Cronin. NATIONAL JOURNAL REPRINTS (1974-75): entire issue.

Casserly, John J. THE FORD WHITE HOUSE: THE DIARY OF A SPEECHWRITER. Boulder: Colorado Associated University Press, 1977. xi, 374 p.

Casserly was senior editor on Ford's speechwriting staff.

Collins, Paul. GERALD R. FORD: A MAN IN PERSPECTIVE: AS PORTRAYED IN THE GERALD R. FORD MURAL BY PAUL COLLINS. Photography by John R. Fulton, Jr., and Candace Brown; text by Tom LaBelle; design by Candace Brown; preface by Fred Myers; poetry by W. Randolph Brown. Grand Rapids, Mich.: Eerdmans, 1976. 39 p. Illus.

Cronin, Thomas E., and Tugwell, Rexford G., eds. THE PRESIDENCY REAPPRAISED. 2d ed. New York: Praeger Publishers, 1977. xii, 371 p.

See chapter 2, "Appraising Presidential Power: The Ford Presidency," by Philip Shabecoff; and chapter 8, "White House Staffing: The Nixon-Ford Era," by Dom Bonafede.

Hartmann, Robert T. PALACE POLITICS: AN INSIDE ACCOUNT OF THE FORD YEARS. New York: McGraw-Hill, 1980. 451 p.

Hartmann was chief-of-staff for Vice President Ford and counsellor to President Ford.

Head, Richard G.; Short, Frisco W.; and McFarlane, Robert C. CRISIS RESOLUTION: PRESIDENTIAL DECISION MAKING IN THE MAYAGUEZ AND KOREAN CONFRONTATIONS. Westview Special Studies in International Relations. Boulder, Colo.: Westview Press, 1978. xxv, 323 p.

Herbers, John. NO THANK YOU, MR. PRESIDENT. New York: W.W. Norton and Co., 1976. 192 p.

An assessment of the flaws of the press and the presidency during the Nixon-Ford period. Chapters 13, 14, and 15 deal with the Ford administration.

Hersey, John Richard. THE PRESIDENT. New York: Knopf, 1975. xi, 153 p. Illus.

An account of a typical work week during the Ford administration. Originally appeared in the NEW YORK TIMES MAGAZINE, 20 April 1975.

Johnson, Haynes. THE WORKING WHITE HOUSE. New York: Praeger Publishers, 1975. 185 p. Illus.

A behind-the-scenes look at how the White House was managed during the Ford administration. Includes housekeeping functions and personnel.

MacDougall, Malcolm D. WE ALMOST MADE IT. New York: Crown Publishers, 1977. 244 p.

President Ford's advertising man tells the personal story behind the 1976 Republican campaign for the presidency.

Medved, Michael. THE SHADOW PRESIDENTS: THE SECRET HISTORY OF THE CHIEF EXECUTIVES AND THEIR TOP AIDES. New York: Times Books, 1979. xi, 401 p.

Chapter 9, pages 331-47, is devoted to Richard Cheney, who is called Ford's secret weapon.

Mollenhoff, Clark R. THE MAN WHO PARDONED NIXON. New York: St. Martin's Press, 1976. 312 p.

An indictment of Ford's credibility by a well-known Washington bureau chief and investigative reporter for the DES MOINES REGISTER and TRIBUNE.

Moore, Jonathon, and Fraser, Janet, eds. THE MANAGERS LOOK AT '76. Cambridge, Mass.: Ballinger Publishing Co., 1977. viii, 194 p.

Proceedings of a conference held 3-5 December 1976 at the Institute of Politics, John F. Kennedy School of Government, Harvard University, attended by individuals who had played key decision-making roles in the just-concluded presidential campaign.

Nessen, Ron. IT SURE LOOKS DIFFERENT FROM THE INSIDE. Chicago: Playboy Press, 1978. xv, 367 p.

Nessen was press secretary for President Ford.

Orman, John M. PRESIDENTIAL SECRECY AND DECEPTION: BEYOND THE POWER TO PERSUADE. Westport, Conn.: Greenwood Press, 1980. xv, 239 p.

Chapter 6 is devoted to the Ford administration.

Osborne, John. WHITE HOUSE WATCH: THE FORD YEARS. Washington, D.C.: New Republic Books, 1977. xxxiii, 482 p.

Essays on the Ford presidency originally published in the pages of NEW REPUBLIC by a veteran Washington observer.

Pomper, Gerald, et al. THE ELECTION OF 1976: REPORTS AND INTERPRETATIONS. New York: David McKay Co., 1977. viii, 184 p.

Seven chapters by five authors. Essays by Pomper on nomination process and W.C. McWilliams on the broader meaning of the election are well done.

Porter, Roger B. PRESIDENTIAL DECISION MAKING: THE ECONOMIC POLICY BOARD. Cambridge, Engl.: Cambridge University Press, 1980. xii, 265 p.

Porter was special assistant to President Ford and executive secretary of the Economic Policy Board from 1974 to 1977.

Ralph Nader Congress Project. GERALD R. FORD: REPUBLICAN CONGRESSMAN FROM MICHIGAN. Washington, D.C.: Grossman Publishers, 1972.

Reeves, Richard. A FORD, NOT A LINCOLN. New York: Harcourt Brace Jovanovich, 1975. xi, 212 p.

A journalistic account of Ford's first hundred days in the White House.

Reichley, A. James. CONSERVATIVES IN AN AGE OF CHANGE: THE NIXON AND FORD ADMINISTRATIONS. Washington, D.C.: Brookings Institution, 1981. xiv, 482 p.

Examines the effect of conservative ideology upon specific policies of each president, and under Ford, adjustment to the rise of the Third World and problems with détente, decontrol of oil prices, and the fight against inflation.

Rowan, Roy. THE FOUR DAYS OF MAYAGUEZ. New York: W.W. Norton, 1975. 224 p.

Tells of the recapture of the American cargo ship MAYAGUEZ after it was seized by the revolutionary government forces of Cambodia.

Schoenebaum, Eleanore, W., ed. PROFILES OF AN ERA: THE NIXON/FORD YEARS. New York: Harcourt Brace Jovanovich, 1979. xxiv, 787 p.

Contains 450 biographies of men and women who helped to shape America's destiny from 1968 to 1976.

Sobel, Lester A., ed. PRESIDENTIAL SUCCESSION: FORD, ROCKEFELLER AND THE 25TH AMENDMENT. New York: Facts on File, 1975. 225 p.

Spragens, William C. FROM SPOKESMAN TO PRESS SECRETARY: WHITE HOUSE MEDIA OPERATIONS. Lanham, Md.: University Press of America, 1980. xiv, 243 p.

See chapter 5, "Gerald Ford's Press Office, 1974-1977" and chapter 10, "Background of Press Secretaries (IV): Gerald R. Ford's Press Secretaries, 1974-1977."

______. THE PRESIDENCY AND THE MASS MEDIA IN THE AGE OF TELEVISION. Washington, D.C.: University Press of America, 1978. vi, 425 p.

Summarizes Ford's approach to the presidency, pages 133-39, and relation to the media, pages 80-85 and pages 279-83.

U.S. White House. Office of Communications. "The Ford Presidency: A Portrait of the First Two Years." Edited by Stefan A. Halper et al. Washington, D.C.: 1976. Typescript.

Wayne, Stephen J. THE LEGISLATIVE PRESIDENCY. New York: Harper and Row, 1978. xiv, 240 p.

See pages 21-22 (Ford and Congress); pages 51-62 (Ford's White House staff); and pages 121-31 (Ford and the Domestic Council).

Weidenfeld, Sheila Rabb. FIRST LADY'S LADY. New York: G.P. Putnam's Sons, 1979. xii, 401 p.

Weidenfeld was press secretary for Betty Ford.

Winter-Berger, Robert N. THE GERALD FORD LETTERS. Secaucus, N.J.: L. Stuart. 1974. 235 p.

An expose of corruption in Washington. Attempts to implicate Congressman Ford. Evidence shoddy and arguments overstated.

Witcover, Jules. MARATHON: THE PURSUIT OF THE PRESIDENCY, 1972-1976. New York: Viking Press, 1977. xvii, 684 p.

A Washington reporter's detailed account of the race between Ford and Carter.

ARTICLES

Bailey, Gil. "Congress or the White House: The Contest for Leadership in Energy Policy." CRY CALIFORNIA 10, no. 3 (1975): 13-17.

Reports on programs of the Ford administration and the Democratic-controlled Congress to deal with both the economic and energy crises.

Baldwin, Hanson W. "The Future of Intelligence." STRATEGIC REVIEW 4 (Summer 1976): 6-24.

Evaluates Ford's plan for reorganization of the intelligence community and reviews changes implemented since Ford's order. Cites omissions in Ford's program and suggests new reform proposals.

Balz, D.J. "Ford Continues to Refine Legislative Proposals for Message." NATIONAL JOURNAL 7 (11 January 1975): 39-46.

Deals with economic and energy proposals to be submitted to Congress.

Barber, James David. "Ford: Will He Turn Tough?" U.S. NEWS AND WORLD REPORT, 2 September 1974, pp. 22-26.

Interview.

Baroody, William J., Jr. "Gerald R. Ford and the New Politics." PRESIDENTIAL STUDIES QUARTERLY 7 (Spring-Summer 1977): 91-95.

Baroody was a senior staff member of the Ford administration. He presents President Ford as a leader of a coalition which favors restoring the balance between the public and the private sectors, and between government and the people.

Bell, D. Bruce, and Bell, Beverly W. "Desertion and Antiwar Protest: Findings from the Ford Clemency Program." ARMED FORCES AND SOCIETY 3 (Spring 1977): 433-43.

Suggests Vietnam deserters who took part in Ford's clemency program deserted more for personal than political reasons and they resembled deserters from other eras more than they did antiwar activists.

Bierce, William B. "A New Era in International Aviation: CAB Regulation, Rationalization and Restrictions on the North Atlantic." NEW YORK UNIVERSITY JOURNAL OF INTERNATIONAL LAW AND POLITICS 7, no. 2 (1974): 317-60.

Argues that the defensive policies of the CAB and the Ford administration raised new hope for a rationalization of the economic chaos resulting from route saturation, foreign subsidies, and the scheduled carriers' suicidal attempts to compete with charter carriers at unprofitable rates. Based upon primary and secondary materials.

Bissell, Richard E. "United States Policy in Africa." CURRENT HISTORY 73 (December 1977): 193-95, 224-25.

Reviews and compares Africa policy of Ford administration with that of the early Carter administration. Discusses Kissinger's limited effectiveness in Africa.

Bonafede, Dom. "Ford Administration Promises Reformation, Restoration." NATIONAL JOURNAL 6 (17 August 1974): 1217-22.

______. "Ford and Staff Tend to Business . . . and Wait." NATIONAL JOURNAL 6 (10 August 1974): 1179-90.

Eight months after becoming vice president, Ford was well-informed on administration policies and worked hard to improve his understanding of economics and foreign policy should he be called upon to succeed Nixon.

______. "Ford Begins Moves to Reshape His Administration." NATIONAL JOURNAL 6 (7 December 1974): 1825-30.

On talent hunt to put Ford appointees in the new administration.

______. "Ford Leaves Office Structure Intact." NATIONAL JOURNAL 7 (28 June 1975): 974.

No basic charges found between the Nixon and Ford administrations.

______. "Ford Reverses Trend in Strengthening Cabinet Role." NATIONAL JOURNAL 7 (3 May 1975): 652-56.

Ford met more often with Cabinet and had more contact with the secretaries than his predecessors.

______. "Ford's First 100 Days Find Skepticism Replacing Euphoria." NATIONAL JOURNAL 6 (16 November 1974): 1711-14.

Much of the criticism of Ford stemmed from his unwillingness or inability to free himself from the personnel and policies he inherited from President Nixon.

______. "Inside the White House." WASHINGTONIAN 10 (September 1975): 80-83.

A comparison of the Ford staff with previous presidential staffs.

______. "Presidential Staff Continues Growth under Ford." NATIONAL JOURNAL 7 (2 August 1975): 1110-11.

Despite a pledge to reduce the White House staff by 10 percent, Ford's staff was larger than Nixon's staff.

______. "Rumsfeld Looks for Efficiency in Decision Making." NATIONAL JOURNAL 7 (5 April 1975): 518-21.

______. "Speech Writers Shun Flourishes in Molding Ford Image." NATIONAL JOURNAL 7 (25 January 1975): 123-27.

Describes procedures used in writing Ford speeches and his staff of speech writers and editors. Also mentions Ford's speaking style and preferences.

______. "Staff is Organized to Ensure Accessibility to Ford." NATIONAL JOURNAL REPORTS 6 (28 December 1974): 1954-58.

Ford organized his White House staff to avoid some of the excesses of the Nixon staff.

Brown, Seyom. "A Cooling-Off Period for U.S.-Soviet Relations." FOREIGN POLICY 28 (Fall 1977): 3-21.

Argues that it was apparent during the Ford administration that many of the objectives of détente were unobtainable. Suggests the lowering of expectations and the turning away from the theme of superpower interdependence.

Buckley, William F. "Reflections on the Resignation." NATIONAL REVIEW 26 (30 August 1974): 954.

Cameron, Juan. "The Management Problem in Ford's White House." FORTUNE, July 1975, pp. 74-81, 176.

______. "Nelson Rockefeller's Metamorphosis as Vice President." FORTUNE, October 1975, pp. 118-23, 201-7.

_____. "Suppose There's a President Ford in Your Future." FORTUNE, March 1974, pp. 103-5+.

Campbell, John. "European Security after Helsinki: Some American Views." GOVERNMENT AND OPPOSITION (Great Britain) 11, no. 3 (1976): 322-26.

Examines the policy of the Ford administration toward European security and American public opinion on the subject.

Cannon, L. "Nessen's Briefings: Missing Questions (and Answers)." COLUMBIA JOURNALISM REVIEW 14 (May-June 1975): 12-16.

Carter, L.J. "President Ford: Maine Street to Pennsylvania Avenue." SCIENCE 185 (30 August 1974): 764-66.

"Cartoonists Have a Field Day with Athlete-President." U.S. NEWS AND WORLD REPORT, 2 September 1974, p. 14.

Chamberlain, J. "Ford's Hundred Days." NATIONAL REVIEW 27 (28 March 1975): 329-32.

Collier, P. "Ford and the Media: CBS Declares a Honeymoon." RAMPARTS 13 (October 1974): 45-50.

"Congressman Ford." NEW YORKER, 12 November 1973, pp. 40-43.

Corrigan, Richard. "Ford Position Strengthened by Lack of Consensus in Congress." NATIONAL JOURNAL 7 (7 June 1975): 837-41.

Ford's position on energy policy helped by lack of agreement among Democratic members who controlled both House and Senate.

Cronin, Thomas E. "An Agenda for Ford." COMMONWEAL 100 (6 September 1974): 472-75.

Evans, Rowland, Jr., and Novak, Robert D. "Jerry Ford: The Eisenhower of the Seventies?" ATLANTIC MONTHLY 234 (August 1974): 25-32.

Feuerwerger, Marvin C. "The Ford Administration and Israel: Early Signals." MIDSTREAM 20, no. 10 (1974): 13-19.

Forbes, M.S., and Forbes, M.S., Jr. "Forbes Interviews the President." FORBES 115 (1 June 1975): 15-17.

______. "Ford and Israel." MIDSTREAM 21, no. 8 (1975): 30-36.

Discusses the changes in President Ford's attitudes toward American foreign policy regarding Israel, 1974-75.

"Ford's Economic Team: A Firm with One Client." CONGRESSIONAL QUARTERLY WEEKLY REPORT 32 (23 November 1974): 3173-79.

On Ford's economic aides, L. William Seidman, William E. Simon, Alan Greenspan, and Arthur Burns.

Frank, R.S. "U.S. Takes First Hesitant Steps toward Shift in Commodities Policy." NATIONAL JOURNAL REPORTS 7 (21 June 1975): 913-21.

"Gerald Ford: A New Conservative President." CONGRESSIONAL QUARTERLY WEEKLY REPORT 32 (10 August 1974): 2077-82.

Goodman, W. "Authorized Autobiography." NEW YORK TIMES BOOK REVIEW, 27 May 1979, p. 3.

Graham, Donald. "The Vice Presidency: From Cigar Store Indian to Crown Prince." WASHINGTON MONTHLY 6 (April 1974): 41-44.

Hahn, Dan F. "Corrupt Rhetoric: President Ford and the MAYAGUEZ Affair." COMMUNICATION QUARTERLY 28 (Spring 1980): 38-43.

Hamm, Michael J. "The PUEBLO and MAYAGUEZ Incidents: A Study of Flexible Response and Decision-Making." ASIAN SURVEY 17 (June 1977): 545-55.

Says Ford was successful in the MAYAGUEZ incident because of the military options and political tensions present after the end of the Vietnam war.

Hartmann, Robert, et al. "How Ford Runs the White House: Interview with President's Three Top Advisors." U.S. NEWS AND WORLD REPORT, 23 September 1974, pp. 28-33.

Havemann, Joel. "Ford Endorses 172 Goals of 'Management by Objective' Plan." NATIONAL JOURNAL REPORTS 6 (26 October 1974): 1597-605.

______. "OMB's New Faces." NATIONAL JOURNAL REPORTS 7 (26 July 1975): 1071-77.

The Office of Management and Budget remained powerful even under President Ford whose advisers told him to reduce its influence.

Head, S. "Pardoner's Tale." NEW STATESMAN 88 (13 September 1974): 335-36.

Heclo, Hugh. "OMB and the Presidency--The Problem of 'Neutral Competence.'" PUBLIC INTEREST 38 (Winter 1975): 80-98.

Hodges, Tony. "The Struggle for Angola: How the World Powers Entered a War in Africa." ROUND TABLE (Great Britain) 66 (April 1976): 173-84.

Traces the development of great power involvement in the Angolan War. Domestic opposition to Ford's Angolan policy and the backfiring of South African intervention forced the western powers to pull back, and enabled the Soviet Union to score a diplomatic triumph.

Hoffman, Daniel N., and Halperin, Morton H. "Top Secret: National Security and the Right to Know." DISSENT 24, no. 3 (1977): 241-47.

Discusses secrecy in the Johnson and Nixon administrations (continued in the Ford administration) over the bombing of Cambodia, 1969-70; also mentions the 1975 intervention in Angola.

Hughes, Peter C., and Lehman, Christopher M. "U.S. Deterrence Doctrine--Continuity and Change." JOURNAL OF SOCIAL AND POLITICAL STUDIES 2 (Spring 1977): 3-16.

By the close of the Ford administration equivalence had come to be used as the ultimate criterion for measuring the strategic balance, the adequacy of the U.S. strategic posture, and the U.S. objectives at SALT.

Ichord, Robert F., Jr. "Pacific Basin Energy Development and U.S. Foreign Policy." ORBIS 20 (Winter 1977): 1025-43.

In December 1975 President Ford proclaimed a "New Pacific Doctrine" which stressed (1) partnership with Japan; (2) a desire to normalize relations with China; (3) a commitment to South Korea; and (4) more economic cooperation. The energy situation in the Pacific basin is creating a new balance of power in the region. The U.S. must work international development of energy in the area in concert with Japan, Indonesia, and Australia.

Ikle, Fred C. "Illusions and Realities about Nuclear Energy." BULLETIN OF THE ATOMIC SCIENTISTS 32 (October 1976): 14-17.

Discusses the issue of nuclear energy and world order from the perspective of the U.S. administration under President Ford.

"An Inside Look at How the White House is Run." U.S. NEWS AND WORLD REPORT, 17 March 1975, pp. 57-60.

Interview with Donald Rumsfeld, assistant to the president.

Johannes, John R. "From White House to Capitol Hill: How Far Will the Pendulum Swing?" INTELLECT 103 (March 1975): 356-60.

After the Nixon "imperial presidency," Congress regains some of its lost powers and improves its capabilities under the Ford administration.

Jordan, Amos A.; Komer, R.W.; Aspin, Les; and Ravenal, Earl C. "Soviet Strength and U.S. Purpose." FOREIGN POLICY 23 (Summer 1976): 32-52.

Presents a number of views on whether the Soviet Union is outspending the United States for defense.

Kolodney, D. "Gerald Ford: Understudy for Defeat." RAMPARTS 13 (October 1974): 8-13.

Kraft, Joseph. "Rising of Lowered Expectations: One Year of Ford." NEW YORK TIMES MAGAZINE, 3 August 1975, p. 7.

Laird, Melvin R. "America's New Leadership: The President I Know." READER'S DIGEST, November 1974, pp. 97-104.

A favorable biographical sketch of President Ford by a congressional associate and informal adviser.

Leeds, Roger S. "The Panama Canal Treaty: Past and Present United States Interests." FOREIGN SERVICE JOURNAL 53, no. 3 (1976): 6-11, 27.

Examines President Ford's noncommittal attitude and Congress' generally aggressive attitude toward American interests in Panama.

Mashek, John. "A Day in the Life of the President: Minute-by-Minute Report from Inside the White House." U.S. NEWS AND WORLD REPORT, 24 February 1975, pp. 12-19.

Mitchell, C. "Mr. Ford and Civil Rights: A Mixed Record." CRISES 81 (January 1974): 7-11.

Moyer, Wayne. "Iowa Dateline." FOREIGN POLICY 19 (Summer 1975): 178-88.

The Ford administration's decision to use food exports as a diplomatic weapon ran counter to the interests of American farmers who believed their interests were not being considered at the policy-making level. Their movement to limit production could have undercut the administration's diplomatic ventures.

Natoli, Marie D. "The Vice Presidency: Gerald R. Ford as Healer." PRESIDENTIAL STUDIES QUARTERLY 10 (Fall 1980): 662-64.

Naughton, J.M. "In the Wake of the Assassins." NEW YORK TIMES MAGAZINE, 19 October 1975, pp. 18-20.

O'Flaherty, Daniel J. "Finding Jamaica's Way." FOREIGN POLICY 31 (Summer 1978): 137-58.

United States-Jamaican relations are examined in light of Jamaica's support for Cuba's African policy and its declaration of socialism. Unlike the Nixon-Ford administration, the Carter administration tried to formulate a policy toward Jamaica that would not repeat the U.S. experience in Allende's Chile.

"The Public Record of Gerald R. Ford." CONGRESSIONAL QUARTERLY WEEKLY REPORT 31 (20 October 1973): 2759-71.

Ravenal, Earl C. "After Schlesinger: Something Has to Give." FOREIGN POLICY 22 (Spring 1976): 71-95.

Ford's firing of Schlesinger raised basic questions over détente and renewed the debate over defense spending. The central questions were what do we need and what can we afford. Ford realized that what he wanted in the defense budget and what Congress and the people would accept were different things.

_____. "Secrecy, Consensus, and Foreign Policy: The Logic of Choice." TOWSON STATE JOURNAL OF INTERNATIONAL AFFAIRS 10, no. 1 (1975): 1-12.

Compares the use of secrecy in the foreign policy of the Nixon and Ford administrations, emphasizing the style of Henry Kissinger.

Reischauer, Edwin O. "Back to Normalcy." FOREIGN POLICY 20 (1975): 199-208.

Says U.S. intervention in Vietnam was based on false premises as events in Southeast Asia contradicted the domino theory. Failure of the Ford administration to understand the world situation led it into the ill-advised MAYAGUEZ affair.

Rosenfeld, Stephen S. "Washington Report: Money, Morality and the Boycott." PRESENT TENSE 3 (Winter 1976): 16-18.

Discusses the impact of the Arab states' primary and secondary boycotts on Israel and on U.S. domestic and foreign relations. The Ford administration, backed by the American public and Congress, favored a policy of Israeli competition in the non-Arab marketplace.

Shearer, Lloyd. "Don Rumsfeld--He's President Ford's Number One." PARADE, 2 February 1975.

Smith, Gerald C. "SALT after Vladivostok." JOURNAL OF INTERNATIONAL AFFAIRS 29 (Spring 1975): 7-18.

Discusses the joint U.S.-Soviet statement limiting offensive strategic arms and other strategic arms control issues.

Spragens, William C. "Political Impact of Presidential Assassinations and Attempted Assassinations." PRESIDENTIAL STUDIES QUARTERLY 10 (Summer 1980): 336-47.

Sprague, R.E. "Nixon, Ford, and the Political Assassinations in the U.S." COMPUTERS AND PEOPLE 24 (January 1975): 27-31.

"Spring Break for Nation's Best-Known Athlete." U.S. NEWS AND WORLD REPORT, 14 April 1975, pp. 50-51.

Stelzner, Hermann G. "Ford's War in Inflation: A Metaphor That Did Not Cross." COMMUNICATION MONOGRAPHS 44 (November 1977): 284-97.

Ford's war metaphor for fighting inflation in 1974 was a poor choice politically because it reminded the public of the Vietnam war, and a poor choice rhetorically because it did not characterize the actions of the Ford administration.

Stever, H. Guyford. "Science Advice: Out of and Back into the White House." TECHNOLOGY IN SOCIETY 2, nos. 1 and 2 (1980): 61-75.

Stever was science adviser to President Ford and the first director of the White House Office of Science and Technology Policy established in 1976.

Strausz-Hupé, Robert. "Reflections on the Quarter: The North Atlantic Committment." ORBIS 22 (Spring 1978): 3-10.

The Ford administration reaffirmed the North Atlantic Alliance and passed on to the Carter administration a confident spirit of close cooperation.

Suttmeier, Richard P. "Japanese Reactions to U.S. Nuclear Policy: The Domestic Origins of an International Negotiating Position." ORBIS 22 (Fall 1978): 651-80.

President Ford's 1976 statement about nuclear nonproliferation made the Japanese uneasy. The Japanese view of the energy question is reviewed.

Swanson, Linda L., and Swanson, David L. "The Agenda-Setting Function of the Ford-Carter Debate." COMMUNICATION MONOGRAPHS 45 (November 1978): 347-53.

Swanson, Roger Frank. "The Ford Interlude and the U.S. Canadian Relationship." AMERICAN REVIEW OF CANADIAN STUDIES 8 (Spring 1978): 3-17.

U.S.-Canadian relations fell to a low point under President Nixon. Ford held five meetings with Prime Minister Trudeau to improve a deteriorating relationship. Ford's approach was positive and effective and normalized an unstable period. Article is based in part on private interviews and confidential sources.

terHorst, Jerald F. "The Shaping of the President: Ford's Early Years." NEW YORK (26 August 1974): 25-34.

Covers Ford's life from his birth in Nebraska, to his wedding, and first campaign for Congress.

Van der Kroef, Justus M. "Southeast Asia: New Patterns of Conflict and Cooperation." WORLD AFFAIRS 138 (Winter 1975-76): 179-200.

Ford's talks with Suharto of Indonesia and United States moves to extend diplomatic recognition to Cambodia were attempts to show that American disengagement from Vietnam did not presage a lessened interest in Southeast Asia.

Wayne, Stephen J. "Running the White House: The Ford Experience." PRESIDENTIAL STUDIES QUARTERLY 7 (Spring-Summer 1977): 95-101.

Ford was open and accessible, but too tolerant and unable to pick quality senior staff. He was unable to adjust to changing public expectations or to articulate a sense of direction. Article based on interviews with the White House staff.

Chapter 49

JIMMY CARTER, 1977-81

BIBLIOGRAPHY

Lankevich, George J., ed. JAMES E. CARTER, 1924--: CHRONOLOGY-DOCUMENTS-BIBLIOGRAPHICAL AIDS. Presidential Chronologies Series. Dobbs Ferry, N.Y.: Oceana Publications, 1981. vi, 153 p.

SOURCE MATERIALS

Carter, Jimmy. A GOVERNMENT AS GOOD AS ITS PEOPLE. New York: Simon and Schuster, 1977. 262 p.

_____. "I'LL NEVER LIE TO YOU": JIMMY CARTER IN HIS OWN WORDS. Compiled by Robert L. Turner. New York: Ballantine Books, 1976. x, 178 p.

_____. KEEPING FAITH: MEMOIRS OF A PRESIDENT. New York: Bantam, 1982. 622 p.

_____. PUBLIC PAPERS OF THE PRESIDENTS OF THE UNITED STATES, JIMMY CARTER, 1977-1981. 8 vols. Washington, D.C.: Government Printing Office, 1977-82.

_____. WHY NOT THE BEST? New York: Bantam Books, 1976. 179 p.

_____. THE WIT AND WISDOM OF JIMMY CARTER. Edited by Bill Adler. Secaucus, N.J.: Citadel Press, 1977. 141 p.

Congressional Quarterly. PRESIDENCY 1977. Washington, D.C.: 1978. 52, 196A p.

_____. PRESIDENT CARTER. Washington, D.C.: 1977. 92 p.

_____. PRESIDENT CARTER, 1978. Edited by John L. Moore. Washington, D.C.: 1979. 86, 165A p.

_____. PRESIDENT CARTER, 1979. Edited by John L. Moore. Washington, D.C.: 1980. 119, 124A p.

_____. PRESIDENT CARTER, 1980. Edited by Margaret Thompson. Washington, D.C.: 1981. 187 p.

Klenbort, Marcia. THE ROAD TO PLAINS: A GUIDE TO PLAINS AND NEARBY PLACES OF INTEREST IN SOUTHWEST GEORGIA. Text, Marcia Klenbort and Daniel Klenbort; drawings and map, Jack Smith; photographs, Daniel Klenbort. Atlanta: Avery Press, 1977. 32 p.

Lott, Davis Newton. JIMMY CARTER AND HOW HE WON: A PICTORIAL DOCUMENTARY. Los Angeles: Petersen Publishing Co., 1976. 128 p.

Nielsen, Niels Christian, Jr. THE RELIGION OF PRESIDENT CARTER. Nashville: T. Nelson, 1977. 162 p.

1977 Inaugural Committee. "A NEW SPIRIT, A NEW COMMITMENT, A NEW AMERICA": THE INAUGURATION OF PRESIDENT JIMMY CARTER AND VICE PRESIDENT WALTER F. MONDALE. Washington, D.C.: Duo-Books, 1977. 128 p.

THE PRESIDENTIAL CAMPAIGN, 1976. 2 vols. Compiled under the direction of the Committee on House Administration, U.S. House of Representatives. Washington, D.C.: Government Printing Office, 1978. 1,267 p.

BIOGRAPHIES

Baker, James Thomas. A SOUTHERN BAPTIST IN THE WHITE HOUSE. Philadelphia: Westminster Press, 1977. 154 p.

Glad, Betty. JIMMY CARTER: IN SEARCH OF THE GREAT WHITE HOUSE. New York: W.W. Norton, 1980. 546 p.

The first academic biography.

Kucharsky, David. THE MAN FROM PLAINS: THE MIND AND SPIRIT OF JIMMY CARTER. New York: Harper and Row, 1976. ix, 150 p.

Analyzes the impact of Jimmy Carter's fundamentalism on his political beliefs and action.

Mazlish, Bruce, and Diamond, Edwin. JIMMY CARTER: A CHARACTER PORTRAIT. New York: Simon and Schuster, 1979. 288 p.

Miller, William Lee. YANKEE FROM GEORGIA: THE EMERGENCE OF JIMMY CARTER. New York: Time Books, 1978. 247 p.

Neyland, James. THE CARTER FAMILY SCRAPBOOK: AN INTIMATE CLOSE-UP OF AMERICA'S FIRST FAMILY. New York: Grosset and Dunlap, 1977. viii, 101 p.

Walker, Barbara J. THE PICTURE LIFE OF JIMMY CARTER. New York: Watts, 1977. 46 p.

Wooten, James T. DASHER: THE ROOTS AND THE RISING OF JIMMY CARTER. New York: Summit Books, 1978. 377 p.

> A journalist's book based upon interviews with the Carter family and experience as Atlanta bureau chief and White House correspondent.

MONOGRAPHS

Collins, Tom. THE SEARCH FOR JIMMY CARTER. Director of photography, Charles M. Rafshoon with Algimantas Kezys. Waco, Tex.: Word Books, 1976. 192 p.

DEFENSE POLICY AND THE PRESIDENCY: CARTER'S FIRST YEARS. Westview Special Studies in National Security and Defense. Edited by Sam C. Sarkesian. Boulder, Colo.: Westview Press, 1979. xv, 341 p.

deMause, Lloyd, and Ebel, Henry, eds. JIMMY CARTER AND AMERICAN FANTASY: PSYCHOHISTORICAL EXPLORATIONS. New York: Two Continents, 1977. 136 p.

> Five essays which probe the psychology of Carter's leadership.

Fink, Gary M. PRELUDE TO THE PRESIDENCY: THE POLITICAL CHARACTER AND LEGISLATIVE LEADERSHIP STYLE OF GOVERNOR JIMMY CARTER. Westport, Conn.: Greenwood Press, 1980. 248 p.

> The first in-depth examination of Carter's four years as governor of Georgia. Includes a dozen vignettes of Carter's political advisers and intimates.

Hefley, James, and Hefley, Marti. THE CHURCH THAT PRODUCED A PRESIDENT. New York: Wyden Books, 1977. 265 p.

> Examines the spiritual roots of Jimmy Carter.

Isaacs, Harold. JIMMY CARTER'S PEANUT BRIGADE. Edited and arranged by Doris Mack Isaacs. Dallas: Taylor Publishing Co., 1977. 150 p.

Jennings, Genelle. INTO THE JAWS OF POLITICS: THE CHARGE OF THE PEANUT BRIGADE. Huntsville, Ala.: Strode Publishers, 1979. 215 p.

Lynn, Laurence E., Jr., and Whitman, David deF. THE PRESIDENT AS POLICYMAKER: JIMMY CARTER AND WELFARE REFORM. Philadelphia: Temple University Press, 1981. 332 p.

Schram, Martin. RUNNING FOR PRESIDENT: A JOURNAL OF THE CARTER CAMPAIGN. New York: Pocket Books, 1976. xi, 276 p.

Shoup, Laurence H. THE CARTER PRESIDENCY AND BEYOND: POWER AND POLITICS IN THE 1980S. Palo Alto, Calif.: Ramparts Press, 1980. 319 p.

> A case study of Jimmy Carter's political roots, presidency, and 1980 election prospects.

Stroud, Kandy. HOW JIMMY WON: THE VICTORY CAMPAIGN FROM PLAINS TO THE WHITE HOUSE. New York: Morrow, 1977. 442 p.

Witcover, Jules. MARATHON: THE PURSUIT OF THE PRESIDENCY, 1972-1976. New York: Viking Press, 1977. xvii, 684 p.

> A detailed account of the 1976 campaign for the presidency by a veteran Washington correspondent.

ARTICLES

Davis, Eric L. "Legislative Liaison in the Carter Administration." POLITICAL SCIENCE QUARTERLY 94 (Summer 1979): 287-302.

Erickson, Keith V. "Jimmy Carter: The Rhetoric of Private and Civic Piety." WESTERN JOURNAL OF SPEECH COMMUNICATION 44 (Summer 1980): 235-51.

Fagen, Richard R. "The Carter Administration and Latin America: Business as Usual?" FOREIGN AFFAIRS 57, no. 3 (1978): 652-69.

Han, Yung-Chul. "The Carter Administration's Policy toward East Asia: With Focus on Korea." AMERICAN STUDIES INTERNATIONAL 18 (Autumn 1979): 35-48.

Havic, John J., and Heffron, Florence. "The Iowa Caucuses: Carter's Early Campaign for the Presidential Nomination." MIDWEST QUARTERLY 20 (Autumn 1978): 32-48.

Lee, David D. "The South and the American Mainstream: The Election of Jimmy Carter." GEORGIA HISTORICAL QUARTERLY 61 (Spring 1977): 7-12.

Patton, John H. "A Government as Good as Its People: Jimmy Carter and the Restoration of Transcendence to Politics." QUARTERLY JOURNAL OF SPEECH 63 (October 1977): 249-57.

Pearson, Frederick S.; Reynolds, J. Martin; and Meyer, Keith E. "The Carter Foreign Policy and the Use of International Organization: The Limits of Policy Innovations." WORLD AFFAIRS 142 (Fall 1979): 75-97.

Spalding, Phinizy. "Georgia and the Election of Jimmy Carter." GEORGIA HISTORICAL QUARTERLY 61 (Spring 1977): 13-22.

Sudel, Ronald A. "The Rhetoric of Strategic Retreat: Carter and the Panama Canal Debate." QUARTERLY JOURNAL OF SPEECH 65 (December 1979): 379-91.

Chapter 50

RONALD REAGAN, 1981--

SOURCE MATERIALS

Reagan, Ronald. CREATIVE SOCIETY: SOME COMMENTS ON PROBLEMS FACING AMERICA. 2d rev. ed. Old Greenwich, Conn.: Devin-Adair, 1981. 178 p.

______. PUBLIC PAPERS OF THE PRESIDENTS OF THE UNITED STATES, RONALD REAGAN, 1981--. Washington, D.C.: Government Printing Office, 1982--.

______. SINCERELY, RONALD REAGAN. Edited by Helene Von Damm. New York: Berkley Books, 1980. xiii, 224 p.

______. WHERE'S THE REST OF ME? THE AUTOBIOGRAPHY OF RONALD REAGAN. With Richard D. Hubler. New York: Karz Publishers, 1981. 316 p.

U.S. President (1981-- : Ronald Reagan). AMERICA'S NEW BEGINNING: A PROGRAM FOR ECONOMIC RECOVERY. Washington, D.C.: The White House, Office of the Press Secretary, 1981. Var. pag.

BIOGRAPHIES

Boyarsky, Bill. RONALD REAGAN: HIS LIFE AND RISE TO THE PRESIDENCY. New York: Random House, 1981. 205 p.

Cannon, Lou. REAGAN. New York: G.P. Putnam's Sons, 1982. 464 p.

______. RONALD REAGAN. Washington, D.C.: Political Profiles, 1980. 32 p.

Edwards, Lee. RONALD REAGAN: A POLITICAL BIOGRAPHY. Ottawa, Ill.: Caroline House, 1981. 307 p.

Smith, Hedrick; Clymer, Adam; Silk, Leonard; Lindsey, Robert; and Burt, Richard. REAGAN THE MAN, THE PRESIDENT. New York: Macmillan, 1980. 186 p.

Ronald Reagan

MONOGRAPHS

Bartlett, Bruce R. REAGANOMICS: SUPPLY SIDE ECONOMICS IN ACTION. Foreword by Jack Kemp. Westport, Conn.: Arlington House, 1981. ix, 229 p.

Broder, David, et al. THE PURSUIT OF THE PRESIDENCY. Edited by Richard Harwood. New York: Berkley Books, 1980. xv, 427 p.

Congressional Quarterly, Inc. PRESIDENT REAGAN. Washington, D.C.: 1981. 123 p.

Evans, Rowland, and Novak, Robert. THE REAGAN REVOLUTION. New York: Dutton, 1981. xiv, 257 p.

THE FUTURE UNDER PRESIDENT REAGAN. Edited by Wayne H. Valis. Westport, Conn.: Arlington House, 1981. xiii, 194 p.

Germond, Jack W., and Witcover, Jules. BLUE SMOKE AND MIRRORS: HOW REAGAN WON AND WHY CARTER LOST THE ELECTION OF 1980. New York: Viking Press, 1981. xviii, 337 p.

Hobbs, Charles D. RONALD REAGAN'S CALL TO ACTION: REALISTIC DEMOCRACY. Chicago: Nelson-Hall, 1976. 190 p.

Lewis, Joseph. WHAT MAKES REAGAN RUN: A POLITICAL PROFILE. New York: McGraw-Hill, 1968. xi, 211 p.

MANDATE FOR LEADERSHIP: POLICY MANAGEMENT IN A CONSERVATIVE ADMINISTRATION. Edited by Charles L. Heatherly. Washington, D.C.: Heritage Foundation, 1981. xviii, 1,093 p.

Van Der Linden, Frank. THE REAL REAGAN: WHAT HE BELIEVES, WHAT HE HAS ACCOMPLISHED, WHAT WE CAN EXPECT FROM HIM. New York: William Morrow, 1981. 288 p.

Wead, Doug, and Wead, Bill. REAGAN IN PURSUIT OF THE PRESIDENCY. Plainfield, N.J.: Logos, 1980. 241 p.

ARTICLES

Blumenthal, Sidney. "Marketing the President." NEW YORK TIMES MAGAZINE 42 (13 September 1981): 43, 110-18.

Reagan as communicator-in-chief.

Bonafede, Dom. "As Pollster to the President, Wirthlin is Where the Action Is." NATIONAL JOURNAL 13 (12 December 1981): 2184-88.

Richard B. Wirthlin provides the White House with crucial political intelligence.

______. "Deaver at the Hub." NATIONAL JOURNAL 13 (15 August 1981): 1461-65.

Deaver enjoys a closer relationship with Reagan than any other aide. He has the largest staff and the broadest mandate.

______. "From a 'Revolution' to a Stumble'--The Press Assesses the First 100 Days." NATIONAL JOURNAL 13 (16 May 1981): 879-82.

______. "He's on His Own." NATIONAL JOURNAL 13 (4 July 1981): 1217.

Suggests Reagan is at a turning point in his presidency.

______. "Reagan and His Kitchen Cabinet are Bound by Friendship and Ideology." NATIONAL JOURNAL 13 (11 April 1981): 605-9.

______. "The Reagans Bring a New Ambience to the Washington Social Scene." NATIONAL JOURNAL 23 (6 June 1981): 1021-24.

______. "Reagan's Economic Advisers Share Task of Shaping and Explaining Reagohomics." NATIONAL JOURNAL 14 (6 February 1982): 245-48.

______. "The Selling of the Executive Branch: Public Information or Promotion?" NATIONAL JOURNAL 13 (27 June 1981): 1153-57.

Brown, Lorenzo. "Reaganomics. The Reagan Economic Proposals and Their Implications for Black America." CRISIS 88 (April 1981): 138-45.

Cannon, Lou. "The Reagan Years: An Evaluation of the Governor Californians Won't Soon Forget." CALIFORNIA JOURNAL 5 (November 1974): 360-66.

Chapman, Stephen. "Governor vs. Governor: Reagan's and Carter's Performances." ATLANTIC 246 (October 1980): 6-16.

Clark, Timothy B. "Reagan's Budget: Economic, Political Gambles." NATIONAL JOURNAL 14 (13 February 1982): 268-85.

Conaway, James. "Looking at Reagan." ATLANTIC 246 (October 1980): 32-45.

Congressional Quarterly, Inc. "Reagan Proposes a New Federalism." CONGRESSIONAL QUARTERLY WEEKLY REPORT 40 (30 January 1982): 147-54.

_____. "Reagan's Executive Agency Lobbyists." CONGRESSIONAL QUARTERLY WEEKLY REPORT 39 (5 December 1981): 2387-92.

_____. "Reagan Shooting Aftermath." CONGRESSIONAL QUARTERLY WEEKLY REPORT 39 (4 April 1981): 579-87.

_____. "Reagan's Legislative Liaison Team Profiled." CONGRESSIONAL QUARTERLY WEEKLY REPORT 39 (2 May 1981): 747-51.

_____. "Voting Record of '81 Shows the Romance and Fidelity of Reagan Honeymoon on Hill." CONGRESSIONAL QUARTERLY WEEKLY REPORT 40 (2 January 1982): 18-24.

"The Decision Makers." NATIONAL JOURNAL 13 (25 April 1981): entire issue.

> Profiles of major appointees in Executive Office of the President, departments, independent agencies, and regulatory commissions.

"The Decision Makers." Supplement. NATIONAL JOURNAL 13 (19 September 1981): 1677-88.

> Profiles forty-seven persons appointed since April 1981.

Donovan, Hedley. "Reagan's First 200 Days." FORTUNE, 21 September 1981, pp. 62-72.

Drew, Elizabeth. "1980: Reagan." NEW YORKER, 29 September 1980, pp. 106-8, 125.

Greenstein, Fred, and Wright, Robert. "Reagan . . . Another Ike?" PUBLIC OPINION 3 (December-January 1981): 51-5.

Holden, Constance. "The Reagan Years: Environmentalists Tremble." SCIENCE 210 (28 November 1980): 988-89.

"Into Reaganland [Symposium]." DISSENT 28 (Spring 1981): 135-63.

Kirschten, Dick. "After a Year, the Reagan White House May Be Beginning to Feel the Strain." NATIONAL JOURNAL 14 (23 January 1982): 140-44.

> New Right is upset, and some embarrassing presidential decisions have fallen between the cracks of the White House command structure.

______. "The Communicator President." NATIONAL JOURNAL 13 (10 January 1981): 66.

______. "Fridays at Blair House." NATIONAL JOURNAL 14 (6 February 1982): 251.

______. "In Reagan's White House, It's Gergen Who's Taken Control of Communications." NATIONAL JOURNAL 13 (25 July 1981): 1329-31.

With Brady still recovering, it's Gergen who is chief spokesman and director of communications.

______. "Putting the Social Issues on Hold: Can Reagan Get Away with It?" NATIONAL JOURNAL 13 (10 October 1981): 1810-15.

______. "Reagan and the Federal Machine." NATIONAL JOURNAL 13 (17 January 1981): 88-93.

______. "Reaganomics Puts Business on the Spot." NATIONAL JOURNAL 13 (19 December 1981): 2229-32.

______. "Reagan's Battle Plan." NATIONAL JOURNAL 13 (21 February 1981): 300, 302-3.

______. "Reagan's Cabinet Councils May Have Less Influence than Meets the Eye." NATIONAL JOURNAL 13 (11 July 1981): 1242-47.

Final decisions may depend more on White House staff headed by James A. Baker III.

______. "Reagan Sends a Message--In Spite of the Bullet, He's Still in Charge." NATIONAL JOURNAL 13 (4 April 1981): 562-63.

______. "Reagan's 'Revolution.'" NATIONAL JOURNAL 13 (29 August 1981): 1532-36.

______. "The Reagan Team Comes to Washington." NATIONAL JOURNAL 12 (15 November 1980): 1924-26.

______. "Watergate Survivor Fielding Guards against Abuses of White House Power." NATIONAL JOURNAL 14 (13 February 1982): 289-92.

Ladd, Everett Carll. "The Brittle Mandate: Electoral Dealignment and the 1980 Presidential Election." POLITICAL SCIENCE QUARTERLY 96 (Spring 1981): 1-25.

Lanouette, William J. "Reagan in the White House: Don't Look for Change Overnight." NATIONAL JOURNAL 12 (8 November 1980): 1872-75.

Lindsey, Robert. "What the Record Says about Reagan." NEW YORK TIMES MAGAZINE, 29 June 1980, pp. 12-20, 32-34.

McCurdy, Howard E. "Crowding and Behavior in the White House." PSYCHOLOGY TODAY, April 1981, pp. 21-25.

The history of the White House depicts a constant struggle to prevent crowding from affecting the public's business. Reagan may decide he needs a new working wing.

"One of Their Own in the White House." BROADCASTING 100 (26 January 1981): 23-24.

Peirce, Neal R. "Reagan to Nation's Governors--The Federal Aid Cupboard is Bare." NATIONAL JOURNAL 48 (28 November 1981): 2109-13.

Interview.

Peirce, Neal A., and Hagstrom, Jerry. "The Voters Send Carter a Message: Time for a Change--to Reagan." NATIONAL JOURNAL 12 (8 November 1980): 1876-78.

How Reagan put his landslide together.

"Reagan Chooses a Mainstream Cabinet." NATIONAL JOURNAL 12 (20 December 1980): 2174-79.

Draws heavily from ranks of business and law and Republican mainstream who favor a more limited federal role.

Reichley, A. James. "The Conservative Roots of the Nixon, Ford, and Reagan Administrations." POLITICAL SCIENCE QUARTERLY 96 (Winter 1981-82): 537-50.

Robinson, Michael J., and Sheehan, Margaret. "Brief Encounters with the Fourth Kind; Reagan's Press Honeymoon." PUBLIC OPINION 3 (December-January 1981): 56-59.

Samuelson, Robert J.; Madison, Christopher; and Gordon, Michael R. "Memo to: President-Elect Ronald Reagan." NATIONAL JOURNAL 47 (22 November 1980): 1968-79.

Outlines hard choices he must face in four central policy areas: economy, energy, the environment, and foreign affairs, plus a hidden agenda of major laws up for renewal in 1981 and 1982 on which administration must take a stand.

Smith, Martin. "Lessons from the California Experience." CHANGE 12 (September 1980): 32-39.

Stang, Alan. "Matter of Ronald Reagan and Henry Kissinger." AMERICAN OPINION 23 (June 1980): 47-54.

Tuchman, Mitch. "Ladies and Gentlemen, the Next President of the United States." FILM COMMENT 16 (July-August 1980): 49-58.

Weisman, Steven R. "Test of the Man and the Presidency." NEW YORK TIMES MAGAZINE, 26 April 1981, pp. 51-56, 76-84.

Wilson, James Q. "Reagan and the Republican Revival." COMMENTARY 70 (October 1980): 25-32.

INDEXES

AUTHOR INDEX

This index includes all authors, editors, compilers, and other contributors to works cited in the text. It is alphabetized letter by letter and references are to page numbers.

A

Author Index

C

D

E

F

G

H

I

L

M

N

O

P

Q

R

S

T

U

V

W

Y

Z

TITLE INDEX

This index includes titles of books cited in the text. All titles are listed in their shortened form except when full titles are necessary to distinguish among works with similar titles or when the full title is needed for a clear understanding of the subject of the text. Titles of journals and titles of articles in journals are not listed. References are to page numbers and alphabetization is letter by letter.

A

Title Index

B

C

D

E

F

G

H

I

J

M

P

Q

R

S

U

V

W

SUBJECT INDEX

This index includes subject areas of interest. Alphabetization is letter by letter and references are to page numbers. Readers should note that the table of contents (pp. vii-ix) has been arranged in outline form and may be used as an optional guide to this index.

A

B

C

D

E

F

P

R

T

V

W